STRATEGIC AIR POWER
in
DESERT STORM

CASS SERIES: STUDIES IN AIR POWER
(Series Editor: Sebastian Cox)
ISSN 1368-5597

STRATEGIC AIR POWER
in
DESERT STORM

JOHN ANDREAS OLSEN

With a Foreword by
EDWARD N. LUTTWAK

FRANK CASS
LONDON • PORTLAND, OR

First published in 2003 in Great Britain by
FRANK CASS PUBLISHERS
Crown House, 47 Chase Side
Southgate, London N14 5BP

and in the United States of America by
FRANK CASS PUBLISHERS
c/o ISBS, 5824 N.E. Hassalo Street
Portland, Oregon, 97213-3644

Website: www.frankcass.com

British Library Cataloguing in Publication Data

Olsen, John Andreas
  Strategic air power in Desert Storm. – (Cass series.
  Studies in air power; no. 12)
  1. Persian Gulf War, 1991 – Aerial operations, American
  I. Title
  956.7'0442'48

ISBN 0-7146-5193-1 (cloth)
ISBN 0-7146-8195-4 (paper)
ISSN 1368-5597

Library of Congress Cataloging-in-Publication Data

Olsen, John Andreas, 1968–
  Strategic air power in Desert Storm / John Andreas Olsen.
    p. cm. – (Cass series–studies in air power, ISSN 1368-5597;
  12)
  Includes bibliographical references and index.
  ISBN 0-7146-5193-1 – ISBN 0-7146-8195-4 (pbk.)
  1. Persian Gulf War, 1991–Aerial operations, American. 2. Air
  power–United States–History–20th century. 3. United States. Air
  Force. I. Title. II. Series.
  DS79.744.A47 O47 2003
  956.7044'248–dc21

                                                                    2002191220

Typeset in 11/12 Monotype Imprint by Cambridge Photosetting Services
Printed in Great Britain by MPG Books Ltd, Victoria Square, Bodmin, Cornwall

To my wife, Tine.

Contents

Illustrations

Figures and Tables

FIGURES

TABLES

Series Editor's Preface

Political and military analysts and historians have all subjected the use of air power against Saddam Hussein's regime in 1991 to intense scrutiny and the conclusions have run the entire gamut from hostile to laudatory.[1] There is little doubt, however, that in the minds of the public and politicians images of the 1991 campaign are firmly associated with air power, which is generally perceived, and not without reason, as having won the war. This belief was to become an influential feature of the international scene over the following decade as air power was deployed in attempts to achieve a wide range of political effects, most notably in the Balkans, with varying degrees of success. As John Olsen points out, historically air power proponents and enthusiasts such as Colonel John Warden have frequently claimed more than they subsequently delivered for the strategic effectiveness of air power. They have also nearly always had to mount a political struggle within their own politico-military hierarchies to be able to put their ideas into practice. The principal reason for this is that two of air power's great strengths, its inherent flexibility and reach, have also led ineluctably to arguments over what should be attacked. As Olsen shows these ancient arguments resurfaced in the Gulf War, with arguments amongst the airmen themselves as to whether the proper focus of the air campaign should be strategic or tactical. Warden was to prove no exception to this historical trend, and pressed the strategic case with such vigour and so little regard for the niceties of rank and hierarchy that he made himself unpopular in many quarters inside the USAF as well as in the wider Pentagon community. Indeed, Warden suffered one of his most notable early setbacks at the hands of the most senior United States Air Force commander in Saudi Arabia, the CENTAF Air Commander himself, General Chuck Horner. In Olsen's words, Horner and Warden were 'far apart both intellectually and emotionally': Horner's focus was on the Iraqi Army and Warden's on Baghdad. Horner's suspicion that Warden represented the thin end of a wedge of Washington-based interference with his ability as air commander to select targets added to the tension between the two men. Yet again a recurrent theme from air power history and one that re-emerged in the NATO air campaign in Kosovo when the SACEUR, General Wesley Clark, insisted on involving himself directly in the targeting process, much to the consternation of his commander, General Mike Short.[2] The influence of personality and the intellectual battle to establish the locus of air power's role are themes which recur continually in air power history: two other strategically minded airmen, Billy Mitchell and Sir Arthur Harris, shared Warden's propensity to press their case to the very limits of acceptability and beyond.

Here also John Olsen traces the complex inter-relationship between the various senior allied figures in the Administration, the Pentagon, and Central Command, and the way these interacted and influenced the air campaign. It was an immensely complicated and dynamic situation in which he demonstrates that, not only the major players themselves, but also the international media, public opinion, and the weather could and did have important and direct effects which are not always properly appreciated.

The debates which raged subsequently over the efficacy of air power in the Gulf, and afterwards the Balkans, cannot always be separated from the age old inter-service debates and arguments over 'resource allocation' or, put more simply, money. Once the factor of future budget appropriations enters the equation it is usually safe to assume that some at least of the debate and the debaters will skew the argument over actual effects to suit their particular domestic political ends. Add to this brew the wider debates over the morality of the use of strategic air power, themselves stretching back to the earliest attempts to use air power in such a manner, together with nationalism and propaganda, and the result is a potent brew worthy of Macbeth's witches. Too much of the extant writing on the 1991 air campaign thus far has been influenced by such factors and both the academic and air power communities, not to mention the foreign policy analysts, have cause to be grateful to John Olsen for his careful and dispassionate analysis, not only of the planning and effects of the strategic air campaign masterminded by men such as Dave Deptula and John Warden, but also of the target systems they aimed at, most particularly the Iraqi state and the hydra of the Baath Party. His analysis of the latter, drawing on a wide range of sources including highly placed sources within the Iraqi regime, is in itself of enormous value and importance. As the Iraqi leadership and the Baath party were in theory and reality a prime target of Warden, Deptula and the other air planners, an informed understanding of this aspect of the campaign should be central to our understanding of air power's successes and failures during the war. The author has been able to show not only what the US air planners in the famous Black Hole thought was happening, but also what senior figures in the Iraqi leadership, including Saddam, believed. The result is a much more rounded picture than before.

By analysing the structure of the Iraqi State in such depth Olsen is able to reach conclusions on the effectiveness of the air campaign which rest on better foundations than much of the more speculative writing of recent years.

This alone should make this volume required reading for those who are charged with thinking about the ways in which the international community should deal with the Iraqi regime of Saddam Hussein or those like him in the near future.

NOTES

1. Readers of this work will find reference to all the major commentaries on the subject, but for a flavour of the very great width of the spectrum of opinion see on the one hand Richard P. Hallion, *Storm Over Iraq: Air Power in the Gulf War* (Washington DC: Smithsonian Institution Press, 1992) and on the other Robert A. Pape, *Bombing to Win: Air Power and Coercion in War* (Ithaca: Cornell University Press, 1996).
2. For insights on the Kosovo air campaign see Sebastian Ritchie, *Air Power Victorious? Britain and NATO Strategy during the Kosovo Conflict*, in Sebastian Cox and Peter Gray (Eds) *Air Power History: Turning Points from Kitty Hawk to Kosovo* (London: Frank Cass, 2002).

Foreword

In January 1945 after five years of increasingly heavy Anglo-American air bombardment, Berlin was devastated with most buildings in the central districts reduced to burnt-out shells. Yet Hitler in his bunker and the Wehrmacht High Command in nearby Zossen could still send out orders to hundreds of units and receive reports by teleprinter and telephone landlines as well as by radio, and the German army could still move its forces by rail through Berlin's often bombed but still operating marshalling yards. Nazi Germany's Minister of Propaganda Josef Goebbels could still broadcast nation-wide, and by short-wave radio heard around the world. Electrical power, the telephone service, public transport, piped water, sewage disposal, and the supply of basic necessities were still functioning with only brief interruptions, as did many cinemas: on 30 January 1945, the great colour spectacular *Kolberg* had a well-attended gala premiere.

Less than 48 hours after the air offensive against Iraq started on 17 January 1991, Baghdad was still mostly intact as it was to remain throughout the Gulf War, but all major military headquarters were wrecked, Saddam Hussein and his spokesmen could no longer broadcast on television or radio, and Baghdad was left without electricity, telephone service, public transport, piped water, or sewage disposal. Military telecommunications no longer worked, so that Iraq's leader and his military commanders were blind, deaf and mute in their paralysed capital city, unable to find out what was happening quickly enough to react usefully, unable to send out orders except by despatch-riders, and over a fibre-optic network that only reached a few headquarters. After another month of much less concentrated bombing, the vast Iraqi armed forces had lost virtually all their fighting capability, so that the American and coalition ground offensive that closed the war was virtually unopposed.

The 1991 air offensive was a very great victory, but a widespread misconception obscured its true meaning, with grave consequences for US military policies in the aftermath, eventually deforming the conduct of the 1999 Kosovo air war. It attributed the victory of air power to technological progress more than anything else, and specifically to the advent of precision-guided munitions, in the shape of laser-homing bombs, variously guided air-launched missiles, and sea-launched cruise missiles. Actually, air-launched missiles were used with much success as far back as 1943, and laser-homing bombs specifically were first used in the Vietnam war, without changing its outcome. Moreover, only a fraction of the air munitions used in the 1991 Gulf War were precision weapons, while the much higher proportion of precision weapons used in the 1999 Kosovo air war did not make it any more successful – in fact that torturous 11-week air campaign is now universally viewed as a catalogue of errors. That is sufficient evidence that the victory of air power in 1991 was not determined by the technology but rather by its radically innovative application, both strategically and operationally.

But therein lies a mystery that requires explanation: for if that strategy and those operational methods had been shaped by established US military doctrines, methods, and procedures, there is no doubt whatever that the 1991 Gulf War would have degenerated into a grinding combat of attrition, probably with significant casualties, in spite of the acute shortcomings of the Iraqi armed forces.

The answer is contained in John Andreas Olsen's book. His careful research unravels a fascinating tale of radical military innovation by a handful of airmen united by a bold vision of how air power could be applied to change war itself, and who had the sheer drive to overcome all manner of bureaucratic obstacles. These officers, mostly of middling rank, simply refused to accept the established order of things, in which even the top leadership of the US Air Force itself viewed its role as that of a mere ancillary to ground operations, except in the delivery of nuclear weapons – the only 'strategic' function then recognised.

Aided by the vast dimensions of the Iraqi armed forces which made established doctrine seem very unpromising, Olsen's small band of determined officers succeeded in persuading the most senior military leaders of the nation, and their commander-in-chief the President, to scrap existing notions and instead adopt their entirely new concept of war. It was a most remarkable achievement. The ideas they forged in the crucible of a dangerous crisis remain the best guides for the strategic planning and conduct of air operations.

It was not an easy success. At many points, the outcome hung by a thread, as relatively low-ranking officers had to face all the power and authority of far more senior officers armed only with their totally untested ideas. Moreover, those ideas were bound to be resisted – or simply ignored – by the senior officers, commands and indeed entire service branches they would inevitably downgrade.

Olsen's highly readable work is clearly an important contribution to the history of war, and of military innovation, for he uncovers the true dynamics at work: the interaction between ideas and personalities, rank and character, and the temporary contexts, eternal realities and current tools of war, old, new and newest.

Unfortunately, the failure to fully comprehend what really happened in 1990–91 also endows this book with radically different qualities. It is not only an excellent history, but also an urgently needed corrective to misconceptions old and new, and a guide to how modern war should be planned and fought. Just because everything can be centralised nowadays, it does not mean that it should be: decentralised execution is the effective counterpart to centralised control. Just because targets can be hit with great precision, it does not mean that anything can be achieved thereby, unless the targets are selected with equal precision in the fluid turmoil of war, in accordance with a valid theory of victory.

All readers can enjoy John Andreas Olsen's work for it is so well written, but for all who are professionally concerned with military matters, it is a truly essential text.

Edward N. Luttwak
Senior Fellow,
Centre for Strategic and International Studies.

Acknowledgements

The study for this book derives from the Ph.D. thesis, which was submitted to De Montfort University, England, in March 2000. My deep and sincere gratitude on that research goes to my two supervisors Dr David J. Ryan and Dr H. P. Willmott. Dr Ryan was the first supervisor providing all the help I could have asked for, while Dr Willmott deserves special thanks for having provided exhaustive insight that was not part of any official accord. Their commitment, patience, high standards and provocative arguments guided me through the journey, and no student could have asked for a better team.

I am grateful to all the people who took the time to be interviewed or engage in discussions on the various subjects related to the Iraqi regime and US air power. They have truly been a major part of this work, and inspiration was found in their enthusiasm for my research. I would particularly like to mention: Dr Amatzia Baram, Dr Richard G. Davis, Brigadier General David A. Deptula, Dr Michael Eisenstadt, Aras Habib, Dr Richard P. Hallion, General (ret.) Charles A. Horner, Colonel Allan W. Howey, Faleh al-Jabbar, Colonel (ret.) Phillip S. Meilinger, Dr Kenneth Pollack, Dr Diane T. Putney, Brigadier General (ret.) Wafiq Samarrai, Dr Wayne W. Thompson, Colonel (ret.) John A. Warden and Lieutenant Colonel (ret.) Barry D. Watts. I owe Patricia Aresvik, Øistein Espenes, Tor Martin Ingebrigtsen, Dr Ian Jackson, Einar Larsen, William S. Lind, Vice Air Marshal (ret.) Tony Mason, Major Ole Jørgen Maaø, Dr Nils E. Naastad, Dr Alan Stephens, Colonel (ret.) Richard Szafranski and Major General (ret.) Olav F. Aamoth for having commented on drafts through which this study has benefited. I am also immensely thankful to my friend Sebastian Cox who made this publication possible and the editor at Frank Cass, Louise Hulks.

I have been fortunate to be surrounded by supportive families and good friends. Those people who I would acknowledge as those to whom I owe a special debt of gratitude are Terje Erikstad, Wenche, Varg and Torbjørn Forseth, Atle P. Larsen, Inge Håvard Lind, Svein-Arne Reinholdtsen, Hugo M. Strand and my brother Claus Ivar Olsen. I am forever grateful to my parents, Nikolai Bøe and Karin Anne Olsen, for all the support and encouragement they have given me over the years. My deepest affection and love goes to my wife, Tine, to whom I dedicate this work. She stands by me with patience, provides me with immense inspiration and has made this endeavour an enjoyable and fulfilling task.

Introduction

On 8 August 1990, six days after Iraqi troops invaded Kuwait, US President George Bush declared four national policy objectives: to effect the immediate, complete and unconditional withdrawal of all Iraqi forces from Kuwait; to restore Kuwait's legitimate government; to protect the lives of American citizens abroad; and to promote the security and stability of the Persian Gulf area.[1] During the following months the United Nations Security Council passed 12 condemning resolutions, demanding an Iraqi withdrawal from Kuwait, culminating on 29 November 1990 with the authorisation for the US-led Coalition to use 'all means necessary' if Iraqi forces did not leave Kuwait by 15 January 1991.[2] When this ultimatum expired, the Coalition embarked on an offensive military campaign code-named Operation Desert Storm. The offensive consisted of four phases: (1) the strategic air campaign, which focused on the Iraqi regime; (2) gaining air superiority over Kuwait; (3) the preparation of the battlefield, which focused predominantly on Iraqi troops in Kuwait; and (4) the ground campaign, which eventually saw the Iraqi Army retreat in fewer than 100 hours of battle.[3]

This study concerns itself primarily with the first phase of Operation Desert Storm – the air campaign against the Iraqi leadership. It examines the genesis, evolution and execution of the strategic air campaign plan, which was directed against the Iraqi regime, and it examines the Iraqi perception of that effort. As part of that process the book seeks to examine the validity of the concept of operations behind a plan that sought to register 'strategic paralysis'. While it was successful in its overall contribution in degrading Iraqi war-making capabilities and inducing fog and friction on a strategic level, the heart of the strategy, the attacks against Saddam Hussein's political power base, did not meet the hoped for, but unstated, objective of changing the regime. The immediate explanation of such a state of affairs rests in the fact that the US political and military establishment did not appreciate the nature of the regime: Saddam Hussein's political structure was far more complicated and resistant to precision bombing than assumed. The US intelligence institution was focused more on 'order-of-battle' assessments than on the make-up and nature of political regimes, and therefore the planners were provided with very little insight on the non-material dimension of the authoritarian political system. Only by examining the Iraqi political power structure and organisation in detail can one begin to understand the context that is required for appreciating the 1991 strategic air offensive.

While the thesis is a case study of one aspect of the 1991 Gulf War, the air power concept that evolved has wider implications. Increasingly, in the past decade air power has become the instrument of choice for US and European policy-makers in dealing with recalcitrant regimes. It was the principal instrument of force in Operation Desert Storm (1991) and the only one, with the exception of special operation teams, in Deliberate Force (1995), Desert Fox (1998), Allied Force (1999) and Enduring Freedom (2001). Despite air power's increasing prominence in crisis management, its employment has been shrouded in controversy and certain analysts contend that air power is not widely understood even among professional military officers.[4] David MacIsaac argues that air power continues to pose problems for analysts because of 'its vocabulary, mystique, and remoteness from the day-to-day experience of most scholars'.[5] Robin Higham has observed that 'The history of air power has been much confused, both by the glamour surrounding flight and by a lack of historical perspective on the part of its exponents.'[6] Be that as it may, political leaders seem to find air power an unusually seductive instrument of force as 'It appears to offer the pleasures of gratification without the burdens of commitment.'[7] Air power seems not only to offer the prospect of decisive action without the accompanying risk of unacceptably heavy casualties, but it has the attraction of being relatively easy to control in terms of application and degree of intensity, and, as a result, political and military commanders have come to look to air power as a quick and cheap solution to otherwise complex international problems. The shift in air power's role during the 1990s has led some analysts to conclude that the changes that have taken place in the conduct of war amount to a major transformation in the nature of war.[8] To such people the offensive concept of 1991 introduced a new aerospace era in which the combination of stealth, precision and stand-off capability, over-laden by information dominance, provided air power with unprecedented leverage in meeting political objectives. As emerging technologies promise to make air power ever more flexible, mobile and lethal, it is important that those associated with the formulation of national security policy understand what modern air power can and cannot achieve in terms of realising political objectives.

The book is divided into five chapters. Chapter 1 is an examination of the process whereby the United States established a military presence in the Middle East and key Arab states during the same period witnessed radical and nationalist movements that played an important role in militarising and polarising the whole region. It examines aspects of the political, social, military and internal security systems in a Middle East context, providing a rationale and setting for the Iraqi invasion of Kuwait. The chapter also explores main features of US military thinking during the Cold War's last decade. By such means, the extent by which air power in Operation Desert Storm departed considerably from both the contingency plans for the region and the established military doctrine will be illustrated.

Chapter 2 begins by providing a doctrinal point of departure for the new ideas on strategic air power that surfaced in certain parts of the United States Air Force during the latter half of the 1980s. It examines the controversy that the concept provoked in the early days of the crisis over Kuwait and how it emerged as the most attractive option available to an army-dominated military leadership. While most of the opposition to the propositions came from within the USAF, the chapter suggests that the conceptual basis, as manifested in the theory of the Five Rings Model, the policy of Global Reach Global Power and the concept of Instant Thunder, amounted to nothing less than a major doctrinal change. The chapter also suggests that the opposition to the strategic air plan was based not only on doctrinal disagreements, but also on the fact that the concept was developed outside the military command tasked with the planning.

Chapter 3 examines how the initial concept evolved into a workable plan over the next months by identifying key briefings during that period. It discloses how certain critically important air planners managed to keep the original focus as political, inter-service and operational concerns played into the overall planning effort. The chapter emphasises that while one group of planners focused on the operational aspects of the strategic air campaign, developing the Master Attack Plan and the Air Tasking Order in Riyadh, another group set out to sell the concept to decision-makers in Washington. Together with Chapter 2, this develops the argument that Operation Desert Storm would not have taken the form it did had it not been for the initiative, persistence and conviction of a few unorthodox airmen.

Chapter 4 explores the inner workings of the Iraqi regime, which the strategic air campaign intended to change by inducing a coup or a revolt. While the air planners based their assumptions on limited knowledge of the social fabric of the Iraqi state, this chapter presents a profile of Saddam Hussein and examines in turn each of the regime's five overlapping pillars of power: the Ba'ath Party, the government, the military apparatus, the security and intelligence network and the informal kinship complex. The chapter explains that the Iraqi leader first established and then maintained himself in power by creating a persuasive and seemingly omnipotent internal security and intelligence network, strengthened by the wider control of the republic through Ba'ath Party, and government and military institutions. To fill the ranks of these organisations, Saddam Hussein drew largely from key Sunni tribes, a small number of Shia tribes, non-tribal elements, loyal Ba'athists, and, perhaps most important of all, individuals from the same family, clan and region as himself. Together these arrangements amounted to Saddam Hussein's personal and political power base, and the relationship between the sole leader and that power base was there- fore the Iraqi regime's centre of gravity – the system on which Saddam Hussein's rule depended.[9]

Chapter 5 discusses what the strategic attacks against the Iraqi regime accomplished in order to determine the validity of the applied strategy of 'strategic paralysis'. It identifies the Iraqi perception of air power prior to the war, and how the bombing of the Iraqi leadership's command and communication facilities affected its decision-making with regard to the occupation of Kuwait. The chapter argues that there were three major factors that prevented the execution of the new concept from being optimal: limited understanding of the nature of the regime, inadequate intelligence and political restraints from Washington. The chapter suggests that the political outcome of bombing had little to do with sorties flown, buildings struck and tanks destroyed, but much to do with the intangibles of politics that in no small part were divorced from realities on the military battlefield.

This study is the story of the birth, development and execution of the first phase of Operation Desert Storm, with a critical analysis of that concept's validity, as it faced a regime that did not lend itself to change through the application of air power. It is also the story of how air operations, for the first time in history, became the backbone of the entire war effort.

The opinions and conclusions expressed in this study are those of the author. They do not represent or reflect the official position of the Royal Norwegian Air Force or any other government agency.

NOTES

1. George Bush, 'Address to the Nation Announcing the Deployment of United States Armed Forces to Saudi Arabia', 8 August 1990, in *Public Papers of the Presidents of the United States: George Bush, 1990* (Washington, DC: Government Printing Office, 1991), p. 1108.
2. The United Nations Security Council Resolution (UNSCR) 678 was adopted by 12 votes in favour, Cuba and Yemen against and China abstaining. For the full text

of UNSCR 678, see E. Lauterpacht, C. J. Greenwood, M. Weller and D. Bethlehem, *The Kuwait Crisis: Basic Documents*, Cambridge International Documents Series, Vol. I (Cambridge: Grotius Publications, 1991), p. 98; and Dilip Hiro, *Desert Shield to Desert Storm: The Second Gulf War*, (London: Paladin, 1992), p. 538.

3. Eliot A. Cohen *et al.*, *The Gulf War Air Power Survey: Volume II: Part II: Effects and Effectiveness* (Washington DC: Government Printing Office, 1993), p. 79.

4. Phillip S. Meilinger (ed.), *The Paths of Heaven: The Evolution of Airpower Theory*, (Maxwell Air Force Base, AL: Air University Press, 1997), p. ix. See Cohen, 'The Mystique of US Air Power', *Foreign Affairs* 73, No. 1 (January/February 1994), pp. 108–23; and Colin S. Gray, *Explorations in Strategy*, (Westport, CT: Greenwood Press, 1996), pp. 55–82.

5. David MacIsaac, 'Voices from the Central Blue: The Air Power Theorists', 1st pub. 1986, in Peter Paret (ed.), *Makers of Modern Strategy: From Machiavelli to the Nuclear Age* (Oxford: Oxford University Press, 1994), p. 624. See also Phillip S. Meilinger, 'Towards a New Airpower Lexicon', *Airpower Journal*, 7, No. 2 (Summer 1993), pp. 39–47.

6. Robin Higham, *Air Power: A Concise History* (London: Macdonald, 1972), p. 1.

7. Thomas A. Keany and Eliot A. Cohen, *Revolution in Warfare? Air Power in the Persian Gulf*, (Annapolis, MA: Naval Institute Press, 1995), p. 213.

8. Richard P. Hallion, *Storm over Iraq: Air Power and the Gulf War*, (Washington, DC: Smithsonian Institution Press, 1992), pp. 180–200; Richard G. Davis, *Decisive Force: Strategic Bombing in the Gulf War* (Washington, DC: Air Force History and Museums Program, 1996), p. i; Air-Vice Marshal (ret.) Tony Mason, 'The Air War in the Gulf', *Survival* 33, No. 3 (May–June 1991), pp. 211–29; Alan Stephens, 'The Implications of Modern Air Power for Defence Strategy', No. 5 (Fairbairn, Canberra: RAAF Air Power Studies Centre, 1992), pp. 21–4; and Gary Waters, *Gulf Lesson One – The Value of Air Power: Doctrinal Lessons for Australia* (Fairbairn, Canberra: RAAF Air Power Studies Centre, 1992), pp. 161–72.

9. Daniel Byman, Kenneth Pollack and Matthew Waxman, 'Coercing Saddam Hussein: Lessons from the Past', *Survival* 42, No. 3 (Autumn 1998), pp. 127–51; Michael Eisenstadt, 'Like A Phoenix From the Ashes: The Future of Iraqi Military Power', *Washington Institute for Near East Policy* 36 (1993), pp. 7–16; and Amatzia Baram, 'Building Toward Crisis: Saddam Husayn's Strategy for Survival', *Washington Institute for Near East Policy* 47 (1998), pp. 7–64.

1

The Politicomilitary Context of Operation Desert Storm

Throughout the Cold War successive US administrations consistently sought to pursue a two-strand policy in the Middle East: to exclude or minimise Soviet presence and influence in the area and to ensure the free flow of oil to Western countries. The process was complicated by the creation of the state of Israel, which in turn led to several Arab states embracing increasingly hard-line radical and nationalist agendas. These agendas, combined as they were with regional militarisation and polarisation through arms sales, further hardened support among national leaders for violent means to realise political objectives. Consequently, the Middle East area ensured that diplomatic solutions to both domestic and regional problems were undermined. As the level of inter-communal violence in the region increased, so did state security measures, and the result was that key regimes became extremely strong at the expense of their populations. These regional developments produced highly authoritarian and deeply entrenched regimes that were not always in harmony with US objectives. In the Iraqi case unprecedented problems followed in the wake of the war with Iran, and this at a time when the hitherto relatively close relationship with Washington was deteriorating. The Iraqi predicament, which culminated in the invasion of Kuwait, came at a period when the increased US defence budget of the Reagan years materialised and the United States found itself as the sole superpower. This chapter will examine these various developments and thereby establish the political and military framework for the analysis of the first phase of Operation Desert Storm – the strategic air campaign directed against Iraq and the Saddam Hussein regime.

US PREPONDERANCE IN THE MIDDLE EAST

The first contact between the United States and the Arab world, in the early part of the nineteenth century, can hardly be said to have been auspicious, even if 'the Shores of Tripoli' are remembered to this day in the Marine Corps' hymn.[1] The second was somewhat more fortunate, establishing as it did diplomatic relations between the United States and the Sultan of Muscat in September 1833.[2] Throughout the remainder of the century, however, the US interest and involvement in matters Middle Eastern was minor even though the area experienced great changes and instability at the time.[3] From the early 1880s onward the region, specifically Egypt and the fertile areas of the Arabian Peninsula, increasingly fell under British sway. After 1919 and the elimination of the Ottoman Empire, Britain and France were without rivals in the area though in this inter-war period the United States, on account of its oil interests, became increasingly involved in the Persian Gulf. It was the Second World War, however, that gave expression to direct US commitments, initially because it provided via Iran the only undeviating overland line of communication with the Soviet Union, but in the longer term because in the course of this war the end of US self-sufficiency in oil came into view. The US entry into the Second World War redefined the importance of the Middle East, according to Daniel Yergin, as oil became the critical commodity for the conduct of the war itself, for national power and international predominance.[4]

Another matter was the weakening of the British position throughout the Middle East.[5] For most of the Second World War, albeit not without certain problems, Britain was able to retain control of the Middle East: the two main threats to its position were in 1941 in Iraq, which witnessed military intervention to forestall either a coup or an Axis challenge, and the following year in Egypt, when the tide of Axis conquest reached El Alamein. The defeat of Axis power in North Africa and the subsequent elimination of the Axis threat throughout the eastern Mediterranean was critically important in loosening the ties that bound various Middle East states and communities to Britain. In this respect, such matters, as well as the Atlantic Charter in 1941 and the formation of the United Nations four years later, served notice of the aspirations of national self-determination felt by various societies under British domination.[6]

Up to late 1941 President Franklin D. Roosevelt had shown little interest in Saudi Arabia, which was 'a little far afield', but on 18 February 1943 he authorised land-lease assistance, and diplomatic relations improved.[7] The deepening US interest in the region promoted an immediate confrontation with Britain. According to Douglas Little, 'To forestall British encroachments in Saudi Arabia, the United States wooed King Ibn Saud with military assistance.'[8] The British Prime Minister, Winston Churchill, virtually accused the United States of seeking to undermine Britain's rights, whereupon Roosevelt replied that the British wished to 'horn in on Saudi Arabia's oil-reserves'.[9] To resolve wartime differences an Anglo-American oil agreement was negotiated in late 1943, and two years later, en route from the Yalta conference, Roosevelt met King Abdul Aziz Ibn Saud in the US heavy cruiser *Quincy* in the Suez Canal and affirmed that the United States had lasting interests in the security of the kingdom. In the event this dispute was quickly overshadowed by the Soviet Union's refusal to consider an evacuation of northern Iran with the end of the war in Europe, the series of demands made on Turkey and the civil war in Greece.[10] The free flow of oil in the Gulf grew in importance, the perception of a Soviet threat to the region seemed evident, and as the British and French were unable to retain their positions in the Middle East the United States found itself obliged to assume a higher profile in the area.[11] Consequently they were no longer prepared to play the role of the 'No. 2 Englishmen'.[12]

These various matters came together in the immediate post-war period as the victorious allied powers confronted one profound truism: allies are not necessarily friends, a fact never more evident than when the common threat that ensured their previous solidarity was gone. The Bolshevik Revolution of 1917 introduced communism as a formidable political force, and by the end of the Second World War the United States and capitalist European countries viewed the Soviet Union as a direct threat to their own ideology. Although the Soviet forces were exhausted after three traumatic decades, the Red Army, which had pushed German forces from the outskirts of Moscow to Berlin, was impressive. As the Cold War took shape and substance, Washington sought to build a security system in the region that would serve as a check upon perceived Soviet expansionism.

The policy adopted was one of containment, formulated by George F. Kennan at the American Embassy in Moscow in early 1946.[13] Although Kennan argued that the policy was designed primarily for Europe, a point he continued to make well into the 1970s, Paul H. Nitze universalised containment through the National Security Council (NSC-68) four years later.[14] It was, nevertheless, for all practical purposes, applied to the Middle East in March 1946 when the Soviet Union opposed withdrawing troops from the Iranian province of Azerbaijan.[15] In this event, Marshal Josef Stalin chose to pull back when faced by a resolute response from Teheran, London and Washington – as anticipated by Kennan in his famous 'Long Telegram' of 22 February 1946. Although Iran had been the diplomatic focus of the first Cold War crisis, the United States was also concerned about Greece and Turkey, which the British were no longer capable of subsidising. The US support for these two countries, the articulation of the Truman Doctrine of 1947 and the implementation of the Marshall

Plan the same year, formed the first part of a policy of containment, by which the United States sought to prevent the spread of communism, forestall Soviet aggrandisement, and in effect defeat the Soviet Union in a confrontation that would involve the use of all resources short of war itself.[16] According to Scott Lucas, this was the first time the United States Joint Chiefs of Staff (JCS) and National Security Council recognised Middle Eastern security as 'vital' to US defence.[17] The nature of Soviet intentions in the region has sparked much scholarly debate: while Bruce R. Kuniholm argues that Washington managed to thwart a very real Soviet threat through military aid and hard-line diplomacy, Melvyn P. Leffler contends that US officials exaggerated the Kremlin menace in order to legitimise their own desire for strategic bases in the Middle East.[18]

Whether the Soviet threat was real or imagined, in terms of the Middle East the new thrust of US policy took the best part of a decade to fully manifest itself, but at the same time Washington set out the two markers that were to last for more than 40 years and which were to impose themselves on successive administrations: containing the Soviet Union and ensuring the free flow of oil to the West at reasonable prices.[19] Within that framework, different policies and strategies were applied as international, regional and domestic circumstances in the area changed. Admittedly a US naval presence in the Gulf was established after 1947, but with Soviet forces obliged to withdraw from northern Iran in 1946 there was no immediate challenge in the Middle East to the United States' policy of containment.[20] Washington's concern for the security of western Europe was ensured with the formation of the North Atlantic Treaty Organisation (NATO) in April 1949, an alliance to which Greece and Turkey subscribed in 1952, while the more immediate concern came in the Far East with the communist victory in the Chinese civil war (1948–49) and the outbreak of the Korean war in June 1950. With President Harry Truman's new hard-line approach towards the Soviet Union, the United States assumed preponderance in the Middle East and the Western world as a whole.[21]

Although the Truman Doctrine was most welcome in London, another focal point of tension during the transition from British to US dominance in the region was the formation of a separate Jewish state in Palestine. While President Truman suggested that some 100,000 displaced European Jews should be settled in Palestine, the British opposed such a massive immigration. Truman continued to favour the Jewish pledge, and despite opposition from the British and prominent members in his own administration – including Secretary of State George Marshall, Under Secretary of State Dean Acheson and head of Policy and Planning Staff George Kennan – Truman declared, in agreement with the United Nations, the de facto recognition of Israeli independence on 14 May 1948.[22] The new state was immediately attacked by over 30,000 troops from the neighbouring Arab countries, but the new state prevailed.[23] By the time the United Nations managed to achieve an armistice in July 1949, Israel had expanded beyond the area it had originally been designated – although it remained without strategic depth. The conception of an Israeli state completely rearranged the political landscape as it polarised the region and led the United States into a more active role in the Middle East.[24] While Truman reaffirmed his predecessor's commitment to Saudi Arabia,[25] Washington's approach to the Middle East would increasingly be related to what Acheson termed the 'Puzzle of Palestine'.[26]

The weakening of the British position in the region and the perceived Soviet threat led the Eisenhower administration in July 1953 to define US interests in terms of having access to the region's resources and strategic positions while denying them to the Soviet Union.[27] With the US primacy in Iran, established when Muhammad Reza Shah Pahlavi replaced Muhammad Mosaddiq in the American-supported coup of 1953, the Turkish–Iraqi alliance of 1955 became the basis of the Baghdad Pact, formed when Britain, Iran and Pakistan adhered to the already established bilateral agreement.[28] Although not a member, it was the Eisenhower administration that orchestrated these arrangements. John Foster Dulles, the Secretary of State, together with Nuri al-Said, the Iraqi Prime Minister, were the real founders of the Northern Tier concept of area defence against perceived Soviet aggression.[29] As reliance on military power increasingly became part of US policy, President Dwight D. Eisenhower came to regard Iraq as 'a bulwark of stability and progress in the region'.[30] However, Iran was defined as the most reliable new partner in the area, and after the 1953 coup the Shah of Iran received political, economic and military support for as long as he remained in power.[31]

Iraq was ironically the only Arab state in the Baghdad Pact, but in the period of the Hashemite Kingdom it was one of the United States' closest associates in the Arab Middle East. However, when King Faisal II and Nuri al-Said were overthrown in 1958, Iraq left the alliance and joined Egypt and Syria in the proclamation of revolution, both domestically and throughout the Arab world. The growing nationalism that arose in the Middle East during the Eisenhower years manifested itself in particular in the person of Gamal Abdul Nasser. Although Iranian nationalisation of oil in 1951 and the forced abdication of King Farouk of Egypt in July 1952 had proved worrying, it was the emerging authority of Nasser in 1954 that was perceived as the biggest threat to Western interests. The Egyptian leader took advantage of the bitterness and humiliation that developed as a result of the 1949 defeat and he became the symbol of the pan-Arab movement. In the process Soviet–Arab relations improved at the expense of the United States. The Western withdrawal from the funding of the Aswan Dam project, Nasser's nationalisation of the Suez Canal and the abortive Anglo-Franco-Israeli intervention in Egypt in October–November 1956 provided the Soviet Union with its first tentative foothold in the Arab Middle East.[32] The Israeli government believed that a major show of force at the time would coerce Arab governments into acknowledging Israel's existence, but rather than being defeated – in large parts a result of US negotiations – Nasser emerged from the Suez debacle as an Arab hero. Moreover, the crisis was a fatal undermining of the British and French position in the Middle East.[33]

The Eisenhower administration went beyond the terms of reference supplied by its predecessor by actually encouraging a regional security system.[34] The Eisenhower Doctrine of 1957 widened US involvement in the region by stating a willingness to use armed force in defence of any country in the Middle East 'requesting such aid against overt armed aggression from any nation controlled by International Communism'.[35] When the monarchy was overthrown in Iraq the following year, it was discussed whether an intervention should take place,[36] but the obvious popularity of the new Qassem regime in Baghdad persuaded Washington not to intervene. Nevertheless, when the Christian President in Lebanon, Camille Chamoun, sought assistance in quelling a revolt that followed the unrest in Baghdad in 1958, Eisenhower decided to dispatch some 15,000 American Marines. The intervention, although supported by pro-Western states such as Iran and Saudi Arabia, witnessed much criticism, as the Marines scrambled up the beach crowded with sunbathers. However ridiculed, it demonstrated for the first time that the United States was determined to use force to defend its interests in the region, but if this and the British intervention in Kuwait in 1961 in some way served to check revolutionary impulses for the moment, the fact was that the tide generally ran against Western interests. Nevertheless, two things had become clear by the late 1950s: as the Arab world divided into revolutionary and conservative states, Saudi Arabia emerged as the only Arab state of real significance that had any affinity with the Western powers, and the United States was the only Western country with real power and influence in the area. From the late 1950s to the late 1970s, the United States relied on a 'three pillar system' in the region: Israel, Iran and Saudi Arabia.

The various rights and wrongs concerning the creation of Israel in May 1948 and its continued existence do not form a proper part of this story. It is sufficient to note certain matters in seeking to set out an account of the process by which the United States came to be directly involved in the affairs of the Middle East.[37] These matters were, first, the deep sense of injustice felt throughout the Arab world at the creation of Israel that was born of the belief that the attempt to provide European Jewry with a state was achieved at the expense of the Palestinian Arabs, and thus by giving deliberate offence to the Arab nations as a whole.[38] Second, the Arab failure in the war of 1948–49 was in large measure responsible for the upsurge in revolutionary strife throughout the Arab world, as discredited regimes in Egypt and Syria were overthrown and the ruler of Jordan assassinated. The two matters came together in proclaimed anti-Western feeling, though until the early 1960s this was not particularly important as far as the United States was concerned. From the time that the state of Israel was proclaimed, Washington was its most important supporter and was committed to ensure the new state's survival. Direct US intervention to ensure this survival never proved necessary, but after the 1949 armistice the United States, in association with Britain and France, sought to ensure peace and stability in the Middle East by arms embargoes that largely curtailed the military capacity of Israel and its neighbours. With the Suez episode and Soviet encroachment in the area, which took the form of supplying modern weaponry to such countries as Egypt and Syria, the US attitude slowly underwent change.[39]

Burton I. Kaufman argues that the Eisenhower administration seemed not to distinguish nationalism from communism, since one was perceived as reinforcing the other.[40] Others have challenged that view, using the Suez crisis to argue that top officials at the time 'drew clear distinctions between Nasserism and Soviet subversion'.[41] Either way, John F. Kennedy attacked the previous administration for having dealt with the Arab world 'almost exclusively in the context of the East–West struggle'.[42] Kennedy sought to establish a working relationship with Nasser, but reassured Israel about defending its national security and agreed to sell it HAWK surface-to-air missiles (SAMs).[43] The deal was a major departure from previous policy, and marked the administration's concerns about the military build-up in Egypt under Soviet auspices.[44] By 1963 relations with Egypt had deteriorated to the point that Congress moved to cut off economic assistance to Cairo. The Kennedy administration, contrary to intention, found itself involved in a major military build-up of regional forces. The United States' relationship with Saudi Arabia nevertheless remained strong and the 1960s brought the two parties closer as they had mutual interests in downplaying radical movements in the region.[45]

The Johnson administration witnessed a new Arab–Israeli war, and with that war American leaders found themselves once again reassessing their Middle East policy. By early 1967 there was a rising tide of rhetoric against Israel in Egypt, Syria and Jordan under the leadership of Nasser, and as discussions intensified Israel came to the conclusion that a war was in the making, and that a pre-emptive strike was required.[46] The Six-Day War had a major impact on the region, as it struck at the heart of Arab values and self-image. It firmly established Israel as the primary military power in the Middle East, as it took Sinai from Egypt, the West Bank from Jordan and the Golan Heights from Syria, and a divided Jerusalem came under Israeli control.[47] Air power proved itself as an instrument of national security, and not until 1991 would the world witness a comparable operational success from the air.[48]

Paradoxically, the Arab defeat strengthened a growing nationalism under the unifying theme of a sovereign state for the Palestinians, and with little access to Israel the Palestinian question was internationalised.[49] Hostility towards Israel in the Arab world became ever stronger, and with Israel occupying areas with large numbers of Palestinians it also created an internal security problem. While the Palestinian Liberation Organisation (PLO), which was established in 1964 as an umbrella organisation for a number of clandestine resistance groups, initially turned to guerrilla warfare, they soon preferred international terrorism in order to draw attention to their cause.

The United States clearly welcomed Israel's victory in 1967,[50] but at least three factors forced a reappraisal: the British pullout from east of Suez announced in January 1968 and completed by 1971; the deployment of Soviet warships to the Indian Ocean in March 1968; and the effects of the Vietnam war on American society in general.[51] Convinced that it could not avoid a military build-up of regional forces, the Johnson administration decided to follow a policy of ensuring if not peace then an absence of war through *imbalance of power*: it sought to arm Israel to the extent that Israeli superiority over its Arab neighbours would ensure it was not attacked. Thus, while the Soviets rearmed Syria and Egypt in the wake of their 1967 defeat, the United States replaced France as Israel's main arms supplier.[52] In this way Washington came to reaffirm its reliance on the 'three pillars' in the Middle East. The increased support for Israel was essentially driven by three main factors: a strong emotional affiliation for the young state; the strength of the Jewish lobby in US politics; and the perception of Israel as a reliable strategic ally in a volatile region which would weaken Soviet influence and undermine Arab radicalism.[53] Iran was kept as an ally for geo-strategic security purposes, while the relationship with Saudi Arabia had direct economic imperatives through oil. The division within the Arab world between conservative monarchies and revolutionary regimes did, however, enter a new phase of intensity after 1967 and therein remained the 'Puzzle of Palestine'. It is worth noting that in one sense the United States escaped the full consequences of its support for Israel by virtue of the divisions within the

Arab world between radical and conservative parties, because the Arab states in direct confrontation with Israel were not the states with which Washington dealt in pursuit of its two overarching objectives of containing communism and securing oil.

One was gradually witnessing an increased acceptance for armed conflict as a means of problem-solving throughout the Middle East: while radical regimes' willingness and ability to use military power grew, they also relied increasingly on a strong security force to maintain their power against internal and external threats. The trend manifested itself over the next two decades as several regimes in the region used violent means to suppress domestic discontent, civil wars erupted, terrorism increased and a series of armed Arab–Israeli conflicts continued to unfold. With increased arms supply the means became increasingly lethal and the overall process influenced the mentality of the leaders as to what the accepted norm was in ensuring personal survival. Although these trends had been in the making for some time,[54] the Israeli victory in 1967 resulted in a higher degree of polarisation, radicalisation and militarisation of the region.[55]

President Richard M. Nixon, who took office in January 1969, continued to rely on Iran, Saudi Arabia and Israel as regional allies. He stated in a letter to King Faisal 'I can assure your majesty of the constancy of our strong interest in Saudi Arabia's security and welfare.'[56] The Nixon administration continued to support the pro-Western Shah of Iran with military and financial incentives, and with regard to Israel the new Republican administration maintained the policy of its predecessor.[57] The administration changed, however, in one critical respect as the Vietnam war had taken its toll: it concluded that the United States had to reconsider its commitments in Asia.[58] On 25 July 1969 Nixon remarked to the press at Guam that henceforth Asian nations would have to accept greater responsibility for their own defence,[59] and six months later, during the State of the Union Address, he formulated what was to become known as the Nixon Doctrine:

> Neither the defense nor the development of other nations can be exclusively or primarily an American undertaking. The nations of each part of the world should assume the primary responsibility of their own well-being; and they themselves should determine the terms of that well-being. We shall be faithful to our treaty commitments, but we shall reduce our involvement and our presence in other nations' affairs.[60]

In Indochina the Americans started training the South Vietnamese to sustain the war on their own, and in the Middle East the Nixon administration sought to prevent an escalation of the War of Attrition between Egypt and Israel which had started in late 1969. Nasser's pan-Arab dreams had survived the Six-Day War, and his new strategy was to wear out the Israelis by conducting military advances and strikes across the Suez Canal.[61] Israel began to construct a defensive line near the Suez Canal, known as the Bar-Lev Line, and Egypt attempted to impede its construction by commando raids and artillery bombardments.[62] Rather than remain passive and accept a prolonged war, the Israelis countered by attacking targets deep in the Egyptian homeland, including Cairo and its telephone and communication network. Egypt, facing defeat, humiliation and growing losses, secured modern SAMs from the Soviet Union. The United States for its part supplied the Israelis, and, as the crisis reached its peak, war erupted in Jordan between the royal forces and the Palestinians.[63] The two came together with the end of the war over the canal and Nasser's death during Black September in 1970.

Nasser's successor, Anwar Sadat, was concerned predominately with Egypt's economic and social problems and less with pan-Arab obligations. To Sadat, Egypt's overriding need was peace with Israel, and peace in his view could only come about through Washington. Sadat had a clear strategy in mind and was therefore ready to work more closely with the United States, though in the event his attempt to secure superpower intervention to reverse the verdict of past wars and to set the basis for a general peace in the area came to little in the beginning.[64] The United States saw no good reason to intervene in order to secure Israeli concessions and sought to maintain the policy of preventing war through the *imbalance of power*. The Soviet Union, embarking on the policy of détente, likewise had no incentive to challenge the present situation. Thus, by the end of 1972, Sadat had come to the conclusion that only through war could Egypt ensure US intervention.

On 6 October 1973 Egyptian forces crossed the Suez Canal while Syrian forces pushed across the Golan Heights. Although the Israelis managed to fight back and defeat their mortal enemies they witnessed the loss of 2,500 men and almost one quarter of their aircraft. Syrian and Egyptian losses were higher still, but Israel had lost face and with that the Arab forces perceived it as a political victory. According to Lawrence Freedman, some of the big military lessons to be drawn from October 1973 were 'the fluidity, tempo and intensity of contemporary war, which suggested that concepts based on holding a line and imposing attrition on the enemy were outdated'.[65] Egypt's and Syria's SAMs had posed a formidable threat to Israeli planes, and combined with the widespread portable anti-tank missiles the Arab forces challenged Israel's mechanised assets.

Politically the Yom Kippur War changed the situation in the Middle East considerably.[66] The Israeli vulnerability and defeat in the opening days of the war, which came as a great surprise to both the Soviet

Union and the United States, called into question the whole concept of stability through *imbalance*.[67] From that point, President Nixon, and next the Ford administration, acknowledged that a policy of regional *balance of power* was the way forward.[68] This marked the ground for what was to become the Camp David Agreement in September 1978,[69] and in the process Egypt severely reduced the Soviet connection and became a major recipient of US aid.[70] As Egypt was frozen out of the Arab League for its separate peace with Israel, the United States had thus developed four major friendships in the Middle East, but when the Shah of Iran was overthrown only months after Camp David, the Carter administration had to reconsider the strategic situation.[71] The sudden change in the regional balance of power was even more critical than the change in 1958. Faced with anti-American resentment in Iraq and Iran, and the Soviet invasion of Afghanistan, Carter decided to form a new military theatre command – the Rapid Deployment Joint Task Force (RDJTF). It was, in effect, the genesis of the structure that became the Central Command in 1983 and which in turn was the military command during Operations Desert Shield and Desert Storm.

The creation of that command led to a change in military strategy from regional stability through assistance and aid to deterrence and defence through force projection. The dominant military force would be the ground element with the priority mission to deter aggression or defend against a Soviet thrust from Iran to Saudi Arabia.[72] On 23 January 1980, before the Joint Session of Congress, President Carter declared:

> Let our position be absolutely clear: An attempt by any outside force to gain control of the Persian Gulf will be regarded as an assault on the vital interests of the United States of America, and such an assault will be repelled by any means necessary, including military force.[73]

The declaration, now known as the Carter Doctrine, was, according to National Security Advisor Zbigniew Brzezinski, 'modelled on the Truman Doctrine, enunciated in response to the Soviet threat to Greece and Turkey'.[74] In truth, however, it represented something entirely new: it assigned the United States a direct role in the Gulf, and US policy-makers seriously considered having ground troops in the region. Soviet forces moving into Afghanistan to support a falling communist regime were perceived as another step in an attempt to establish a stronghold in the Gulf, and this fear was supported by increased Soviet influence and war by proxy in Yemen, Angola and the Horn of Africa. The declaration of an Islamic Revolution by the new Iranian leader, Ayatollah Ruhollah Khomeini, and the subsequent Iraqi invasion of Iran on 22 September 1980, led the new Reagan administration in 1981 to reconsider still further its choice of associates.[75]

Ronald Reagan's presidency roughly coincided with the Iran–Iraq War, which became the centre stage of Washington's Persian Gulf policy. Initially, Reagan sought a posture of neutrality, but Henry Kissinger summed up the general preference when he indicated that the best outcome would be for both sides to lose.[76] While Iran was radical and aggressive in its rhetoric on expanding Islam, Iraq was viewed as an agent of Soviet subversion. There was never harmony in the Reagan administration on which party posed the biggest threat to the region, but ultimately it sought Iraqi goodwill to ensure 'security of access to [the] Persian Gulf'.[77] It hoped Saddam would eventually join the 'moderates' led by Egypt and Saudi Arabia, and by February–March 1982 Washington began its tilt towards Baghdad.[78] It was predominantly the Iranian counteroffensive that convinced Washington that the perceived spread of Islamic fundamentalism was far more damaging to their oil interests than an Iraqi victory that might further Soviet advances. The policy of supporting Iraq continued after the war ended in August 1988, but as the Bush administration would discover, Iraqi and US interests in the Persian Gulf began to separate.

In brief, the domestic and regional developments in the Middle East, in their interaction with US policy, shaped the very survivability that has come to characterise many of the Arab nations. Perhaps of all the countries thus affected in this process, Iraq was most profoundly changed in terms of coming into possession of a radical, nationalist stridency and unprecedented military power. In reality these elements entwined, along with a regime containing an infrastructure that made for unsuspected powers of recuperation and resilience, in the course of the war with Iran. The very possession of immense oilfields strengthened the authoritarian administration in Iraq, because it could pay for large army and security forces without relying on taxes and foreign subsidies. Thus, oil revenues made the state independent of society.[79] As Operation Desert Storm eventually demonstrated, the United States was able to gather unprecedented support for military action against Saddam's leadership, but the regime was one that a high-technological air campaign plan complemented by ground operations ultimately did not alter. The resilience and stamina of the regime will be detailed later, but it is all-important to appreciate that Saddam's durability is a reflection not only of personal characteristics, but of the regions' reliance on intimidation to express political opinion, and elaborate security means to ensure survival. Ironic as it may be, the United States played an important role in enabling that process, and the Iraqi leader proved throughout the 1980s that he was a man with whom the Western world could do business.

THE IRAQI PREDICAMENT – SADDAM'S BLITZKRIEG

During the 1970s Iraq was closely associated with the Soviet Union, while Iran was a US ally. The overthrow of the Shah at the end of 1978 seriously damaged the latter friendship, and with the revolution in Iran in February 1979 and the Soviet invasion of Afghanistan in December the same year, Washington looked to Baghdad for an alternative partner in the region. Saddam Hussein had become president of Iraq in July 1979, and on the night of 21–22 September 1980 he ordered Iraqi forces to move into Iranian territory to halt the perceived ideological threat posed by Ayatollah Khomeini, reverse minor border skirmishes and, importantly, secure the Shat al-Arab waterway, which provided access to the Persian Gulf. Analysts disagree on the causes of the war, but some of the explanation resides with the two predominant individuals. Saddam believed in the supremacy of the state, while Khomeini, who arrived in Iraq in 1964 and spent several years in the most religious parts of the country before he was expelled, viewed state and religion as one entity. It was essentially a secular Sunni Arab ruling over a traditional Shia majority in Iraq, confronting a Shia Persian 'cleric with a direct line to Allah'.[80]

The Iraqi leader was concerned that Iraq would disintegrate from within, and quickly established himself as the defender of the modern state system against fundamentalism, and when his secular Ba'ath regime had failed to prevent the Iranians from making inroads into Iraqi territory by the end of 1982, Washington decided to take sides. The Iraqi leader was perceived as a man with whom the West could reason and as the Iran–Iraq War progressed a rather close relationship between Baghdad and Washington developed in four distinct phases, according to Bruce W. Jentleson. From 1982 to 1984 Washington provided political support and allowed Iraq gradually to import US commodities on credit. Between 1984 and 1986 Washington resumed arms sales to Baghdad and fully restored diplomatic relations that had been weak ever since the monarchy fell in 1958, but completely severed since June 1967. From 1986 to 1988 the two countries almost formed an alliance in which the United States became one of Iraq's main supporters, and finally, between 1989 and the invasion of Kuwait, the Bush administration, although freezing loan guarantees and considering a ban on technology that could be used both commercially and militarily, continued to provide Saddam with both economic and political assistance. A brief examination of how the Iraqi regime was transformed from ally to adversary within a decade is thus required in order to put the military endeavour of 1991 into perspective.

The informal opening to Iraq started in 1977, when President Carter sent an American surgeon and his team to treat Saddam's back problem.

In mid 1979 the number of diplomats and staff members from US delegations in Baghdad was larger than in most Western Embassies, and American businessmen frequently visited Baghdad. Saddam announced that relations with the United States were better than ever,[81] but the official opening to Iraq started on 26 February 1982, when the Reagan administration took Iraq off the list of state sponsors of terrorism.[82] Although it would later admit that 'the real reason for the decision was to help [the Iraqis] succeed in the war against Iran',[83] the decision opened the market for US companies exporting agricultural products and technology. Iraq received credit guarantees from the Export-Import Bank (Eximbank), and the new Iraqi market promised prosperity for American farmers. Products like rice, wheat, corn, sugar and tobacco were, however, soon accompanied by computers, helicopters, machine tools and high technology. The Secretary of State, George P. Shultz, sent a memorandum to the US Embassy in Baghdad in January 1983, suggesting a meeting with the Iraqi Secretary of Foreign Affairs, Saadoun Hammadi, and the first meeting between the two took place the following month.[84] It was suggested that if a 'tilt towards Iraq' was necessary, because of increased Soviet influence or Iranian gains in the war, it might include financial, diplomatic and military action. Shortly afterwards, the Iraqis were given further loans, dual-use technology restrictions were loosened, and in 1984 President Reagan signed National Security Decision Directive 99 (NSDD-99) formally authorising a 'limited intelligence sharing program for Iraq'.[85] Shultz used NSDD-99 the following year to argue that the United States had the opportunity to pull Iraq further away from the Soviet Union and help restrain its behaviour.[86] The United States assisted Iraq militarily, high-technology export licences which previously had been held back were approved, and it encouraged other countries to supply aircraft, missiles and helicopters.[87] The United States was, according to Kenneth R. Timmerman, by the mid 1980s literally arming Iraq to prevent Iran from winning the war.[88]

The Iraqi Ambassador to Washington, Nizar Hamdoun, befriended a range of opinion- and policy-makers, and he was one of the first Arab ambassadors to really understand the intricate workings of the US political system. He quickly established himself as an articulate and popular figure in Washington, arguing that Iraq was a moderate state and thereby influencing Congress, media and public opinion.[89] The *Wall Street Journal* even referred to him as 'the best foreign ambassador ever posted to the United States'.[90] The shift in US policy towards Iraq was the subject of a May 1985 memorandum in which William Casey, director of the Central Intelligence Agency (CIA), concluded 'the tilt to Iraq was timely when Iraq was against the ropes and the Islamic revolution was on a roll'.[91] Two months later Shultz requested the Department of Defense's assistance 'in expediting licensing of exports to Iraq "without impositions of impractical conditions", in order to increase our influence in Iraq to the detriment of the Soviet Union'.[92]

There was, however, never consensus on policy towards Iraq in the early Reagan years. While George Shultz and his Assistant Secretary of State Richard Murphy were promoting closer ties with Iraq, Secretary of Defense Casper Weinberger 'went ballistic when he heard about the [Bell-214] helicopter sales'.[93] Both Richard Perle and Stephen Bryan, high-ranking members in the Department of Defense, criticised the embrace of Iraq from a perspective of realpolitik.[94] In 1985 they had argued that Iraq was pursuing an interest in nuclear weapons that would threaten US national security interests separately from the Cold War context. Despite their efforts, a new National Security Directive was issued the following year, stating that all government agencies should 'be more forthcoming on Iraqi licence requests'.[95] Others, including national security advisors Richard V. Allen, Robert McFarlane and Admiral John M. Poindexter, argued that Iran was basically more hostile to Moscow than Washington, and thus deals could be made with Teheran.[96] Some took the issue further, and the November 1986 revelation of arms sales to Iran, known as the Irangate or the Iran-Contra affair, sent shock-waves through the American people. Although it upset Baghdad, the Iraqis were deeply dependent on continued US military support against their neighbour,[97] and therefore Saddam limited himself to rhetorical misgivings about the deal. According to Barry Rubin, Saddam believed the United States was capable of ending the Iran–Iraq War whenever it chose, and the fact that it did not stop the war combined with American arms deals with Iran, implied to the Iraqi leader 'a U.S. conspiracy to weaken Iraq'.[98]

Congress was also divided over Iraq, but on the whole sceptical towards the State Department's endorsement. Reports had reached its members that chemical bombs and artillery shells had been used against Iranian troops since 1983,[99] and although Amnesty International, the United Nations and the press raised their concerns, the Reagan administration did little more than send a formal protest and tighten control on chemical exports.[100] There were further reports on Saddam violating human rights issues domestically and by March 1988 the gassing of the Kurdish population of Halabja had reached such a level that the Senate unanimously passed the Prevention of Genocide Act of 1988 calling for tough economic sanctions on Iraq. Despite the strong violation of the Geneva Convention, and Khomeini having accepted a cease-fire after eight years of war, Shultz argued that to impose sanctions was 'premature', and that 'there should be no radical policy change now regarding Iraq'.[101] When Saadoun Hammadi met with Shultz after the cease-fire he expressed genuine concerns on whether the United States might consider Iraq as the new threat, but Shultz assured him that 'we do not want to tame Iraq, nor concede anything to Iran'. Shultz further contended that 'we have no desire to bring Iraq down to earth. We would like to see Iraq develop.'[102]

The Bush administration, which came into office in January 1989, decided to follow the previous administration's attempt to 'bandwagon Iraq'[103] by re-socialising the leadership through a policy of 'constructive engagement', but there was never full consensus on the issue.[104] Zalmay Khalilzad, a member of the Department of State's Policy Planning Staff who specialised on the Gulf region, supported the tilt towards Iraq during the war on the basis of regional balance, but now that Iran was seriously weakened he argued that Saddam would exploit the opportunity. The Iraqi leader was allegedly determined to build a non-conventional programme, which would turn Iraq into a regional superpower, and Khalilzad argued that Iraq needed to be contained.[105] George Shultz strongly opposed the conclusion,[106] and his successor, James Baker, continued to develop strong ties with Baghdad.[107]

On 2 October 1989, President Bush signed National Security Directive 26 (NSD-26), which proposed 'economic and political incentives for Iraq to moderate its behavior and to increase [American] influence in Iraq'.[108] The directive was a continuation of the Reagan administration's policy, and Bush contended that the whole idea was to bring Saddam Hussein 'into the family of nations'.[109] NSD-26 set the stage for the Bush administration's decision to follow its predecessor, committing itself to a policy of improving US–Iraq relations. It suggested that 'normal relations between the United States and Iraq would serve our longer-term interests and promote stability in both the Gulf and the Middle East'.[110] The policy was consistent with previous presidential doctrines and viewed as a natural extension of a strategic review (NSR-10), which emphasised the economic and security importance of the oil reserves to the United States.[111] Three days after the President's approval of NSD-26, on 5 October 1989, Baker hosted an Iraqi delegation to discuss bilateral relations.[112] An internal Department of State memorandum followed shortly after, recommending the administration to commit $1 billion of Commodity Credit Corporation (CCC) loan guarantees for Iraq.[113]

While US–Iraqi relations seemed reasonably good on the surface, the Iraqi regime was less happy with the domestic situation. Iraq undoubtedly emerged from the war with Iran as a major military power, but it was economically impoverished and its social fabric was over-stretched.[114] Paradoxically, the post-war situation disclosed serious challenges to the Iraqi leadership that had been curtailed during the war. Saddam had managed to mobilise considerable Iraqi patriotism during the war by balancing the relationship between nationhood and religion, but the fact that at least 200,000 were killed, about 400,000 were wounded and 70,000 were taken prisoner, seriously weakened the country.[115] By mid 1989 Iraq owed some $40 billion to the Arab Gulf States and another $40 billion to non-Arab countries.[116] Heavy war debts, reluctance by regional and Western banks to give new loans and declining oil prices resulted in a severe lack of cash. Consequently, national enterprises went into recession and signs of private dissatisfaction followed.[117]

In an attempt to pre-empt discontent the Iraqi leader had called for constitutional reforms which the Revolutionary Command Council (RCC) discussed on 22 December 1988 and 16 January 1989.[118] The members divided themselves into two orientations: the hard-liners and the moderates. The former group argued against change while the latter, which included Saadoun Hammadi, Nizar Hamdoun and Tariq Aziz, argued that a multiparty system and more freedom for the press was the right way forward. Saddam never gave the project high priority, but at the time there was some hope for change.

The perceived victory over Iran provided for another security challenge for the Iraqi leader. The military troops became popular and highly respected throughout the society, and to make sure that no officer would challenge his own position he allegedly had prominent generals such as Mahir Abdul Rashid put under house arrest and Thabit Sultan killed in a helicopter crash.[119] Many others were arrested, and on 5 May 1989 Baghdad Radio announced that Secretary of Defence, Adnan Khayr Allah al-Tilfah, Saddam's cousin and brother-in-law, had been killed in a helicopter crash. It is still contested whether this was an accident or arranged from the Office of the Presidential Palace (OPP),[120] but either way, Saddam's wife (Adnan's sister) and Saddam's foster-father and early mentor, Khayr Allah al-Tilfah (Adnan's father), blamed Saddam for the death. This gave rise to unprecedented tension between the two core families on which Saddam's power relied (al-Majid and al-Tilfah). These tensions within the core families, combined with economic difficulties, amounted to a very real threat for the Iraqi leader.

With economic stagnation, inflation reaching some 40 per cent per annum and increasing unemployment,[121] Saddam was reluctant to demobilise his armed forces, possibly fearing wider social unrest.[122] From August 1988 to August 1990 the Popular Army was demobilised,[123] but only 250,000 were released from the regular army, leaving over 1 million in uniform.[124] Keeping such a large military force during a time of economic hardship needed justification, and therein one finds some of the explanations for Saddam's overt criticism of Zionist and Anglo-American imperialism. Those who had been demobilised returned, however, to find that over 1 million Egyptian immigrants had taken their jobs, and consequently violent clashes took place resulting in hundreds of Egyptian deaths.[125] Mohammad-Mahmoud Mohamedou argues in his dissertation that 'The attempt to annex Kuwait was promoted by the serious and pressing need to give a mission to the Iraqi army', and thus keep it 'away from urban centers, where it was poised, upon its return from the Iranian front, to engender socioeconomic problems of re-integration and political concerns about the regime's security'.[126] Although most of the political opposition had been driven abroad by the late 1980s, alleged assassination attempts were discovered in early and late 1989, resulting in arrests and execution of Army and Air Force officers. For example, in January 1990, on the Iraqi Army day, a young Colonel in the Republican Guard, Sattam Ghanim al-Jubburi, tried to take matters into his own hands. He placed a small missile in his tank, planning to blow up the podium where Saddam was to give a speech, but the secret police discovered him in an unexpected security check.[127] Saddam executed 26 members of the Jubburi tribe and arrested alleged collaborators of the Ubeidi tribe. The events, in effect, suggested the first cracks in the politically important tribal power base, and fear of social unrest was further strengthened by the fate of Romania's Nicolai Ceaucescu on 25 December 1989.

Early 1990 also witnessed Turkey closing the Euphrates River for 30 days to flood a lake behind the new Attaturk Dam, causing severe hardship for some of Iraq's farmers.[128] Additionally, some 13 million date trees had been destroyed during the war with Iran, seriously undermining other aspects of agricultural production.[129] The leadership briefly tried a free-market economy, selling state enterprises en masse and cheaply, but, when that proved disastrous, it reintroduced strict price control.[130]

Acknowledging these growing domestic issues, Saddam tried to secure a higher regional profile for Iraq. On 16 February 1989 the Arab Co-operation Council (ACC) was formed between Iraq, Egypt, Jordan and Yemen. Saddam proposed that it should include a military dimension, but President Mubarak managed to limit it to the economic field. Iraq nevertheless continued its quest for military technology, and on 5 December 1989 Hussein Kamel was able to claim that they had launched their first space rocket, Tammuz I, and that they had developed missiles that could reach Israel. Since 1972, Saddam Hussein, as Vice President, had given great priority to developing the first Arab atomic bomb, and throughout the 1980s such research increased. Nuclear weapons were part of the Iraqi leader's instruments for becoming the new pan-Arab leader, but events in 1989 and early 1990 undermined such ambitions.

Although Ayatollah Khomeini accepted United Nation Security Council Resolution 598,[131] he refused to reopen the Shat al-Arab waterway and the exchange of prisoners of war was slow. This impaired

Saddam's regional authority, as did the failure to evict Syria's army from Lebanon. The following months witnessed the beginning of an intensive Iraqi intervention in the Lebanese civil war in the form of financial and military support to General Michael Aoun.[132] The campaign was not very successful, but to make matters worse, President Hafiz Assad arrived in Cairo on 14 July 1990 for discussions on improving Syrian–Egyptian relations.[133] The Kuwaitis and the Iranians on their part started bilateral negotiations, and additionally Baghdad seemed to conclude that Washington was less willing to help Iraq now that the war with Iran had ended. Tariq Aziz told James Baker: 'Frankly speaking in the spirit of friendship, Iraq has not seen enough improvements in the relationship since the ceasefire.'[134] He observed that the United States 'seemed to have a negative approach to Iraqi post-war efforts to develop its industry and technological base'. There was therefore, in essence, by early 1990 no compensation for the domestic problems in the foreign field, and gradually the Iraqi leader looked for alternative solutions to his economic problems.

According to General Wafiq Samarrai, former chief of Iraqi Military Intelligence, the creation of the ACC was the point in time when Saddam seriously started thinking of Kuwait as the solution to Iraq's strategic and financial problems.[135] As the war with Iran ended, the Iraqi–Kuwait relationship in effect became increasingly more distant. The Emir of Kuwait, for example, was the only Arab leader who did not accept Saddam's invitation to visit Iraq to celebrate the proclaimed victory over Iran. Still, when the Emir decided to come, on 23 September 1989, he was given a warm reception, including the highest Iraqi decoration in appreciation of the support they had received in the war.[136] The border dispute was discussed, and so was a non-aggression pact,[137] but when Saadoun Hammadi visited Kuwait three months later, Iraq had expanded the subjects for discussion to include restoring the Organisation of Petroleum Exporting Countries (OPEC) oil prices, in addition to requesting a loan of $10 billion for reconstruction.[138] When the Kuwaiti Secretary of Foreign Affairs suggested settling the subject of borders according to the 1963 Agreement, Hammadi simply replied that no such agreement existed:

> What you are talking about is neither an agreement nor a treaty because the draft that was drawn then was not ratified by any legislative source in Iraq. This means that it did not acquire any legal status according to the Iraqi constitution. Frankly what you are talking about and call the 1963 Agreement does not exist legally or historically.[139]

The Iraqi regime insisted that the war with Iran had cost some $102 billion in military hardware, and during those eight years Iraq had further lost some $106 billion in oil revenues.[140] Saddam became increasingly frustrated with the low oil prices and his Arab Gulf colleagues' reluctance to grant his country more loans, or even forgive old war debts. In sum, while the Kuwaitis wanted to settle the border dispute, the Iraqi leadership wanted to settle its wider economic problems. Moreover, Saddam believed Kuwait could not possibly be doing this on its own initiative.

John Kelly, who replaced Richard Murphy in 1989 as Under Secretary of State for Near Eastern Affairs, visited Baghdad on 12 February 1990, and for the first time a US official voiced misgivings about the use of chemical weapons and other human rights records. He emphasised that the US administration was 'committed to the relationship for the long haul, but that in every respect it will have to be a two-way street ... benefits for US interests must outweigh concerns over Iraq's behaviour in some areas'.[141] Kelly told Saddam that he was a 'force for moderation in the region, and the United States wishes to broaden its relations with Iraq'.[142] Despite these assurances the Iraqi leader remained uncertain of American intentions, because three days later *Voice of America* condemned him as one of the worst tyrants in the world, running a 'ruthless secret police regime', and on 21 February the State Department published a report in which the Iraqi regime was described as 'the worst violator of human rights'.[143]

In response, early 1990 witnessed increased hostile rhetoric from the Iraqi leader. He questioned the US naval presence in the region and seriously threatened 'to burn half of Israel' if attacked.[144] Saddam was genuinely concerned that Israel was about to attack Iraq's nuclear facility now that it had one of the most right-wing coalition governments in its history: Yitzak Shamir was Prime Minister, David Levy Foreign Minister and Ariel Sharon Housing Minister.[145] This was a transition government, as had been the case with Israeli premier Menachem Begin a decade earlier. The Israeli air attack on Iraq's nuclear reactor, Osirak, on 7 June 1981, had indeed helped Begin in the following election.[146] Israel responded to Saddam's threat by launching a satellite in orbit for military reconnaissance. According to Hazim Abd al-Razzaq al-Ayyubi, who was the commander of the Iraqi surface-to-surface missiles corps, exercises were held throughout 1989 and early 1990 for the purpose of retaliation. Maps and target-information were continually updated, especially for Tel-Aviv and Haifa.[147] Prince Bandar, the Saudi Ambassador to Washington, intervened for the time being, assuring the Iraqi leader on behalf of Washington that Israel would not attack Iraq. But while this may have provided Saddam with domestic popularity and some room for manoeuvre, he was apparently convinced that the world was largely against him. Without the common cause previously found in the perceived Iranian threat, US–Iraqi relations increasingly suffered from mutual distrust, which manifested itself in the absence of constructive dialogue.[148] The Iraqi leader's relationship with President Mubarak was also becoming ever more complicated, and in the process Saddam identified increasingly with the Palestinian cause and Yassir Arafat, who once stated 'I can't sleep peacefully except in Baghdad.'[149]

With the increased tensions the US strategy of 'constructive engagement' was consequently replaced by one of reassurance,[150] and the immediate diplomatic move by Washington was to send a bipartisan delegation of senators to meet Saddam Hussein in Mosul on 12 April 1990. The delegation, which was headed by Senator Robert J. Dole, sought to assure Saddam that the United States was committed to working closely with Iraq.[151] In a prepared statement the Bush administration desired 'to improve relations between [the] two countries'.[152] Senator Dole further assured the Iraqi leader that even if Congress voted in favour of economic sanctions, Bush would oppose them.[153] When Dole reported back to President Bush he argued that Saddam was the kind of leader the United States could 'easily be in a position to influence', and in return Bush sent a message to the Iraqi leader, expressing the hope that 'ties between the United States and Iraq would contribute to the peace and stability of the Middle East'.[154] In early May, Saddam seemed rather confident, promising Arafat nothing less than Jerusalem, the Gaza Strip and the West Bank.[155]

With assurances from the United States that Israel would not attack Iraq,[156] Saddam shifted his effort eastwards. At the opening of the Arab summit in Baghdad on 28 May 1990 he accused both Kuwait and the United Arab Emirates (UAE) of overproduction of oil and stealing through lateral drilling, causing the price to fall from the OPEC agreed $18 a barrel to $7. He emphasised that he considered these actions as an economic war against Iraq, and consequently the Iraqis would take action if it did not stop.[157] The threat was followed by military deployment on the Kuwaiti border. The Department of State responded with a prompt warning, arguing that they were determined to ensure the free flow of oil through the straits of Hormuz; to defend the principles of freedom of navigation; and to 'support the individual and collective self-defence of our friends in the Gulf, with whom we have deep and long-standing ties'.[158] Saddam described the message as implying 'clear alignment against Iraq',[159] but he still believed he could enter Kuwait *and* satisfy the US concerns.

Saadoun Hammadi embarked on a tour throughout the Gulf States, arguing that Iraq was drained of resources. When he came back from talks with the Kuwaitis in June 1990 the Iraqi leader felt that the Emir had been arrogant and indifferent to Iraqi needs.[160] Saddam's anti-Israel speeches earned him some admiration among the Arab masses, and on 27 June 1990 he felt confident enough to launch his own doctrine: 'Whoever strikes at the Arabs we will strike back from Iraq.'[161] The doctrine was proclaimed only hours after a limited meeting in the RCC where the proposal for a partial invasion of Kuwait was ratified.[162] Iraq had substantial support in Jordan and Yemen, but to safeguard Arab support for an invasion the Iraqi leader tried to convince President Mubarak that Arab wealth should be redistributed, and for a start he gave the Egyptian leader $25 million with the promise of more to come.[163] Saddam was, therefore, facing a post-war social–economic–political crisis, and he felt he deserved more gratitude after having defended the Fertile Crescent in an historical war against the Persians.[164] He decided not to stay passive as international developments upset him further: the decline of the Soviet Union had left the United States as the only superpower in the region, and to add insult to injury, Soviet-Jewish immigration to Israel increased. When the Iraqi leadership failed in having the United Nations High Commission for Refugees condemn the immigration, Saddam might have perceived an Anglo-US-Zionist threat to his pan-Arab visions. The domestic, regional and international developments that followed the war with Iran strengthened his conviction that Kuwait should be 'Iraq's port' and 'the Arab brothers should eat off the same dish'.[165] There was also the popular sentiment among the Iraqis that Kuwait really belonged to Iraq.

The Iraqi leadership initiated contacts with Iran after Khomeini died on 3 June 1989, but the Iranian leadership was slow in responding. Saddam sent several delegations and in the spring of 1990 he wrote a letter to the new Iranian leader, Ali Akbar Hashemi Rafsanjani, suggesting direct talks. In the following months senior officials from both parties engaged in discussions, and the Iraqi leader seems to have concluded that only the United States could pose a problem to his regional ambitions. Consequently, the Iraqi leadership gradually engaged in a media campaign against the economic policies of the Gulf Arab states, at the same time as it probed Washington's position.

On 16 July 1990, the Iraqi Secretary of Foreign Affairs Tariq Aziz issued a note to the General Secretary of the Arab League, accusing the Kuwaiti government of having adopted an unjust policy whose object was to undermine the Arab nations and especially Iraq. The argument was that Kuwait, and to some extent the other Gulf States, were waging an economic war against Iraq. This was followed up by a speech wherein the Iraqi leader publicly threatened Kuwait and the United Arab Emirates with war,[166] accusing them of shoving a 'poisoned dagger' into Iraq by overproduction that resulted in low oil prices.[167] He further accused the Kuwaitis of working with Israel and the United States in a conspiracy against Iraq.

Being well aware of these disagreements, and despite knowing that 150,000 Iraqi troops were massed on the Kuwaiti border by late July 1990, the world's major political powers were preoccupied with Europe and the changes that were evolving in one communist regime after the other. President George Bush personally had been giving priority to the hostage-taking in Trinidad, the civil war in Liberia and the domestic budget battle.[168] Although some military analysts, on 19–20 July, started arguing that Iraq would most likely invade the whole of Kuwait, they were not able to convince the wider intelligence community.[169] It was, however, serious enough for the Defense Intelligence Agency (DIA) to declare Watchcon III, the lowest level of alert, noting that 'this relocation [of Republican Guard forces] does significantly reduce warning time if the Iraqis were to decide to conduct cross border operations'.[170] Three days later, on 24 July, the DIA raised the alert level to Watchcon II, noting that sufficient logistics were in place and that those forces could 'initiate military operations against Kuwait at any time with no warning'.[171] On the same day, James Baker issued guidance to US Embassies, on 'US Reactions to Iraqi Threats In the Gulf'. The cable stated that they were concerned about the Iraqi threats, and 'While we take no position on the border delineation issue raised by Iraq with respect to Kuwait, or on other bi-lateral disputes, Iraqi statements suggest an intention to resolve outstanding disagreements by the use of force, an approach which is contrary to UN-Charter principles.'[172]

When the American Ambassador to Iraq, April Glaspie, met Saddam the next day, she delivered those points without realising that Saddam was trying to get a feel for an American reaction to his secret plan of invasion.[173] She reported back to Washington that Saddam sought to settle the crisis with Kuwait at the upcoming Jedda meeting. The Arab leaders furthermore reassured President Bush that no Arab country had ever invaded another,[174] that the military training in the desert around Basra was not abnormal, and that the eight Republican Guard divisions at the northern Kuwaiti border were merely part of gunboat diplomacy. King Hussein, President Mubarak and King Fahd all contended that an invasion would not take place, because Saddam Hussein had given his word.[175] Although some defence analysts argued that Iraq was going to invade,[176] the Arab leaders insisted that the United States should not get involved, and the Bush administration adhered to the advice of the latter.[177] Saddam seems to have been convinced by late July 1990 that the United States would not seriously intervene in what was to him an Arab affair.[178] There was at best an ambiguous US commitment to Kuwait territory, and therein Saddam may have perceived a reasonable case: the US–Iraqi relationship was not bad, and it was Saudi Arabia that was the vital US interest, not

Kuwait. With a non-aggression pact with Saudi Arabia from February 1989 and no immediate intention of going into that country,[179] Saddam possibly calculated that any reaction to an invasion would be manageable. The only thing that could prevent him from invading the emirate was unconditional economic grants from the Kuwaiti side.

A close examination of the meeting between the Iraqi leader and April Glaspie reveals that he was feeding her false information. He told her that if the Kuwaitis did not meet his demands he would destroy Kuwait and conquer it physically, but he promised not to use force until after meetings were held at Jedda and in Baghdad. He knew he was misleading her, and when Glaspie provided a fairly mild response, restating the US policy, that it did not want to be involved in inter-Arab border issues, Saddam seems to have concluded that the official United States position was that he would get away with invading Kuwait. In other words, he provided false information, and when her response was based on those lies he seems to have taken it as the genuine United States position.

The Iraqi–Kuwaiti negotiations were hosted by King Fahd at Jedda in Saudi Arabia on 30–31 July. The Emir decided not to attend the summit, sending his brother Crown Prince Sheikh Saad instead. Saddam was allegedly 'deadly insulted' and sent a trio as his replacement.[180] Izzat Ibrahim, Vice Chairman of the RCC, headed the Iraqi delegation, accompanied by Saadoun Hammadi and Ali Hasan al-Majid. The latter was most likely sent with the intention of intimidation, as he had been in charge of gassing the Kurds in March 1988, earning him the nickname of Chemical Ali (*Ali al-Kimyawi*). Saddam's representatives demanded a $10 billion 'loan', the redrawing of the border, including the disputed oilfields, and at least a leasing agreement of the islands of Warba and Bubiyan. Izzat Ibrahim seems to have been instructed not to agree to anything less than concessions on all issues. The meeting was tense and with no agreements on the two islands the Iraqi leader chose to order the delegation back to Baghdad. This was sufficient for the DIA to raise the level of alert to the highest, Watchcon I:

> Although there is as yet no evidence of a direct move against Kuwait, the combination of the breakdown in the talks, the latest Iraqi military moves, and the resumption of harsh Iraqi rhetoric all point towards military action by Iraq, although these developments may only be part of an escalation in psychological pressure by Baghdad. Saddam is undoubtedly prepared to cross the border in force. In fact, the Iraqi force now assembled is sufficient not only to overrun all of Kuwait, but the Eastern Province of Saudi Arabia if necessary.[181]

The military analysts in the CIA and the DIA argued that the deployment on the Iraqi border was unprecedented: never before had the Iraqi President ordered all eight of the Republican Guard divisions to one place. He had even called for the division in the west facing Israel, and he did not keep a division or two outside Baghdad for security measures, as he had always done during the war with Iran. Furthermore, according to some reports, the deployment area was not the traditional exercise ground for these elite forces, and exercises of this size did not normally take place in summer.[182]

In essence, although Saddam held his cards close to his chest, it was the scope of the invasion rather than invasion itself that came as a surprise. The Iraqi leader had engaged in hostile rhetoric for some time, and his troop movements were closely monitored by US intelligence. Some of the intelligence reports warned about Iraqi intentions, but the White House chose to trust the Arab leaders who argued that a full occupation of Kuwait was not conceivable. It begs the obvious question of whether warning the Iraqi President, or deploying military forces, would have deterred aggression. The USS *Independence* could have been deployed, and the 82nd Airborne Division could have been despatched – although agreeing on a suitable base for such a deployment could have proved difficult in the first place – but it might additionally have provided support for Middle East fears of conspiracy. The display of US military force in the region would further have been against the wishes of the other Arab leaders at the time, and it might therefore have created a reason for Saddam to engage in pre-emptive strikes.

The White House has faced some criticism for not having been able to predict Iraq's regional ambitions, but the senior military leadership regarded a full invasion as unlikely. Based on the intelligence, they argued that if an invasion were to take place it would at most involve the disputed Rumalia oilfield, and the two islands in the north, Bubiyan and Warba. Much of the same attitude was reflected in a classified information report by the Department of Defense in late July. The report stated that 'the goal of Iraqi president Hussein is to be the leader of the Arab world', and that within two years he would have the strongest army in the region, including the capability of threatening Israel with ballistic missiles.[183] The report further stated that Iraq was not 'particularly pressed for currency at this particular time', so the economic demands would most likely be 'for the continued development of the Iraqi military machine (for example, nuclear weapons or more chemical weapons)'. The report concluded that the 'goal would likely be focused on obtaining a port on the Persian Gulf, rather than completely conquering Kuwait'. In a post-war interview April Glaspie too seems to have given the game away when she responded 'We never expected they would take all of Kuwait.'[184]

It has been argued thus far that the Reagan administration fully embraced Iraq as their regional partner out of fear of Iranian dominance. While the decision made sense in terms of realpolitik at the time, the Bush administration's decision to continue to improve relations with Saddam's secular Ba'ath regime represented a serious misreading of the Iraqi leader's concerns and ambitions following the end of the Cold War and the Iran–Iraq War. Although some of the miscalculations were founded in different 'mind-sets', the Bush administration was not willing to challenge a relationship that had served it well in the past until it was too late. Bruce W. Jentleson suggests that the administration was caught up in a self-perpetuating operational tautology: 'We know the policy is working because we believe it is the right policy; we believe it is the right policy because we know it is working.'[185] Thus, although the Iraqi regime claimed victory after the war with Iran, the socio-economic problems that followed led it into a new crisis. In simple terms the Iraqi people wanted the fruits of victory, and Saddam needed to deliver. As the regime was denied further loans, and there were few prospects for immediate incentives in the talks with the Kuwaitis, Saddam came to the conclusion that an occupation of Kuwait was the solution. It is reasonable to argue that the idea of occupying Kuwaiti territory had been considered by Saddam at least since 1989, but 'the political decision to enter Kuwait was not open for discussion [in the RCC] until 27–29 June 1990'.[186] A few days later, the commander of the Republican Guard, Lieutenant General Ayad Futayih al-Rawi, his son-in-law, Hussein Kamel, and his cousin, Ali Hasan al-Majid,[187] were ordered to prepare plans for a possible invasion of Kuwait. In mid July the RCC adopted the option of using some sort of military force if Kuwait denied them access to the South Rumalia oilfield and the two islands at the Jedda meeting.[188]

Egyptian author Mohamed Heikal claims the original plan had indeed been to seize only the two islands and the Rumalia oilfield, but that Saddam had proposed a change of plans only a few days before the invasion.[189] Key individuals such as Secretary of Defence Abdel Jabber Shansal, Secretary of Foreign Affairs Tariq Aziz and Armed Forces Chief of Staff Nazir al-Khazzraji were not informed,[190] and the Iraqi Ambassador to Tunisia, Hamed al-Jabouri, argued that the invasion took the Iraqi people, its military officers and even high-ranking politicians completely by surprise.[191] Brigadier General Tawfiq al-Yasari, who served as political advisor to the Republican Guard's Medina division during the invasion, was only informed of parts of the plan just prior to the advance.[192] Tariq Aziz described taking the whole of Kuwait as Saddam's own 'last-moment' decision.[193] Since Iraq had all kinds of military contingency plans for the region, and given the relative size of Kuwait, such an operation would not need much coordination.[194]

According to Tariq Aziz, the philosophy behind the last-minute decision was that such an invasion would bring about a military coup, through which 'a new indigenous government' would replace the ruling family. As a result, 'in the ashes of the ruins we will build a politics of understanding rather than a politics of confrontation, to unite, to become one after the long separation, and finally, Iraq will be able to solve its economic problems with a lung open to the sea.'[195] Although an interesting mixing of metaphors, the move was according to Saddam's definition of realpolitik: 'Politics is when you say you are going to do one thing [not invade Kuwait] while intending to do another [partial occupation]. Then you do neither what you said or what you intended [full occupation].'[196] Although one does not know the seriousness behind this definition, it suits a pattern of behaviour based on amorality and cynicism.

The Iraqi leader had managed to keep his decision to invade Kuwait highly secret, and since the Kuwaitis had no defence line of substance, the occupation was completed within hours. Kuwait maintained only three active brigades, a small Air Force and a Navy, so militarily it was no opposition. Without exception, all officers were genuine Kuwaitis, and above the rank of colonel almost all officers had close ties to the royal family or members of prominent families. With most of them abroad on holiday during the invasion, it was, according to Lieutenant Colonel Fred L. Hart, an American eyewitness, hard to even find anyone above the rank of major around.

Three Republican Guard divisions crossed the border en masse on 2 August 1990. The mechanised Tawakala division and the armoured Hammurabi division conducted the main attack along the four-lane highway from Safwan, while the armoured Medina division crossed further to the west through the Rumaylah oilfields. These Republican Guard divisions were ordered to enter and capture strategic positions throughout the country, while the others remained in reserve. One division crossed the Kuwaiti–Iraqi border and headed south to al-Jahrah, and then moved to occupy key government buildings in Kuwait city. Another armoured division entered south below the Gulf of Kuwait to deal with the remaining resistance from the Kuwaiti Army, and the remaining divisions stayed more or less in the rear. These ground operations were coupled with special operations, amphibious landings and the use of helicopter airborne units. The latter occupied three sites: the Kuwaiti airfields, to secure landing facilities for the invading forces; the Emir's Dasman and Bayan palaces in the hope of capturing the Emir; and units that went to break into the National Bank. The Bank assets proved to be disappointing to Saddam. He believed that the Kuwaitis had the same practice as he did, where gold reserves were in the main bank buildings, but the Kuwaitis kept most of their reserves in Western banks. Thus, although he found some gold, and transported it to Baghdad, it was a relatively small amount.

With the important exception of not succeeding in capturing the Kuwaiti Emir and his family, and getting huge amounts of gold bars, the military operation was reasonably well executed at a tactical level. On an operational level, however, one might question why Iraq attacked frontally, rather than encircling to ensure the blockage of an escape, which could easily have been done by two divisions.[197] Furthermore, the Iraqis did not seal the border with Kuwait until 12 August: the Iraqi troops decided to go straight for the capital, and the operational error of not bypassing Kuwait city permitted the bulk of the Kuwaiti 15th Brigade, located near the al-Ahmadi oilfields, to escape to Saudi Arabia.

The single most important destination for the helicopter-borne commandos was the Emir's palace.[198] Saddam seems to have been convinced that if he managed to capture the Kuwaiti Emir, he would have the upper hand in any further negotiation. Without al-Sabah, there would be no focus for loyalty, and no symbol of state legitimacy. The Kuwaiti Air Force's brief resistance may have saved the Emir as he managed to escape with some 25 members of his family.[199] The secrecy of the operation was, in retrospect, at the expense of succeeding in the most important objective. One might question whether there were other, less violent instruments, that could have been used, but according to Tariq Aziz, it was not sufficient to simply capture the Emir: a full occupation was required to ensure a strategic blow.[200] Next, by taking the National Bank, Saddam seems to have concluded that he could offer the regional opposition financial incentives, and by seizing those assets he believed he could divert them to Iraq with immediate effect.

The military strategy was supplemented by a strong and consistent media campaign, which relied on a range of controlled agencies to support its case. According to newspapers, radio and television, there had been a revolution in Kuwait against the Emir's family, and a new interim government had seized power. This new government had in turn requested military support from their Arab brothers, to prevent any foreign country from intervening, and Iraq had consequently only answered to their national duty. Baghdad Voice of the Masses stressed the temporary nature of the occupation by stating that 'We will withdraw when the situation becomes stable and when Kuwait's provisional government asks us to do so.'[201] The *Baghdad Observer*, also reflecting the Iraqi leadership's position, argued that 'A group of Kuwaiti revolutionaries on Thursday [2 August] toppled the subservient monarchic regime ... and established a new Interim Free Government of Kuwait.'[202] It argued that the new government would ensure an even distribution of wealth among the Arab nations, and that free national elections would be held to decide on the form and substance of a new government. Overall, a well-planned media campaign emphasised that the Iraqi engagement was temporary, popular, a subject of invitation and an internal affair.[203] Baghdad argued it was a defensive action against foreign intervention,[204] and the following day the papers further condemned the Kuwaiti monarchy for corruption and accused it of having 'close links with the United States, the strategic ally of Israel'.[205] Another reason for establishing a Revolutionary Kuwaiti Government was that with the Emir out of the country, the new government would ensure that Kuwaiti foreign assets were sent to Kuwait city, and thus Baghdad.

Saddam's precondition for success was an Iraqi installed puppet regime, but there was no indication of this requiring a permanent military presence or a formal annexation. It was, for example, only after the US deployment to Saudi Arabia that Saddam announced further mobilisation: forces that were sent into Kuwait were neither prepared nor trained for the occupation in which they had engaged.[206] However, when Iraqi forces failed to capture the Kuwaiti Emir and his family, things went wrong for Saddam Hussein. Although the Kuwaiti National Assembly had been abolished in 1986, and the Emir had faced some internal political opposition in the late 1980s, the Iraqi regime could not find a single senior Kuwaiti politician who was willing to take the job of running the 'new government'. According to Saad al-Bazzaz the Iraqi leader considered Prince Fahd al-Ahmad al-Sabah likely to replace the Emir, and when he died outside the Dasman Palace on the opening night of the invasion the Iraqi leader turned to Aziz al-Rashid and Faisal al-Sanii, but both rejected cooperation with Saddam. Desperate for options, the regime captured some Kuwaiti officers, who were members of the Kuwaiti Ba'ath Party, to head the provisional government; 31-year-old Alaa Hussein Ali al-Jabur was summoned to Baghdad, promoted to colonel and put in charge of the new government, reporting directly to Hussein Kamel, then Secretary of Defence, and Abid Hamid Mahmoud, Secretary at the Office of the Presidential Palace.[207]

Analysts have argued that the Iraqi leader should never have gone for the whole of Kuwait, and although that might well be the case with the advantage of hindsight, the Iraqi leader believed at the time that capturing the Emir was manageable and would make all the difference. Saddam Hussein later told King Hussein that he expected the United States to defend the Emirate with force, and if that were to be the case, he would be left in a better bargaining position if he held the whole of Kuwait rather than only parts of it.[208] According to Mohamed Heikal, Saddam argued that a limited operation would

leave the al-Sabah family in power in Kuwait, and they would undoubtedly mobilise world opinion and use their relationship with Washington
to ensure a US military response. Kuwait would then become a US base
threatening Iraq. It seemed better to move decisively.[209]

In addition, to Saddam the option of a limited invasion, occupying
only the northern part of Kuwait, would not have solved Iraq's acute
cash-flow problem.[210] Saddam wanted to teach the dynasty of al-Sabah
an unforgettable lesson. He wanted to transform Kuwait into an extension of Iraq's will, thereby increasing oil prices. This essentially required
an Iraqi-installed puppet regime.[211] In essence, therefore, Saddam had
come to the conclusion that a full occupation would increase the chances
of a military coup. It would increase his bargaining power, be a demonstration of strength, and allow for immediate access to Kuwaiti assets.
He had also come to the conclusion that he would get away with it,
and, against that background, any limited invasion seemed like an unnecessary half-measure. Saddam's reasoning then, seems to have been
that Washington need only be assured that he had no intention of
touching Saudi Arabia and that the flow of oil was guaranteed at
reasonable prices. Finally, an editor of an Iraqi newspaper argued that
Iraqi troops chose to stay in Kuwait, even though it knew it had to go
to war with a superior enemy, because of tribal honour (*al-sharaf al-
ashairi*): 'The Iraqis, whose tribal honour was injured by the lowly
Kuwaitis, had no choice but to act, no matter what the consequences.'[212]

Saddam miscalculated the regional and international response on
several levels, and within 48 hours he faced four surprises. First, Britain
and the United States froze all Iraqi and Kuwaiti assets, thereby
denying him immediate access to newly gained wealth. Second, a harsh
condemnation from the United Nations Security Council followed
through Resolution 660, demanding immediate, complete and unconditional withdrawal. Third, a joint condemnation by the United States
and the Soviet Union was issued by Secretary of State James Baker
and Secretary of Foreign Affairs Eduard Schevardnadze, which in effect
reduced the chance of playing the superpowers off against each other.
Fourth, an unprecedented condemnation by the Arab League followed,
insulting Saddam. The latter was the most important at the time.

King Hussein of Jordan arrived in Baghdad on the afternoon of
3 August receiving an agreement from the Iraqi President that the crisis
would be settled within an Arab framework during the following two
days. The initial withdrawal plan arranged by King Hussein, and
reportedly blessed by both Egypt and Kuwait,[213] failed in part because
the Iraqi condition agreed upon by the King, that no Arab public
condemnation should occur before the pullback, was not met when
President Mubarak issued a separate statement denouncing the

invasion.[214] The RCC had indeed announced that 'If there are no threats against Iraq or Kuwait, Iraqi forces will start withdrawal tomorrow [4 August].'[215] Saddam's resolve may have hardened with Mubarak's response, but if he had been successful in establishing a new Kuwaiti government he might well have decided to stay in Kuwait even if Mubarak had not criticised him. After all, he needed oil, the geo-strategic position and the harbour. Additionally, he had good reason to believe that annexing Kuwait would prove popular with the Iraqis, as many genuinely believed that Kuwait was part of Iraq.

President Mubarak explained to an angry King Hussein that he was 'under great pressure', and insisted on Iraq's unconditional withdrawal from Kuwait and the immediate restoration of the Kuwaiti ruling family.[216] The Egyptian stand was next endorsed by a majority vote through Arab League Resolution 3036 on 3 August.[217] For symbolic reasons, the evacuation of a tank brigade was shown on Iraqi television on 5 August, but Saddam counterattacked by announcing further mobilisation of Iraqi troops, honouring his warning that he would not concede to 'threats, provocation or condemnation'.[218] The Arab stand was one of Saddam's major miscalculations, but at the end of the day, through military might, he believed he could sustain the occupation against any Arab opposition. Moreover, Jordan, Yemen and Arafat did not denounce the Iraqi action. The real challenge, nevertheless, would be the United States' reaction.

Although Saddam had responded to the freezing of Iraqi and Kuwaiti assets by freezing payments of debts to the United States in return,[219] he was careful not to provoke Washington. On 6 August, Saddam met with the US chargé d'affaires, Joseph Wilson, in Baghdad. He promised that Iraq had no hostile intent towards Saudi Arabia: 'We will tell our brothers in Saudi Arabia that we were prepared for any assurances required to remove their worries and to make them calm.'[220] He offered Iraqi friendship, arguing that Iraq was a better partner in the region than Saudi Arabia:[221] 'Iraq is firmly willing to respect the United States' legitimate international interests in the Middle East, and is interested in establishing normal relations with the United States on the basis of mutual respect.'[222] Saddam further proposed to Wilson: 'Tell me what ... would remove your anxiety, and I will give it.'[223] In the meeting Saddam offered the United States the two things he believed were crucial: free flow of oil, and at reasonable prices. He promised that he would provide the world with sufficient oil at $25 per barrel. Saddam, realising that the adventure had taken a different turn than planned, was ready to appease, rather than confront the United States, and he sought to buy time and defuse the crisis, rather than escalate it. He simply believed that he could strike a compromise with the Bush administration, and when the deployment of some

250,000 US troops was announced two days later, on the request of King Fahd, the Iraqi leader felt trapped.[224] He continued to repeat, however, that he could give any guarantee necessary that he would not invade Saudi Arabia, because, unlike Kuwait, it had never been part of Iraq.[225] Throughout August and September the Iraqi leader was indulging 'in a flurry of activity to negotiate a settlement',[226] never refusing to discuss a conditional withdrawal. He was not willing to withdraw unconditionally, however, particularly after the annexation, because withdrawing would be too humiliating. The Iraqi leadership turned to the French, and although Tariq Aziz seemed to understand that Iraq might have to withdraw without incentives, it was at least a matter of finding an 'honourable way'. In Saddam's mind, 'wanting to humiliate him is the same as not wanting a peaceful solution'.[227]

The United States' decision to send forces to the region caused Saddam to shift his strategy. The story of a revolution in Kuwait was dropped, and so was the temporary status of the occupation. In response to the US visit to Saudi Arabia the RCC stated that they had agreed 'to return the part of the branch, Kuwait, to the whole root, Iraq'.[228] Saddam's strategy was one of brinkmanship accompanied by great willingness to have a protracted process of negotiations with the United States. The Iraqis continued to complain that the Bush administration was not willing to negotiate, but Washington knew that the Iraqi method was to trap it into endless negotiations to gain time, and eventually stay in Kuwait after the US resolve evaporated. Whatever Saddam's original plans, he believed that the annexation would escalate the crisis to a level beyond US willingness to act forcefully. With worldwide condemnation and socio-economic problems at home, Saddam found it too humiliating to withdraw under pressure with nothing in return. According to Amatzia Baram there were at least four mutually reinforcing calculations behind the decision to annex Kuwait: he wanted to send a message that if attacked he would respond forcefully; to ensure domestic support by finally fulfilling the long-lasting dream of unity; to encourage the soldiers to fight for something that they would keep; and to deter President Bush by 'burning his boats'.[229] Moreover, in addition to the international confrontation Saddam could not siphon the Kuwaiti economic assets from the West, and thus he had nothing to lose by annexing Kuwait. It would prove to everybody that he was absolutely adamant on staying in Kuwait, and thus possibly dissuade threats of war.[230] There is also the possibility that Saddam believed that if he withdrew unconditionally, short of a fight, his own military forces would challenge him.[231] The announcement, difficult to understand from an international point of view, made a great deal of sense to the domestic audience at whom it was directed. Saddam's decision to annex Kuwait and George Bush's announcement that the aggression would not stand, in combination with deployment of forces to defend Saudi Arabia, raised the stakes considerably for both parties and Iraqi intransigence persisted until February 1991.

Although the Iraqi leader seems not to have decided from the outset that he was formally going to annex Kuwait, the firm regional and international condemnation in essence forced Saddam's hand. As Washington committed itself to the liberation of Kuwait the road to war was quickly opened, but although the Iraqi leader underestimated international resolve and US determination to see the crisis through, his perception that air power could not be a decisive instrument of force in the event of war did in fact coincide with overall US military thinking at the time.

FROM ROLLING THUNDER TO JUST CAUSE

The 1970s, which started with President Richard Nixon's détente, ended in what Zbigniew Brzezinski called 'the Arc of Crisis': the crisis of 1978–79 in the two Yemens, the Soviet airlift to Ethiopia, the Iranian Revolution, and the dispatch of Soviet combat forces to Afghanistan.[232] The worsening of East–West relations, sometimes referred to as the 'Second Cold War', had a strong impact on US policy towards the Middle East, and the decade proved relevant to Operations Desert Shield and Desert Storm in three ways. First, as the war with Vietnam drew to a close, the United States' military services embarked on much soul searching, and in 1973 new war-fighting doctrines were developed at a time when conscription was abolished. Second, the Israeli vulnerabilities witnessed by the combined Egyptian–Syrian attack in October the same year, led to a reconsideration of US relations with the Arab world. Third, as the Soviet Union showed increased interest in the region, in conjunction with the crises in Iran and Afghanistan, President Carter authorised reinforcement of the Middle East Force in 1979. In order to understand the military and political interaction that characterised the administrations from Nixon to Bush one needs to examine the evolution of the military doctrine in the post-Vietnam era, US military engagements in the 1980s and post-Cold War contingency planning in the Persian Gulf. These three aspects form the baseline for military thought that dominated when Iraq invaded Kuwait.

The US military emerged from Vietnam with damaged confidence and little credibility. Drug abuse, racial violence and crime in general were high in the military community. These social problems added to low self-esteem and increased frustration over military strategy and political purpose. It was, however, the Arab–Israeli War in October 1973 that 'jolted the Army out of the doctrinal doldrums and forced it to face the reality'.[233] According to the author of the official United States Army account of Operation Desert Storm, Brigadier General Robert H. Scales:

> The [Yom Kippur] war influenced the Army's effort towards reform for two reasons. First, it was the first large-scale confrontation between two forces equipped with modern weapons representative of those found in NATO and the Warsaw Pact. As such, the battle was a propitious window on the future. Second, the battle was so bloody, intense, and close-run that policymakers outside the Army began to seriously question the ability of a seemingly moribund American Army to fight a war of similar intensity. The war prompted a compelling argument for sweeping modernization and reform.[234]

The experience convinced the US armed forces that they could not rely solely on superior technology to win against the quantitatively superior Soviet forces. Another troubling factor was that the technological improvements witnessed at the time made war enormously lethal. It gave incentives to the Army's Training and Doctrine Command (TRADOC), that had been established in July 1973, to deal with the required reform. TRADOC's first commander, General William Depuy, set out to redirect the Army's focus from jungle warfare to a possible ground war with the Soviets on the plains of Central Europe, reflecting the East–West tensions. The new doctrine went back to the basics of high-intensity warfare and became known as Active Defense. In essence it sought to interpret the NATO strategy of flexible response by ensuring battlefield success by the conduct of the defensive battle in depth through the employment of the combination of massed firepower and mobile formations.[235] When TRADOC approached the USAF Tactical Air Command (TAC), in order to make the doctrine joint, they established the AirLand Forces Application (ALFA) in June 1975.[236] The new Army war-fighting doctrine resulted in the field manual (FM) 100-5 *Operations* in July 1976, and although it emphasised mobility, firepower and tactical defence, it acknowledged that 'the Army cannot win the land battle without the Air Force'.[237] For all practical purposes, the strategy was to defend Europe by engaging Soviet forces, ensuring that the first battle would not be lost, without thinking too much about the next one.

The doctrine clearly defined the enemy as the Warsaw Pact and therein three axes of attack: the North German Plain, the Fulda Gap and the Hof Corridor. As the inter-German border became the assumed location for a future ground war,[238] the new doctrine faced considerable opposition from both within and outside the Army. The NATO bases, a legacy of the British and US depots from the Second World War, were certainly not providing for the operational depth required by the Cold War threat. The most severe criticism was nevertheless that the concept was based on attrition, which left the initiative in the hands of the enemy. It was argued that NATO would exhaust itself, as the basic problem was to get US reinforcement to the European battlefield in time to fight the second and third echelon of Soviet forces.[239] The critical question was whether the offensive could be held in check, and while geography favoured the Warsaw Pact there were doubts as to whether Western technology could compensate through superior weapon platforms.

The alternative was presented as the Maneuver Warfare School, and the new concept, the AirLand Battle Doctrine, was the accepted norm in the revised FM 100-5 of 1982. The new manual proposed two approaches of attack. The first was to use long-range and electronic warfare to slow, confuse and damage arriving forces. The object was to create gaps in the enemy's battle array that could be exploited by the second means of attack: lightning-fast offensive manoeuvre using mechanised forces with tactical air support. William S. Lind, Colonel (ret.) John R. Boyd and the other founding fathers of the doctrine argued that initiative, creativity and mission-type tactics had to replace procedures and fixed methods, as the Germans had done in their *Blitzkrieg* of 1939. In order to succeed they argued that one had to focus on the importance of time and the enemy's decision-making process rather than on mere physical strength.[240] It has been observed that the doctrinal shift represented both material and intellectual processes, to the extent that the United States Army discovered the art of operational warfare.[241]

> The Operational Manoeuvre Group (OMG) concept was designed to use tanks in an offensive mode, so that the attacking force could be compact enough to be truly manoeuvrable but powerful enough to be decisive. It involved a spearhead force of light tanks, possibly supported by paratroops or heliborne forces, making the first deep penetration. This would then be filled out using a mechanized division, bringing forward artillery in order to keep open the original axis and further develop the offensive.[242]

The new concept sought ways to fight with inferior numbers and superior technology without having to use nuclear weapons. The NATO first-line forces would engage and hold the Warsaw Pact first echelon, and next use their technological edge for deep attacks upon the reinforcing second and third echelons, causing confusion that would lead to victory. Similar doctrinal discussions took place in Europe under the term 'follow-on-forces attack', but there was at least one element of the European idea that was more appealing to airmen. While TRADOC focused on planning and execution at the *corps level*, where the corps commander would have full control of the battlefield, the NATO scheme concentrated on the *theatre level*.

Military success following the reform in doctrine that had started in 1973 was, however, slow to surface. The first post-Vietnam engagement ended in broken Marine helicopters and crashed C-130 aircraft in the aborted attempt to rescue American hostages in revolutionary Iran in 1980.[243] The criticism following Operation Desert One and the losses Iraq witnessed in its war with Iran by 1982, convinced the Reagan administration of the need to redesign the temporary task force structure to a permanent unified and central command (CENTCOM). Ever since the Second World War, the United States has divided the world into a number of regions and CENTCOM was given geographical responsibility for military operations in most of the Middle East and Southwest Asia. The European Command held on to Israel, Lebanon and Syria, while the Pacific Command continued to hold on to the Indian Ocean and the Arabian Sea.[244] CENTCOM's headquarters were located at MacDill Air Force Base (AFB) in Tampa, Florida and, in a time of crisis, each service would make forces available to the commander-in-chief.[245] Secretary of Defense Casper Weinberger declared that the new organisation 'marks the first geographic unified command created in over thirty-five years and highlights the importance we have placed on Southwest Asia and our ability to deter and oppose Soviet aggression in the region'.[246]

In the autumn of 1983, US forces engaged in three overt armed conflicts, all of them with mixed results, indicating that there was still much work to be done to get out of the doldrums of Vietnam. The first was a Marine force dispatched to Beirut, despite opposition from both the Secretary of Defense and the JCS, as part of a multinational peace-keeping force.[247] A terrorist bomb killed 241 Marines on 23 October and by February 1984 the troops had pulled out short of ever having been given a clear purpose or mission for deployment in the first place.

The second engagement was the airborne *coup de main* in Grenada, code-named Operation Urgent Fury. Tens of thousands of sailors, marines, soldiers and airmen were ultimately involved to achieve three official objectives: to rescue 1,000 Americans to prevent hostage-taking; to restore order; and to return Grenada to a US-friendly government.[248] Although the 'rescue mission' was formally requested by the Organization of Eastern Caribbean States (OECS),[249] and a majority in polls and surveys, both in Grenada and America, favoured the operation, it witnessed world-wide opposition.[250] The United Nations General Assembly condemned the US action in Grenada as a 'violation of international law', voting 108 to 9: the resolution was approved by a larger majority than the one that had earlier condemned the Soviet invasion of Afghanistan.[251] The legal aspect of the operation remains disputed, as does the military aspect. The US invasion was fraught with operational difficulties despite the relatively light Grenadian–Cuban force being outnumbered ten to one and operating without air power or even heavy weapons.[252] The deputy commander in the theatre, Major General Norman Schwarzkopf, would later confess that 'We lost more lives than we needed to', and that shortcomings were revealed in inaccurate intelligence, poor communication and logistics, and 'flareups of interservice rivalry, interference by higher headquarters in battle-field decisions, [and] our alienation of the press'.[253] The assessment is supported by the official United States Army source,[254] but stands in strong contrast to Casper Weinberger's statement that in both military and political terms, the operation on Grenada was a success. He would later dub the Grenada invasion 'the complete model for future such activities',[255] and President Reagan stated in his memoir that the operation was a 'textbook success'.[256] These statements are, however, widely disputed, and one such counteropinion is found in Hugh O'Shaughnessy's account of the operation: 'Three conclusions can fairly be drawn about the invasion of Grenada in October 1983; it was illegal, it was unnecessary as far as rule of law in Grenada was concerned and it set back the cause of political democracy and long-term economic development in the region.'[257] While one would expect 'textbook success' comments from the administration, and the military difficulties should be acknowledged, the cumulative impact of Operation Urgent Fury on the United States' self-image should not be underestimated. It was a resounding political success from the White House's point of view,[258] and for the armed forces it was progress from the failed attempt to rescue hostages in Iran.

The third engagement in late 1983 was a United States Navy response to surface-to-air missiles fired at low-flying reconnaissance aircraft. The Sixth fleet launched air strikes against Syrian gun and radar positions, resulting in one US airman killed, one immediately rescued and one hostage held in Syria for months.[259] These episodes raised questions about the legitimacy of US involvement overseas, and in November 1984 Weinberger identified six tests that should be met before committing overt substantial forces overseas: are US vital interests at stake; are the issues so important that the Americans will commit enough forces to win; are the military and political objectives clearly defined; are the forces sized to achieve the objectives; do the American people support the objectives; and are forces to be committed only as a last resort?[260] Weinberger was later to argue that the liberation of Kuwait following the Iraqi occupation some six years later was 'An Ideal Case for Military Intervention',[261] and his military advisor in 1984, Colin Powell, was to regard the tests as 'useful guidelines'.[262]

In April 1986, the USAF faced its first extensive employment of force since Vietnam: Operation Eldorado Canyon. The objective was to send a message to Libya's Muammar Qaddafi, who allegedly had been sponsoring and encouraging terrorism for some time.[263] Since 1985 tensions had increased between the two countries, including some military confrontations such as the Battle of Sidra and the 'Line of Death' debacle.[264] Libya was accused of supporting Palestinian attacks on Jewish targets at Rome and Vienna airports, and the United States had suspended economic relations with the country. On 4 April 1986 Qaddafi's regime arguably orchestrated a bombing of a discotheque in West Berlin, killing two American soldiers.[265] Although some argue that Syria was responsible, the US, Italian, Israeli, UK and German governments were convinced otherwise.[266] There was consensus in the White House that retaliation was necessary to reduce terrorism, and with no military option other than air strikes seriously discussed, the Pentagon was given full responsibility for the planning, including selection of targets.[267] The target list included the Bab al-Aziziyya complex in Tripoli, a site for terrorist training and known as the 'nerve centre' of the regime. Within the site there were communications and intelligence centres, a barracks of revolutionary guards, headquarters for the military and Qaddafi's working and living quarters. Although removing Qaddafi from power was desirable, the planners felt that by hitting his nerve centre his means to operate would be reduced, and the attack would have an intimidating effect on the leader whether he was present or not.[268] On 14 April 1986 the United States launched a joint Air Force–Navy strike against air defences and targets in Tripoli and Benghazi.[269] Although operational problems manifested themselves, for example only two of the nine planned F-111s succeeded in bombing the Bab al-Aziziyya complex, and some collateral damage occurred, Reagan's approval rating rose to 70 per cent.[270] Several alleged terrorist training camps were attacked, and considering the modern and extensive Libyan air defence system, and threat of retaliation, the operations may have indicated, despite operational problems, US determination in the use of military force as an instrument of foreign policy.

Nine months later, in January 1987, CENTCOM faced its first major challenge. Kuwait asked for their tankers to be re-flagged, to avoid the Iranian air and naval attacks in the Gulf.[271] Since the command's mission was to deter direct conflict, rather than get involved, it declined – until the Soviets showed interest. In July 1987 the Reagan administration agreed to re-flag Kuwaiti tankers as US merchant vessels, and to provide naval escorts for them. Operation Earnest Will lasted until the end of the Iran–Iraq war, and it helped shift the Iranian bombing away from Basra and the Gulf. In the meantime, an Iraqi aircraft, on 17 May 1987, fired two Exocet missiles into USS *Stark*, resulting in 37

Americans killed. Embarrassed by the Iran-Contra affair, Washington accepted the Iraqi leader's apology, and two smaller incidents with Iran in 1988 were further settled short of military escalation: the USS *Samuel B. Roberts* ran across an Iranian-laid mine and an Iranian Airbus commercial airliner was shot down by USS *Vincennes*.

The first major military test for the new Bush administration was, however, closer to its own shores and under the auspices of the Southern Command. The intervention in Panama, Operation Just Cause, was ordered on 20 December 1989, and, despite ending in a desperate man-hunt, Manuel Noriega was detained two weeks later.[272] The operation did not have its roots in a military threat, but a growing disenchant-ment with Noriega's government and its public criticism of US intentions in the country. Noriega was a former intelligence officer for the United States, but a series of violent incidents – including altering election results, televised beatings of rival candidates, an abortive coup, the death of an US Marine who had violated a road block, and the assault of a naval officer and his wife – served as justification for the Bush administration to engage in a military offensive. The operational plan was a joint *coup de main* where the primary objective was to eliminate Noriega and the Panamanian Defense Force (PDF).[273] The plan included simultaneous airborne operations against 27 objectives spread across the country – and all the attacks were executed at night.[274] Operation Just Cause witnessed several operational problems, but partly because of overwhelming force the objectives were achieved.[275] The manhunt itself gave rise to concern during the crisis over Kuwait: if one experienced trouble in catching Noriega in a relatively small and well-known country in Central America with some 13,000 pre-positioned troops, how could one catch Saddam in the unknown Iraq?[276] Although the F-117s stealth aircraft made their debut, Just Cause was pre-dominately an army operation.

The United States Army, which had the rare opportunity of being stationed in the theatre of operations and knowing the area well prior to engagement, had come a long way with regard to training, discipline and leadership after 16 years of reform. US support of its own military forces reached a new post-Vietnam high,[277] the political leadership did not interfere in the military operations, and the military leadership for its part established a working relationship with the press. President Bush followed Reagan's approach, in that, once having made the decision to conduct a military operation, he left it to the military to carry it out. Although one should be careful not to draw too many conclusions from military operations against such a small force, Lieutenant General Carl W. Stiner argued that it was 'the largest, most sophisticated contingency operation conducted over the longest distances in the history of the US armed forces. It succeeded because of tough young soldiers, sailors, airmen, and marines.'[278] General Colin Powell for his part was also satisfied, but concluded that relations with the press had to be improved, and that the enemy should not be allowed to communicate pre-recorded propaganda.[279] Furthermore, the press-pool system used during Operation Just Cause became the preferred choice during the liberation of Kuwait less than a year later.

By early 1990 the Soviet Union's geo-political influence was clearly disintegrating, and with Iran remaining militarily weak, the US contingency plans for the Soviet/Iranian threat to the region were given less attention.[280] Since US policy towards Iraq was one of moderation, and Iran posed no immediate threat, the JCS suggested downgrading the US posture in the region.[281] Secretary of Defense Richard Cheney opposed the JCS review,[282] and supported Under Secretary of Defense for Policy, Paul Wolfowitz, who recommended a shift towards emphasising the Iraqi threat in the new Defense Planning Guidance for FY 1992-97.[283] On 16 October 1989, the Chairman of the JCS, General Colin Powell, ordered General Norman Schwarzkopf, who had been in charge of CENTCOM since 23 November 1988, to update the existing contingency plans for the region reflecting the new political–military situation.[284] The shift towards Iraq as the new regional threat followed only two weeks after President Bush signed NSD-26, in which political incentives were sought to moderate Iraq's behaviour.

The revision included updating the Joint Strategic Capabilities Plan (JSCP) which provides guidelines for US contingency plans, and by late 1989 CENTCOM had begun to devote much effort to updating these plans. Schwarzkopf appeared several times before the Senate Armed Services Committee in the following spring, suggesting that Iraq was the primary military power in the region, and that the Iraqi leader had regional ambitions.[285] The contingency plan that Powell wanted Schwarzkopf to update was OPLAN 1002-88: Operations to Counter Intraregional Persian Gulf Conflict Without Direct Soviet Involvement. Faced with the new guidelines that shifted the focus of regional threat to Iraq, there was an increase in the number of forces, and OPLAN 1002-90: Operations to Counter an Intraregional Threat to the Arabian Peninsula, was built on three operational phases with the stated mission to 'counter Iraqi intraregional threat to Kuwait/ Saudi Arabia'.[286] The first phase was based on deterrence whereby the US forces would attempt to discourage an aggressor who had already demonstrated hostile intent or action by deploying forces. The next phase was based on defensive operations in which the United States would gain air superiority, protect their naval and air bases used for debarking forces, interdict enemy lines of communication and supply, and provide close air support. The third phase was based on counteroffensive action, but received little attention in the plan.[287] The contingency plan was primarily a deployment document, heavily geared towards troop deployment and logistic support, and although there was a vague notion of how to use air power in combination with ground forces, there was no mention of a distinct offensive air campaign.[288] The contingency plan anticipated 30 days warning of an invasion of Saudi Arabia. It encompassed several hundred pages and covered many administrative aspects such as which divisions should go to Saudi Arabia, what radio frequencies would be used, where the soldiers would get their water, how they would treat their casualties, and how they would handle the news media.[289]

These contingency plans had been developed in conjunction with the Army's war-fighting doctrine – the AirLand Battle.[290] Although FM 100-5 had been updated both in 1982 and 1986, the military scenario was still one where the Warsaw Pact countries were arrayed against NATO in Central Europe. Since the former were numerically superior in tanks, artillery, aircraft, armoured personnel carriers and soldiers, the doctrine supported the notion of the extended and deep battlefield.[291] In 1984 the Army and Air Force Chiefs of Staff announced the acceptance of 31 Initiatives particularly designed to enhance the joint employment of the AirLand Battle Doctrine.[292] The initiatives later expanded to 35, and among others Initiative 21 established a new category, battlefield air interdiction (BAI):

> Air action against hostile surface targets nominated by the ground commander and in direct support of ground operations. It is the primary means of fighting the deep battle at extended ranges. BAI isolates enemy forces by preventing their reinforcement and supply and restricting their freedom of manoeuvre.[293]

Although the doctrine was 'stressing unified air and ground operations throughout the theater',[294] air power was a subordinate element of the AirLand team. The doctrine assumed that a future war would involve ground forces against enemy ground forces, and the key to success would be to out-manoeuvre the enemy on the battlefield. Although air power was to be used in close air support and interdiction, it was basically perceived as fire support for the ground forces. The Navy for its part did not have an air power doctrine separate from naval doctrine and its maritime strategy,[295] and consequently the Army was allowed to dominate military thinking on air power.

Tactical Air Command, which was responsible for developing air power doctrine, agreed to air power having this subordinate role. The 31 Initiatives became the skeletal framework on which the Army and Air Force based their work on air support doctrine and planning.[296] When General Norman Schwarzkopf and his air commander, Lieutenant

General Charles A. Horner, met in March 1990 to prepare for the up-coming military exercise considering the increased dangers presented by the regional powers, these ideas governed their planning.[297] The main purpose of Joint Exercise Internal Look, which ran from 23 to 28 July 1990, was to test the unfinished OPLAN 1002-90. The scenario was a six-division Iraqi invasion of Kuwait and Saudi Arabia, in which the XVIII Airborne Corps was given sufficient time to deploy to the region and establish a defence in eastern Saudi Arabia before the attack began.[298] Horner's comment in the margin during one of the briefings was indicative of his mission: 'Build a hose and point it where the ground commander sees that it's needed.'[299] For political reasons, Schwarzkopf's foreign policy advisor Gordon Brown underlined that the exercise was not aimed at Saddam, but at a future Iraqi regime that was hostile to Western interests.[300] In April 1990, CENTCOM planners were directed to drop the countries' identifications, and substitute them with colour codes. Iraq was RED, Iran ORANGE and Yemen YELLOW.[301] The exercise proceeded through its phases, and on the final two days the National Command Authority granted the players 'cross-border authority', which included strategic attacks on RED's homeland.[302] Although strategic targets were not mentioned in the AirLand Battle, a number of non-nuclear attacks were 'executed' at the end of the military exercise. This was regarded as a last effort to win a war in the event of trouble arising on the battlefield. The decision to wait until the final hours of the exercise to authorise action into Iraq reflected sensitivity about bombing an Arab state, and the lack of air power doctrine with regard to strategic conventional employment.

Thus, the most likely threat to the Persian Gulf resources was perceived as an Iraqi invasion of Saudi Arabia. In such an event, the planned use of air power was essentially to support ground forces that would be deployed, in accordance with the AirLand Battle philosophy. Air power was, as such, defined within a supportive posture, with little thought given to offensive employment against strategic targets in Iraq proper. Chapter 2 will explain why the air campaign that started on 17 January 1991 was so different from the doctrine and contingency plans that constituted common belief at the time of the invasion.

NOTES

1. Following the war with the Barbary pirates in 1805, when Lieutenant Pressely N. O'Bannon and his small force of Marines participated in the capture of the Derne and hoisted the US flag for the first time over a fortress in the region, the Colours of the Corps was inscribed with the words: 'To the Shores of Tripoli'. The words remain in the first line of the hymn to this day.

2. Michael A. Palmer, *On Course to Desert Storm: The United States Navy and the Persian Gulf* (Washington, DC: Naval Historical Center, 1992), p. 3.
3. In this work, the term 'Middle East' refers to the region from Libya in the west through Iran in the east, from Turkey in the north to the Arabian Peninsula in the south.
4. Daniel Yergin, *The Prize: The Epic Quest for Oil, Money and Power* (New York: Simon & Schuster, 1991), pp. 393–5; Douglas Little, 'Gideon's Band: America and the Middle East Since 1945', in Michael J. Hogan (ed.), *America in the World: The Historiography of American Foreign Relations Since 1941* (Cambridge and New York: Cambridge University Press, 1995), p. 464; and Melvyn P. Leffler, *A Preponderance of Power: National Security, the Truman Administration, and the Cold War* (Stanford, CA: Stanford University Press, 1992), pp. 237–6. Douglas Little's article can also be found in *Diplomatic History* 18, No. 4 (Fall 1994), pp. 513–40.
5. For a discussion on the British mandatory period, see for example Aharon Cohen, *Israel and the Arab World* (London: W. H. Allen, 1970), pp. 165–220.
6. Little, 'Gideon's Band', p. 464.
7. Yergin, *The Prize*, p. 397.
8 Little, 'Gideon's Band', p. 466.
9. Aaron David Miller, *Search for Security: Saudi Arabian Oil and American Foreign Policy* (Chapel Hill, CA: University of South Carolina Press, 1980), pp. 101–2. See also Yergin, *The Prize*, pp. 391–409.
10. For a comprehensive background, see for example Bruce R. Kuniholm, *The Origins of the Cold War in the Near East: Great Power Conflict and Diplomacy in Iran, Turkey and Greece* (Princeton, NJ: Princeton University Press, 1980), pp. 6–208.
11. See for example Elizabeth Monroe, *Britain's Moment in the Middle East, 1914–1971* (London: Chatto and Windus, 1981); and Glen Balfour-Paul, *The End of Empire in the Middle East: Britain's Relinquishment of Power in her Last Three Arab Dependencies* (Cambridge: Cambridge University Press, 1994).
12. The term 'No. 2 Englishmen' is borrowed from Palmer, *On Course to Desert Storm*, pp. 3–10.
13. John Lewis Gaddis, *Strategies of Containment: A Critical Appraisal of Postwar American National Security Policy* (New York: Oxford University Press, 1985), pp. 25–53.
14. Paul Nitze, then chairman of the Department of State's Policy Planning Staff, led an ad hoc study group which formulated the policy of National Security Council (NSC) directive number 68 in April 1950 (NSC-68: United States Objectives and Programs for National Security). The directive was not publicly released until 1975. The content of the directive is available as 'NSC-68: A Report to the National Security Council', reprinted in *The Naval War College Review* 27, No. 2 (May–June 1975), pp. 51–108. For more on NSC-68, see Leffler, *A Preponderance of Power*, pp. 312–61. Note that Kennan gave several lectures on his perception of the US role in the world. These lectures appear in print in George F. Kennan, *American Diplomacy*, 1st edn 1951, expanded in 1984 (Chicago, IL: University of Chicago Press, 1984).
15. Fred Halliday, 'The Middle East, the Great Powers, and the Cold War', in Yezid Sayigh and Avi Shlaim (eds), *The Cold War and the Middle East* (New York: Oxford University Press, 1994), p. 10; and Kuniholm, *The Origins of the Cold War in the Near East*, pp. 304–41.
16. Leffler, *A Preponderance of Power*, pp. 141–80; Kuniholm, *The Origins of the Cold War in the Near East*, pp. 410–24 and 458–64; and William L. Cleveland, *A History of the Modern Middle East* (Boulder, CO: Westview Press, 1994), p. 260.

17. W. Scott Lucas, *Divided We Stand: Britain, the US, and the Suez Crisis* (London: Hodder and Stoughton, 1991), pp. 6–8.
18. See in particular Kuniholm, *The Origins of the Cold War in the Near East*; and Leffler, *A Preponderance of Power*. This study does not seek to enter that debate, but rather illustrate how the United States became the dominating power in the region. Two writers who over time have been extremely critical of US involvement are Gabriel Kolko and Noam Chomsky. See for example Gabriel Kolko, *Century of War: Politics, Conflicts, and Society Since 1914* (New York: The New Press, 1994); Noam Chomsky and Michael Albert, 'Gulf War Pullout', *Z Magazine* (February 1991); Noam Chomsky, '"What We Say Goes": The Middle East in the New World Order', *Z Magazine* (May 1991); and Noam Chomsky, 'Aftermath', *Z Magazine* (October 1991).
19. See Barry Rubin, 'Middle East: Search for Peace', *Foreign Affairs* 64, No. 3 (Fall 1986), pp. 583–4.
20. Leffler, *A Preponderance of Power*, p. 150.
21. Palmer, *On Course to Desert Storm*, pp. 41–8.
22. Burton I. Kaufman, *The Arab Middle East and the United States: Inter-Arab Rivalry and Superpower Diplomacy* (New York: Twayne Publishers, 1996), p. 6; Steven P. Spiegel, *The Other Arab–Israeli Conflict: Making America's Middle East Policy from Truman to Reagan* (Chicago, IL: Chicago University Press, 1985), p. 17; and Kathleen Christison, *Perceptions of Palestine: Their Influence on U.S. Middle East Policy* (Berkeley, CA: University of California Press, 1998), pp. 61–94.
23. Daniel Moran, *Wars of National Liberation* (London: Cassell, 2001), p. 162.
24. Lucas, *Divided We Stand*, p. 7.
25. Harry S. Truman to King Abdul Aziz, letter of 31 October 1950, cited in Congress, Senate, 'Secretary of Defense Richard Cheney Speaking on the Crisis in the Persian Gulf Region: U.S. Policy Options and Implications to the Committee on Armed Services', S. Hrg. 101–1071, 101st Cong., 2nd sess, *Congressional Record*, pt. 642 (3 December 1990).
26. Dean Acheson, *Present at the Creation: My Years in the State Department* (New York: W. W. Norton & Co., 1969), p. 169. For an Arab perspective on the Palestinian question, see for example Said K. Aburish, *A Brutal Friendship: The West and the Arab Elite* (London: Victor Gollancz, 1997), pp. 147–87. For an historical account, see Cleveland, *A History of the Modern Middle East*, pp. 222–56.
27. Kaufman, *The Arab Middle East and the United States*, p. 18.
28. For general accounts, see Magnus Persson, *Great Britain, the United States and the Security of the Middle East: The Formation of the Baghdad Pact*, Lund Studies in International History, No. 3 (Stockholm: Almquiest and Wiksell Intl., 1998); and John W. Young, *The Foreign Policy of Churchill's Peacetime Administration 1951–1955* (Worcester: Leicester University Press, 1988). See in particular Lucas, *Divided We Stand*, pp. 45–6, 66–7, 74–7 and 105–10; Ernest Stock, *Israel on the Road to Sinai, 1949–1956* (Ithaca, NY: Cornell University Press, 1967), pp. 115–16; and Kuniholm, *The Origins of the Cold War in the Near East*, pp. 304–50.
29. Persson, *Great Britain, the United States and the Security of the Middle East*, pp. 9–10. John Foster Dulles coined the term 'Northern Tier' to describe the states in the Middle East that lay close to the southern border of the Soviet Union. States frequently included in the various definitions of the Northern Tier encompass Greece, Turkey, Iran, Pakistan and Afghanistan. For discussion on the term, see for example Kuniholm, *The Origins of the Cold War in the Near East*, pp. xv–xvi.
30. Kaufman, *The Arab Middle East and the United States*, p. 27; and Kolko, *Century of War*, p. 415.

31. Palmer, *On Course to Desert Storm*, pp. 49–59. For a discussion on whether Mosaddiq presented a real or exaggerated threat, see Little, 'Gideon's Band', pp. 470–3.

32. Lucas, *Divided We Stand*, pp. 78–9, 113–14 and 135–40. For documents and official speeches on the Suez crisis, see John Norton Moore (ed.), *The Arab–Israeli Conflict: Readings and Documents*, abridged and revised edn (Princeton, NJ: Princeton University Press, 1977), pp. 999–1034.

33. Cohen, *Israel and the Arab World*, pp. 515–520; Menachem Z. Rosensaft, *Not Backward to Belligerency: A Study of Events Surrounding the 'Six-Day War' of June, 1967* (New York: Thomas Yoseloff, 1969), pp. 21–2; John Dickie, *'Special' No More: Anglo-American Relations: Rhetoric and Reality* (London: Weidenfeld and Nicolson, 1994), pp. 86–104; and Lucas, *Divided We Stand*, pp. 324–30.

34. See Stephen J. Genco, 'The Eisenhower Doctrine: Deterrence in the Middle East, 1957–1958', in Alexander L. George and Richard Smoke (eds), *Deterrence in American Foreign Policy: Theory and Practice* (New York: Columbia University Press, 1974), pp. 309–62; and Carl F. Salans, 'Gulf of Aqaba & Strait of Tiran: Troubled Waters', in Moore, *The Arab–Israeli Conflict*, p. 186.

35. Stephen E. Ambrose, *Eisenhower*, Vol. II (New York: Simon & Schuster, 1984), pp. 381–8. For a discussion of Ambrose's thesis and the historiography on the Eisenhower years, see Stephen G. Rabe, 'Eisenhower Revisionism: The Scholarly Debate', in Michael J. Hogan (ed.), *America in the World*, pp. 300–25.

36. Palmer, *On Course to Desert Storm*, pp. 67–8; and Little, 'Gideon's Band', pp. 488–90.

37. For an overview of the first Arab–Israeli conflict (1948–49), see for example, Shimon Shamir, 'The Arab–Israeli Conflict', in A. L. Udovitch (ed.), *The Middle East: Oil, Conflict and Hope* (Lexington, MA: Lexington Books, 1976), pp. 195–231.

38. See for example Charles W. Yost, 'The Arab-Israeli war: How it Began', in Moore, *The Arab–Israeli Conflict*, pp. 293–309.

39. Lucas, *Divided We Stand*, pp. 104–5; and Victor Israelyan, *Inside the Kremlin During the Yom Kippur War* (University Park, PA: Pennsylvania State University Press, 1995), pp. 56–61.

40. Kaufman, *The Arab Middle East and the United States*, p. 31.

41. For a discussion on whether the Eisenhower administration distinguished Arab nationalism from communism, see Little, 'Gideon's Band', pp. 485–6.

42. Little, 'The New Frontier on the Nile: JFK, Nassar and Arab Nationalism', *Journal of American History*, 75, No. 3 (September 1988), p. 502; Christison, *Perceptions of Palestine*, pp. 104–5; Little, 'Gideon's Band', pp. 491–4; and Spiegel, *The Other Arab–Israeli Conflict*, pp. 94–5.

43. Christison, *Perceptions of Palestine*, pp. 107–8.

44.

	1957	1967	1977	1987	1997
Iraq	4.8 mill	8.3 mill	11.2 mill	15.9 mill	22.4 mill
	50,000	82,000	188,000	1.0 mill	387,500
Syria	3.9 mill	5.6 mill	7.7 mill	11.2 mill	15.3 mill
	25,000	60,500	227,500	470,500	320,000
Egypt	23.2 mill	31 mill	35.8 mill	52.0 mill	63.0 mill
	100,000	180,000	345,000	445,000	450,000

The table illustrates each of these countries' population compared to number of armed forces in the period 1957–97. Note, for example, that Iraq increased their number of forces more than five-fold between 1977 and 1987. While the numbers of armed forces increase substantially after 1967, the quality and lethality of weapons also improved. For more details, see the Military Balance series produced by the International Institute for Strategic Studies (IISS) from 1967. For the figures on 1957, see S. H. Steinberg (ed.), *Statesman's Year-Book: Statistical and Historical Annual of the States for the Year 1957* (London: Macmillan, 1957), pp. 948–58, 1129–37, and 1408–13.

45. Little, 'Gideon's Band', p. 493.
46. Lawrence Freedman, *The Cold War: A Military History* (London: Cassell, 2001), p. 156.
47. For consequences of war, see for example Itamar Rabinovich, *Waging Peace: Israel and the Arabs at the End of the Century* (New York: Farrar, Straus and Giroux, 1999), pp. 11–18. For documents and speeches, see Moore, *The Arab–Israeli Conflict*, pp. 1035–184. For background, see for example Carl L. Brown, 'Origins of the Crisis', in Richard B. Parker (ed.), *The Six-Day War: A Retrospective* (Gainesville, FL: University Press of Florida, 1996), pp. 13–71.
48. Edward N. Luttwak, 'Air Power in US Military Strategy', in Richard H. Shultz Jr and Robert L. Pfaltzgraff Jr (eds), *The Future of Air Power in the Aftermath of the Gulf War* (Maxwell Air Force Base, AL: Air University Press, 1992), p. 21. See also Rick Atkinson, *Crusade: The Untold Story of the Gulf War* (London: HarperCollins, 1994), p. 48. On air power in 1967, see R. A. Mason, 'Air Power as a National Instrument: The Arab-Israeli Wars', in Alan Stephens (ed.), *The War in the Air 1914–1994* (Fairbairn, Canberra: RAAF Air Power Studies Centre, 1994), pp. 181–200; M. J. Armitage and R. A. Mason, *Air Power in the Nuclear Age, 1945–84: Theory and Practice* (London: Macmillan, 1985), pp. 114–43; and Major Ronald E. Bergquist, *The Role of Airpower in the Iran–Iraq War* (Maxwell AFB: Air University Press, 1988), p. 8.
49. See, for example, Donald Neff, *Fallen Pillars: U.S. Policy towards Palestine and Israel since 1945* (Washington, DC: Institute for Palestinian Studies, 1995), pp. 107–66; and William B. Quandt, *Camp David: Peacemaking and Politics* (Washington, DC: The Brookings Institute, 1986), p. 20.
50. On President Johnson's personal affiliation for Israel, see for example, Spiegel, *The Other Arab–Israeli Conflict*, pp. 118–20; Christison, *Perceptions of Palestine*, pp. 95–123; and Rosensaft, *Not Backward to Belligerency*, pp. 62, 119.
51. Palmer, *On Course to Desert Storm*, p. 75; and Balfour-Paul, *The End of Empire in the Middle East*, pp. 96–136.
52. Martin Van Creveld, *Command in War* (Cambridge, MA: Harvard University Press, 1985), p. 203; Kaufman, *The Arab Middle East and the United States*, p. 45; and Israelyan, *Inside the Kremlin During the Yom Kippur War*, pp. 53–86.
53. Kaufman, *The Arab Middle East and the United States*, p. 64; and Spiegel, *The Other Arab–Israeli Conflict*, pp. 381–94.
54. See Said K. Aburish, *Saddam Hussein: The Politics of Revenge* (New York: Bloomsbury, 2000), pp. 1–8.
55. For a view on the Johnson administration's role in 1967, see, for example, Donald C. Bergus, 'The View from Washington', in Parker, *The Six-Day War*, pp. 189–236.
56. Richard M. Nixon to King Faisal, letter of 31 August 1973, cited in Congress, Senate, 'Secretary of Defense Richard Cheney speaking on the Crisis in the Persian Gulf Region', pt. 642.
57. Spiegel, *The Other Arab–Israeli Conflict*, pp. 166–8.
58. Henry Kissinger, *White House Years* (Boston, MA: Little, Brown and Company, 1979), pp. 223–5.
59. Richard M. Nixon, *Public Papers of the Presidents of the United States: Richard M. Nixon, 1969* (Washington, DC: US Government Printing Office, 1971), p. 549.

60. Nixon, *Public Papers of the Presidents of the United States*, p. 9.
61. Abdel Magid Farid, *Nasser: The Final Years* (Reading: Ithaca Press, 1994), pp. 91–2, 153–4; C. Ernest Dawn, 'The Other Arab Responses'; Parker, *The Six-Day War*, pp. 161–2; and Armitage and Mason, *Air Power in the Nuclear Age, 1945–84*, pp. 118–19.
62. Freedman, *The Cold War*, p. 158.
63. Farid, *Nasser*, pp. 205–11. For an argument on Palestinian self-determination, Kuniholm; and Michael Rubner, *The Palestinian Problem and United States Policy: A Guide to Issues and References* (Claremont, CA: Regina Books, 1986), pp. 5–38. For a collection of American official statements in regards to the United Nation Security Council Resolution 242, which was issued 22 November 1967 and has been the basis for peace-talks since, see for example, Jody Boudreault, Emma Naughton and Yasser Salaam (eds), *U.S. Official Statements: U.N. Security Council Resolution 242* (Washington, DC: Institute for Palestinian Studies, 1992).
64. Spiegel, *The Other Arab–Israeli Conflict*, p. 266.
65. Freedman, *The Cold War*, p. 166.
66. Spiegel, *The Other Arab–Israeli Conflict*, pp. 245–72. For insight into the Yom Kippur War, see for example, Creveld, *Command in War*, pp. 203–26; The Insight Team of the *Sunday Times*, *The Yom Kippur War* (London: André Deutsch, 1975); and Rabinovich, *Waging Peace*, pp. 18–24. For documents and speeches, see Moore, *The Arab–Israeli Conflict*, pp. 1185–250. For implications on strategy, see for example Edward N. Luttwak, *Strategy: The Logic of War and Peace* (Cambridge, MA: Harvard University Press, 1987), pp. 225–30.
67. Israelyan, *Inside the Kremlin During the Yom Kippur War*, p. 53.
68. Christison, *Perceptions of Palestine*, pp. 124–56. For a Soviet view on the changes of Nixon's policy toward the Middle East, see Israelyan, *Inside the Kremlin During the Yom Kippur War*, pp. 115–50.
69. Quandt, *Camp David*, pp. 237–58 and 376–87; and Rabinovich, *Waging Peace*, pp. 27–8.
70. Rabinovich, *Waging Peace*, pp. 20–1.
71. Christison, *Perceptions of Palestine*, pp. 157–94.
72. Cohen, *et al.*, *Gulf War Air Power Survey: Planning Report*, p. 18.
73. Jimmy Carter, *State of the Union Address*, 23 January 1980, cited in Kuniholm, 'The U.S. Experience in the Persian Gulf', in Robert F. Helms and Robert H. Dorff (eds), *The Persian Gulf Crisis: Power in the Post-Cold War World* (London: Praeger, 1993), p. 65.
74. Zbigniew Brzezinski, *Power and Principle: Memories of National Security Advisor, 1977–1981* (New York: Farrar Straus & Giroux, 1985), p. 444.
75. For a military account on the Iran–Iraq War, see Anthony H. Cordesman and Abraham R. Wagner, *The Lessons of Modern War, Volume II: The Iran–Iraq War* (Boulder, CO: Westview Press, 1990).
76. Avi Shlaim, *War and Peace in the Middle East: A Concise History* (New York: Penguin Books, 1995), p. 77. For an overview of the first Reagan administration's Middle East policy, see Rubin, 'Middle East', pp. 483–604.
77. Pentagon statement of defence priorities for 1984–88, cited in Barry Rubin, 'The United States and the Middle East', in Robert O. Freedman (ed.), *The Middle East After the Israeli Invasion of Lebanon* (Syracuse, NY: Syracuse University Press, 1986), p. 84.
78. Amatzia Baram and Barry Rubin, 'Introduction', in Amatzia Baram and Barry Rubin (eds), *Iraq's Road to War* (London: Macmillan, 1993), p. ix.
79. Andrew Cockburn and Patrick Cockburn, *Out of the Ashes: The Resurrection of Saddam Hussein* (New York: Harper Collins, 1999), p. 66.

80. Aburish, *Saddam Hussein*, p. 192.
81. Baram, correspondence with author, 14 April 2002.
82. Bruce W. Jentleson, *With Friends Like These: Reagan, Bush and Saddam, 1982–1990* (New York: W. W. Norton & Company, 1994), p. 31.
83. Noel Koch, former Assistant Secretary of Defense, quoted in Guy Gugliotta *et al.*, 'Air War, Iraq Courted U.S. into Economic Embrace', *Washington Post*, 16 September 1990.
84. George P. Shultz, cable to the United States Embassy in Baghdad, 'Visit of Iraqi Foreign Minister', 11 January 1983, Joyce Battle (ed.), *Iraqgate: Saddam Hussein, US Policy and the Prelude to the Persian Gulf War (1980–1994)* (Alexandria, VA: Chadwyck-Healey, 1994), document number 94. The meeting took place on 14 February 1983 in Washington, DC.
85. Colonel Muhammed Ali (former commander in the Republican Guard), interview with author, tape-recording, London, 23 August 1998. See also Jentleson, *With Friends Like These*, p. 46.
86. George P. Shultz, letter to Casper Weinberger, 'High Technological Dual-Use Export to Iraq', 30 April 1985, *Iraqgate*, document No. 262.
87. Elaine Sciolino, *The Outlaw State: Saddam Hussein's Quest for Power and the Gulf Crisis* (New York: John Wiley and Sons, 1991), p. 166. Note that light aircraft and helicopters under 10,000 lbs were defined as dual-use.
88. Kenneth R. Timmerman, *The Death Lobby: How the West Armed Iraq* (London: Bantam Books, 1992), pp. 233–5.
89. Barry Rubin, 'The United States and Iraq: From Appeasement to War', in Baram and Rubin, *Iraq's Road to War*, p. 258.
90. Cited in Pierre Salinger with Eric Laurent, *Secret Dossier: The Hidden Agenda Behind the Gulf War* (London: Penguin Books, 1991), p. 29.
91. James Ridgeway (ed.), *The March to War* (New York: Four Walls Eight Windows, 1991), p. 13.
92. George P. Shultz, letter to Weinberger, 'High Technological Dual-Use Export to Iraq', 30 April 1985, *Iraqgate*, document No. 262.
93. Timmerman, *The Death Lobby*, p. 235. See also pp. 93–6, 178, 292.
94. Rubin, 'The United States and Iraq', p. 256.
95. Timmerman, *The Death Lobby*, pp. 312–13.
96. Shlaim, *War and Peace in the Middle East*, p. 81.
97. Adam Tarock, *The Superpowers' Involvement in the Iran–Iraq War* (Commack, NY: Nova Science Publishers, 1998), pp. 91–122.
98. Rubin, 'The United States and Iraq', p. 257.
99. George P. Shultz, *Turmoil and Triumph: My Years as Secretary of State* (New York: Charles Scribner's Sons, 1993), p. 238.
100. Jentleson, *With Friends Like These*, p. 49.
101. Shultz, *Turmoil and Triumph*, p. 241.
102. George P. Shultz, cable to the United States Embassy in Iraq, 'Secretary's Meeting with Iraqi Minister of State for Foreign Affairs, Saadoun Hammadi', 10 September 1988, *Iraqgate*, document No. 633.
103. Jentleson, *With Friends Like These*, pp. 90–1; Shultz, *Turmoil and Triumph*, p. 243; and Zalmay Khalilzad, interview with author, tape-recording, Washington, DC, 3 March 1999.
104. Richard Haass, interview with BBC Frontline, transcript, p. 1. For confirmation of argument, see Alexander L. George, *Bridging the Gap: Theory and Practice in Foreign Policy* (Washington, DC: United States Institute of Peace, 1993); and Richard Herrmann, 'Coercive Diplomacy and the Crisis over Kuwait, 1990–1991', in Alexander L. George and William E. Simons (eds), *The Limits of Coercive*

Diplomacy (Boulder, CO: Westview Press, 1994), pp. 229–64.

105. Alan Friedman, *Spider's Web: Bush, Saddam, Thatcher and the Decade of Deceit* (London: Faber and Faber, 1993) p. 133; Don Oberdorfer, 'Missed Signals in the Middle East', *Washington Post Magazine*, 17 March 1991, pp. 19–41, and Zalmay Khalilzad, correspondence with author, transcript, 3 March 1999

106. Shultz, *Turmoil and Triumph*, p. 243.

107. According to Secretary of State James Baker, 'the U.S. values its relationship with Iraq and wants to see it strengthen and broaden'. See James Baker, 'Secretary's October 6 [1989] Meeting with Iraqi Foreign Minister, Tariq Aziz', 13 October 1989, *Iraqgate*, document No. 1063.

108. George Bush, 'U.S. Policy Toward the Persian Gulf', National Security Directive (NSD) 26, 2 October 1989, pp. 1–2.

109. Laurie Mylroie, 'Why Saddam Hussein Invaded Kuwait', *Orbis* 32, No. 4 (Winter 1993). James Baker's 29 October 1990 statement is cited in Thomas L. Friedman, 'Baker Seen as Balancing Bush's Urge to Fight Iraq, *New York Times*, 3 November 1990.

110. Bush, 'U.S. Policy Toward the Persian Gulf', pp. 1–2.

111. George Bush and Brent Scowcroft, *A World Transformed* (New York: Alfred A. Knopf, 1998), p. 305.

112. James Baker, 'Secretary's October 6 Meeting with Iraqi Foreign Minister Tariq Aziz', 13 October 1989, in Jentleson, *With Friends Like These*, p. 130.

113. United States Department of State, 'The Iraqi CCC program', memorandum, 26 October 1989. The memo is reproduced in Alan Friedman, *Spider's Web*, p. 323.

114. Faleh al-Jabbar, 'The Invasion of Kuwait: Iraqi Political Dynamics', in Victoria Brittan (ed.), *The Gulf Between Us: The Gulf War and Beyond* (London: Virago Press, 1991), p. 31; and Saad al-Bazzaz, cited in Samaan B. Samaan and Abdullah H. Muhareb (eds), *An Aggression on the Mind: A Critical Study of Sa'd al-Bazzaz's Book 'A War Gives Birth to Another'*, translated Mohammad Sami Anwar (Kuwait City: Center for Research and Studies on Kuwait, 1995), pp. 33–4.

115. Baram, 'The Iraqi Invasion of Kuwait: Decision-making in Baghdad', p. 6. See also Helen Chapin Metz *et al.*, *Iraq: A Country Study* (Washington, DC: Government Printing Office, 1993), pp. 245–6.

116. Patrick Clawson, 'Iraq's Economy and International Sanctions', in Baram and Rubin, *Iraq's Road to War*, pp. 81–2.

117. Mohammad-Mahmoud Mohamedou, *Iraq and the Second Gulf War: State Building and Regime Security* (Bethesda, MD: Austin and Winfield, 1998), p. 124; Baram, 'Calculation and Miscalculation in Baghdad', in Alex Danchev and Dan Keohane (eds), *International Perspectives on the Gulf Conflict 1990–1991* (London: Macmillan, 1994), p. 24; and Faleh al-Jabbar, 'The Invasion of Kuwait', p. 33.

118. Majid Khadduri and Edmund Ghareeb, *War in the Gulf, 1990–1991: The Iraq–Kuwait Conflict and its Implications* (New York: Oxford University Press, 1997), pp. 81–2; and Faleh al-Jabbar, interview with author, tape-recording, London, 19 August 1998.

119. Hiro, *Desert Shield to Desert Storm*, p. 75.

120. Ibid. p. 58; and Cockburn and Cockburn, *The Resurrection of Saddam Hussein*, pp. 155–6.

121. Phebe Marr, 'Iraq in the '90s', *Middle East Executive Report* (June 1990), p. 13; and General Wafiq Samarrai, interview with BBC Frontline, transcript, p. 2.

122. Baram and Rubin, 'Introduction', p. xiii.

123. Colonel Muhammed Ali, interview with author, tape-recording, London, 23 August 1998; and Haider al-Moussawi (Lieutenant in the Iraqi Army), interview with author, tape-recording, London, 25 January 1999.
124. Baram, 'The Iraqi Invasion of Kuwait', p. 7; Faleh al-Jabbar, 'The Invasion of Kuwait, p. 34; Hiro, *Desert Shield to Desert Storm*, p. 56; General Wafiq Samarrai, interview with BBC Frontline, transcript, p. 2; and Tariq Aziz, interview with BBC Frontline, transcript, p. 1.
125. Colonel Muhammed Ali, interview with author, tape-recording, London, 23 August 1998. For confirmation, see for example, Hiro, *Desert Shield to Desert Storm*, p. 62; and Ghazi A. Algosaibi, *The Gulf Crisis: An Attempt to Understand* (London: Kegan Paul International, 1998), p. 60.
126. Mohamedou, *Iraq and the Second Gulf War*, p. 4.
127. Salah Umar al-Ali (former member of the Regional Command), interview with author, tape-recording, London, 13 May 1999; and Aras Habib (member of the Iraqi National Congress), interview with author, tape-recording, London, 17 May 1999. See also Scott Ritter, *Endgame: Solving the Iraq Problem – Once and for All* (New York: Simon & Schuster, 1999), p. 97. Note that Ritter argues that it was the Amn al-Khas (of which Hussein Kamel was in charge) that discovered the plot, but the author's sources argue that it was al-Mukhabarat.
128. Saad al-Bazzaz, cited in Samaan and Muhareb, *An Aggression on the Mind*, p. 117.
129. Mohamedou, *Iraq and the Second Gulf War*, p. 122.
130. Faleh al-Jabbar, 'The Invasion of Kuwait', p. 33; Hiro, *Desert Shield to Desert Storm*, pp. 81–2; and Efraim Karsh and Inari Rautsi, *Saddam Hussein: A Political Biography* (London: Brassey's, 1991) p. 197.
131. On resolution, see Lauterpacht, Greenwood, Weller and Bethlehem, *The Kuwait Crisis*, p. 61.
132. Karsh and Rautsi, *Saddam Hussein*, p. 201.
133. Hiro, *Desert Shield to Desert Storm*, p. 88.
134. United States Department of State, 'Secretary's October 6 Meeting with Iraqi Foreign Minister Tariq Aziz', 13 October 1989, reprinted in *Congressional Record* (2 March 1992), pp. H864–866.
135. General Wafiq Samarrai, interview with BBC Frontline, transcript, p. 3.
136. Khadduri and Ghareeb, *War in the Gulf, 1990–1991*, p. 84; and Mohamed Heikal, *Illusions of Triumph: An Arab View of the Gulf War* (London: HarperCollins, 1993), pp. 206, 223.
137. *Baghdad Observer*, 10 September 1990, p. 1.
138. Khadduri and Ghareeb, *War in the Gulf, 1990–1991*, p. 87.
139. Saad al-Bazzaz, cited in Samaan and Muhareb, *An Aggression on the Mind*, p. 79. See also Heikal, *Illusions of Triumph*, 210.
140. Hiro, *Desert Shield to Desert Storm*, p. 89.
141. Laurence Pope (NEA/NGA) to Ambassador Kelly, 'Your Visit to Iraq', memorandum, *Iraqgate*, document number 1198. Alternatively, see Lawrence Freedman and Efraim Karsh, *The Gulf Conflict 1990–1991: Diplomacy and War in the New World Order* (London: Faber and Faber, 1994), p. 259.
142. Salinger with Laurent, *Secret Dossier*, p. 4.
143. Ibid., pp. 4–5.
144. *Iraqi News Agency*, 'President Warns Israel, Critiques US 1 April 1990', in *FBIS-NES-90-064*, 3 April 1990.
145. Shlaim, 'Israel and the Conflict', in Danchev and Keohane, *International Perspectives on the Gulf Conflict 1990–91*, p. 60; and Hiro, *Desert Shield to Desert Storm*, p. 89.

146. Amatzia Baram, interview with author, 19 February 1999. For an account of the actual air attack, Operation Babylon, see, for example, Dan McKinnon, *Bullseye One Reactor* (San Diego, CA: House of Hits, 1987), pp. 150–77.

147. Staff Lieutenant General Hazim Abd al-Razzaq al-Ayyubi, *Forty-Three Missiles on the Zionist Entity*, transl. *FBIS*, 25 October–12 November (Amman: Amman al-Arab al-Yawm, 1998), pp. 4–8. The author is thankful to Michael Eisenstadt who made this text available.

148. Aburish, *Saddam Hussein*, p. 273.

149. Ibid., p. 255.

150. US News and World Report [Brian Duffey *et al.*], *Triumph Without Victory: The Unreported History of the Persian Gulf War* (New York: Times Books, 1992), p. 19.

151. The four other Senators were James A. McClure, Alan K. Simpson, Howard M. Metzenbaum and Frank H. Murkowski. See for example, Freedman and Karsh, *The Gulf Conflict*, p. 37; Friedman, *Spider's Web*, p. 160; and Heikal, *Illusions of Triumph*, pp. 164–8.

152. Iraqi News Agency, 'Saddam Hussein Addresses Visiting US Senators 12 April 1990', in *FBIS-NES-90-074*, 17 April 1990. Senator Dole emphasised that Saddam Hussein was 'the kind of leader the United States can easily be in the position to influence'. See Salinger with Laurent, *Secret Dossier*, p. 25.

153. Iraqi News Agency, 'Saddam Hussein Addresses Visiting US Senators 12 April 1990', in *FBIS-NES-90-074*, 17 April 1990.

154. Salinger with Laurent, *Secret Dossier*, pp. 26–7.

155. Amatzia Baram, 'An Analysis of Iraq's WMD Strategy', in *The Non-proliferation Review* 8, No. 2 (Summer 2001).

156. Bob Woodward, *The Commanders* (London: Simon & Schuster, 1991), pp. 199–204.

157. 'Saddam Hussein Addresses Arab Summit', 28 May 1990, Duffey, 'The World's Most Dangerous Man', *U.S. News and World Report*, 4 June 1990, pp. 28–51.

158. Baram, 'Calculation and Miscalculation in Baghdad', pp. 26–7.

159. Saad al-Bazzaz, cited in Samaan and Muhareb, *An Aggression on the Mind*, p. 128.

160. Saad al-Bazzaz, 'An Insider's View of Iraq', *Middle East Quarterly* 2, No. 4 (December 1995), p. 67; and Salinger with Laurent, *Secret Dossier*, pp. 30–4.

161. *Baghdad Radio*, 18 June 1990, cited in Baram, 'The Iraqi Invasion of Kuwait', p. 14.

162. Saad al-Bazzaz, cited in Samaan and Muhareb, *An Aggression on the Mind*, p. 105.

163. Baram, 'The Iraqi Invasion of Kuwait', p. 18.

164. Iraqi News Agency, cited in *FBIS*, 8 Feb 1989, pp. 21–2.

165. Saad al-Bazzaz, cited in Samaan and Muhareb, *An Aggression on the Mind*, p. 24.

166. The date is not accidental, 17 July is the day the Ba'ath Party came to power in 1968.

167. Baghdad Radio, 17 July 1990, cited in *The Guardian* (London), 19 July 1990.

168. Bush and Scowcroft, *A World Transformed*, p. 303.

169. Kenneth Pollack (former CIA analyst), interview with author, tape-recording, Washington, DC, 24 February 1999.

170. Michael R. Gordon and General Bernard E. Trainor, *The Generals' War: The Inside Story of the Conflict in the Gulf* (Boston, MD: Little, Brown and Company, 1995), p. 17.

171. Gordon and Trainor, *The General's War*, p. 17.

172. Ibid., p. 20.

173. United States Department of State, 'Meeting between President Saddam Hussein and the American Ambassador to Baghdad', 25 July 1990, *Iraqgate*, document number 1482.

174. The possible exception is Syria's offensive actions in Lebanon in 1982, but the circumstances were quite different from the Iraqi invasion of Kuwait. President Assad had for example been invited by the then current government and ensured approval in the Arab League.
175. Bruce W. Nelan, 'Who Lost Kuwait', *Time Magazine*, 1 October 1991.
176. Woodward, *The Commanders*, pp. 216–17; and Kenneth Pollack, interview with author, tape-recording, Washington, DC, 24 February 1999; and confirmed by Horner, correspondence with author, transcript, 18 March 1999.
177. King Fahd, speech, 27 November 1990, cited in Nasser Ibrahim Rashid and Esber Ibrahim Shaheen, *Saudi Arabia and the Gulf War* (Joplin, MO: International Institute of Technology, 1994), p. 154. See also Congress, Senate, 'Secretary of Defense Richard Cheney Speaking on the Crisis in the Persian Gulf Region', pt. 22; James A. Baker with Thomas M. DeFrank, *The Politics of Diplomacy: Revolution, War, and Peace, 1989–1992* (New York: G.P. Putnam's Sons, 1995), p. 260; and Bush and Scowcroft, *A World Transformed*, p. 313.
178. Tariq Aziz, interview with BBC Frontline, transcript, p. 7; and Baram, interview with author, tape-recording, Washington, DC, 19 February 1999. See also Edward Heath: *The Course of My Life: My Autobiography* (London: Hodder and Stoughton, 1998), p. 651; Kenneth Pollack, interview with author, tape-recording, Washington, DC, 24 February 1999; Michael Eisenstadt, interview with author, tape-recording, Washington, DC, 25 February 1999; and Baram, 'The Iraqi Invasion of Kuwait', p. 24.
179. Saddam Hussein noted on 6 August that Kuwait had also been offered such an agreement, but they declined. He contends that had such an agreement been made, he would not have attacked Kuwait. See 'Meeting Between President Saddam Hussein and American Chargé d'Affaires Wilson on 6 August 1990', cited in Baram, 'The Iraqi Invasion of Kuwait', p. 10.
180. Salinger with Laurent, *Secret Dossier*, p. 69.
181. Gordon and Trainor, *The Generals' War*, p. 27.
182. Kenneth Pollack, interview with author, tape-recording, Washington, DC, 24 February 1999; Colonel Muhammed Ali, interview with author, tape-recording, London, 23 August 1998; and Baram, interview with author, tape-recording, Washington, DC, 19 February 1999.
183. King Fahd seems to have been more surprised by the extent of the invasion than anything else when he called King Hussein and 'urged [Saddam] to limit the invasion to the extent of the disputed boundaries between Iraq and Kuwait until the whole dispute could be resolved peacefully'. See The Government of the Hashmitie Kingdom of Jordan, 'Jordan and the Gulf Crisis August 1990 – March 1991', *White Paper*, Amman (1991), p. 3.
184. Robert Fisk, 'Saddam Hussein: The Last Great Tyrant', *The Independent*, 30 December 2000.
185. Jentleson, *With Friends Like These*, p. 217.
186. Saad al-Bazzaz, cited in Samaan and Muhareb, *An Aggression on the Mind*, p. 39; and Tariq Aziz, interview with BBC Frontline, transcript, p. 3.
187. Saad al-Bazzaz, 'An Insider's View of Iraq', p. 67.
188. Robert H. Scales, *Certain Victory: The U.S. Army in the Gulf* War (London: Brassey's, 1997), p. 44; Saad al-Bazzaz, cited in Khadduri and Ghareeb, *War in the Gulf, 1990–91*, p. 121; and Kevin Don Hutchinson, *Operation Desert Shield/Desert Storm: Chronology and Fact Book* (London: Greenwood Press, 1995), p. 1.
189. Heikal, *Illusions of Triumph*, p. 244. See also statement from former Egyptian Secretary of Defence, Mohammud Fawzi, *Baghdad Observer*, 8 October 1990, p. 1.

190. Amatzia Baram, interview with author, tape-recording, Washington, DC, 19 February 1999. This is confirmed by Nabeel Musawi (member of the Iraqi National Congress), telephone interview with author, notes, 8 March 1999.

191. Hamed al-Jabouri, interview with author, tape-recording, London, 15 August 1998.

192. Brigadier General Tawfiq al-Yasiri, interview with author, tape-recording, London, 6 August 1998.

193. Tariq Aziz, interview with Milton Viorst, the *New Yorker*, 30 May 1991, pp. 64–7; and Baram, interview with author, tape-recording, Washington, DC, 19 February 1999.

194. Aras Habib, interview with author, tape-recording, London, 14 May 1998; and Saad al-Bazzaz, cited in Samaan and Muhareb, *An Aggression on the Mind*, p. 105. General Samarrai argues that the regime started thinking of Kuwait after the end of the war with Iran. See General Wafiq Samarrai, interview with BBC Frontline, transcript, pp. 3–4.

195. Tariq Aziz, interview with Saad al-Bazzaz, cited in Musallam Ali Musallam, *The Iraqi Invasion of Kuwait*, p. 87. See also Mohamedou, *Iraq and the Second Gulf War*, p. 134.

196. Cockburn and Cockburn, *The Resurrection of Saddam Hussein*, p. 7.

197. Khaled Bin Sultan with Patrick Seale, *Desert Warrior: A Personal View of the Gulf War by the Joint Forces Commander* (London: HarperCollins, 1995), p. 5.

198. Heikal, *Illusions of Triumph*, 248.

199. Colonel Faisal S. al-Adwani (Kuwaiti Ambassador in London), interview with author, tape-recording, London, 14 February 1999; Kuwaiti Embassy in Washington, interview with author, tape-recording, Washington, DC, 3 March 1999; Tom Clancy with Chuck Horner, *Every Man a Tiger* (New York: G. P. Putnam's Sons, 1999), p. 555; and Heikal, *Illusions of Triumph*, p. 248.

200. Tariq Aziz, interview with BBC Frontline, transcript, p. 2.

201. *Baghdad Voice of the Masses*, 3 August 1990, cited in Karsh and Rautsi, *Saddam Hussein*, p. 217.

202. *Baghdad Observer*, 3 August 1990, p. 1.

203. Ibid.

204. The Iraqis even had the city of al-Ahmadi renamed the 'City of the Call', and an Iraqi newspaper which began to be published in Kuwait was named *The Call*. See Algosaibi, *The Gulf Crisis*, p. 69.

205. *Baghdad Observer*, 4 August 1990, p. 1.

206. Norman Cigar, 'Iraq's Strategic Mindset and the Gulf War: Blueprint for Defeat', *Journal of Strategic Studies* 15, No. 1 (March 1992), p. 3.

207. Faisal S. al-Adwani, interview with author, tape-recording, London, 14 February 1999.

208. *Jordanian Times* (Amman), 17 October 1990, cited in the Cohen *et al.*, *Gulf War Air Power Survey: Planning*, p. 63.

209. Heikal, *Illusions of Triumph*, p. 244.

210. Baram, 'The Iraqi Invasion of Kuwait', p. 25.

211. Lisa Beyer, 'The Crude Enforcer', *Time Magazine*, 6 August 1990, pp. 32–4; Lisa Beyer, 'Iraq's Power Grab', *Time Magazine*, 13 August 1990, pp. 8–12; Karsh and Rautsi, *Saddam Hussein*, p. 218.

212. Amatzia Baram, 'Neo-Tribalism in Iraq: Saddam Hussein's Tribal Policy 1991–1996', *International Journal of Middle East Studies* 29, No. 1 (February 1997), p. 13.

213. Mohamedou, *Iraq and the Second Gulf War*, p. 135.

214. Kingdom of Jordan, 'Jordan and the Gulf Crisis', p. 4. See also, Mohamed

Heikal, *Illusions of Triumph*, pp. 249–70; and Salinger with Laurent, *Secret Dossier*, pp. 96, 102.

215. Mohamedou, *Iraq and the Second Gulf War*, p. 135; and Heikal, *Illusions of Triumph*, p. 265.
216. Kingdom of Jordan, 'Jordan and the Gulf Crisis', p. 5; Heikal, *Illusions of Triumph*, pp. 260–2; and Salinger with Laurent, *Secret Dossier*, p. 114.
217. Kingdom of Jordan, 'Jordan and the Gulf Crisis', pp. 19–20.
218. Ibid., p. 3. For Mubarak's view, see for example Dean Fischer, 'An Urgent Call to Negotiate', *Time Magazine*, 10 September 1990, pp. 30–1.
219. *Baghdad Observer*, 3 August 1990, p. 1.
220. Saad al-Bazzaz, cited in Samaan and Muhareb, *An Aggression on the Mind*, p. 142. See also Baram, 'Calculation and Miscalculation in Baghdad', p. 30; Heikal, *Illusions of Triumph*, pp. 311–17; and Salinger with Laurent, *Secret Dossier*, pp. 138–48.
221. Baram, 'Calculation and Miscalculation in Baghdad', p. 30.
222. Karsh and Rautsi, *Saddam Hussein*, pp. 220, 289.
223. Heikal, *Illusions of Triumph*, p. 317.
224. Beyer, 'The World Closes In', *Time Magazine*, 20 August 1990, pp. 15–18.
225. *Baghdad Observer*, 27 October 1990, p. 1.
226. Aburish, *Saddam Hussein*, p. 293.
227. Ibid., 297–8.
228. Karsh and Rautsi, *Saddam Hussein*, p. 222.
229. Baram, 'Calculation and Miscalculation in Baghdad', p. 31. See also Heikal, *Illusions of Triumph*, p. 288.
230. Amatzia Baram, correspondence with author, 14 April 2002.
231. Thasin Mualla (member of the Iraqi National Accord), interview with author, tape-recording, London, 14 August 1998.
232. Brzezinski, 'The Premature Partnership', *Foreign Affairs* 73, No. 2 (March/April 1994), pp. 67–82.
233. Scales, *Certain Victory*, p. 9.
234. Ibid.
235. H. P. Willmott, 'When Men Lost Faith in Reason: Reflections on Warfare in the Twentieth Century', unpublished manuscript, ch. 5, p. 5.
236. Richard G. Davis, *The 31 Initiatives: A Study of Air Force–Army Cooperation* (Washington, DC: Office of USAF History, 1987), pp. 25–7.
237. Department of the Army, Field Manual (FM) 100-5, *Operations* (Washington, DC: Department of the Army, 1976), as cited in Hallion, *Storm over Iraq*, p. 76.
238. Scales, *Certain Victory*, p. 13.
239. Willmott, 'When Men Lost Faith in Reason', p. 5.
240. William S. Lind, 'The Origins of Maneuver Warfare and its Implications for Air Power', in John Andreas Olsen (ed.), *From Manoeuvre Warfare to Kosovo?* (Trondheim: The Royal Norwegian Air Force Academy, 2001), pp. 19–38.
241. Willmott, 'When Men Lost Faith in Reason', p. 4. See Colonel (ret.) Harry G. Summers Jr, *On Strategy II: A Critical Analysis of the Gulf War* (New York: Dell Publishing, 1992), pp. 139–50; and John L. Romjue, *From Active Defense to AirLand Battle: The Development of Army Doctrine 1973–1982* (Fort Monroe, VA: United States Army Training and Doctrine Command, 1984).
242. Freedman, *The Cold War*, p. 141.
243. The military code-name for the operation was Desert One, but sometimes it is referred to as Operation Eagle Claw. The attempted rescue of American hostages on 24–25 April 1980 was aborted, however, after eight American servicemen were killed, and others injured.
244. Gordon and Trainor, *The General's War*, p. 42.

245. The Army Component (ARCENT) headquarters was at Fort McPherson, Georgia. The Air Force Component (CENTAF) headquarters was at Shaw Air Force Base, South Carolina. The Navy Component (NAVCENT) headquarters was at Pearl Harbour, Hawai. The Marine Component (MARCENT) headquarters was at Camp Pendelton, California. The Special Operations Component (SOCENT) headquarters was at MacDill Air Force Base, Florida.

246. Report of the Secretary of Defense, cited in Sheila Ryan, 'Countdown for a Decade: The U.S. Build-Up for War in the Gulf', in Phyllis Bennis and Michel Moushabeck (eds), *Beyond the Storm: A Gulf Crisis Reader* (New York: Olive Branch Press, 1991), p. 93.

247. Hallion, *Storm over Iraq*, p. 99.

248. Hugh O'Shaughnessy, *Grenada: Revolution, Invasion and Aftermath* (London: Sphere Books with *The Observer*, 1983), p. 174.

249. The OECS was established in 1981 and includes seven member states: Antigua/Barbuda, Dominica, Grenada, Montserrat, St. Kitts/Nevis, St. Lucia, and St. Vincent and the Grenadines. Grenada is a sovereign state of 133 square miles and approximately 110,000 citizens.

250. Robert J. Beck, *The Grenada Invasion: Politics, Law, and Foreign Policy Decision-making* (Boulder, CO: Westview Press, 1993), pp. 2–6. For Ronald Reagan's account of the events, see Ronald Reagan, *An American Life: The Autobiography* (London: Arrow Books, 1991), pp. 449–57. For Prime Minister Margaret Thatcher's disapproval, see for example, Dickie, *'Special' No More*, pp. 187–9.

251. John Norton Moore, 'Grenada and the International Double Standard', *American and International Law* 78, No. 1 (January 1984), p. 153.

252. John H. Cushman Jr, 'Pentagon Study Faults Planning on Grenada', *New York Times*, 12 July 1986; Steven Emerson, 'What Went Wrong on Grenada?', *U.S. News & World Report*, 3 November 1986, p. 42; and George C. Wilson and Michael Weisskopf, 'Pentagon, Congress Seek Cure to Shortcomings Exposed in Grenada Invasion', *Washington Post*, 20 February 1986.

253. H. Norman Schwarzkopf with Peter Petre, *It Doesn't Take a Hero* (London: Bantam Books, 1993), p. 258.

254. Scales, *Certain Victory*, pp. 29–31.

255. Casper Weinberger, *Fighting for Peace: Seven Critical Years in the Pentagon* (New York: Warner Books, 1990), p. 126.

256. Reagan, *An American Life*, p. 455.

257. O'Shaughnessy, *Grenada*, p. 217.

258. Ibid., p. 173.

259. Hallion, *Storm over Iraq*, pp. 102–3.

260. Ibid., p. 90.

261. Casper Weinberger, 'An Ideal Case for Military Intervention', *Los Angeles Times*, 9 August 1990.

262. Atkinson, *The Crusade*, p. 122.

263. According to Ronald Reagan, 'the attack was not intended to kill Qaddafi, that would have violated our prohibition against assassination. The objective was to let him know that we were not going to accept his terrorism anymore, and that if he did it again he could expect to hear from us again'. See Reagan, *An American Life*, p. 519. For US–British relations, see for example, Dickie, *'Special' No More*, pp. 187–9.

264. Brian Lee Davis, *Qaddafi, Terrorism, and the Origins of the U.S. Attack on Libya* (New York: Praeger, 1990), pp. 101–32; and Mansour O. El-Kikhia, *Libya's Qaddafi: The Politics of Contradiction* (Gainesville, FL: University Press of Florida, 1997), p. 140.

265. Geoff Simons, *Libya: The Struggle for Survival*, 1st edn 1993 (London: Macmillan, 1996), p. 335; and Davis, *Qaddafi, Terrorism, and the Origins of the U.S. Attack on Libya*, pp. 115–27.
266. According to Chancellor Helmut Kohl 'the trail of blood from the Berlin disco bombing leads to Tripoli', as cited in Davis, *Qaddafi, Terrorism, and the Origins of the U.S. Attack on Libya*, p. 118. On lack of evidence, see Simons, *Libya*, pp. 341–2; and El-Kikhia, *Libya's Qaddafi*, p. 141.
267. Davis, *Qaddafi, Terrorism, and the Origins of the U.S. Attack on Libya*, p. 119; and Simons, *Libya*, p. 341.
268. Davis, *Qaddafi, Terrorism, and the Origins of the U.S. Attack on Libya*, p. 122; and Simons, *Libya*, pp. 336–7; See also Tim Zimmermann, 'The American Bombing of Libya: A Success for Coercive Diplomacy?', *Survival* 29, No. 2 (June 1987), pp. 195–224.
269. On operational aspects, see William R. Doerner, 'In the Dead of the Night', *Time Magazine*, 28 April 1986, pp. 28–31; and William R. Doerner, 'Getting Rid of Kaddafi', *Newsweek*, 28 April 1986, p. 18.
270. Davis, *Qaddafi, Terrorism, and the Origins of the U.S. Attack on Libya*, p. 145.
271. Tarock, *The Superpowers' Involvement in the Iran–Iraq War*, pp. 123–58; Anthony H. Cordesman and Abraham R. Wagner, *The Lessons of Modern War: Volume IV: The Gulf War* (Boulder, CO: Westview Press, 1996), p. 73.
272. For a general account, see for example, Thomas Donnelly, Margaret Roth and Caleb Baker, *Operation Just Cause: The Storming of Panama* (New York: Lexington Books, 1991).
273. Colin Powell with Joseph E. Persico, *My American Journey* (New York: Ballantine Books, 1995), p. 410. For the increased tension between the Washington and Noriega in the latter part of the 1980s, see for example Margaret E. Scranton, *The Noriega Years: U.S.–Panamanian Relations, 1981–1990* (Boulder, CO: Lynne Rienner Publishers, 1991), pp. 105–84; and Michael L. Conniff, *Panama and the United States: The Forced Alliance* (Athens, GA: The University of Georgia Press, 1992), pp. 154–68.
274. Scales, *Certain Victory*, pp. 32–5; Scranton, *The Noriega Years*, pp. 195–207; and Conniff, *Panama and the United States*, pp. 163–6.
275. Horner, correspondence with author, transcript, 26 August 1999.
276. Bush and Scowcroft, *A World Transformed*, pp. 463, 489.
277. Hallion, *Storm over Iraq*, p. 115; Scales, *Certain Victory*, pp. 32–5; and Woodward, *The Commanders*, pp. 45–196.
278. Lieutenant General Carl W. Stiner, 29 December 1989, as quoted in TRADOC Just Cause briefing, 4 May 1990, cited in Scales, *Certain Victory*, p. 35.
279. Powell, *My American Journey*, p. 418.
280. United States Department of Defense, *Conduct of the Persian Gulf War: Final Report to Congress* (Washington, DC: Government Printing Office, 1992), p. 333.
281. Zalmay Khalilzad, correspondence with author, transcript, 26 April 1999.
282. Ibid.
283. The Defense Planning Guidance was signed by Richard Cheney on 24 January 1990.
284. Cohen *et al.*, *Gulf War Air Power Survey: Planning*, p. 20.
285. Congress, Senate, 'Commander in Chief Central Command H. Norman Schwarzkopf Speaking before the Committee on Armed Services', 101st Cong., 2nd sess, *Congressional Record*, pt. 22–6 (12 December 1989); pt. 2 (30 January 1990); pt. 6–8 (22 February 1990); and pt. 21–2 (7 March 1990).
286. Cohen *et al.*, *Gulf War Air Power Survey: Planning*, p. 39.
287. Keaney and Cohen, *Revolution in Warfare*, pp. 24–5.

288. Cohen *et al.*, *Gulf War Air Power Survey: Planning*, p. 21.
289. Michael Klare, *Rogue States and Nuclear Outlaws: America's Search for A New Foreign Policy* (New York: Hill and Wang, 1995), p. 36.
290. Department of the Army, *Operations*.
291. General Donn A. Starry, USA, 'Extending the Battlefield', *Military Review* 61, No. 3 (March 1981), pp. 31–50.
292. Scales, *Certain Victory*, pp. 25–7.
293. Davis, *The 31 Initiatives*, pp. 58–9.
294. Department of the Army, *Operations*, p. 7–1.
295. Robert Komer, 'Maritime Strategy vs. Coalition Defense', *Foreign Affairs* 61, No. 2 (Summer 1982), pp. 1124–44; Willmott, 'When Men Lost Faith in Reason', pp. 13, 42.
296. Hallion, *Storm over Iraq*, p. 80.
297. Lieutenant General Charles A. Horner, 'Desert Shield/Desert Storm: An Overview', *Air Power History* 38, No. 3 (Fall 1991), p. 5.
298. Schwarzkopf with Petre, *It Doesn't Take a Hero*, pp. 285–95 (300,000 men, 3,200 tanks and 640 combat planes); and Scales, *Certain Victory*, pp. 43–4.
299. Edward C. Mann, *Thunder and Lightning: Desert Storm and the Airpower Debates* (Maxwell Air Force Base, AL: Air University Press, 1995), p. 28.
300. Gordon and Trainor, *The Generals' War*, p. 46.
301. Richard M. Swain, *'Lucky War': Third Army in Desert Storm* (Fort Leavenworth, KA: United States Army Command and General Staff College Press, 1997), p. 6.
302. Cohen *et al.*, *Gulf War Air Power Survey: Planning*, p. 46.

2

The Genesis of the Strategic Air Campaign Plan

In response to the Iraqi invasion of Kuwait on 2 August 1990, a small team of air power advocates in the Pentagon, meeting in the office space occupied by an organisation known as Checkmate, proposed a conventional strategic air campaign to liberate the Emirate. The team, which was under the guidance of Colonel John Ashley Warden III, sought to force Saddam Hussein's army out of Kuwait by applying air power directly against the sources of Iraqi national power. The concept, Iraqi Air Campaign Instant Thunder, called for focused and intense attacks on the Iraqi leadership and its associated command, control and communication systems. It concentrated on concurrent and precise targeting of the regime itself, and rather than apply air power in a gradual and demonstrative fashion, it articulated an all-out offensive against 84 critical targets in Iraq. Instant Thunder was originally proposed as a six to nine days stand-alone war-winning option, which would induce the Iraqis to leave Kuwait without being defeated on the battlefield. The concept was therefore a significant departure from the established military doctrine at the time, in which air power played a supporting role to ground operations, and consequently it received severe criticism for its impertinence. It subsequently underwent several changes prior to the execution of the air war, but the overall concept remained at the heart of what became the strategic air campaign – the first phase of Operation Desert Storm.[1]

This chapter seeks to examine the genesis of this approach to warfare, and thereby disclose *why*, *where* and *how* the plan emerged as the most attractive option, if not from conviction at least from necessity, in the early days of the crisis over Kuwait. It suggests that Instant Thunder was not a momentary lapse of creativity, but the solidification of a process that had been going on for the previous two years in the Checkmate environment. The story is one of an important strategic innovation that almost did not happen, but for the initiative, persistence and conviction of a few unorthodox airmen.[2]

FROM THE INDUSTRIAL WEB THEORY TO AIRLAND BATTLE

When Colonel Warden suggested a strategic air campaign plan, which could achieve the US President's four national security objectives without substantial ground operations, most military officers saw another air power zealot who promised much more than could be delivered.[3] One was reminded of General Giulio Douhet, General William Mitchell and Major Alexander de Seversky who all advocated that air power could be decisive if applied directly against the enemy's vital centres.[4] Ever since its inauguration, the air power debate has been dominated by that overarching question: to what extent can air power achieve political objectives without defeating the enemy on the battlefield? While these visionaries had their premonitions, conventional wisdom adhered to air power being part and parcel of a larger scheme of manoeuvre, as realised in the *Blitzkriegs* of 1939–40, wherein air power spearheaded an attack by providing ground forces with the element of speed and surprise, combined with long-range firepower.

It is difficult to measure how much impact Douhet, Mitchell and de Seversky had on modern air power thought, but perhaps the first collective effort in developing a theory on strategic bombing was found at the Air Corps Tactical School (ACTS), Maxwell, Alabama. In the inter-war period the ACTS developed a theory based on the idea that one could cause social collapse through the bombing of key industrial nodes. It became known as the Industrial Web Theory, and the assumption was that an industrial state's economy was fragile, and if certain critical industry nodes were hit, the entire economic system would collapse. Economic disintegration, in turn, would render the enemy incapable of sustaining military operations, and thus incite the civilian population to put pressure on the government to stop the war. The doctrine that followed from the theory was 'unescorted high altitude precision daylight bombardment' against the key economic, industrial and societal nodes of a hostile opponent.

Deriving from the ACTS the Air War Plans Division (AWPD) staff formulated the United States' first strategic air campaign plan, AWPD-1, in August 1941,[5] which predicted that an initial consignment of 6,860 bombers massed against 154 German target-sets would produce victory in six months.[6] The Industrial Web Theory was embodied in the AWPD-1, and the target priorities recommended were the German Air Force (aircraft and ammunition factories, aluminium and magnesium plants), followed by the electric power grid, the transportation network (rail, inland waterways and highways) and the petroleum industry.[7] The objective of bombing the air force was to ensure air superiority, while downgrading electricity would alter weapon manufacturing, food storage, living and working conditions, and lines of communication in general. Crippling the transportation network would deny the military and civilian population access to coal for heating, and distribution of food would be further complicated. Importantly, the theory was based on the assumption that bombers would be able to both locate and destroy specific factories and commodities. In other words, the planners postulated reasonable intelligence and adequate precision.[8]

The four main architects behind this strategy of economic deprivation were Harold L. George, Laurence S. Kutter, Haywood S. Hansell and Kenneth N. Walker. They were also authors of a more extreme version developed four months later, which emphasised that strategic bombardment could win the war in Europe more or less on its own. The plan faced much opposition and the air campaign that was finally executed became, as is so often the case, a compromise. For a variety of reasons, the first attack on Germany, 27 January 1943, involved 54 heavy bombers and the few targets that were hit during the following months were not the ones posed by AWPD-1. Bombers did not number in the thousands until late 1944, at which time most of the AWPD-1 targets came under attack (except electricity), and the war ended less than six months later. The effectiveness of the strategic air campaigns against both Germany and Japan remains widely disputed,[9] because there are no common criteria on which to base an objective assessment. Importantly, however, a *negative* image of strategic bombing embedded itself in the public mind. Dresden, Hamburg, Tokyo, Nagasaki and Hiroshima represented pictures of horror rather than the precise targeting of industrial nodes. Although air power played an all-powerful part in defeating the fascist regimes, air power advocates seemed to have promised more than they were able to deliver, although they were not allowed to execute as planned.

The Industrial Web Theory became a popular concept among airmen, but its limitations were obvious: it assumed that war could be treated in a scientific manner, it believed in high-technological solutions to complex matters on the ground, it assumed that the enemy was a passive system and it underestimated the strength of the population. Advocates of strategic bombardment believed society could be viewed as a mechanical piece of clockwork that would stop if certain physical elements were eliminated, not appreciating the resilient nature of the German economy and society. According to David R. Mets, this mechanical approach stems from the fact that these advocates were not much concerned with the possibilities of air defences or intelligence, which were required ingredients for identifying and finding the vital targets. Rather, they acknowledged only three impediments to the fulfilment of what they viewed as a revolution in the conduct of war: the need for further development of aircraft engine and airframe technology; the acceptance of a doctrine of independent strategic bombing; and the creation of autonomous air organisations under the auspices of a centralised department of defence.[10] While all three impediments were important factors in developing air power as a decisive instrument of force, they narrowed their vision into technology and targeting. It was simply assumed that vital targets could be identified, found and destroyed without thorough examinations of what the truly vital targets were or what the political effects of such bombing would be.

This single-mindedness had severe consequences for the legacy of air power, according to Carl Builder. Although air power theory was a pertinent factor in the establishment of the USAF as an independent military service in September 1947, there was a subsequent abandonment of air power theory during the Cold War period in the face of competitive *means*, such as missiles and nuclear devices, and *ends*, such as deterrence and a tactical orientation to warfare. This in turn separated the USAF from those commitments that had ensured its creation in the first place.[11] In the 1950s and 1960s the USAF apparently shifted its focus from the conceptual thinking of winning wars to the business of procuring bigger and faster aircraft in a nuclear context on the one hand, and merely supporting the ground commander's scheme of manoeuvre on the other. Thus, throughout the inter-war period and the Cold War the popular perception has been that airmen have been more concerned with the technological aspects of the aircraft and nuclear weapons than with the conceptualisation of air power strategy, theory and doctrine. This notion became an integrated part of the institutional culture, but in order to fully understand the criticism that the Instant Thunder proposal faced in August 1990 one must take a closer look at the impact of the nuclear bomb on strategic thought in general, and the devastating legacy of Vietnam in particular.

The idea that it was possible to force an enemy to surrender by bombing alone received renewed attention with the technological improvements of the 1960s. Rolling Thunder, the bombing campaign against North Vietnam between 1965 and 1968, was designed to dissuade the North from sending men and supplies into the South, and to force Hanoi into a peace agreement.[12] Beyond that, although some argued it would strengthen morale in the South, weaken it in the North and reaffirm US credibility and commitment, these objectives were secondary and not inconsistent with the primary aim of an 'independent, stable, non-communist South Vietnam'. The debate within the administration at the time was not so much about aims, but how these aims were to be realised.[13] According to Mark Clodfelter, several negative objectives limited President Lyndon B. Johnson's ability to pursue his positive goals: Johnson aimed to avoid active Chinese or Soviet involvement in order to prevent a possible Second World War; he wanted to maintain a positive image of the United States on the world stage; and he wanted to keep the American public's focus on his Great Society programmes for domestic and social reform rather than on a war 8,000 miles away.[14] President Johnson remained torn between the competing negative and positive goals, arguing:

> I knew from the start that I was bound to be crucified either way I moved. If I left the woman I really loved – the Great Society – in order to get involved in the bitch of a war on the other side of the world, then I would lose everything at home. All my programs ... Yet everything I knew about history told me that if I got out of Vietnam and let Ho Chi Minh run through the streets of Saigon, then I'd be doing exactly what Chamberlain did in World War II. I'd be giving a big fat reward to aggression.[15]

General John P. McConnell, the USAF Chief of Staff during Rolling Thunder, proposed to make the air campaign fast and hard-hitting against 94 targets over a period of 28 days,[16] while his predecessor General Curtis E. Lemay even declared that the best way to liberate South Vietnam was to bomb North Vietnam 'back into the Stone Age'.[17] President Johnson, for his part, perhaps because of such sentiments, stated: 'I won't let those Air Force generals bomb even the smallest outhouse without checking with me.'[18] While airmen preferred to attack with mass and intensity, going in with all resources available, President Johnson, Secretary of Defense Robert McNamara and Secretary of State Dean Rusk seem to have waged a war in order to send signals and messages to improve their bargaining position with the North Vietnamese.[19]

The list of 94 targets was never implemented as proposed by Army General Earle Wheeler, the CJCS, and consequently, air power advocates have ever since dismissed the limitations of air power as the fault of micro-management from Washington.[20] The outcome was demonstrative attacks to send messages, followed by further escalation until compliance, or more specifically, to gradually increase the scope and intensity of the bombing until Hanoi stopped supporting the Viet Cong.[21] Originally planned to succeed within weeks, it became a three and a half year ad hoc programme with hundreds of thousands of bombs dropped and close to 900 aircraft lost.

The theory behind the executed Rolling Thunder campaigns was founded in the so-called graduated and reciprocated initiatives in tension (GRIT), a reduction strategy for conflict management introduced by political psychologist Charles Osgood in 1962, and expanded by political scientist Thomas C. Schelling.[22] The GRIT strategy was based on one side announcing a unilateral conciliatory gesture while at the same time threatening to escalate if the opponent tried to exploit the situation.

Schelling based his theory on the idea of manipulating the risk of punishment for political purposes.[23] The overall idea was to raise the risk of civilian damage gradually, by altering between bombing pauses and threats of further strikes, compelling the enemy to concede. It might be that this strategy did not work in Rolling Thunder in part because it was not politically acceptable for Washington to increase the level of bombing to the point where the North Vietnamese leadership was forced to comply. In reality, the bombing pauses provided the North Vietnamese with the chance to repair damage and move supplies to safety, which in turn resulted in a war of attrition. There was, furthermore, a sufficient supply of goods and arms arriving from neighbouring countries, undermining the US strategy of interdiction. To many, this deprived air power of its main *characteristics*, such as height, speed and reach, and key *capabilities*, such as responsiveness, flexibility, ubiquity, precision, mobility and concentration.

From a political standpoint, the Johnson administration felt constrained to limit the bombing, both to avoid China and the Soviet Union getting further involved, and because there was little support for massive conventional bombing among the American public.[24] This was reminiscent of the Korean War where the North had an under-developed industrial base, and its sources of military equipment came from communist production centres outside Korea.[25] As these centres were off-limits, the North Koreans had a logistic and industrial sanctuary – constraints that were not applied to planners of either the Second World War or the Gulf War of 1991. It was, according to the CJCS, General Omar Bradley, 'a war against the wrong enemy, at the wrong place, at the wrong time',[26] and with concepts, weapons and aircraft from the Second World War one might add. Nevertheless, one should not automatically dismiss the overall strategy of gradualism, as it was the *practice* that failed, and not the *principle*. In order for the theory to work certain preconditions for bombing-halts are required, but in this case the United States allowed the Vietnamese to reinstall, resupply and reinforce. Moreover, Washington established sanctuaries and put key cities and airfields off-limits. These factors undermined the desired effect, and airmen were consequently right to argue that many of their efforts were compromised, but one should be careful to condemn gradualism as the concept itself provides great flexibility if adequately used together with diplomacy.[27] Added to this, it might sometimes be the only feasible political option.

Although North Vietnam was devastated, the United States' air campaign failed in its aims, as witnessed by the Tet Offensive in 1968 and the inability to get the North Vietnamese to comply with Washington's objectives.[28] Part of the failure can be explained by the fact that the Viet Cong, not the North Vietnamese, were the primary enemy, and most of the troops did not fight because they strongly believed in Ho Chi Minh's ideology, but because of the corrupt and brutal nature of the Saigon government that was associated with the United States.[29] According to Truong Nhu Tang, 'the Southern revolution was generated of itself, out of the emotions, conscience, and aspirations of the Southern people'.[30] Moreover, the bombing campaigns focused on destroying North Vietnamese resources for fighting a conventional war, while the type of war that the enemy fought was one of guerrilla warfare and the 'hearts and minds' of the people. Consequently Rolling Thunder contributed only partly to reducing the Viet Cong's capacity and desire to fight. Although Rolling Thunder is widely ridiculed, one might add that the North Vietnamese seem to have been able to launch a successful ground attack on the South only after US air power was withdrawn. Thus, the impact of air power on the Viet Cong remains contested.

The subsequent Linebacker campaigns, which began in January 1972, were based on continuous and massive force against the North Vietnamese. The campaigns were more successful on a political level, but importantly, the Americans were engaged in an optional conflict with limited and loosely defined objectives, while the North Vietnamese were in a total war of national survival.[31] The Linebacker campaigns were again predominantly interdiction, but the gradualist approach was replaced by sustained and heavy bombing. Combined with resolute diplomacy, an agreement between the United States and the Vietnamese was achieved in October 1972, but it took further violent actions to compel Hanoi to actually sign the accord in Paris on 27 January 1973. From an air strategy perspective, the Linebacker campaigns were far more successful than the Rolling Thunder campaigns, but one cannot evaluate the achievements in isolation from the changes that had occurred in the political situation. President Nixon's détente with the Soviet Union and China, coupled with his agreement to leave without having ensured South Vietnam's security against perceived communist aggression, created conditions that favoured bombing for limited ends.[32] Nixon's notion of victory differed greatly from that of his predecessor, who sought independence for a stable non-communist South Vietnam. Finally, there had been an improvement in precision technology over the years, and North Vietnam was far more industrialised in 1972 than it had been seven years earlier. All these changes increased the effectiveness of air power, but whether air power was not allowed to be decisive, or whether other circumstances combined to reduce its effectiveness, the outcome of the Vietnam War was not determined by air power. The political and cultural circumstances blended with technical, organisational and doctrinal issues have left the lessons learned from Vietnam an unclosed affair.

Nevertheless, the legacy of Vietnam seems to have provided crucial points of reference for the Iraqi and US leaderships in 1990. Washington stated time and again that the crisis over Kuwait would not be another Vietnam, and General Norman Schwarzkopf asserted that he measured everything in life against the experience of Vietnam.[33] Both his chief air planner, Brigadier General Buster Glosson, and the Joint Force Air Component Commander (JFACC), Lieutenant General Charles Horner, had been in Vietnam and argued that they were determined to 'do it right this time'.[34] The latter uses strong words in describing his hatred for the generals, admirals and politicians who were responsible for the loss of some 58,000 American lives in a conflict that resulted in several million being killed:

> If I had to be a killer, I wanted to know why I was killing; and the facts didn't match the rhetoric coming out of Washington ... They just did not know what they wanted to do ... they came up with strategies almost on a day-to-day basis ... Our generals were bad news ... I hated my own generals because they covered up their own gutless inability to stand up to the political masters in Washington ... We taught our enemy to endure air attacks, we taught our enemy how to best defend against the world's greatest air power, and we taught our enemy how to defeat us in the end ... I lied ... I stripped myself of integrity... I learned that you cannot trust America ... The result was that we were living a lie and had lost our pride ... The policy of Vietnamization was a sham ... We had become a Communist nation within the very organization that was to protect our nation from the threat of communism.[35]

When Colonel Warden suggested a strategic air campaign in response to the Iraqi invasion, it was a complete rejection of Rolling Thunder in name and content. He chose to sell his new concept as the very antithesis of the image of the Vietnam experience. Instant Thunder was 'a focused, intense air campaign designed to incapacitate Iraqi leadership and destroy key Iraqi military capability, in a short period of time', and not a 'graduated, long-term campaign plan designed to provide escalation options to counter Iraqi moves'.[36]

One of the problems in Vietnam was that there was no guidance for either conventional strategic air power or limited war. The USAF doctrine dated back to 1959, and stated that 'the best preparation for limited war is proper preparation for general war',[37] ignoring the fact that the very nature of war might change in the process. The lack of a coherent and unified concept of operations stemmed partly from the USAF having divided the doctrine programmes into two separate commands. The Strategic Air Command (SAC), based in Omaha, Nebraska, was responsible for developing the single integrated operations plan (SIOP), which dealt with notions, principles and policies of how to develop and employ nuclear weapons against the Soviet Union and the Warsaw Pact. In 1948 the Air Force Chief of Staff, Hoyt S. Vandenberg, argued that 133 bombs against urban, industrial, government control, petroleum, transportation and electric power targets in 70 cities 'could well lead to Soviet capitulation and in any event would destroy their overall capability for offensive operations'.[38] Soon the term 'strategic air power' was perceived as 'nuclear air power', and the doctrines adhered to the overarching policy of the time: first there was the New Look which manifested itself in Massive Retaliation during the Eisenhower administration, and next Flexible Response during the Kennedy succession. When examining the different SIOPs from 1960 to 1983 one finds one strand arguing in favour of 'counter-value' targeting and another adhering to the principle of 'counter-force'. While General Vandenberg told a Senate sub-committee in June 1953 that 'the proper role of air forces is to destroy the enemy's industrial potential', Robert McNamara argued in the often-quoted Ann Arbor speech of 1962 that 'principal military objectives, in the event of a nuclear war stemming from a major attack on the Alliance, should be the destruction of the enemy's military forces, not his civilian population'.[39] The two strands strike at the core of air power theory: should one aim for the enemy's *will*, or should one settle for targeting physical manifestations of the abstract and intangible will, namely the *capability*.

SAC's counterpart, the Tactical Air Command, located at Langley, Virginia, developed air power doctrines that were concerned with close air support, interdiction and counter air, and these roles became known as 'tactical operations' to distinguish them from the SIOPs.[40] Since the mid 1950s TAC had both plans and aircraft for nuclear weapons, but its predominant focus was on conventional air power supporting ground forces, while SAC for its part basically dealt with tankers and air power as a nuclear instrument. Consequently, when the Army's training and doctrine team, TRADOC, developed the AirLand Doctrine in the 1980s and defined conventional air power as 'fire support', it found much support among the TAC officers. TAC essentially prepared for a war with the Soviet Union in a limited geographical area, while SAC was concerned with nuclear strikes in a global context. An almost theological division within the USAF therefore emerged over the proper use of air power: should it be used independently in a nuclear framework, or in support of ground operations on a conventional basis? Consequently, the theory of using conventional strategic air power had lost its stand with the nuclear capacity and the perceived failures of Vietnam. Warden's Checkmate team sought to change all that.

THE FIVE RINGS MODEL AND GLOBAL REACH –
GLOBAL POWER

Although the execution of the air campaign against Iraq was to involve airmen from all services and from several countries, the *strategic* air campaign against the Iraqi regime was predominately based on resources from the USAF. The most influential individuals in terms of the role their ideas subsequently played in the planning and execution were all USAF officers: Lieutenant General Charles Albert Horner, Brigadier General Buster Cleveland Glosson, Colonel John Ashley Warden and Lieutenant Colonel David Albin Deptula.[41] All four were important in making the strategic air campaign possible, as were others, but Warden is of particular interest in this case since he initiated the concept.

Warden was born in McKinney (Texas) in 1943, the third generation of military officers. His military and academic background stems from the USAF Academy, Colorado Springs, where he received his Bachelor of Science degree in 1965. His overall class rating was well in the mainstream, but his yearbook reveals that he was on the Dean's List in five out of eight semesters, appearing on both the Commandant's List and the Superintendent's List several times, indicating that within the academic and military he was occasionally in the top 10 per cent of the cadet wing. As he moved through the engineering curriculum, however, he found that he was really more interested in military history than science. He selected as many courses as possible within history and paid close attention to what made legendary military commanders successful. He studied Major General John Frederick Charles Fuller's analyses in some depth and was particularly concerned with *The Generalship of Alexander the Great*. He studied closely the genius and strategy of the King of Macedon, focusing on the Battle of Arbela (Erbil in modern Iraq), in which Alexander the Great defeated Darius III by going for the leader directly rather than focusing on the battlefield. Additionally, although he did not explore the matter at the time, he registered that there was a tendency in historical accounts to downplay the significance of the strategic bombing against Germany and Japan during the Second World War.[42]

Although having developed an interest for books and academia, Warden decided to become a fighter pilot before he entered the Academy, and the four years at Colorado Springs did not change his determination. In July 1965 he embarked on pilot training at Laredo (Texas), graduating in August 1966. He then attended a two-month school for F-4 backseaters at Davis Monthan AFB (Arizona) before entering the full five-month training programme at MacDill AFB (Florida) from which he graduated in April 1967. His first operational

assignment was as an F-4 pilot at the 4th Tactical Fighter Wing at
Seymour-Johnson AFB (North Carolina), deploying to South Korea
in response to the 1968 Pueblo Incident. His team was struck by the
fact that they were able to deploy on such short notice, arriving with
nearly 100 fighters ready for combat in the theatre within 48 hours,
only to discover that they were left with no reasonable plan for their
actual employment. Moreover, they were all parked wing-tip to wing-
tip on the runway at Kunsan, disclosing that nothing had been learned
from the Pearl Harbour experience and the Israeli attack on Egypt the
previous year. Returning from Korea that summer, First Lieutenant
Warden went through OV-10 training and next served for 12 months
as Forward Air Controller over Vietnam and Laos, accumulating 266
combat missions. He spent half the time at Tay Ninh with the 1st Air
Cavalry and the rest targeting the Ho Chi Minh Trail, during which
he experienced, together with all the other pilots, the frustration of
going after individual trucks just south of the border while lines of
trucks 2 or 3 miles further north, preparing for advance, were defined
as 'off-limits'. Allowed to operate only in support of ground forces or
in interdiction operations at the most unlikely places, they started to
question the lack of strategic overlay, some of the operational procedures and the limits of air power. As was the case for many of the
officers who participated in Vietnam, Warden resolved that if he ever
went to war again he would not accept such an ill-defined strategy.[43]
Later, as an F-4 pilot at Torrejon AFB in Spain he participated in
operations and training towards Iran, arguing at the time that there
were logical flaws in some of the SIOP concepts and in parts of the
US thinking about conventional war with the Soviets. In essence,
Warden recognised that air power was either planned to be used to
support the ground commander or as a key element within a nuclear
context, and he started to commit some of his observations to paper.

Warden was, however, still predominantly concerned about air power
at the tactical level at this time. In his third year at Torrejon, he was
offered the opportunity to attend graduate school in residence. At first
he was reluctant to accept, as it meant time away from flying and the
operational command, but the prospect of one year of full-time
studying was simply too tempting. He began a course in Political Science
at Texas Tech in the summer of 1974, graduating a year later having
compressed the normal two-year programme into a single year.

In August 1975 he submitted his Master of Arts thesis, 'The Grand
Alliance: Strategy and Decision'. Captain Warden focused on the
highest level of decision-making in the Second World War, discussing
how countries go to war and how they win wars. The thesis, supervised
by Fredrick Hartman, who was on sabbatical from the Navy War College,
questioned why President Franklin D. Roosevelt and Prime Minister

Winston Churchill accepted the Soviet occupation of Berlin, and Warden explored 'a continuing Western failure to integrate military and political affairs into a grand strategy'.[44] Although examining military and political compromises, he argued that the desired end-state should be the focus of all decision-making and strategy: 'The indispensable need for a sound coalition [is] to find a long term grand strategy which looks beyond the war to the peace which will inevitably follow it.'[45] In completing his degree in international relations he gradually started to develop distinct ideas on how one ought to wage war in order to win, and he became increasingly interested in Liddell Hart's strategy of The Indirect Approach and General MacArthur's thoughts on warfare. Warden developed a genuine interest in military and political theory, and explored books written by Dean Acheson, Graham Allison, Bernard Brodie, Edward M. Earle, Samuel Huntington, Henry Kissinger, Henry Morgentheau and Harry Truman among others. Although focusing on grand strategy, Warden did not link the issue at that time to air power.

After his Master's degree Major Warden was assigned to the Air Staff where he served as an action officer in the Directorate of Plans (XOXXM) with specific responsibility for the Middle East politico-military planning. When the Carter administration came to power, it began a review of national strategy which at that time was focused on a two and a half war strategy with the half war being a deployment to the Middle East followed by redeployment to fight in Central Europe. Warden believed that this half war concept made little sense and that national strategy at that point had missed the very real dangers that the Soviet Union could pose to the strategic flank of the West. He argued, moreover, that the overall war-planning focus was misconceived, as there were many other threats to US interests than the Fulda Gap scenario across the borders between the German states. Importantly, there were oil interests and warm water ports in the Persian Gulf, and the Soviet Union would easily control those locations if it decided to seize the Straits of Hormuz. In Warden's mind, war planning should not be focused on territory per se, but the underlying strategic interests. With the help of key individuals working in and for the National Security Council, Warden's team successfully proposed a change in the national strategy to focus on the Persian Gulf. Having succeeded in changing the focus, it became necessary to create realistic war plans, and Warden next suggested a plan to his superiors whereby 13 tactical fighter wings were to be deployed into Saudi Arabia and southern Iran. The first part of the plan, 'to leap-frog those forces forward' as air superiority was extended, in order to drive the Soviet forces back, was highly welcomed.[46] The second part was far more controversial, as it suggested a direct attack on the Soviet Union. It reflected Warden's belief in massive and offensive use of air power, and ultimately, that there was no such thing as a limited war: 'If you weren't prepared to expend the effort that was going to assure victory, then you shouldn't play.'[47] The late 1970s convinced Warden that if the President was ready to commit forces to war, one should do everything to win it short of nuclear attacks. There was no way one could win by constantly worrying about escalation. During this period Warden and his colleagues in the Directorate of Plans strongly recommended a separate command for the Persian Gulf, thus taking part in forming what later became the US CENTCOM.[48]

Warden next served as the Assistant Executive officer to the Air Force Chief of Staff, Wing Chief of Inspections at 33rd Tactical Fighter Wing (F-15 Eagle), Deputy Commander for Operations of the 34th Tactical Fighter Wing (F-4 Phantoms) and Commander of the US Forces at Deccimomanu in Italy. By the mid 1980s Warden had done well in the USAF: he was hard working, he was recognised for his intellectual grasp of concepts and strategy, he had reasonable operational experience accompanied by good reports, and he definitely stood out as one who was dedicated to the future of the institution. Moreover, he was recognised as an extraordinary staff officer.[49] When offered a place as a student at the National War College in Washington, he finally found himself in a position where he would manage to link his tactical air power experience from Vietnam with matters on strategy identified in his Master thesis.

While a student at the National War College in 1985–86 he embarked on a project for a book to be titled *The Air Campaign: Planning for Combat*, in which he focused on translating national political objectives into theatre campaign plans. Warden emphasised air power's potential contribution to the overall effort, the significance of 'distant interdiction' and the predominant importance of air superiority.[50] He argued that temporary air superiority was a dangerous delusion,[51] and that the least effective way of achieving control of the air was air-to-air combat. He also introduced the concept of reserves in air campaign planning. Discussing air power at the operational level of war, and how an air commander should plan, orchestrate and structure an air campaign, he essentially sought to provide a conceptual framework for thinking about the practice of air warfare beyond the Cold War paradigm, seriously opposing the idea of air power being a mere adjunct to land forces.[52] He did not use the term 'strategic air power', because of its association with massive destruction, but the importance of strategic operations was entwined in the chapters on 'air superiority' and 'interdiction'.

His contemplative life as a student allowed him the opportunity to put into writing what he had thought about for years. His ability to conceptualise complex matters and articulate these with ease gave him a reputation as an able theorist, and on having completed War College in the summer of 1986 he was assigned the position of Vice Commander of the 36th Tactical Fighter Wing in Bitburg, Germany. By all USAF standards, Warden's career was promising: the National Defense University had decided to publish his thesis and his posting was every fighter pilot's dream as it provided for senior responsibility for the USAF's premier air-to-air wing, and thus an almost certain promotion to brigadier general.[53] While most officers would have concerned themselves with assuring that promotion, Warden viewed his assignment as a great opportunity to actually implement some of the ideas that he had articulated in his air campaign thesis.

As Vice Commander, Warden spent the year focusing on what he argued were conceptual flaws in the Wing's war doctrine, and as neither the USAFE nor the EUCOM had an air campaign plan that he viewed as sufficient for winning wars, he set out to develop one.[54] Within a year he became Wing Commander, assuming responsibility for 72 F-15s and some 5,000 personnel. There was much Warden wanted to rectify on the base, so he immediately issued an ambitious memorandum containing some 90 initiatives on what had to be improved. Among other things he suggested modifications to war plans, more realistic exercises, new command and control procedures, improvements within the maintenance system and a systematic strengthening of base survivability. He advocated the idea of using 'big wing' tactics to attack and destroy Warsaw Pact air power, and was deeply concerned with keeping the accident rate low. He intended to get as much mass into the exercises as possible and to develop a genuine offensive capability. Rather than investing in formations of three to four aircraft, Warden emphasised the advantages of large air superiority formations, a concept that was partly tested at Incirlik AFB (Turkey) in the autumn of 1987, with commendation from General William L. Kirk, the USAFE Commander. In essence Warden argued that although the Warsaw Pact outnumbered NATO on a theatre basis, that did not automatically imply the alliance being outnumbered on a tactical level – one just had to make sure the concept of mass was applied at the right focal points. Moreover, Warden disagreed with the established view that the first days of a European air war had to be defensive.

While many of these ideas strengthened the Wing, Warden was unable to convince those who worked for him and for whom he worked that he had their best interests at heart.[55] He had developed these ideas in isolation and was unable to follow up with their complete implementation. Consequently, his subordinates felt uncertain about many of the changes and vocal opponents made themselves heard. For example, Warden introduced a close-circuit TV monitoring system for war exercises, which made it much more convenient for the commander to observe work on the line and give orders, but for many of the personnel the feeling of being watched resulted in suspicion. The most controversial issues, however, were changes that affected daily life on the base. Warden argued that it would be more cost-effective to abandon reserved parking spaces, including his own; he emphasised coat and tie requirements in the officer's club after 16:00; and he preferred pilots to wear flight suits only when they were on mission. Warden found that his subordinates had become 'unofficerlike', but as his subordinates were not involved in suggesting these changes Warden was soon perceived as insensitive to their everyday concerns, and consequently complaints to the Inspector General soon increased significantly. In pursuing ideas for developing his 'big wing' concept he became detached from the fighter community proper and within a few months his leadership came into question. In pushing hard and fast for changes, he seems to have had little sense of proportion and priority, offering 90 initiatives of equal importance. According to Major General (ret.) Perry Smith:

> He tried to initiate major changes in a very short period of time, and it was so disruptive to the wing that the wing undercut him in many ways ... When he is on track for something, he is very hard to move; very hard to move. That is an unfortunate quality. When you are a commander of people, you have got to be flexible. When you do change management, you should do it incrementally, not because you don't need to do things fast, but you need to bring the people along. That, I think, is a part of his personality that worked against him as a commander. He was labelled a 'poor operator' because of his performance as an operational commander.[56]

Thus, John Warden was perceived as a man who was out of touch with many of his colleagues, subordinates and superiors. He was perceived as lacking the deep sense of camaraderie, game playing and affection for flying that is highly valued in the world of fighter pilots.[57] According to Colonel Richard T. Reynolds, Warden was recognised as 'unable to relate to people's personal concerns, which in turn marginalized the effectiveness of his intellectual capabilities'.[58] For sure, Warden proved more concerned with ideas and concepts than people, and in the process he was regarded as arrogant and disrespectful. Indeed, to some extent his intellect and insight were perceived as intimidating.[59] There was no doubt in Warden's mind that his business was warfare, but with his strong focus on concepts he did not fill the classic criteria for being credited as a successful operational commander. Six months into his tour as the 36th Commander he was told by General Kirk that he was to leave his post and start working on a project in the Pentagon. Although recognised as an innovative and brilliant theorist, 'Genghis', as his call sign was, became 'an intellectual maverick who did not fit in'.[60]

Some individuals who are visionary and creative are often incapable of separating 'the wheat from the chaff'. This is the 'Churchill syndrome', wherein the originator does not distinguish between his good and bad ideas. Warden seems in part to have suffered from this: within a day he would initiate and propose a number of ideas, some brilliant and some rather far-fetched, but he would not be able to distinguish between them. Added to this, some of Warden's observations were never given proper attention simply because the people around him focused on the more daily matters such as dress codes and parking spaces. Warden, being a revolutionary at heart, seems to have overlooked the fact that most changes seldom work when the people affected are not involved from the beginning. The dismissal from Bitburg had a crucial effect on Warden and his career. He concluded that one should never suggest new ideas without getting the people who will be affected involved at an early stage. But, perhaps even more importantly, his prompt return had a negative effect on his reputation since his credibility was called into question. His superiors in the Pentagon, his peers and his subordinates all became familiar with rumours of his misfortunes as a commander, be they exaggerated or not. To many he became the theorist who did not have the skills of team building and personal bonding, and within the fighter community he was simply 'not one of them'. General Robert D. Russ, who had held the position as commander of TAC since May 1985, concluded six years later that the fighter pilots

> had a feeling that he [Warden] was from academia. They had a feeling that he sat in an ivory tower and thought about all these grand and glo-rious things, but when it got down to fighting and dropping bombs and shooting people, that he just didn't understand.[61]

Another observer within the TAC 'brotherhood' argued that his strength was insight and enthusiasm for air power, but he lacked credibility with his peer group because he to a great extent refused to listen to opposing views.

The reassignment would later prove to be a setback to a promising military career, but at the time Warden was simply told that his exper-tise was needed in Washington. Rather than speculate he was deter-mined to make a difference. Warden strongly believed that his ideas were applicable, and therefore the misfortunes at Bitburg were a failure of communication on his part more than anything else. On his return to Washington he also found that a few generals had taken a keen interest in 'The Air Campaign' thesis. When Lieutenant General Michael J. Dugan became deputy Chief of Staff for plans and operations on the Air Staff in March 1988, he issued copies to all his subordinates. Warden was first assigned director of the Constant Demo air base operability exercise – 'an exercise to study the effects of battle damage and possible defensive measures on a single NATO air base'.[62] Ever full of energy, he proposed to increase the utility of the exercise to include several bases, and to focus on the operational aspects of the air campaign. According to USAF historian Richard G. Davis, several generals were impressed with his foresight and Dugan immediately made him his personal assistant.[63] During May and June 1988 Warden was asked to write a paper about what the USAF ought to do in order to improve its organisation from an operational standpoint. After having discussed Warden's ideas on the strategic and operational value of air power with Major General Charles Boyd, they concluded that Warden had rather unique qualities. The challenge was to find a position in which Warden would be able to develop his theoretical skills. They agreed that he should elevate some of the ideas from the book to make them applicable for the USAF at a military–strategic level, and thus he became the director for war-fighting concepts developments (XOXW).[64] By July 1988 Warden was deeply involved in developing USAF strategies, doctrines and long-range planning, charged with suggesting new air power concepts that were not beholden to either TAC or SAC. From his position as director of XOXW he became responsible for some 80 officers divided into six divisions: the Doctrine Division, the Strategy Division, the Requirements Division the Long-range Planning Division, the Concepts Division, and the Force Assessment Division.[65] The latter dealt with war-gaming and simulation, originally with a focus on the Soviet Union, and was simply referred to as Checkmate.[66] It was not originally part of XOXW and reviews had concluded that it should be shut down, but Warden insisted that he would be able to make it useful. Although Checkmate was only one of the six divisions, its physical layout made it the central location for what became the air campaign planning during the crisis over Kuwait. Consequently, the overall XOXW has since then simply been referred to as the Checkmate team.

From this new position Warden encouraged free and innovative thinking, and argued that only by stretching current ideas could the USAF improve as an institution. The potential, not the limitations of air power should be the driving force, but in all strategy, he stressed, the political purpose had to be identified. Operating from the basement of the Pentagon, exploring all kinds of ideas, was the perfect environment for Warden. While perceived as one who could not relate to the daily concerns of his troops in Bitburg, he quickly established a reputation for himself in the Pentagon as one with intellectual openness, creativity and energy. He cared about important air power ideas and was willing to debate them and refine them with anyone, including captains, majors and lieutenant colonels.[67] He learned the names and backgrounds of his subordinates, focusing on individual potential rather than rank, and genuinely listening rather than dictating.[68] He established great authority as a man of firm convictions, and not only was he tenacious in promoting his views, but he proved himself to be a superb communicator. He seems to have inspired considerable respect and passion among those who worked with him on a daily basis, particularly those who were part of his team or those with whom he exchanged ideas, while those viewing him from afar seem to have perceived him as obsessively intense, and too serious and business-like.

Those academically inclined found Warden 'mentally stimulating', as he promoted and challenged his immediate colleagues to think, and through brainstorming and analysis he created unique circumstances for developing alternative ideas on air power and strategy.[69] To some, that was the very definition of ideal leadership, as they were given a legitimate mandate to criticise existing patterns and promote institutional change.[70] They would basically discuss grand strategy with Warden and then go off to examine the suggestions in detail, without interference. He was to them a mentor and facilitator. To others Warden appeared to involve himself in matters far beyond his position and committed himself too strongly to ideas that had not been tested. While parts of Checkmate almost worshipped him for his dedication to air power, others saw him as a zealot arguing that air power could do the impossible. For sure, when Warden decided that an idea was worth selling it could be very difficult to change his mind.[71] He managed to get the best out of some, but his loose-rein leadership style also resulted in a certain amount of friction. Warden was not good at delegating tasks, and consequently there would be rivalry among his subordinates in trying to gain control of interesting projects. The less interesting ones were left largely untouched and in this respect Warden's management by 'chaos theory' did not suit everyone.

Just a couple of months before Warden arrived in his new position then Major David A. Deptula had been assigned to the Air Force doctrine division. Deptula had earned his wings in 1977, was an F-15C instructor pilot, a graduate of the elite USAF Fighter Weapons School, and an F-15C aerial demonstration pilot who had attended Armed Forces Staff College in the autumn of 1987. His first assignment from Warden was to review, comment and provide edits on the manuscript of 'The Air Campaign', and to write a paper on how best to use air power at the operational level of war.[72] Warden became Deptula's mentor and, contrary to prevailing opposition, Warden and Deptula believed it was essential to attack the enemy's political leadership directly in order to provide US policy-makers with options beyond the clash of forces on the battlefield. Neither of the two would accept conventional wisdom without a challenge, and they strongly opposed the 'yes-men' syndrome that stifles new ideas.

In August 1988 Warden finished writing a paper, 'Centers of Gravity – The Key to Success in War', in which he articulated a concept for describing a modern state as a system.[73] At this point, Warden became convinced that strategic air warfare was *the* form of warfare, and at the heart of his thinking lay Carl von Clausewitz' notion of 'centres of gravity'. The Prussian defined it as 'the hub of all power and movement, on which everything depends ... the point against which all our energies should be directed'.[74] One of the great debates at the time, especially with the Army, was whether there could be more than one centre of gravity. Those endorsing Clausewitz argued there could be but one, whereas Warden and Deptula argued that there could be several.

Warden first applied his theory to a real world problem through his Checkmate Division in 1989. They started with the hypothesis that fuel was a centre of gravity, that is, a vital necessity for the Soviet Army. According to intelligence reports, the Soviet Union had some six months of fuel supply buried in hardened storage tanks in East Germany, and consequently it was not realistic to attack all the supply units. The challenge would therefore be to examine how the fuel would get from the storage to the main tanks at the front. In approaching the distribution, it was established that there were 25 operational-level fuel depots that stretched from the Baltic in the north to the Alps in the south. A further examination revealed that there was no north–south connection between the depots, and that each depot had only about three output manifolds. Having further established that there was no elasticity in the Soviet system, one could bomb the depot fuel manifolds, and the tactical commanders would run out of fuel in four to five days. The essence was not that there would be no fuel left, but that because of lack of oil the commander would have to await supply rather than advance. Thus, 'a handful of fighter-bomber sorties properly employed against operational centers of gravity could have a hugely disproportionate effect on fighting at the front itself'.[75] Although simple in concept and opposed by intelligence officers at the time, these ideas were used in planning Desert Storm, when 'bombing for effect' rather than destruction on a strategic level was to become the guiding line.[76] The whole approach was clearly inspired by the AWPD's scheme to mount 'a sustained and unremitting Air Offensive ... [which would] destroy the will and capability to continue the war; and to make an invasion either unnecessary or feasible without excessive cost'.[77] Interestingly, Warden and the Checkmate team presented the concept to senior Air Force officers, including the Chief of Staff. The team also visited Europe, where it briefed the four star commander of the

USAREUR. This Army officer was delighted with the briefing and asked Warden to develop it further and extend it to Soviet weapon storage in East Germany – a task that was overtaken by the collapse of the Soviet Union and the exigencies of the Gulf War.

While Warden and Deptula were undertaking their studies there was a struggle over revising the *Air Force Manual 1-1: Functions and Basic Doctrine of the United States Air Force*.[78] The version that existed when Iraq invaded Kuwait dated from 1984, and although some changes in the revision process reflected the XOXW studies, and included a few lines about conventional strategic bombardment, this document was not well known among Air Force officers.[79] In fact, offensive and independent use of conventional air power that was not applied only to gain air superiority, had not been seriously considered since the perceived failures of the Rolling Thunder and Linebacker campaigns in the late 1960s and early 1970s. As previously noted, while SAC focused on nuclear strikes in a global context, TAC prepared for a war of attrition in which US warplanes would knock out the Soviet airfields, achieve air superiority and destroy the enemy forces and supplies. As late as 1988 the head of TAC, General Robert Russ, stated that the mission of his command was to support the army in the destruction of the enemy army.[80] Thus, conventional strategic air power was in a doctrinal vacuum, and the theories launched by Warden and Deptula were closer to the ideas of Mitchell, de Seversky and the AWPD architects, than the current thinking represented by the doctrine groups at TAC and SAC.

In the period July 1988 to July 1990, Warden and the Checkmate team spent a great deal of time discussing what was to become known as The Five Rings Model.[81] Warden insisted that one could analyse the enemy as a system by picturing the state's centres of gravity as five concentric circles. The central circle was defined as the political decision-making apparatus and its ability to command, control and communicate. It was the state's national leadership, the collection of individuals invested with the power to initiate, sustain and terminate wars. It gave the state its strategic direction and helped it respond to external and internal changes and challenges. Warden equated the leadership of a state to the brain of a human body: it was the most important organ, generating and controlling all physical motions. Surrounding this core he identified the second circle as the state's energy facilities – oil, gas and electricity – the organic essentials with the function of converting energy from one form to another. The third circle contained the state's infrastructure, primarily industry and transportation links such as roads, bridges and railways, the instruments that kept a society interconnected and enabled mobility and movement. The fourth circle focused on the demographic elements, the population – the very citizens of the state. Unlike Giulio Douhet, Warden did not find it politically acceptable to target citizens directly with anything but psychological means. The final ring was the state's fielded military forces, the entity whose purpose was to protect the state and society from external aggression. Warden argued that traditionally the fifth ring had been at the centre of struggle, where huge armies fought against each other, moving towards the cumulative clash on the battlefield. Warden would argue that relying on targeting the population, the economy, or military forces were all *indirect* attempts to evoke concessions, while going after the national leadership presented a *direct* approach. Targeting the leadership directly, in addition to the notion of mass and intensity from the opening moments of war, without pauses, was at the core of the model. The model was basically an expansion and elevation of the operational concepts that Warden had developed in *The Air Campaign*.

Figure 1: The Five Rings Model

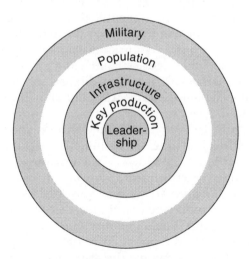

Moreover, in order to accurately identify the critical vulnerabilities within each ring, Warden proposed the further breakdown of each ring into five sub-rings based on the same structure, until the true centre of gravity was disclosed. Warden referred to these as 'fractals' or structures that repeat themselves as their size grows or shrinks. The number of fractals can be indefinite and all expose centres of gravity at different levels – strategic, operational and tactical – all of which relate to each other. When these multiple targets were struck simultaneously, the enemy system would be incapacitated through the rapid imposition of either total or partial paralysis. The intention was to create so much confusion and disorder in the enemy system at the strategic level that it would react inappropriately to US activities that appeared simultaneously. In essence, Warden sought to change a 'system' by focusing on critical leverage points, exploiting the principle of exponential strategic impact. Warden further stressed that since human behaviour and national *will* were unpredictable and intangible, the enemy *capability* should be the overall focus.

In Warden's mind the four outer rings should be attacked only as far as was necessary to expose the leadership ring to offensive action. The priority given to the 'inner ring' resulted in terms like 'inside-out warfare' and 'bombing for [political] effect'. By going for the leadership directly, attacking several target-sets hard and fast from the opening moment of war, Warden argued that one could achieve 'strategic paralysis' of the state's war-making capabilities with decapitation as one possible outcome. Thus, he did not argue a 'decapitation strategy' per se, but a larger strategic air campaign in which 'decapitation' was but one element.[82] He stressed that long-range aircraft and precision targeting made it possible to translate this theory effectively into practice. He favoured carrying the war to the enemy's state organisation (system warfare), rather than to the enemy's armed forces (military warfare). The selection of targets would make sure that one rendered the enemy's strategy and decision-making irrelevant. In order to be successful, however, Warden emphasised that 'Military objectives and campaign plans must be tied to political objectives *as seen through the enemy's eyes, not one's own.*'[83] In effect, he argued that one could defeat a state without seeking to destroy its forces in the field. The occupying forces were therefore only a manifestation of the real problem, which resided with the leadership that ordered the occupation in the first place. Consequently, the purpose of war was not even to defeat the enemy's ground forces, but to force the decision-makers to do one's own will.

Unlike the Industrial Web Theory, which sought industrial and economic collapse, Warden argued that such targets should only be bombed as a means of isolating the leadership and depriving it of communication.[84] Moreover, Warden emphasised, as he had done in his Master's degree more than a decade earlier, that it is the desired political end-state that should govern the rationale behind the target selection, and herein targeting had to be identified in terms of political effects rather than physical destruction. The concept that Warden worked on was a complete rejection of the AirLand Battle doctrine that had gained wide acceptance in the USAF's TAC community.[85] Moreover, it was diametrically opposed to the contingency plans that were being developed in the Persian Gulf region. Operational Plan 1002-90 suggested defensive actions in which ground forces would conduct counterattacks with air power in a supporting role focusing on the theatre of operation only. Warden and his team challenged these doctrines and concepts by claiming that the true strength of air power was its ability to strike deep inside the enemy territory,[86] and that by going for the battlefield and the periphery, the doctrines of the other services were based on *war fighting* rather than *war winning* strategies. Warden became the proponent of 'strategic paralysis', although he remained quite vague on how such an achievement was going to translate into getting the enemy to surrender.[87]

Deptula took many of these ideas with him when he left his position in the Doctrine Division in late 1988 to work for the policy group guided by Donald B. Rice, the Secretary of the Air Force. Rice, who came into office on 22 May 1989, strongly believed in conventional strategic capabilities.[88] Rice observed that both the Navy and the Army were well versed in discussing military strategies, while airmen discussed nothing but aircraft.[89] He was determined to change that, and initiated several projects that would look into the future role of air power. At the time there was no general acceptance of the terms 'strategic operations' and 'air campaign', as air power's role was perceived predominantly to support the ground commander's scheme of manoeuvre.[90] Despite these disagreements, Rice sent an information memorandum, drafted by Deptula on 'the Potential of Air', to the Secretary of Defense on 28 March 1990. The effort resulted in the white paper *Global Reach – Global Power: Reshaping for the Future*, which was published in June 1990.[91] Deptula became a principal author of that paper, which stressed that one should focus on 'airpower's inherent strengths – speed, range, flexibility, precision and lethality' and that should include, among other things, the ability to 'inflict strategic and operational paralysis on any adversary by striking key nodes in his war-making potential'.[92]

These initiatives were not only a result of new visions being committed to paper: but to a large extent were a reaction against growing concerns about the future of the USAF. It was in particular a counter-argument to an unpublished paper entitled 'A View of the Air Force Today', written by some Air Staff officers in the autumn of 1989. The paper was remarkable for its direct criticism of the Air Force and its leadership, and it concluded that it was widely believed by other services that the Air Force should be abolished as a separate institution, and that air power was neither distinctly decisive nor influential in battle. One such criticism was that 'the US Air Force was created to honor a false premise that should have been discredited long ago; that premise is the efficacy of airpower as an independent war-winning doctrine'.[93]

The paper stressed that the USAF had lost its identity, and did not have a coherent concept or doctrine. It argued that unlike 'The

Maritime Strategy' or the AirLand Battle Doctrine, the Air Force was run by pilots who gave priority to their love for the aircraft and technology, at the expense of a holistic concept. Military analyst Jeffrey Record also raised the question whether one should 'abolish the Air Force?'[94] Global Reach – Global Power for its part argued that 'a new Air Force' was in the making and that by taking advantage of 'airpower's inherent strengths', it would be not only one of four services, but the dominating one.[95] While the AirLand Battle foresaw USAF elements as working largely in support of ground forces, a doctrine based on mobility and deep-strike firepower delivered by both ground and air power,[96] the Marine doctrine was built around the expeditionary qualities of the Marine Air Ground Task Force (MAGTF) concept, wherein air power was the supporting element.[97]

Warden and Deptula were involved in briefing the CENTCOM, the CENTAF and a range of other parts of the military establishment on these new ideas, but they were not appreciated.[98] General Robert Russ, and Warden's boss, Lieutenant General James Adams, strongly disagreed with the new focus.[99] The latter even told them to terminate the project of advancing strategic air operations, something neither Warden nor Deptula were willing to accept.

This was very much the state of the debate in the USAF when Iraq invaded Kuwait. There was no up-dated conceptual military contingency plan, no coherent air policy and the majority of military and air planners believed that air power should be supporting ground forces. Warden and Deptula had remained in close contact throughout this period, and a few days after the invasion they met and developed the basis for Instant Thunder, which was founded on the theory of the Five Rings construct, and the policy of Global Reach – Global Power.[100] They were, however, confronted with two principal problems: the concept ran counter to ongoing planning and deployment, and they had no mandate to involve themselves in war-planning. Before one deals with how they involved themselves in the planning, the following section will establish the initial US political and military response to the Iraqi invasion of Kuwait.

RESPONDING TO THE IRAQI INVASION

Although the Office of the Secretary of the Air Force and the Air Staff had been working on ideas related to strategic use of air power, neither of these institutions was part of the command structure that was responsible for developing war plans or implementing contingencies. Indeed, the Goldwater–Nichols Act of 1986 gave unprecedented power to the CJCS and the Commander-in-Chief (CINC) of the respective regions.[101] Consequently, it was for General Colin Powell and General Norman Schwarzkopf to provide the political leadership with military options. Schwarzkopf, who was in charge of CENTCOM, would further be given military forces from all services on request. By default, the air service was the responsibility of Lieutenant General Charles Horner, who since March 1987 had held the dual-hat position at Shaw AFB as commander of the 9th Air Force and commander of Central Command Air Forces, reporting in peacetime to General Russ, the commander of TAC.

While the Department of State in late July 1990 argued that the 'administration continues to desire better relations with Iraq',[102] General Powell summoned General Schwarzkopf to come up with a 'two-tiered response' in case Iraqi troops entered Kuwaiti territory. One would be based on retaliation options if Saddam 'commits a minor border infraction', and the other would focus on 'how we'd stop him and protect the region'.[103] When the Iraqis put artillery forward with reinforced logistics and linked up communication lines, Schwarzkopf notified Washington that a threat 'appeared imminent'.[104] Schwarzkopf and Powell briefed Secretary of Defense Richard Cheney on 1 August, whereupon the CINC predicted that Iraq would invade the Warba and Bubiyan islands of Kuwait, and perhaps the disputed Rumalia oil field on the Kuwaiti–Iraqi border, but not the whole country.[105] Later that evening, Brent Scowcroft, the National Security Advisor, and Richard Haass, the National Security Council Middle East expert, briefed President Bush, and they agreed to contact Saddam 'to try to convince him not to attack'.[106]

Within the hour, however, 02:00 on Thursday 2 August (21:00 on 1 August, United States Eastern Standard Time), 80,000 of Iraq's Republican Guard headed towards Kuwait City. The first National Security Council (NSC) meeting in response to the Iraqi invasion was held 11 hours later. The meeting in the White House Cabinet Room revealed many of the uncertainties that characterised the military and political leadership at the time, but much of the political framework was already taking shape. By the time the meeting took place, the UN Security Council had voted 14:0 in favour of Resolution 660;[107] Bush had signed an Executive Order freezing the assets of Iraq and Kuwait in the United States; the President banned trade with Iraq altogether; and he ordered a warship from Diego Garcia in the Indian Ocean to the Persian Gulf.[108] General Powell described the contingency plans, but only briefly referred to air power capabilities. The tier one response, which consisted of punitive air strikes against Iraqi targets using American Naval aircraft, had been superseded by events, and tier two, OPLAN 1002-90, designed to defend Saudi Arabia, received most of the attention.[109] Deployment was the immediate challenge, but Saudi

Arabia was not by any means automatically willing to accept US troops into its Holy Land.[110] Although some defensive precautions had been taken, there was a feeling of resignation and fait accompli in the White House. President Bush publicly stated that he was 'not contemplating' an intervention.[111]

At the NSC meeting the following day Bush engaged in telephone conversations with several world leaders. He had been assured that Iran would stay more or less neutral, and that other world leaders supported the defence of Saudi Arabia, but he was told by King Hussein and President Mubarak that they were trying to find an 'Arab solution', and preferred Washington not to act.[112] On the military side, Powell argued that there were two military options: 'to deter further Iraqi action with Saudi Arabia', or 'deploy forces against the Iraqi troops in Kuwait, to defend Saudi Arabia or even strike against Iraq'.[113] There was consensus on the importance of Saudi Arabia, but whether it was 'worth going to war to liberate Kuwait' was not asserted.[114] As 14 of the 21 Arab League secretaries of foreign affairs condemned the invasion, and a strong joint US–Soviet statement also objected to the Iraqi action, Schwarzkopf had asked his team to develop alternative military responses to the crisis. During the night the director of operations (J-3), Major General Burt Moore, and Lieutenant General Horner developed a 15-squadron force structure with the intention of slowing down a possible Iraqi advance into Saudi Arabia, by attacking the second echelon of re-supply rather than the lead elements.[115] The first planning efforts that were initiated were related to a Quick Reaction Package, 1307, in which F-15s or F16s, depending on the situation, would deploy rapidly to the crisis area.

On 4 August, the third NSC meeting in three successive days was held at Camp David, and the focus turned to military options.[116] Colin Powell's suggestion was that they should be ready to defend Saudi Arabia on the one hand, and simultaneously lay the foundation for moving north into Kuwait, on the other.[117] This concept was in harmony with President Bush's view that the first objective was to keep Iraq out of Saudi Arabia, while the second was to protect the Saudis against retaliation when Iraq's export capability was shut down. Bush further contended that 'We have a problem if Saddam does not invade Saudi Arabia but holds on to Kuwait',[118] indicating that defending Saudi Arabia was only a partial solution, and that ultimately Iraq would have to leave Kuwait.

Schwarzkopf had brought Horner to the meeting, and they both argued that air power was the only military option that could be employed if the Iraqis chose to invade Saudi Arabia before the United States managed to deploy ground forces to the region. Horner presented the early options that involved air power according to the unfinished

OPLAN 1002-90: gaining air superiority, interdiction of attacking Iraqi forces, and defending ports and rear areas. Horner focused on a delaying action wherein air power would cut Iraqi forces, but also suggested offensive retaliatory strikes against 17 targets in Iraq, *if* Iraq used chemical weapons against friendly forces. Both Secretary of Defense Richard Cheney and General Colin Powell argued that air power by itself was not sufficient to do the job, and that ground power was the key backup to air power success anyway.[119] President Bush acknowledged that air power would play an important part if it came to a military option,[120] but Cheney, Scowcroft and Powell cautioned the President on the limits of air power to achieve national security objectives without the ground element.[121] Schwarzkopf, who had worked closely with Horner throughout the year, reassured: 'I am not an advocate of air power alone. But this is a target-rich environment. There is no cover in the desert. Their army has never operated under attack, and we have sophisticated munitions.'[122] Both Powell and Baker warned that going after Baghdad directly might be counter-productive in terms of public relations, while White House Chief of Staff John Sununu suggested 'sending B2s to bomb Iraq'. Cheney pointed out, however, that they had only one such aircraft available, as the others had not been tested sufficiently to be considered ready for combat.[123] As the discussion developed Schwarzkopf stressed that the plan was about defending Saudi Arabia, and that if military force were to be used to get Saddam Hussein out of Kuwait, that would be an offensive option which required many more troops and some eight to ten months of preparations.[124] At the end of the meeting Bush decided to send Cheney and a small delegation to Saudi Arabia to convince King Fahd that they should ask the United States for help.[125] In the meantime, Cheney instructed Powell and Schwarzkopf 'to develop an offensive option that would be available to the President in case Saddam chose to engage in further aggression or unacceptable behaviour such as killing Kuwaiti citizens or foreign nationals in Kuwait or Iraq'.[126]

There seems to have been consensus that if Iraq attacked Saudi Arabia, then military action would need no further justification. With only Kuwait occupied, further provocation would be needed for an offensive action.[127] President George Bush, a former Navy pilot with experience in the Second World War, was the most determined in the senior political leadership.[128] Within the first three days, Bush had gone from the position that he was 'not contemplating intervention' to 'this will not stand, this aggression against Kuwait'.[129] The latter comment was a personal determination that had not resulted from consultation. Powell felt Bush had declared war, and done it without Saudi Arabia formally having requested help, and more importantly, without consulting the military leadership.[130] However, on 6 August King Fahd received a team led by Secretary Cheney and upon being presented with satellite photos of the Iraqi occupation, he immediately accepted the offer of US forces. Cheney next ordered Schwarzkopf to take the necessary actions to deploy and Schwarzkopf in turn told Horner, who he had brought along, to get started.[131] While Schwarzkopf returned to the United States he left Horner in the theatre as CENTCOM Forward.[132] One might have expected the CINC to place his deputy in such a position, but the fact that he chose Horner shows the high degree of trust and confidence he held in his JFACC. As the deployment for Saudi Arabia started, Powell's and Schwarzkopf's major concern was that *if* Iraq decided to take immediate action against Saudi Arabia, started killing American hostages, exposed troops to chemical weapons, or torched Kuwaiti oil wells, their only option was Horner's retaliation plan.[133]

In the meantime, Colonel Warden and his Checkmate team had been developing their own ideas about what could be done to eject the Iraqi forces from Kuwait. Although not aware of the military options presented to the President, Warden was sure that they would be founded on the AirLand Battle doctrine or OPLAN 1002-90, both based on a military philosophy of which he strongly disapproved.[134] Warden believed that no real concept of operations for offensive action existed in the war plans and he was determined to change that.[135] On Monday 6 August he told the director of plans, Major General Robert M. Alexander, 'I don't have any idea how it's going to come out, but we are going to put it [an air plan] together anyway and see what happens.'[136] Rather than await instructions, which would most likely not come his way, Warden decided to take matters into his own hands. He gathered, without higher authorisation, a 20-man strong air force team that was comfortable with the Five Rings approach and convinced that air power alone could achieve the political objective of liberating Kuwait.[137] Based on the five strategic rings, the group started to gather people from the intelligence community for target selection, and operators who understood weapon and system capabilities, in order to match operational campaign planning to the overall theoretical construct. Since Warden was well aware of the controversy over his ideas on strategic air power, he was not only concerned about putting the plan together, but was also concerned about selling it to the military leadership. As the group managed to gather information about the deployment, they realised that there was a focus on the traditional tactical application of air power. Deptula observed that substantial numbers of B-52s were not in the deployment plan, and that F-117s were not even on the list. Importantly, F-111s were, but the D-version was on the deployment list versus the F-version, which had a precision weapon capability.[138] Major General Alexander informed General John

M. Loh, the Vice Chief of the Air Staff, on 6 August, that his team was dealing with some options on Kuwait, but there seemed to be no way that a think-tank in the Air Staff could interfere in such a vast process.

Schwarzkopf, who had no idea of the airmen's efforts, was getting desperate for an immediate rapid air power option. Since Horner was working 18–20 hour days, preoccupied with responsibilities of deploy- ment and mobilisation in Riyadh, in addition to setting up relations with Saudi Arabia, ensuring the defence of Saudi Arabia and establish- ing headquarters, Schwarzkopf and Powell agreed that they should call the Air Staff and ask 'what air could do in Iraq'.[139] Horner disapproved of this decision when Schwarzkopf informed him: 'Sir, the last thing we want is a repeat of Vietnam, where Washington picked the targets! This is the job of your Air Force commander.'[140] Schwarzkopf promised that this would be preliminary work, and that it would be handed over to Horner as soon as possible.[141] On 8 August, Schwarzkopf called the Air Staff and asked to talk to 'whoever was in charge'.[142] General John Loh took the call where Schwarzkopf in a 10-minute long conversation requested a 'retaliatory air campaign'.[143] Schwarzkopf asked for a 'retaliation capability' in case Saddam Hussein committed a 'heinous' act, such as taking hostages or using chemical weapons.[144] Schwarzkopf argued that his team had a reasonable plan for 'AirLand operations', but that he did not have the required expertise for developing a broader set of targets.[145] Loh, recalling his brief conversation with Alexander, told Schwarzkopf that he already had a team working on a strategic air campaign, and Schwarzkopf confirmed that what he needed was a quick and decisive response. According to Loh, Schwarzkopf said:

> We are doing a good job on AirLand Battle – on tactical application – but I need a broader set of targets, a broader air campaign; and I need it fast because if he [Saddam Hussein] attacks with chemicals or nuclears, I have got to be able to hit him where it hurts right away, and that is a strategic air campaign ... We can't go out in piecemeal with an AirLand Battle plan. I have got to hit him at his heart! ... I need it kind of fast because I may have to attack those kinds of targets deep, that have value to him as a leader.[146]

General Loh could not believe what had just happened: a four-star infantry Army general had, on his own initiative, called and asked if he could provide him with a plan in which air power would be used independently of ground forces.[147] As soon as the conversation ended, General Loh ordered Alexander to prepare 'a strategic air campaign'.[148] Since much of the basis for a proposed air campaign against Iraq had already been developed over the previous two days, and Checkmate had been thinking in these terms for over two years, Warden was able to provide General Loh and others in the Air Staff with a rather comprehensive presentation within 24 hours; Schwarzkopf on 10 August and Powell on 11 August. For Warden, Schwarzkopf's request was heaven sent: 'The man and the moment met and jumped as one.'[149]

INSTANT THUNDER

Warden gathered his team and through discussions and drawings they developed ideas on what needed to be done. In typical fashion he did not order anyone in particular to do anything, but several small groups developed proposals according to the overarching focus found in the Five Rings model. The brain power that contributed to assembling the initial strategic air campaign plan came from each of the six divisions in the XOXW, and, additionally, individuals with particular knowledge would be drawn into the planning effort. Learning from the Bitburg experience, Warden based the forthcoming work on the principle of 'open planning':

> I briefly considered gathering a very small group of people around me, closing the doors, and doing it all in great secrecy. Quickly, however, I realized that this didn't make much sense – I was certainly no expert on Iraq, I needed a lot of help, but didn't even have a way of knowing who or what I needed. I decided to open the doors of a big briefing room we had in the basement of the Pentagon and gather as many people as possible. Right from the start, everyone in the group was involved in almost everything that took place. This way, everybody understood not only the decisions but also the thinking and discussions associated with them. So they were able to do most of their work without reference to any higher authority, secure in the knowledge they were doing the right thing.[150]

The group that Warden assembled had a clear purpose in mind: to force Iraq's army from Kuwait by applying air power in a strategic offensive directly at the sources of Iraqi national power. In essence, actions in one major geographic sector (Iraq proper) would force reaction in another (Kuwait). The plan, which Warden termed Instant Thunder, envisioned unrelenting pressure on the Iraqi state and Saddam's regime until the latter accepted Washington's demands. Targets were selected according to the Five Rings Model for their presumed effect on the national leadership, and the implementation was to be made possible through precision. The political–military leadership organs of Saddam's regime, together with its associated means of command and control, were viewed as the 'central nervous system'. This system, as the 'political centre of gravity' of Iraq, was seen by Checkmate as offering the quickest and cheapest way to achieve the national security objectives.[151]

The centrepiece of Instant Thunder was to discredit and isolate the Iraqi regime, in addition to eliminating its offensive and defensive capability, in order to create conditions leading to Iraqi withdrawal from Kuwait, through long-range pinpoint bombing. They wanted to present a *war-winning* rather than a *war-fighting* plan that Schwarzkopf could implement within a week or two if required, and in essence they believed that six to nine TAC fighter wings against strategic centres of gravity would make all the difference.[152] To the architects of Instant Thunder, modern air power could strike directly at the Iraqi regime's decision-making body, and thus the Iraqi ground forces in Kuwait were not important.

Briefing the Air Staff: 8–9 August 1990

On 9 August 1990, less than 24 hours after Schwarzkopf's request for retaliation options, Colonel Warden briefed General Loh.[153] Warden's team had taken the four political objectives from Bush's 8 August speech and formulated four military objectives for the secret plan code-named Instant Thunder: A Strategic Air Campaign Proposal for CINCCENT (Commander-in-Chief of CENTCOM). They were to:

- force Iraqi withdrawal from Kuwait;
- degrade Iraq's offensive capability;
- secure oil-facilities;
- render Saddam ineffective as a leader.[154]

The fourth objective was the centrepiece of Warden's philosophy. There was no doubt in the minds of the planners that the root of the problem was Saddam, and that if they managed to kill the Iraqi leader, a better peace would follow.[155] Originally the term 'kill Saddam' was defined as an objective, and although the wording later changed to 'decapitating', 'render ineffective' and 'incapacitate leadership', these were mere changes of label.[156] Since killing the leader from the air would require luck which the plan could not depend on, Warden argued that one should isolate the regime from its own population and military forces, and thereby facilitate a subsequent overthrow.[157] The whole process of identifying targets was therefore governed by the effect their destruction would have on the Iraqi leadership. By disrupting critical nodes in the air defence system, including radars, and by damaging electricity supplies and communications, the planners sought to maximise friction and confusion within the Iraqi command structure. It would furthermore 'minimize civilian casualties and collateral damage' through precision-guided munitions.[158] In Warden's mind, there was a high probability that there would be a coup of some sort within a week, leading to the overthrow of the Iraqi leader, but, if that did not happen, he would at least be in the process of complying with UN demands.[159] They assumed, correctly, that Kuwait was not something Saddam was willing to die for. Nevertheless, based on intuition, Warden believed that attacks on the Iraqi regime's instruments of political control, combined with a major psychological warfare campaign, were certain to make someone overthrow the Iraqi leader somehow.[160] In the early versions of the air power option Warden had stressed the link between national objectives and the operational centres of gravity, but since Schwarzkopf had requested a strategic air campaign he did not see the need to spend time on justifying the approach.

Warden further argued that cutting the electricity supplies would have a psychological effect on the population and the regime in addition to the physical effects. Importantly, transformers rather than generators were to be targeted. In Warden's mind the bombing would not create too much destruction, and he envisioned a prosperous post-war Iraq which the United States would help reconstruct.[161] This would underline the fact that the regime was the enemy, not the people, and that the desired end-state would be an Iraq with a new leadership that would develop into a new working relationship with Washington. Warden stressed that in this particular case oil targets would have an important effect on Iraqi war-making capability, unlike the case in Vietnam. But he warned against destroying oil facilities that were not related to internal consumption, since that would reduce Iraq's ability to pay war debts or rebuild itself after hostilities. Thus, what was partly new in targeting electricity and oil was the intention of not inflicting long-term damage, and this reflected Warden's belief that the war would be short, and that the bombing could be very precise. Unlike the AWPD's strategy of bombing certain industrial sectors serially, the new strategy aimed at attacking several key areas simultaneously.

Interdiction of supply lines was not a target-set of priority, again because of the anticipated shortness of the war. In Warden's mind 'strategic warfare is only indirectly concerned with what is happening on some distant battlefield',[162] and consequently he suggested leaving the field army that occupied Kuwait intact. According to his theory, when the Iraqi military forces saw their leader embarrassed in front of his own people as his vulnerability surfaced, they would take matters into their own hands, demanding Saddam's resignation. Warden further argued that the military forces were not practical target-sets: the input in terms of effort would be high compared to the effect.[163]

General Loh felt uncomfortable with Warden's optimism, but was impressed by what had been assembled at such short notice.[164] He believed the planning had the right focus, and importantly, he believed this would be useful for Schwarzkopf. He even told Warden that Instant

Thunder was now 'the number one project in the Air Force ... you can call on anybody anyplace that you need for anything'.[165] He approved of the concept with only minor amendments, and agreed on the four suggested centres of gravity:

- Saddam's political and military leadership and internal control network;
- Saddam's strategic chemical warfare capability;
- the telecommunication, industrial and transportation systems that supported his rule;
- critical military systems such as the Iraqi air defence network.[166]

Donald Rice, the Secretary of the Air Force, and General Michael Dugan, by now the Air Chief of Staff, were comfortable with the focus of the planning when they were briefed on 9 August.[167] General Loh also informed General John T. Chain, the commander of SAC, who perceived many of Warden's ideas as in accordance with a conventional SIOP and responded positively by sending 14 members of his staff to support Checkmate in their efforts. General Loh also talked to TAC's commander, General Robert D. Russ, and they agreed to supply Schwarzkopf with 'a broader set of targets', but Russ was not comfortable with the Air Staff doing the actual planning.[168] When Alexander, Warden's immediate boss, next faxed an early version of Instant Thunder, asking for comments from TAC, its director of operations, Major General Michael E. Ryan, a former classmate of Warden's at the USAF Academy, commented that he liked 'everything after the last slide'.[169] This was the general feeling at TAC, and they opposed letting Warden take a plan to Schwarzkopf that they believed basically suggested bombing Iraq into oblivion.[170] General Russ found Instant Thunder too violent to be politically acceptable, and thus not in the best interests of either the Air Force or the country. Russ felt that the American public would not support an all-out war and that one 'couldn't just go in there and start a massive attack to win'.[171] He was not ready to take part in a plan that might put 'the United States in the position of starting World War III'.[172]

Russ ordered his Deputy Chief of Staff for Plans, Brigadier General Thomas R. Griffith, to come up with an alternative to Instant Thunder – CENTCOM Air Campaign Plan. Griffith formed a team and their immediate response was that Instant Thunder lacked tactical perspective:[173] first by failing to commit forces to holding a defence line on the Saudi/Kuwaiti border, second by omitting integration with ground forces in general, and third by not dealing with electronic countermeasures at all.[174] The clash between the Air Staff's effort and TAC was on several levels.[175] First, the former believed in intensive attacks, while the latter believed in gradualism for political reasons. Second, the former advocated attacking the political leadership and its command and control structure, while the latter believed in focusing on the Iraqi Army. While Russ was concerned that simply bombing Baghdad might provoke Saddam into invading Saudi Arabia, Warden felt that no army would move under enemy air superiority. Third, Russ, Ryan and others felt that the Air Staff was interfering in CENTAF's business:[176] after all, in peacetime, CENTAF's forces were responsible to TAC, so if anybody should help with the planning, it should be them. While many disagreed with Warden's offensive thinking, the resentment that developed at the time also resided in the fact that he had played such an important role in the planning.[177]

Within the Air Staff there were two key branches under Lieutenant General James Adams: *Plans* and *Operations*. Warden worked for Major General Alexander in *Plans*, which normally dealt with long-term events, while *Operations*, under the auspices of Major General Richard E. Hawley handled current issues. Thus, Warden was a planner who intruded into current operations, according to Adams, and was therefore perceived as overstepping his bounds. Moreover, *Plans* in the Air Staff was not responsible for strategy and war-planning per se, giving Adams an uneasy feeling about the Pentagon's involvement altogether. CENTCOM had its own planning team for such matters, and if they needed advice on air power they would normally approach either TAC or SAC, ultimately consulting CENTAF. Lieutenant General Adams and his assistant, Major General Charles A. May, were concerned that Warden was out of control again, prying into Horner's business, while Secretary Rice and General Dugan viewed it differently: he was merely lending professional expertise.[178]

The alternative plan to Instant Thunder provided by TAC suggested demonstrative attacks, sending a message to the Iraqi leader as to what US air power could achieve by bombing a few key installations, and then give him a pause in which the Department of State could work for a diplomatic solution. If Saddam did not comply there would be further escalation of offensive operations.[179] Additionally, it called for massive air strikes attacking the Iraqi armed forces in Kuwait.[180] The plan aimed to begin

> with demonstrative attacks against high value targets ... [and then] esca-late as required until the significant targets are destroyed ... This strat-egy allows time and opportunity for Hussein to re-evaluate his situation and back out while there is something to save.[181]

Air efforts would focus on targets 'that reduce his ability to project power, [i.e.] field armies and infrastructure to support offensive operations'.[182] Thus, it was argued that if this was a short-term option, then a demonstrative and gradual strategy was preferable. If it was to be part of an overall campaign, however, then air power should support the ground operations. Either way, the Warden approach was not feasible as it was 'too violent'.[183]

To Dugan, Loh, Alexander, Warden, Deptula and others who believed in a strategic air campaign, this was not only an attempt to make air power an adjunct to ground forces, it was a throw-back to Vietnam and Rolling Thunder.[184] Russ disagreed, arguing that he inserted himself in the planning 'to make sure that we didn't have someone picking targets in Washington like they did in Vietnam'.[185] The TAC planners were cautious and wanted to wait for Schwarzkopf to define his ground plan so that the air component could be developed to support it.[186] Lieutenant General Charles G. Boyd, who was appointed Commandant of the Air University in January 1990, found Instant Thunder right on target,[187] but many of the students at the university, who were given access to the briefing at the time, were sceptical and argued that the plan's strategic objectives were 'inappropriate and probably counterproductive',[188] reflecting the criticism from TAC. Despite the opposition, General Loh decided to send the team to brief Schwarzkopf at MacDill Air Force Base the following day.[189]

Briefing Schwarzkopf: 10 August 1990

Although TAC insisted that the Five Rings Model was an 'academic bunch of crap',[190] Warden believed that its simplicity was a great strength for the planning, and that it provided the basis of Instant Thunder's clear concept of operations: 'conduct powerful and focused attacks on strategic centres of gravity in Iraq over a short period of time (days not weeks)'.[191] Warden referred to the model when he stressed the relationship between the political and military objectives, and the rationale for the air campaign deriving from them. Warden told Schwarzkopf that the air offensive would involve 'round-the-clock operations against leadership, strategic air defence', and electrical targets with the aim of achieving 'strategic paralysis and air superiority'.[192] Warden stressed that war was about gaining political advantages, and the air power concept rested on four principles to realise that end:

- target the Hussein regime, not Iraqi people;
- minimise civilian casualties and collateral damage;
- minimise US and allied losses;
- pit US strengths against Iraqi weaknesses.[193]

Warden also noted that 'psychological operations [would be a] critical element in the command; destroy Iraqi TV and broadcast systems – substitute US broadcasts; separate regime from support of military and people'.[194] These messages would state why they were attacking, and explain what the people in Iraq could do to end the conflict.[195]

The CINCCENT, his deputy General Buck Rogers and Major General Burton Moore were presented with eight target-sets: strategic air defence, strategic offensive capability, leadership, civilian and military telecommunications, electricity, internal consumption of oil, railroads and nuclear, biological and chemical (NBC) research facilities. The attacks against the strategic air defence network were to ensure air superiority, while the attacks against the strategic offensive capability and NBC research facilities were designed to reduce Iraq's alleged short- and long-term threat to the region. The strikes against the tele-communications, electricity, oil and railroad target-sets were intended to disconnect the national leadership from both the people and the military forces in Kuwait. All these strikes were to contribute to the isolation and the incapacitation of the Iraqi leadership and prevent it from taking offensive action.

Warden argued enthusiastically and passionately that the focus of the campaign should be on Iraq's command and control facilities in and around Baghdad: Saddam Hussein's political headquarters, his secret police network and monuments that symbolised the power of the Iraqi leader. The objective was to slow down the Iraqi decision-making process, and hopefully facilitate a change in the leadership. Warden's group advocated a massive and intense application of air power from the start: there would be no gradual increase in military pressure to force the Iraqis to the negotiation table. It was not to be a piecemeal approach designed to send signals and messages: there would be no sanctuaries and no bombing halts. Instant Thunder suggested fast and precise operations, and the original plan was based on using only USAF assets: B-52s, F-117s, F-111s, F-15s, F-16s, A-10s etc. The strategy sought to paralyse the leadership and its command and control, degrade the military capabilities, and thereby neutralise the enemy's capability to fight. It was to be a self-sufficient air offensive whose objectives were directly linked to the four political objectives declared by President Bush. NBC production and research facilities would be destroyed, but air power was not to be diverted against the Iraqi forces in the field.[196]

Schwarzkopf had not asked for an air option that would be capable of ejecting Iraq from Kuwait on its own. Moreover, he had not asked for an extensive air campaign plan, but he had asked for retaliation options that went further than the ones presented by General Horner at Camp David on 4 August. The term 'strategic' meant something different to different people. In Schwarzkopf's mind it was air attacks on the Iraqi homeland that would deflect the Iraqi leadership from the path of further aggression. Instant Thunder was to be a decisive military reaction that would make Saddam change his mind about invading Saudi Arabia or killing hostages. The air campaign had therefore little to do with the occupation of Kuwait per se; it was about presenting immediate options to the President, a plan that would slow down Iraq's movements until the US forces were ready to counter-attack. Among Air Force officers the term 'strategic' also had different connotations. While many thought of 'strategic' as part of limited nuclear action, Colonel Warden, Lieutenant Colonels David Deptula, Ronnie Stanfill and Bernard Harvey, and others who had worked at the XOXW for some time, argued that the term 'strategic' should not be related to the mechanism of force application by air power – nuclear or conventional – but rather the effect that is achieved by its use: strategic, operational or tactical. Therefore, conventional air power, aimed at the enemy's political leadership and its command and control mechanisms, could achieve strategic effects – ergo, strategic air power.[197] It was they who established a concept whereby presidential objectives could be accomplished by using air power as the dominant force, and in essence, air power would ensure that the Iraqi Army withdrew from Kuwait with far fewer casualties on both sides than a ground war would require. It is therefore fair to say that Schwarzkopf asked for one thing, and Warden's team had delivered it, but offered something much more at the same time.

Schwarzkopf was extremely pleased, however, with the 30-minute tabletop presentation. He expressed '100 per cent' approval,[198] and when Warden suggested bombing palace bunkers in Baghdad, Schwarzkopf responded 'This is absolutely essential. I will call the chairman today and have him give you a directive to proceed with detailed planning immediately.'[199] Schwarzkopf further told Warden that 'You guys have restored my faith in the Air Force.'[200]

Much of Schwarzkopf's enthusiasm was based on the fact that there was no real alternative: the Joint Staff had started an analysis to determine the cost of a counterforce ground campaign, and the pre-liminary conclusion was that the casualties would be unacceptably high.[201] The CENTCOM planners also stressed that offensive operations into the Iraqi state involved too much risk. Schwarzkopf, desperate for options, found that Warden was the first one 'leaning forward'.[202] To Schwarzkopf, Instant Thunder was a good retaliation option, and to Warden his approval was the first important step in convincing the senior military leadership that air power could be decisive if applied strategically. Although Schwarzkopf was sceptical about some of Warden's promises,[203] he was pleased to hear that that plan could be executed within a week or two.[204] While some argued that Warden was unrealistic with his six to nine days timeframe, General Schwarzkopf favoured it because he foresaw that it might be the case that the United Nations required an end to the bombing after only a few days, and this would thus allow them to degrade some of Iraq's offensive capability. Indeed, Warden argued that the strategic air campaign should be allowed to run its course even if Saddam chose to surrender already after a day or two, in order to inflict sufficient damage on his offensive capability. Schwarzkopf raised the concern that Saddam might wave the white flag as the bombing commenced, whereupon Warden presented the story of Captain Nelson sailing into Copenhagen to attack the enemy fleet. His flag-lieutenant tapped him on the shoulder and said the admiral was signalling them to break off the action and return. Nelson allegedly asked for the telescope, which he picked up and held to his patched eye and said, 'I see no signal. Proceed'! Thus, Warden recommended to Schwarzkopf that they had to make sure that they did not see the white flag during those opening days.

While TAC felt that Instant Thunder was too violent, Schwarzkopf saw several advantages to it: 'If we invade Kuwait they will destroy it. This might leave Kuwait intact.'[205] Schwarzkopf was also extremely concerned about friendly casualties, so anything that would reduce body-bags was welcomed.[206] Finally, TAC's concern about the necessity of attacking ground forces in order to liberate Kuwait did not bother Schwarzkopf at the time, simply because this was to him a retaliation option, not a comprehensive war plan. Warden, on the other hand, believed that the strategic air campaign would now become the only show for the time being. Schwarzkopf next asked the team to give the same briefing to General Powell, and come back with a more extensive briefing one week later. As they were leaving, Warden told Schwarzkopf 'You have the opportunity now to carry off the most brilliant operation that any American general has executed since Douglas MacArthur went ashore at Inchon.'[207] Schwarzkopf's eyes allegedly lit up and it might be that, for the first time, he realised his potential impact on history.

Briefing Powell: 11 August 1990

Sixteen hours later the same group presented the same concept to General Colin Powell and 12 high-ranking officers and officials in Washington. Powell was less enthusiastic than Schwarzkopf, but he was pleased overall and thought it was a 'good plan, very fine piece of work'.[208] Lieutenant General Tom Kelly, Joint Chief Director of Operations, was reluctant because Warden had no empirical support: 'Airpower has never worked in the past by itself ... airpower can't be decisive.'[209] Powell too was suspicious of air power promises, and questioned what would happen after six days of strategic bombing.

Warden argued with candour that it would induce the Iraqis to withdraw, and that the conscripts in the foremost positions were likely to return home and overthrow Saddam: 'This plan may win the war. You may not need a ground attack ... I think the Iraqis will withdraw from Kuwait as a result of the strategic air campaign.'[210] At this point Powell introduced an added concept to the war planning: 'I don't want them to go home – I want to leave smoking tanks as kilometer fence posts all the way to Baghdad.'[211] Powell made it quite clear at the time that he saw this as punishment for the Iraqis. It was also one of the many debates that would continue throughout the war: what would constitute defeat in the minds of the Iraqis? To Warden, paralysis of an entire nation and destruction of its NBC research, development and production programmes would constitute a real defeat, especially if the Iraqis failed to impose any serious blood penalty on the United States. The other side of the argument was that the Arabs would not feel defeated unless they had fought and lost a man-to-man conflict. Members of Powell's staff criticised the plan for ignoring the troops in Kuwait, but Major General Alexander insisted time and again that the strategic air campaign could not be compromised to include targeting ground forces.[212] Warden argued that prior to the Normandy invasion General Eisenhower, ill advised, pulled significant resources from the strategic bombing against German targets in order to degrade French and Belgian transportation systems.[213] Powell agreed that resources should not be diverted from the strategic operations, but after they had finished that, tanks would have to be destroyed.[214] Thus, Powell argued that he needed more than strategic effects – he also wanted to destroy military equipment as a political signal. Warden's team was ordered to make the planning joint and expand it to include targeting ground forces.

Warden had mixed feelings after the briefing. He was pleased that Powell liked the proposal and that they were to continue with the planning, but he also felt that Powell thought in terms of force-on-force which contradicted the idea of putting all the effort on the enemy's 'inner ring'.[215] Significantly, Powell's comment reflected a political concern in the White House: evicting Iraq from Kuwait would not be sufficient, Iraq's offensive capabilities would need to be degraded. Instant Thunder stated this as one of its objectives, but there was a fundamental difference of opinion: while Warden thought in terms of aircraft and NBC facilities, Powell thought in terms of artillery and tanks. Nevertheless, there seems to have been an understanding even, at this point, that there were objectives beyond those stated by the President: the official objective was to liberate Kuwait, the unofficial one was to degrade Iraq's military capability, while the hoped-for objective was to overthrow the Iraqi leadership.[216]

Although Powell questioned Warden's lack of attention to ground forces, he found that they at least had an option for retaliation. Powell requested a five-slide summary immediately to brief higher authorities,[217] and by ordering the planning to become joint it became an extension of the Joint Staff's Directorate for Operations (J-3), which de facto 'legitimised' further planning. Warden had received a green light from both the JCS and CENTCOM, and could therefore ignore much of the internal USAF disapproval as he continued the planning. Importantly, the new concept had made its presence felt.

Warden realised that he had to come up with a compromise, at least on paper, regarding attacks on Iraqi ground forces in Kuwait. The Checkmate group continued to work predominately on the strategic air campaign, but they also initiated a follow-on phase, 'the operational level campaign', which was to include 'direct attack on the Iraqi army in Kuwait itself'.[218] In making the planning joint, six officers were included from the Navy and six from the Marines, in addition to three from TAC and the ten from SAC. The US Navy proved extremely useful with its information on the TLAMS, which would eventually play such an important part in the air campaign. USAF historian Dr Wayne W. Thompson had already arrived and finally Colonel James R. Blackburn brought a staff of 13 target experts from intelligence, which was to be the basis for the selection of the targets associated with Instant Thunder.[219] Warden's team expanded from 20 to over 100, and the three TAC officers were officers who had suggested an alternative to Instant Thunder under the direction of Brigadier General Griffith. Not at all pleased with their presence, Warden gave them the task of developing Instant Thunder Phase II: KTO Operations Against Iraqi Army, a phase that he believed did not have to be executed. The TAC trio saw their mission as 'putting some tactical sense into the plan', but felt that 'Warden had a plan, and he wasn't going to listen to any outside changes or inputs to his plan.'[220] Although they provided some useful input to the planning they just did not manage to establish a working relationship with the core of Warden's team. Since they kept Major General Ryan continuously updated on their efforts they were simply referred to as the 'TAC spies', reflecting the tacit disagreement between the Air Staff and TAC.[221]

The whole Checkmate effort was an extremely dynamic process, in which everybody talked to everybody, emphasising the importance of networking and pulling in resources. For example, Lieutenant Colonel Rich Stimer, who was responsible for the Concept Division, established close contacts in the intelligence community enabling access to both the National Intelligence Council (Fritz Ermath) and the Central Intelligence Agency (Mary Gambolli and Charlie Allan). It was as such an impressive collective effort that went far beyond the initial team, wherein most contacts were established through personal networks and phone-calls rather than formal requests for support.

Further internal briefings were held during the next few days, including updates and inputs to and from Generals Dugan, Loh and Alexander, in addition to Air Force Secretary Donald Rice and the Vice Commandant of the US Marine Corps, General Alfred Gray. They were all in favour of Warden's emphasis on the strategic realm, and General Dugan stressed that he wanted the planners to remain 'bold and imaginative', insisting that they 'press hard on planning for INSTANT THUNDER'.[222] He also emphasised that Iraqi experts had to be consulted because Saddam 'doesn't care about military or economic targets but about self, family, mistresses'.[223] Dugan wanted to know what kind of targets would play on Arab culture and what would really hurt Saddam. The planners had already talked to several civilians who had involved themselves with strategic thinking over the years, most notably Edward Luttwak, Colin Gray and Eliot Cohen.[224]

On 14 August Schwarzkopf presented his preliminary offensive plan to Powell. It reflected much of Instant Thunder, but importantly, it argued that strategic operations would only be part of an overall campaign.[225] On 15 August General Powell briefed President Bush, Secretary of Defense Cheney and the Joint Chiefs on Desert Shield, and a few briefing slides prepared by Checkmate were presented.[226] These slides predicted that Instant Thunder would 'incapacitate or discredit Hussein's regime', eliminate the offensive/defensive capability and facilitate conditions for an Iraqi withdrawal. The air campaign would not target the population, but render the 'Hussein regime destroyed and impotent'. If Saddam Hussein did not comply, there would be a second phase where bombing would continue against the Iraqi Army in Kuwait. If Saddam managed to survive, he would be very much weakened. Shortly after, Major General James W. Meier, who was heading the joint planning (J-5), received a briefing by Checkmate, and although he opposed much of it, he agreed to let the briefing go without delay to Schwarzkopf.[227] Assembling some 25 Checkmate planners Warden went to brief General Schwarzkopf for the second time in one week accompanied by General Meier.

Briefing Schwarzkopf: 17 August 1990

The 17 August Iraq Air Campaign Instant Thunder briefing was presented in the name of the JCS rather than the Air Staff, as Powell had ordered that the planning was made a joint venture. In Warden's mind, as previously mentioned, the concept might be executed in six to nine days.

What it is: a *focused, intense* air campaign designed to incapacitate Iraqi leadership and destroy key Iraqi military capability, in a *short* period of time and it is designed to leave basic Iraqi infrastructure intact. What it is not: a graduated, long-term campaign plan designed to provide escalation options to counter Iraqi moves.[228]

They identified five goals that were linked directly to Bush's 8 August speech. They were to:

- isolate Saddam;
- eliminate Iraq's offensive and defensive capability;
- incapacitate the national leadership;
- reduce the threat to friendly nations;
- minimise the damage to enhance rebuilding.[229]

The briefing stressed again that the focus should be on the Iraqi regime and that it could be executed in the near term; 84 targets, divided into ten target categories, according to the Five Rings formula, were expected to provide the results described in Table 1.

Table 1: Instant Thunder Target Categories and Expected Strike Results

Target Category	Number	Expected Strike Results
Strategic Air Defense	10	Destroyed
Strategic Chemical	8	Long-Term Setback
National Leadership	5	Incapacitated
Telecommunications	19	Disrupted/Degraded
Electricity	10	60% Baghdad, 35% Country
Oil (internal consumption)	6	70% (Destroyed)
Railroads	3	Disrupted/Degraded
Airfields	7	Disrupted/Degraded
Ports	1	Disrupted
Mil. Production and storage depots	15	Disrupted/Degraded

Source: Warden to General Normal Schwartzkopf, 'Iraq Air Campaign Instant Thunder', p. 5.

All these targets would be attacked on the first two days, and then the round-the-clock attacks would continue with further strikes. The team that developed the plan stressed that through strategic bombing it would be possible to incapacitate the basic physical components of the enemy's overall ability to pursue its political and military goals. These targets would be headquarter organisations, command centres, information-gathering and information-disseminating structures with their telecommunication adjuncts, related public infrastructures and military facilities. Checkmate argued that targeting these physical components would be of particular importance in this case because Saddam's dominant political goal was to conserve enough strength to survive, while the military goal of holding on to Kuwait was secondary. The strategy was consequently to focus on downtown Baghdad from the opening moments, and make air power decisive by using stealth aircraft and precision bombing. It was still based on intensity, gaining and maintaining the initiative, and never pausing until Saddam had withdrawn from Kuwait and acknowledged the UN Resolutions. While bombing a battlefield would have a cumulative effect over time, this campaign was to create instantaneous results. It was an offensive option that did not pay attention to the Iraqi ground threat at the Saudi Arabian border, its most severe weakness according to critics. There was one slide asking 'What if: Iraq attacks Saudi Arabia in response to Instant Thunder', indicating that there were a substantial number of aircraft 'available for immediate engagement'.[230] But Warden chose not to present the added phase, which Powell had requested and TAC developed, since Schwarzkopf did not ask for it.[231] Schwarzkopf was extremely pleased with the briefing, and when questioning whether the 'expected strike results' were realistic Major General Meier endorsed the plan.[232]

By 17 August 1990, 15 days after the Iraqi invasion of Kuwait, there was widespread acceptance of Instant Thunder in the senior military leadership, but importantly – for different reasons. While Warden, the Checkmate group and others who thought favourably of this effort believed there was acceptance for an air plan that could win a war on its own, Schwarzkopf and Powell approved of Instant Thunder for its retaliatory capabilities. Herein lies part of the answer as to why the notion of air superiority was not substantially questioned. While military commanders would argue that air superiority is essential for air, naval and ground operations to succeed, Warden believed that fewer than 20 targets needed to be struck in order to command the skies. Since the United States was technologically superior, and some aircraft had inherent stealth capabilities, Checkmate believed air superiority would be achieved within hours, and therefore the focus of attack should be on the leadership. Schwarzkopf and Powell, for their part, did not give the issue major attention since they did not consider Instant Thunder anything more than a reprisal campaign at the time. There was, however, no disagreement on the necessity of having the air plan ready in a short period of time.[233]

When Schwarzkopf stated that 'This [Instant Thunder] is what makes the US a superpower ... our strengths against their weaknesses ... our air power against theirs',[234] he was talking about retaliation first, and this possibly being part of an overall campaign next. He favoured the fact that the air campaign was designed to exploit air power's strength, which included well-trained aircrews, advanced technology such as stealth, stand-off capability and precision-guided munitions, superior Command and Control, and the ability to operate effectively at night, while at the same time taking advantage of Iraqi weaknesses which included a rigid Command and Control apparatus and a defensive ground orientation. Schwarzkopf liked the idea that air power could be so decisive immediately, with low casualties, but more importantly, if the President ordered immediate action, he now had a good option. Significantly, Schwarzkopf did not accept sending his troops into war without being fully prepared, and Instant Thunder was a way around that encompassing problem. Schwarzkopf never believed that air power could win a war on its own,[235] and he was predominantly concerned with the defensive mission: deterrence and defence of Saudi Arabia. While Warden refused to weaken Instant Thunder by diverting attention to field forces, the 17 August 1990 briefing made Schwarzkopf realise that it could have a dual purpose. It could be a retaliation option for the time being, and the initial phase in a larger campaign if liberating Kuwait by force became necessary. Furthermore, a major premise of Instant Thunder was to ignore the air defences over Kuwait proper. Still, widely influenced by Warden's presentations Schwarzkopf formulated the idea of the four-phased war-strategy, which was to become the substance of Desert Storm:

- Instant Thunder;
- suppression of air defences over Kuwait;
- attrition of enemy forces by 50 per cent;
- ground attack?[236]

Schwarzkopf chose to keep Instant Thunder as the code name for Phase I,[237] and he found the plan so interesting that he decided to send Warden, and a few key members of his team, to Riyadh to brief the air commander, Lieutenant General Charles Horner, and let the planning continue in the theatre as he had promised. It was the 17 August briefing that convinced Schwarzkopf that his war plan would consist of four phases, and although impressed by Warden's efforts he ordered his J-5 staff in secret to develop a four-phased plan at the same time as he sent Warden to Saudi Arabia.[238]

Briefing Horner: 20 August 1990

Horner, who had been in Riyadh since 6 August, was at the time pre-occupied with bedding down forces in the theatre, developing a plan to defend Saudi Arabia in case Iraq chose to attack, and coordinating administrative matters in general.[239] Horner had originally ordered his staff to look into some offensive type of targets, categorising them as military, economic and political, but as soon as they deployed to Riyadh the CENTAF planners were ordered to give priority to developing a defensive plan in case Iraq continued into Saudi Arabia.[240] The CENTAF planners had thus by mid August developed two air options: the D-Day ATO, which would deal with Iraqi forces moving into Saudi Arabia, and the less complete Punishment ATO, which was a limited retaliation strike against the Iraqi homeland.[241] The former was the first air power option presented to the military and political leadership. It was in harmony with the AirLand Battle Doctrine, and it stressed the defensive nature of operations that would be applied in defending Saudi Arabia. At this time Horner's main concern was to be able to prevent an Iraqi attack into Saudi Arabia, and consequently a comprehensive bombing of Baghdad was not on his mind.

When he received an early draft of Instant Thunder from TAC he felt uncomfortable with the focus,[242] and disdainfully penned a note with words to the effect: 'How can a person in an Ivory Tower far from the front, not knowing what needs to be done, write such a message? Will wonders never cease?'[243] This comment presented Lieutenant General James Adams with a dilemma. Schwarzkopf had ordered Warden and some of his team to brief Horner in the theatre, but he knew Horner would see this as a Vietnam-style Washington interference. Consequently, he sent Colonel Steve Wilson from the 'Fighter Mafia' on 12 August as a 'peacemaker' to 'smooth the way for Warden's visit'.[244] Wilson was updated on the Instant Thunder concept by Warden and Deptula. The latter was a very close friend of Wilson, and having been a squadron commander under Horner he was prepared to meet somebody who would 'ask a lot of questions', do 'a lot of screaming' while 'pretending not to listen'.[245]

Horner was given an early version of the briefing by Wilson and was far from happy with the concept: he did not appreciate the Air Staff doing this, and he did not like the content. After having objected harshly several times, Horner told Wilson that he was not interested in giving priority to 'strategic targeting', because the imminent threat was on the Saudi Arabian border.[246] Horner did not like the terms used in the briefing: he argued that 'centre of gravity' was a 'college boy term', that 'strategic' was perceived as 'nuclear' and that the term Instant Thunder reminded him of Vietnam.[247] More importantly, however, to Horner the concept did not amount to a plan: it was bombing Baghdad and hoping to win.

Warden for his part was somewhat sceptical of Horner: he knew that the air commander was close to General Russ and Lieutenant General Adams, who both disapproved of the Instant Thunder initiative and philosophy. Deptula had received feedback from Colonel Wilson on Horner's reaction, but with the endorsement from Powell and Schwarzkopf Warden's team thought they had a good case. In Warden's mind the concept was so good that when given a chance, he would convince Horner of the plan's efficiency. Warden's personal objective was to ensure that there was acceptance for the plan, and that CENTAF would continue the planning as opposed to CENTCOM – hopefully with himself in the driving seat.[248] Warden had brought with him Lieutenant Colonels Deptula, Harvey and Stanfill, the core of the Instant Thunder planning group, and they briefed portions of Horner's CENTAF staff at midnight on 19 August. The senior members of CENTAF argued that the concept was interesting, while the more junior members, who were briefed the following day, argued that the capacity of the Iraqi ground forces should be the essence of the planning effort, and only when the ground war had adequate support should the focus be on targets 'deep inside Iraq'.[249]

Horner was briefed the next day, and although he appreciated some of it, there was a lot he disliked. The tension was high from the beginning, the two men having very different personalities. Horner, 'a combat tested, dyed-in-the-wool, old school fighter pilot who flew F-105s over Hanoi and harbored no illusions about who he was or what he knew' early on stated 'Let's not use the terms "strategic" and "tactical". Targets are targets.'[250] They discussed the importance of 'getting Hussein' as opposed to just 'isolating' the Iraqi leader, in addition to several operational aspects.[251] Horner was very critical of Warden's emphasis on PGM, arguing that the real point was rather 'precision delivery of munitions', stressing that it did not matter what kind of bomb was used as long as it hit the target.[252] Horner felt that the plan lacked depth, and importantly he was very uncomfortable with the lack of focus on the immediate threat of Iraqi forces coming into Saudi Arabia, the very same issue that Powell and the TAC officers had emphasised in their critique.[253] That theme was to be the climax of tension during the briefing. As Warden argued that an offensive application of air power would institute a change in the Iraqi government, Horner argued that Iraqi ground forces had to be dealt with first, and consequently: 'You can't do it with air alone.'[254] Adams had told Warden to drop the prediction that the air campaign would succeed in six to nine days, and rather focus more on destroying Iraqi military forces, but Warden disregarded his boss on both accounts, as he argued that was not the CINC's request. Horner too was indeed sceptical about the idea that it would all be over after a week or so. Horner further stated that while Warden was doing this very presentation, tanks could be rolling into Saudi Arabia, reaching Riyadh within hours. Warden begged to differ: having simulated an Iraqi advance into

Saudi Arabia in Checkmate, he concluded that when attacked by US air power the Iraqi tanks could only move a few miles a day at best in any coherent and coordinated fashion. Thus, the comment from Horner seemed ridiculous to Warden, who, annoyed, replied, 'You're being overly pessimistic about those tanks, Sir!' The tension was at its peak, and Warden next apologised: 'I'm sorry, Sir. I went a little too far.'[255] Horner accepted the apology, but the tension remained throughout the briefing. Not accepting Warden's assumption that the Iraqi ground forces were not really a threat, Horner did not agree that going in deep and destroying a few targets would win the war.[256] Warden argued for complementing the strategic bombing campaign with psychological operations, but Horner insisted 'That's a theatre-level responsibility, and it's concentrated in the Army.'[257]

Horner found that the briefing essentially did not pass the 'common sense' test, and he viewed it as 'incomplete', 'embryonic' and only a 'partial answer'.[258] At the end of the briefing Horner asked some questions: Did Warden know when sufficient supplies would exist in theatre to support such a campaign? What would happen if the Iraqi regime did not collapse after a five or six day campaign and CENTAF had used up its logistic base in theatre? What could CENTAF do against the Iraqi Army with so few ground forces presently in theatre?[259] What is the goal of attacking the railroads? What is the goal of airfield attacks? What is the goal of ports disruption? Why TLAMs? Horner recollects that Warden was unable to answer these practical questions, reinforcing his perception of this being merely an academic study.[260] Warden's recollection, however, is that Horner was firing questions without presenting him with a chance to answer them. Moreover, to Warden the answers were mostly in the briefing that he had already given, and those that were not were quite simple anyhow. In particular, Warden felt that he had addressed explicitly what CENTAF could do against the Iraqi Army by itself: air forces were held in reserve to repel a potential Iraqi offensive, including modelling that showed what it would do to movement rates.

In Horner's mind the main task was to build an ATO, and to him the devil was in the details, while Warden focused on the big picture only. Still, there were elements that Horner liked, especially the target research that had been undertaken, and he acknowledged after the war that Warden's briefing 'contained elements of brilliance', but 'lacked full scope'.[261]

The disagreement between Warden and Horner arose partly from different perspectives on precision bombing. While Warden believed that the bombing could be very precise, Horner was sceptical and argued that although attacking downtown Baghdad would be an advantage in the short term, it might have repercussions for the US–Arab relations for the next 200 years: 'I have trouble with the basic premise, severing the head from the body ... If you're trying to institute a change in his government, you can't leave this to chance.'[262] Horner was furthermore sceptical about going straight after vital centres without paying sufficient attention to the Iraqi air defence system. He was more interested in a sustained air campaign plan rather than one of overwhelming force. Horner appreciated, however, that the concept contained time compressed convergence of technology and strategy, a combination he felt should be explored further. Horner ended the session by saying 'You took and made an academic study. Now I need to turn that into reality. What you've essentially brought me, for all intents and purposes, is a target list, and I thank you for your efforts for doing that. Now I need to turn it into an executable plan.'[263]

There has been much speculation as to why Horner was so critical of the new concept, but some of the explanation resides in his preconception. The Checkmate group was very confident in their concept, among other things because of Schwarzkopf's strong support, but it seems as though the CINC was somewhat more critical when conveying his impression to Horner on 17 August. Schwarzkopf allegedly told Horner that the Instant Thunder proposal was 'too parochial' and 'too focused on the Air Force doing the whole show'.[264] When this perception was combined with his own assessment of operational flaws it becomes less surprising. He believed Warden was a brilliant theorist, but not the right man to translate the concept into something that could be carried out.

In the end Horner chose to keep Warden's key planners, Deptula, Harvey and Stanfill, but not Warden himself. Horner thought that, with some luck, Saddam would withdraw short of a ground war, but he could not allow luck and chance to be dominating criteria for success, and he felt Warden failed to acknowledge such realities. Horner, however, had come to the conclusion that an offensive option should be developed. Within the next two days Horner appointed Brigadier General Buster Glosson, the Deputy Commander of the Joint Task Force Middle East (JTFME), to make an offensive plan effective by early September. With Warden on his way to Washington, thinking about how to gather a constituency for enhancing the campaign planning from within Washington, the future of Instant Thunder was for Glosson to decide.

CONCLUSIONS

The development of a strategic air campaign plan in the early days of the crisis over Kuwait quickly became an encounter between the radical air power ideas articulated by a small group in the Air Staff, and the more conventional thinking that dominated at TAC. While the latter was anchored in existing military doctrine and contingency plans for the region, the advocates of strategic air power managed to present the army-dominated military leadership with an alternative philosophy. When Iraq invaded Kuwait the United States armed services were still thinking in terms of the Cold War where conventional air power would be used in support of ground forces and always start on the defensive. Based on a European scenario, as was the case with the AirLand Battle doctrine, there was no alternative strategy to retaking lost territory piece-meal short of nuclear attacks.

For these reasons Checkmate received much opposition within the USAF when they reintroduced the concept of conventional strategic air power in August 1990: the Instant Thunder concept simply did not adhere to the established Cold War way of thinking.[265] However, when considering the 75 years of air power thought that preceded it, one realises that Instant Thunder was more of a synthesis than something revolutionary. It partly reflected the strategic bombing philosophy of the inter-war period, but focused on regime targets rather than the industrial and economic centres; it partly reflected the SIOP's target lists, but departed from the nuclear framework; it kept the strategic dimension to targeting as reflected in Thomas Schelling's paradigm, but with massive and intense bombing over a short period of time rather than gradual escalation; and it focused on *war-making* facilities rather than *war-fighting* forces. To its critics Instant Thunder was nothing more than a target list, and they are right to suggest that a target list does not make a strategy, but as detailed, Instant Thunder had a clear theoretical foundation.

Although General Horner had a list of high-value targets from Exercise Internal Look prior to Warden's initiative,[266] he thought in terms of limited retaliation as opposed to a comprehensive offensive air campaign plan at the time. Thus, a strategic air campaign proposal beyond demonstrative attacks may not have been presented to the military and political leadership had it not been for the persistence of the small group of airmen in the Air Staff. While all planning was focused on defending Saudi Arabia, only a few individuals were thinking in the strategic realm.[267] Since the JCS, CENTCOM, CENTAF and TAC were all thinking in terms of AirLand Battle doctrine and were well versed in the application of tactical air power, it is by no means certain that the strategic thinking that came to characterise Operation Desert Storm would have taken form within the organisation.[268] It is, nevertheless, interesting that it was a ground commander who took the initiative in calling for an offensive air option, but one cannot help being struck by an irony: as Warden and his team argued that air power could win the war through a strategic air campaign, it was General

Powell and General Schwarzkopf who sought to enhance the wider spectrum of air power capabilities by stressing that also ground forces should be targeted.[269] Before Chapter 3 examines the modifications which Instant Thunder went through it might be worthwhile to reflect on two major issues. Why did General Schwarzkopf decide to take the unprecedented action of asking the Air Staff for a strategic option, and why did Schwarzkopf and Powell like it so much, while Horner did not?

It seems as though Schwarzkopf first became aware of the term 'strategic air operations' when Horner suggested extensive retaliation options during Exercise Internal Look in April 1990.[270] Horner had briefed Schwarzkopf on how to bomb targets deep inside the enemy state, and he had referred to them 'strategic targets'. Thus, when Schwarzkopf was tasked with defending Saudi Arabia, and had no ground forces in place, he wanted to know what retaliation options he could present to the President. Since Horner was heavily preoccupied in Riyadh, he called the Air Staff and asked for a decisive air campaign.[271] He most certainly had in mind the Iraqi military, industrial and communications systems as targets for retaliation or punishment, but when Warden was asked to develop an option he envisioned a full-blown strategic air campaign. There is still uncertainty as to whether Schwarzkopf used the term 'strategic air campaign', but to Warden it did not matter: he was going to present what he believed was the only way forward, whatever the CINC had actually asked for.[272] The Instant Thunder concept has often been criticised for not focusing on the ground force in Kuwait, but the CINC's request was to develop an air campaign that might have to be executed long before US ground forces were in place. Schwarzkopf wanted something that could operate without ground forces, and since he did not view this as a campaign to liberate Kuwait, but a quick and severe retaliation, he was not concerned with the occupying forces. This explains why both Schwarzkopf and Powell were so impressed with the concept in August, but as time went by and other options became available they became more and more reluctant to let air power be the only show.

In essence, Schwazkopf asked for one thing, was presented with something else, and fully appreciated what he received.[273] He had no clear vision of what would happen if the crisis escalated, and suddenly this colonel comes along and provides a lot of answers. Some of the flaws of Instant Thunder will be examined in the succeeding chapters, but at the time, almost out of nowhere, General Powell and General Schwarzkopf received a plan that could, if necessary, be executed by early September. Although both were impressed by Warden's effort, and his thinking on a strategic air campaign strongly influenced their thinking, they were *never* confident with this as a stand alone war-winning solution.

The clarity of the plan was its strength and weakness. Horner, pre-dominantly concerned that the Iraqi forces on the Saudi Arabian border could attack at any moment,[274] saw an intellectual coming down to Riyadh with an academic study, telling him how to do his job.[275] In Horner's mind, this 'superb targeteer' from Washington did not have a sound relationship with reality: he argued that it would be possible just to bomb certain targets in Baghdad over a week or so, and then the Iraqi forces would start withdrawing.[276] Horner knew that in a theoretical world that was possible, but he asked himself what kind of commander he would be if he accepted such a gamble? It reminded him of Vietnam where Washington told the theatre commander what to do.[277] While Deptula has suggested that there is a big difference between advice from the Pentagon on the west side of the Potomac river, and inter-ference in military affairs from the White House on the east side of the Potomac, Horner would treat Washington as one unwelcome entity in planning.[278] One might note, however, that Horner's disgust for Washington inputs also included his colleagues at TAC: to Horner war planning simply needed to be done in the theatre of operations. Ironi-cally, both the Checkmate group and Horner tried to avoid another Vietnam, but while Horner feared Washington was about to grab control of the planning, the Checkmate group tried to avoid the application of air power that had characterised Vietnam.

With the difference in personalities between Warden and himself,[279] Horner chose the middle way: he kept the plan and three of the plan-ners, while sending Warden home. Horner simply did not want the 'intellectual' Warden, and felt more comfortable with somebody who had a better feel for the nitty-gritty of tactics. Consequently, rather than terminate the initiative, Horner decided to establish an offensive planning cell under Brigadier General Buster Glosson. From that time, the fate of the strategic air campaign proposal was in the hands of Glosson, who had no previous relationship with Instant Thunder, or the Checkmate officers who had been working on the ideas of strategic operations for two years. Chapter 3 will explore the continued planning which ultimately formed the content of what became the first phase of Operation Desert Storm.

NOTES

1. Powell with Persico, *My American Journey*, p. 460; Schwarzkopf with Petre, *It Doesn't Take a Hero*, pp. 369–71; Cohen *et al.*, *The Gulf War Air Power Survey: Planning*, pp. 105–43; United States Department of Defense, *Conduct of the Persian Gulf War*, p. 89; Gordon and Trainor, *The Generals' War*, pp. 75–102; Phillip S. Meilinger, 'Air Targeting Strategies: An Overview', in Richard P. Hallion (ed.), *Air Power Confronts an Unstable World* (London: Brassey's, 1997), pp. 61, 77;

Richard T. Reynolds, *Heart of the Storm: The Genesis of the Air Campaign Against Iraq* (Maxwell Air Force Base, AL: Air University Press, 1995), p. 134; Atkinson, *Crusade*, pp. 56, 63; James Blackwell, *Thunder in the Desert: The Strategy and Tactics of the Persian Gulf War* (New York: Bantam Books, 1991), pp. 114–16; Duffey *et al.*, *Triumph Without Victory*, p. 266; and Scales, *Certain Victory*, p. 176. Warden's contribution is also acknowledged by the official USAF historians: Richard G. Davis, 'The Offensive Air Campaign Plan', unpublished paper (1994), p. 2; Hallion, *Storm over Iraq*, appendix between pp. 242–3; and Diane T. Putney, 'From Instant Thunder to Desert Storm: Developing the Gulf War Air Campaign's Phases', *Air Power History* 41, No. 3 (Fall 1994), pp. 39–50.

2. Keaney and Cohen, *Revolution in Warfare?*, p. 25; Barry Watts, correspondence with author, transcript, 4 November 1998; Thomas A. Keaney, interview with author, tape-recording, Washington, DC, 23 February 1999; and Perry Smith, 'Translating Airpower Theory and Practice', *Marine Corps Gazette* (November 1995), p. 79.

3. Richard D. Bristow, interview, *Desert Story Collection,* 9 November 1992, p. 2.; and Warden, interview, *Desert Story Collection*, 22 October 1991, p. 87.

4. Giulio Douhet, *The Command of The Air*, transl. Dino Ferrari (New York: Coward-McCann, 1984). The book was published in 1921 and expanded into a second edition in 1927. He also wrote several articles and memoranda. For an analysis of Douhet, see Frank J. Cappelluti, 'The Life and Thought of Giulio Douhet' (Ph.D. dissertation, Rutgers University, 1967); and Azar Gat, *Fascists and Liberal Visions of War: Fuller, Liddell Hart, Douhet, and other Modernists* (Oxford: Clarendon Press, 1998), pp. 43–79. Brigadier General Mitchell's two most influential books are *Skyways: A Book on Modern Aeronautics* (Philadelphia, PA: J. B. Lippincott, 1930) and *Winged Defense: The Development and Possibilities of Modern Air Power Economic and Military*, 1988 reprint (New York: Dover Publications, 1925). Alexander P. de Seversky is the author of *Victory Through Air Power* (New York: Simon & Schuster, 1942). Walt Disney decided to make it into a film in which cartoon sequences were combined with de Seversky giving lectures on the importance of developing long-range bombers.

5. For insight on planning, see James C. Gaston, *Planning the American Air War: Four Men and Nine days in 1941* (Washington, DC: National Defense University Press, 1982); and Haywood Hansell Jr., *The Air Plan That Defeated Hitler*, 1st edn 1972 (New York: Higgins-McArthur/Longino & Porter, 1980).

6. Peter Faber, 'The Evolution of Airpower Doctrine in the United States: From World War I to John A. Warden's *The Air Campaign*', paper presented at the Netherlands Defence College, *Airpower Theory & Application Proceedings (1)*, Symposium 15–19 April 1996, p. 29; and Hansell, *The Air Plan That Defeated Hitler*, pp. 92–3 (appendix inserted between the two pages). The AWPD War Plan series consists of AWPD-1, -4 and -42: AWPD-1 was written in August 1941, AWPD-4 in December 1941 (in reaction to the Japanese attack on Pearl Harbour) and AWPD-42 in the autumn of 1942.

7. Hansell, *The Air Plan That Defeated Hitler*, pp. 78–88; and Robert A. Pape, *Bombing to Win: Air Power and Coercion in War* (Ithaca, NY: Cornell University Press, 1996), p. 259.

8. Tami Davis Biddle, 'British and American Approaches to Strategic Bombing: Their Origins and Implementation in the World War II Combined Bomber Offensive', in John Gooch (ed.), *Airpower: Theory and Practice* (London: Frank Cass, 1995), pp. 91–144.

9. While Richard Overy concluded that 'the air offensive was one of the decisive elements in Allied victory', Bernard Brodie, after acknowledging that 'air power

had a mighty vindication in World War II', concluded that air power 'came too late to have a clearly decisive effect [against Germany]'. Richard Overy, *Why the Allies Won* (London: W. W. Norton & Company, 1995), p. 133; and Bernard Brodie, *Strategy in the Missile Age* (New York: Princeton University Press, 1959), p. 107. See also John Kenneth Galbraith, *The Affluent Society* (London: Hamish Hamilton, 1958); Stephen Garrett, *Ethics and Airpower in World War Two* (New York: St. Martin's, 1993); Michael S. Sherry, *The Rise of American Air Power: The Creation of Armageddon* (New Haven, CT: Yale University Press, 1987); and Franklin D'Olier, *et al.*, *The United States Bombing Surveys (European War)*, 1st edn September 1945, *Summary Reports* reprinted (Maxwell Air Force Base, AL: Air University Press, 1987). For an interesting analysis of the *Bombing Surveys*, see Gian P. Gentile, *How Effective Is Strategic Bombing? Lessons Learned from World War II to Kosovo* (New York: New York University Press, 2001).

10. David R. Mets, *The Long Search for a Surgical Strike: Precision Munitions and the Revolution in Military Affairs*, CADRE Paper No. 12 (Maxwell AFB, AL: Air University Press, 2001), p. 3.

11. Carl H. Builder, *The Icarus Syndrome: The Role of Air Power Theory in the Evolution and Fate of the U.S. Air Force*, 4th edn (London: Transaction Publishers, 1998).

12. Dennis M. Drew and Donald M. Snow, *Rolling Thunder 1965: Anatomy or Failure* (Maxwell Air Force Base, AL: Air University Press, 1986), p. 29.

13. Pape, *Bombing to Win*, pp. 174–210, for a general and controversial analysis of Vietnam.

14. Mark Clodfelter, 'Air Power Versus Asymmetric Enemies: A Framework for Evaluating Effectiveness', paper presented at the Royal Norwegian Air Force Academy, 6 February 2002, p. 15.

15. Cited in Clodfelter, 'Air Power Versus Asymmetric Enemies', p. 15.

16. Robert F. Futell, *Concepts, Ideas, Doctrine: Basic Thinking in the USAF 1907–1960*, Vol. I (Maxwell Air Force Base, AL: Air University Press, 1989), p. 259.

17. Curtis E. LeMay with MacKinlay Kantor, *Mission with LeMay* (Garden City, NY: Doubleday Books, 1965), p. 565.

18. Lyndon B. Johnson, cited in John D. Morroco, 'From Vietnam to Desert Storm', *Air Force Magazine* 75, No. 1 (January 1992), p. 71.

19. Mark Clodfelter, 'Of Demons, Storms, and Thunder: A Preliminary Look at Vietnam's Impact on the Persian Gulf War Air Campaign', *Airpower Journal* 5, No. 4 (Winter 1991), pp. 17–32; and Hallion, *Storm over Iraq*, p. 19.

20. Drew, 'Air Theory, Air Force, and Low Intensity Conflict: A Short Journey to Confusion', in Meilinger, *The Paths of Heaven*, p. 334.

21. Hallion, *Storm over Iraq*, pp. 17–24.

22. Charles Osgood, *An Alternative to War and Surrender* (Champaign-Urbana, IL: University of Illinois Press, 1962); and Thomas C. Schelling, *Arms and Influence* (New Haven, CT: Yale University Press, 1966).

23. Schelling, *Arms and Influence*, pp. 92–125.

24. Mark Clodfelter, *The Limits of Air Power: The American Bombing of North Vietnam* (New York: Free Press, 1989), pp. 39–72.

25. Futell, *Concepts, Ideas, Doctrine*, p. 251. On air power in Korea, see also Armitage and Mason, *Air Power in the Nuclear Age, 1945–84*, pp. 20–45.

26. Cited in Mets, *The Long Search for a Surgical Strike*, p. 18.

27. Tony Mason, 'Rethinking the Conceptual Framework', in Peter W. Gray (ed.), *Air Power 21: Challenges for the New Century* (Norwich: The Stationery Office, 2000), p. 2. See also Major Martin L. Fracker, 'Psychological Effects of Aerial Bombardment', *Airpower Journal* 6, No. 3 (Fall 1992), pp. 57–8.

28. Willmott, 'From Rolling Thunder to the Tet Offensive', in J. L. Pimlott, *Vietnam: History and Tactics* (London: Orbis, 1982), pp. 40–63; Clodfelter, *The Limits of Air Power*; and Larry Cable, *Unholy Grail: The US and Wars in Vietnam, 1965–1968* (London: Routledge and Kegan Paul, 1991).

29. Clodfelter, 'Air Power Versus Asymmetric Enemies, p. 18.

30. Ibid.

31. Ronald H. Spector, *After Tet: The Bloodiest Year in Vietnam* (New York: Free Press, 1993), p. 314; and Clodfelter 'Molding Airpower Convictions: Development and Legacy of William Mitchell's Strategic Thought', in Meilinger, *The Paths of Heaven*, pp. 134–46.

32. Clodfelter, 'Of Demons, Storms, and Thunder', p. 19.

33. Schwarzkopf, in 'General Admits Vietnam Body Counts Were Lies', *Detroit News*, 11 March 1991, p. 6; and C. D. B. Bryan, 'Operation Desert Storm', *New Republic*, 11 March 1991.

34. Tom Mathews, 'The Secret History of the War', *Newsweek*, 18 March 1991, p. 30.

35. Clancy with Horner, *Every Man a Tiger*, pp. 96–8, 156.

36. Warden to Schwarzkopf, 'Iraqi Air Campaign Instant Thunder', briefing, 17 August 1990 (the author is grateful to Diane Putney for having made parts of the briefing available).

37. United States Air Force Manual 1–2, *United States Air Force Basic Doctrine* (1 December 1959), p. 4, cited in Clodfelter, 'Of Demons, Storms, and Thunder', p. 24.

38. Aron L. Friedberg, 'A History of the U.S. Strategic "Doctrine" – 1945 to 1980', p. 46.

39. Ibid., pp. 41–2.

40. The USAF provided the following mission objectives: 'Counter Air objectives are to gain control of the aerospace environment'; 'Air Interdiction objectives are to delay, disrupt, divert, or destroy an enemy's military potential before it can be brought to bear effectively against friendly forces'; and 'Close Air Support objectives are to support surface operations by attacking hostile targets in close proximity to friendly forces.' See USAF, *Air Force Manual 1-1: Basic Aerospace Doctrine of the United States Air Force* (Washington, DC: Government Printing Office, 1984), pp. 3–3, 3–4.

41. It does not mean that the inputs from Lieutenant Colonel Bernard Harvey, Lieutenant Colonel Ronnie Stanfill, Major Buck Rogers and others were not important, but these played a supportive rather than a leading role.

42. Warden, interview, *Desert Story Collection*, 30 May 1991, p. 2.

43. David Halberstam, *War in a Time of Peace: Bush, Clinton and the Generals* (London: Bloomsbury, 2002), pp. 48–9.

44. Captain John A. Warden, 'The Grand Alliance: Strategy and Decision' (Master of Arts thesis in political science at Texas Tech University, submitted in 1975), p. 5 (the author is grateful to Diane T. Putney for having made the thesis available).

45. Ibid., p. 150.

46. Warden, interview, *Desert Story Collection*, 22 October 1991, pp. 10–11; and 30 May 1991, pp. 39–40.

47. Ibid., 22 October 1991, p. 4.

48. The United States is divided into the following commands: US Pacific Command (Honolulu, Hawaii); US Southern Command (Miami, Florida); US Central Command (MacDill Air Force Base, Florida); US European Command (Stuttgart-Vaihingen, Germany); US Joint Forces Command (Norfolk, Virginia); US Space Command (Peterson Air Force Base, Colorado); US Special Operations Command

(MacDill Air Force Base, Florida); US Transportation Command (Scott Air Force Base, Illinois); US Strategic Command (Offutt Air Force Base, Nebraska); and US Northern Command (location to be determined).

49. Richard T. Reynolds, correspondence with author, 22 April 2002.
50. John A. Warden III, *The Air Campaign: Planning for Combat* (Washington, DC: NDU Press, 1988). See also David R. Mets, *The Air Campaign: John Warden and the Classical Airpower Theorists* (Maxwell Air Force Base, AL: Air University Press, 1998), pp. 55–71.
51. Warden, *The Air Campaign*, p. 130.
52. For two critiques on Warden's *The Air Campaign*, see Niklas Zetterling, 'John Warden, The Air Campaign – en kritisk gransking', *Kungl krigsveteskapsak-ademiens hanlinger och tidsskrift*, No. 1 (1998), pp. 107–30 (in Swedish); and Timothy G: Murphy, 'A Critique of the Air Campaign', *Airpower Journal* 8, No. 1, 1994.
53. Richard T. Reynolds, correspondence with author, transcript, 23 October 2001.
54. USAFE = United States Air Force Command Europe; and EUCOM = European Command.
55. Richard T. Reynolds, correspondence with author, transcript, 23 October 2001.
56. Major General (ret.) Perry Smith, interview, *Desert Story Collection*, 18 June 1992, pp. 5–7.
57. Richard T. Reynolds, correspondence with author, transcript, 23 October 2001.
58. Ibid., 17 April 2002.
59. Steve Wilson, interview, *Desert Story Collection*, 11 December 1991, p. 4.
60. Richard T. Reynolds, correspondence with author, transcript, 23 October 2001.
61. Robert D. Russ, interview, *Desert Story Collection*, 9 December 1991, p. 25.
62. Davis, 'On Target', p. 3.
63. Ibid., p. 4.
64. Lieutenant Colonel (ret.) Barry Watts, 'Doctrine, Technology and Air Warfare', in Hallion, *Air Power Confronts an Unstable World*, p. 20. Lieutenant General Michael Dugan was the Deputy Chief of Staff for plans and operations (XO) 1/3/88-30/4-89, and during the invasion of Kuwait the position belonged to Lieutenant General James V. Adams. Major General Charles Boyd was the Director of Air Force Plans (XOX) 22/5/88-14/8/89, and during the occupation of Kuwait the position belonged to Major General Robert M. Alexander. Major General Hawley was Director of Operations (XOO).
65. Acronyms and responsibility: the Air Force Doctrine Division (XOXWD), Colonel Coffman; the Strategy Division (XOXWS), Colonel Dunn; the Concepts Division (XOXWC) – the top secret part of XOXW, Lieutenant Colonel Stimer; the Long-range Planning Division (XOXWP), Lieutenant Colonel Roe; the Require-ments Division (XOXWR), Colonel Jeffreys; and the Force Assessment Division (XOXWF), Lieutenant Colonel Autry. Colonel Allan W. Howey, telephone inter-view with author, notes, 6 April 1999; and correspondence 18–19 April 2002.
66. Deptula, correspondence with author, transcript, 31 October 1998. For confirmation, see Davis, 'The Offensive Air Campaign Plan', p. 4.
67. Richard T. Reynolds, correspondence with author, 28 October 2001.
68. Deptula, correspondence with author, 11 March 1998.
69. Wayne Thompson, interview with author, tape-recording, Washington, DC, 1 March 1999; Richard G. Davis, interview with author, tape-recording, Washington, DC, 9 March 1998; and Deptula, interview with author, tape-record-ing, Washington, DC, 11 March 1998.
70. Mark B. Rogers, interview, *Desert Story Collection*, 3 June 1991.
71. Mets, *The Air Campaign*, p. 58; and Halberstam, *War in a Time of Peace*, p. 49.

72. The paper, 'Airpower: Concentration, Responsiveness and the Operational Art', was co-authored with General Dugan, published in *Military Review* 69, No. 7 (July 1989), pp. 12–21. Deptula, correspondence with author, transcript, 20 October 1998; and Watts, 'Doctrine, Technology and Air Warfare', p. 20.

73. Warden, 'Centers of Gravity: The Key to Success in War', unpublished paper.

74. Carl von Clausewitz, *On War*, trans. and ed. Michael Howard and Peter Paret (London: Everyman's Library, 1993), p. 595.

75. Warden, in Tom Clancy, *Fighter Wing: A Guided Tour of an Air Force Combat Wing* (New York: Berkley Books, 1995), p. 41.

76. Deptula, 'Parallel Warfare: What Is It? Where Did It Come From? Why Is it Important', in William Head and Earl H. Tilford Jr. (eds), *The Eagle in the Desert: Looking Back on U.S. Involvement in the Persian Gulf War* (Westport, CT: Praeger, 1996), pp. 127–56; Davis, *Decisive Force*, p. 12; and Deptula, interview with author, tape-recording, Washington, DC, 11 March 1998.

77. Hansell, *The Air Plan That Defeated Hitler*, p. 91, cited in Warden, 'The Grand Alliance', pp. 27–8.

78. Hallion, *Storm over Iraq*, p. 118.

79. Watts, correspondence with author, transcript, 28 October 1998.

80. Meilinger, 'Air Targeting Strategies', p. 59; and Robert D. Russ, interview, *Desert Story Collection*, 9 December 1991, p. 23.

81. Warden, interview, *Desert Story Collection*, 30 May 1991, p. 86.

82. John A. Warden, 'Success in Modern War: A Response to Robert Pape's *Bombing to Win*', *Security Studies* 7, No. 2 (Winter 1997/98).

83. Warden *The Air Campaign*, p. 132.

84. James R. Cody, *AWPD-42 to Instant Thunder: Consistent, Evolutionary Thought or Revolutionary Change?* (Maxwell Air Force Base, AL: Air University Press, 1996); and Allan W. Howey, telephone interview with author, notes, 6 April 1999.

85. Davis, 'The Offensive Air Campaign Plan', p. 5.

86. Summers, *On Strategy II*, pp. 139–52.

87. For a discourse on 'strategic paralysis', see David S. Fadok, 'John Boyd and John Warden: Airpower's Quest for Strategic Paralysis', in Meilinger, *The Paths of Heaven*, pp. 357–98.

88. Warden, interview, *Desert Story Collection*, 30 May 1991, p. 78; Deptula, interview with author, tape-recording, Washington, DC, 16 April 1999; and Donald B. Rice, interview, *Desert Story Collection*, 11 December 1991, p. 29.

89. Donald B. Rice, interview with author, tape-recording, Birmingham (England), 17 July 1999. General Dugan made the same observation at the time, see for example Phillip S. Meilinger, 'The Problem with Our Air Power Doctrine', *Airpower Journal* 6, No. 1 (Spring 1992), p. 24.

90. James V. Adams, interview, *Desert Story Collection*, 3 February 1992, p. 2; and Warden, interview, *Desert Story Collection*, 22 October 1991, p. 19.

91. Donald B. Rice, interview with author, 17 July 1999.

92. Secretary of the Air Force Donald B. Rice, *The Air Force and the U.S. National Security: 'Global Reach – Global Power: Reshaping for the Future'* (Washington, DC: Department of the USAF, 1990). The White Paper was first published in June 1990 and updated in September 1991. See also John M. Loh, 'Advocating Mission Needs in Tomorrow's World', *Airpower Journal* 6, No. 1 (Spring 1992), pp. 4–13.

93. USMC Battalion Commander Gary Anderson, cited in Builder, *The Icarus Syndrome*, p. 14.

94. Jeffrey Record, 'Into the Wild Blue Yonder: Should We Abolish the Air Force?', Heritage Foundation, *Policy Review*, No. 52 (Spring 1990), p. 50.

95. Secretary of the Air Force, *'Global Reach – Global Power'*, p. 2.
96. Barry Watts, correspondence with author, transcript, 28 October 1998.
97. Admiral Carlise A. H. Trost, 'Maritime Strategy of the 1990s', *US Naval Institute Proceedings* (May 1990).
98. Ronnie Stanfill, interview, *Desert Story Collection*, 3 June 1991, p. 11; and Warden, interview, *Desert Story Collection*, 30 May 1991, pp. 19–20.
99. Ronnie Stanfill, interview, *Desert Story Collection*, 3 June 1991, pp. 36, 62–3; Warden, interview, *Desert Story Collection*, 30 May 1991, pp. 109–10; and Gordon and Trainor, *The Generals' War*, p. 79.
100. Deptula, correspondence with author, transcript, 31 October 1998; and Lieutenant Colonel William Bruner, interview with author, tape-recording, Washington, DC, 18 February 1998.
101. Harry G. Summers Jr, *The New World Strategy: A Military Policy for America's Future* (New York: Simon and Schuster, 1995), pp. 125–6.
102. Margaret Tutwiler's statement on 24 July 1990, cited in the *New York Times*, 23 September 1990, p. 18; and verified in the *Washington Post*, October 21, 1992, p. A-17.
103. Powell with Persico, *My American Journey*, p. 447.
104. Schwarzkopf with Petre, *It Doesn't Take a Hero*, p. 341.
105. Ibid.; and Powell with Persico, *My American Journey*, p. 448.
106. Bush and Scowcroft, *A World Transformed*, p. 302. Haass, interview with BBC Frontline, p. 9.
107. United Nations Security Council Resolution 660 2 August 1990: 'condemns the Iraqi invasion of Kuwait; demands that Iraq withdraw immediately and uncon-ditionally all its forces to the positions in which they were located on 1 August 1990; calls upon Iraq and Kuwait to begin immediately intensive negotiations for the resolution of their difference and supports all efforts in this regard, and especially those of the League of Arab States'. See for example Lauterpacht, Greenwood, Weller and Bethlehem, *The Kuwait Crisis*, p. 88; and United States Department of Defense, *Conduct of the Persian Gulf War*, p. 320.
108. Bush and Scowcroft, *A World Transformed*, p. 314.
109. Hiro, *Desert Shield to Desert Storm*; and Powell with Persico, *My American Journey*, p. 449.
110. Bush and Scowcroft, *A World Transformed*, p. 316.
111. Ibid., p. 315.
112. Ibid., p. 323.
113. Ibid., p. 324.
114. Powell with Persico, *My American Journey*, p. 451.
115. Reynolds, *Heart of the Storm*, pp. 8–9.
116. Present at the morning meeting: President Bush, Vice President Quayle, White House Chief of Staff John Sununu, National Security Advisor Brent Scowcroft, Secretary of State James Baker, Secretary of Defense Richard Cheney, Under Secretary of Defense Paul Wolfowitz, Middle East Security Advisor Richard Haass, White House Press Secretary Marlin Fitzwater, General Colin Powell, General Norman Schwarzkopf, Lieutenant General Charles A. Horner, Chief of Staff Major General Robert Johnston, JCS J-3 Lieutenant General Thomas W. Kelly, CIA Director William Webster, and JCS J-2 Vice Admiral Michael McConnell.
117. Bush and Scowcroft, *A World Transformed*, p. 327.
118. Ibid., p. 328.
119. Hiro, *Desert Shield to Desert Storm*, p. 110.
120. Horner, correspondence with author, transcript, 17 November 1998. Horner

argues that Bush was the senior politician who resonated most with his briefing at Camp David.

121. Cohen, *et al.*, *Gulf War Air Power Survey: Planning*, p. 107.
122. Bush and Scowcroft, *A World Transformed*, p. 328.
123. Salinger with Laurent, *Secret Dossier*, p. 100.
124. United States Department of Defense, *Conduct of the Persian Gulf War*, p. 66; and Schwarzkopf with Petre, *It Doesn't Take a Hero*, p. 350.
125. The US delegation: Cheney, Wolfowitz, Gates, Schwarzkopf, Horner, Spokesman for the Department of Defense, Pete Williams, Ambassador Charles Freeman and representatives from the Department of State and the CIA.
126. Davis, 'The Offensive Air Campaign Plan', p. 2; and United States Department of Defense, *Conduct of the Persian Gulf War*, p. 65.
127. Bush and Scowcroft, *A World Transformed*, p. 384.
128. Ibid., p. 318.
129. George Bush, 'Remarks and the Exchange With Reporters on the Iraqi Invasion of Kuwait' (5 August 1991), in 'The George Bush Presidential Library'.
130. Bush and Scowcroft, *A World Transformed*, p. 333; and Powell with Persico, *My American Journey*, p. 453.
131. Cohen et al., *Gulf War Air Power Survey: Planning*, p. 108; Woodward, *The Commanders*, p. 273; Schwarzkopf with Petre, *It Doesn't Take a Hero*, p. 354; and Mark D. Mandeles, Thomas C. Hone and Terry S. Sanford, *Managing 'Command and Control' in the Persian Gulf War* (Westport, CT: Greenwood Publishing Group, 1996), p. 122.
132. Mandeles, Hone and Sanford, *Managing 'Command and Control' in the Persian Gulf War*, p. 10. Schwarzkopf was Commander-in-Chief (CINC) of the Central Command (CENTCOM), but since the organisation was based in Tampa, Florida, headquarters would have to be deployed to the theatre (in this case Riyadh). While Schwarzkopf was preparing his departure, Horner was responsible in Riyadh, and thus carried the title CENTCOM Forward (FWD). In this period Major General Thomas R. Olsen was the acting CENTAF. When Schwarzkopf returned to theatre on 24 August 1990, Horner took up his duties as CENTAF.
133. Gordon and Trainor, *The Generals' War*, p. 76.
134. Ronnie Stanfill, interview, *Desert Story Collection*, 3 June 1991, pp. 4, 6; and Warden, interview, *Desert Story Collection*, 22 October 1991, pp. 39, 61.
135. Warden, interview, *Desert Story Collection*, 22 October 1991, p. 10.
136. Robert M. Alexander, interview, *Desert Story Collection*, 30 May 1991, p. 1; and Warden, interview, *Desert Story Collection*, 22 October 1991, p. 40.
137. Warden, interview, *Desert Story Collection*, 22 October 1991, pp. 39, 42.
138. Deptula, interview, *Desert Story Collection*, 1 November 1990, p. 2; and Warden, interview, *Desert Story Collection*, 22 October 1991, p. 42.
139. Gordon and Trainor's *The Generals' War*, p. 76.
140. Schwarzkopf with Petre, *It Doesn't Take a Hero*, p. 371.
141. Ibid., p. 372; and Horner, correspondence with author, transcript, 11 September 1999.
142. Reynolds, *Heart of the Storm*, p. 23.
143. Schwarzkopf with Petre, *It Doesn't Take a Hero*, p. 369.
144. Schwarzkopf, notes from telephone interview with Diane T. Putney, *Desert Story Collection*, 5 May 1992.
145. John M. Loh, interview, *Desert Story Collection*, 26 September 1991, pp. 1–2.
146. Ibid., p. 8.
147. Reynolds, *Heart of the Storm*, p. 24.

148. James V. Adams, interview, *Desert Story Collection*, 3 February 1992, p. 2; and Warden, interview, *Desert Story Collection*, 22 October 1991, p. 49.
149. Davis, 'The Offensive Air Campaign Plan', p. 3.
150. John A. Warden III and Leland A. Russell, *Winning in FastTime: Harness the Competitive Advantage of Prometheus in Business and Life* (Montgomery, AL: Venturist Publishing, 2001), p. 72.
151. Warden, *The Air Campaign*, pp. 10, 40–5, 53–4 and 138–9.
152. Ronnie Stanfill, interview, *Desert Story Collection*, 3 June 1991, p. 33.
153. Deptula, *Desert Story Collection*, 1 November 1990, p. 1.
154. Warden to John M. Loh, 'Iraqi Air Campaign', 9 August 1990, cited in Cohen *et al.*, *Gulf War Air Power Survey: Planning*, p. 109.
155. Warden, interview, *Desert Story Collection*, p. 11. See Keaney and Cohen, *Gulf War Air Power Survey: Summary Report*, p. 68; Cohen *et al.*, *Gulf War Air Power Survey: Effects and Effectiveness*, pp. 240–7 and 284–5; and Cordesman and Wagner, *The Lessons of Modern War, Volume IV: The Gulf War*, pp. 499–500.
156. Warden, interview, *Desert Story Collection*, 22 October 1991, pp. 55–6.
157. Deptula, interview, *Desert Story Collection*, 1 November 1990, p. 2.
158. Putney, 'From Instant Thunder to Desert Storm', p. 41.
159. Warden, interview, *Desert Story Collection*, 22 October 1991, pp. 57–8.
160. Warden, interview with Karl P. Mueller, Maxwell AFB, August 1994, in Karl Mueller, 'Strategies of Coercion: Denial, Punishment, and the Future of Air Power', *Security Studies* 7, No. 3 (Spring 1998), p. 187.
161. Warden to Schwarzkopf, 'Iraqi Air Campaign Instant Thunder', cited in Cohen *et al.*, *Gulf War Air Power Survey: Planning*, p. 116.
162. Atkinson, *Crusade*, p. 59.
163. Warden, interview, *Desert Story Collection*, 22 October 1991, p. 57; Ronnie Stanfill, interview, *Desert Story Collection*, 3 June 1991, p. 29.
164. John M. Loh, interview, *Desert Story Collection*, 26 September 1991, pp. 16–19.
165. Warden, interview, *Desert Story Collection*, 22 October 1991, p. 51.
166. Warden to Schwarzkopf, 'Instant Thunder', briefing, 10 August 1990.
167. Ben Harvey, notes from interview, cited in Reynolds, *Heart of the Storm*, p. 50.
168. John M. Loh, interview, *Desert Story Collection*, 26 September 1991, pp. 9–11.
169. Robert M. Alexander, interview, *Desert Story Collection*, 6 May 1991, p. 11.
170. James V. Adams, interview, *Desert Story Collection*, 3 February 1992, pp. 12, 15; John M. Loh, interview, *Desert Story Collection*, 26 September 1991, pp. 16–17; and Warden, interview, *Desert Story Collection*, 30 May 1991, p. 110.
171. Richard D. Bristow, interview, *Desert Story Collection*, 9 November 1992, pp. 10–11.
172. Ibid., pp. 10–11.
173. Ibid., p. 3.
174. Mainly a group of four: Colonels Richard D. Bristow, Alex Bettinger, Richard Biglow and Doug Hawkins.
175. Robert M. Alexander, interview, *Desert Story Collection*, 3 June 1992, pp. 20–1.
176. James V. Adams, interview, *Desert Story Collection*, 3 February 1992, pp. 6–8 and 22; Robert D. Russ, interview, *Desert Story Collection*, 9 December 1991, pp. 19–20, 49; and Warden, interview, *Desert Story Collection*, 30 May 1991, p. 110.
177. Ronnie Stanfill, interview, *Desert Story Collection*, 3 June 1991, p. 70; and Robert M. Alexander, interview, *Desert Story Collection*, 30 May 1991, p. 8.
178. Donald B. Rice, interview, *Desert Story Collection*, 11 December 1991, p. 8.
179. Robert D. Russ, interview, *Desert Story Collection*, 9 December 1991, pp. 10–14; General Thomas Griffith and Colonel Alex Bettinger, interview, *Desert Story Collection*, 26 September 1991, p. 11. See also Williamson Murray with Wayne

W. Thompson, *Air War in the Persian Gulf*, 2nd edn (Baltimore, MA: The Nautical & Aviation Publishing Company of America, 1995), p. 20.

180. Richard D. Bistow, interview, *Desert Story Collection*, 9 November 1992, pp. 6, 10.
181. Thomas R. Griffith to Robert M. Alexander, 'CENTCOM Air Campaign Plan', 11 August 1990, briefing, cited in Cohen *et al.*, *Gulf War Air Power Survey: Operations*, p. 25; and James V. Adams, interview, *Desert Story Collection*, 3 February 1992, p. 8.
182. Thomas R. Griffith to Robert M. Alexander, 'CENTCOM Air Campaign Plan', 11 August 1990, briefing, cited in Cohen *et al.*, *Gulf War Air Power Survey: Operations*, p. 25.
183. Reynolds, *Heart of the Storm*, p. 39.
184. Robert M. Alexander, interview, *Desert Story Collection*, 30 May 1991, p. 5.
185. Robert D. Russ, interview, *Desert Story Collection*, 9 December 1991, pp. 20–1.
186. Richard D. Bistow, interview, *Desert Story Collection*, 9 November 1992, p. 5.
187. James V. Adams, interview, *Desert Story Collection*, 3 February 1992, p. 14; and Robert M. Alexander, interview, *Desert Story Collection*, 30 May 1991, p. 14.
188. Ronnie Stanfill, interview, *Desert Story Collection*, 3 June 1991, pp. 64–5.
189. Davis, 'The Offensive Air Campaign Plan', p. 12; Deptula, interview, *Desert Story Collection*, 1 November 1990, p. 3.
190. Robert M. Alexander, interview, *Desert Story Collection*, 30 May 1991, p. 13.
191. Warden to the Center for Air Force History, 'Strategic Air Campaign Instant Thunder', unclassified briefing, 6 February 1992 (the slide has been made available to the author). See also quote in Davis, *Decisive Force*, p. 11.
192. Cohen *et al.*, *Gulf War Air Power Survey: Operations*, p. 23.
193. Warden to the Center for Air Force History, 'Strategic Air Campaign Instant Thunder'. See also quote in Davis, *Decisive Force*, p. 11.
194. Cohen *et al.*, *Gulf War Air Power Survey: Operations*, p. 30.
195. Gordon and Trainor, *The Generals' War*, p. 88.
196. Ronnie Stanfill, interview, *Desert Story Collection*, 3 June 1991, p. 29.
197. Deptula, interview with author, transcript, 3 May 2002.
198. Ben Harvey, notes from briefing, cited in Robert M. Alexander, interview, *Desert Story Collection*, 30 May 1991, pp. 29–30. The essence is confirmed in Warden, interview with author, notes, 12 April 1999; and Putney, 'From Instant Thunder to Desert Storm', p. 42.
199. Robert M. Alexander, *Desert Story Collection*, 3 June 1992, p. 16.
200. Warden, interview with Clancy, cited in Clancy's *Fighter Wing*, p. 46; Warden, interview, *Desert Story Collection*, 22 October 1991, p. 65; Major General Michael J. Ryan, interview, *Desert Story Collection*, 4 September 1992, p. 15; Donald B. Rice, interview, *Desert Story Collection*, 11 December 1991, p. 6; and Robert M. Alexander, interview, *Desert Story Collection*, 30 May 1991, p. 19.
201. Colonel John A. Warden, 'Airpower in the Gulf', *Daedalus Flyer* 36, No. 1 (Spring 1996), p. 13.
202. Robert M. Alexander, interview, *Desert Story Collection*, 30 May 1991, p. 18.
203. Schwarzkopf with Petre, *It Doesn't Take a Hero*, p. 369.
204. Warden, interview, *Desert Story Collection*, 22 October 1991, p. 86.
205. Robert M. Alexander, interview, *Desert Story Collection*, 3 June 1992, p. 16.
206. Horner, interview with author, notes, London, 20 July 1999.
207. Warden, interview, *Desert Story Collection*, 22 October 1991, p. 96.
208. Powell, cited in Putney, 'From Instant Thunder to Desert Storm', p. 42; John M. Loh, interview, *Desert Story Collection*, 26 September 1991, p. 21; and Robert M. Alexander, interview, *Desert Story Collection*, 30 May 1991, p. 34.
209. Cited in Mann, *Thunder and Lightning*, p. 90.

210. Warden, cited in Rick Atkinson, *Crusade*, p. 60; and Robert M. Alexander, interview, *Desert Story Collection*, 30 May 1991, p. 36.
211. Powell, cited in Putney, 'From Instant Thunder to Desert Storm', p. 42; Robert M. Alexander, interview, *Desert Story Collection*, 30 May 1991, p. 37; and Atkinson, *Crusade*, p. 60.
212. Ben Harvey, telephone interview with author, notes, 7 April 1999.
213. Davis, 'On Target', p. 16.
214. Robert M. Alexander, interview, *Desert Story Collection*, 30 May 1991, p. 38.
215. Wayne Thompson, interview with author, tape-recording, Washington, DC, 1 March 1999.
216. This was later stated by Deputy Secretary of State, Lawrence Eagleburger, according to Amatzia Baram, interview with author, tape-recording, 19 February 1999, Washington, DC.
217. Davis, 'The Offensive Air Campaign Plan', p. 17.
218. James P. Coyne, *Airpower in the Gulf* (Arlington, VA: Air Force Association Book, 1992), p. 45.
219. Cohen *et al.*, *Gulf War Air Power Survey: Planning*, p. 114.
220. Richard D. Bristow, interview, *Desert Story Collection*, 9 November 1992, pp. 26–7.
221. Ibid., p. 72.
222. Davis, 'On Target', p. 19.
223. Davis, 'The Offensive Air Campaign Plan', p. 19.
224. Robert M. Alexander, interview, *Desert Story Collection*, 3 June 1992, pp. 46–7.
225. Davis, 'The Offensive Air Campaign Plan', p. 19.
226. Cohen *et al.*, *Gulf War Air Power Survey: Operations*, p. 22; and Reynolds, *Heart of the Storm*, p. 95; Davis, 'The Offensive Air Campaign Plan', p. 20; and Major General Buster C. Glosson, interview, *Desert Story Collection*, 4 June 1992, p. 32.
227. Deptula, interview, *Desert Story Collection*, 1 November 1990, p. 3; and Warden, interview, *Desert Story Collection*, 22 October 1991, pp. 88–9.
228. Warden to Schwarzkopf, 'Iraq Air Campaign Instant Thunder', briefing, 17 August 1990, p. 3. See Gordon and Trainor, *The Generals' War*, p. 75; and Atkinson, *Crusade*, p. 60.
229. Warden to General Norman Schwarzkopf, 'Iraq Air Campaign Instant Thunder', p. 5.
230. Ibid., p. 32.
231. Putney, 'From Instant Thunder to Desert Storm', p. 44.
232. Gordon and Trainor, *The Generals' War*, p. 89.
233. According to Schwarzkopf, 'On Thursday, August 16 [*sic*], Colonel John A. Warden and a team of Air Force officers showed up from Washington to brief me on their plan for Instant Thunder, our retaliatory air campaign' (note that the date should be 17 August). See Schwarzkopf with Petre, *It Doesn't Take a Hero*, p. 369.
234. Schwarzkopf, cited in Reynolds, *Heart of the Storm*, p. 110.
235. Schwarzkopf with Petre, *It Doesn't Take a Hero*, pp. 369–71.
236. Ibid., p. 371.
237. Ibid., p. 372.
238. Diane T. Putney, 'Planning the Air Campaign – The Washington Perspective', draft, p. 5.
239. Mandeles, Hone and Sanford, *Managing 'Command and Control' in the Persian Gulf War*, pp. 121–5.
240. James Crigger, interview, *Desert Story Collection*, 2–3 December 1991, pp. 1–15.
241. Keaney and Cohen, *Gulf War Air Power Survey: Summary Report*, p. 33. The ATO provides the flying units with specific orders for their missions, call signs,

frequencies, aircraft, target, target coordination, tanker and refuelling requirements, airspace control and coordination matters, and other specifications. The 'Punishment ATO' was also referred to as the 'ATO BRAVO'.

242. Steve Wilson, interview, *Desert Story Collection*, p. 15–20; and Gordon and Trainor, *The Generals' War*, p. 91.
243. Davis, 'The Offensive Air Campaign Plan', p. 30; and Putney, correspondence with author, transcript, 12 August 1999.
244. James V. Adams, interview, *Desert Story Collection*, 3 February 1992, p. 13.
245. Steve Wilson, interview, *Desert Story Collection*, 11 December 1991, p. 11.
246. Ibid., p. 17.
247. Ibid., p. 27.
248. Deptula, interview, *Desert Story Collection*, 22 May 1991, p. 9.
249. Ibid., pp. 10–12.
250. For quote, Richard T. Reynolds, correspondence with author, transcript, 2 June 2002: and second quote, Deptula, interview, *Desert Story Collection*, 22 May 1991, p. 37.
251. Ben Harvey, notes, cited in Reynolds, *Heart of the Storm*, p. 126.
252. Deptula, interview, *Desert Story Collection*, 22 May 1991, p. 26.
253. Horner, interview with Barry Jamison, Richard G. Davis and Barry Barlow, in *Desert Story Collection*, 4 March 1992, pp. 12–14.
254. Deptula, interview, *Desert Story Collection*, 22 May 1991, pp. 46–8.
255. Warden, interview with author, 4 June 2002; and Warden, interview, *Desert Story Collection*, 22 May October, p. 109.
256. Horner, interview with author, notes, Trondheim, 27 January 1997.
257. Deptula, interview, *Desert Story Collection*, 22 May 1991, p. 38.
258. Horner, cited in Putney, 'From Instant Thunder to Desert Storm', p. 44.
259. Ben Harvey, notes, 20 August 1990, cited in Cohen *et al.*, *The Gulf War Air Power Survey: Operations*, p. 27.
260. Horner, interview with author, notes, London, 20 July 1999.
261. Horner, interview, *Desert Story Collection*, 4 March 1992, p. 31.
262. Deptula, interview, *Desert Story Collection*, 22 May 1991, pp. 26–38.
263. Ibid., pp. 36–7.
264. Glosson, interview, *Desert Story Collection*, 29 May 1991, p. 37.
265. Jack Chain, interview, *Desert Story Collection*, 12 August 1991, p. 15; John M. Loh, interview, *Desert Story Collection*, 26 September 1991, p. 13; Robert M. Alexander, interview, *Desert Story Collection*, 30 May 1991, pp. 1–5; and Bistow, interview, *Desert Story Collection*, pp. 1–10.
266. Horner, interview, *Desert Story Collection*, 4 March 1992, p. 12.
267. Jack Chain, interview, *Desert Story Collection*, 12 August 1991, p. 2.
268. James V. Adams, interview, *Desert Story Collection*, 3 February 1991, pp. 1 and 29; Robert M. Alexander, interview, *Desert Story Collection*, 3 June 1992, pp. 1–3; and John M. Loh, interview, *Desert Story Collection*, 26 September 1991, pp. 1–6.
269. Robert M. Alexander, interview, *Desert Story Collection*, 3 June 1992, p. 10.
270. Horner, interview *Desert Story Collection*, 2 December 1991, p. 34–5.
271. Schwarzkopf's recollection in November 1992 was that he called General John M. Loh and 'requested him to put something together that would show him what air could do'. Buster C. Glosson, interview, *Desert Story Collection*, 31 May 1991, p. 105.
272. Warden, telephone interview with author, notes, 12 April 1999; Ben Harvey, telephone interview with author, notes, 7 April 1999; and John M. Loh, interview, *Desert Story Collection*, 26 September 1991, pp. 1–5.
273. Horner, interview, *Desert Story Collection*, 2 December 1991, pp. 34–5; and Buster C. Glosson, interview, *Desert Story Collection*, 29 May 1991, p. 11.

274. Buster C. Glosson, interview, *Desert Story Collection*, 4 June 1992, p. 62.
275. Horner, interview with author, notes, London, 20 July 1999; and interview, *Desert Story Collection*, 2 December 1991, p. 38.
276. Horner, interview with author, notes, London, 20 July 1999; and interview, *Desert Story Collection*, 4 March 1992, p. 31.
277. According to Horner, 'When you have the people in Washington who think they are running the war, and the people over the battlefield who are fighting the war, and they are not on the same emotional and psychological level, and you don't have trust, you've got *nothing*.' Horner cited in Clancy, *Fighter Wing*, p. 37.
278. Deptula, interview with author, tape-recording, Incirlik (Turkey), 15 August 1999.
279. Michael J. Ryan, interview, *Desert Story Collection*, 4 September 1992, *Desert Story Collection*, p. 27.

3

The Evolution of the Strategic Air Campaign Plan

By examining how the concept that was articulated in Instant Thunder evolved into Phase I of Operation Desert Storm, this chapter suggests that the strategic air campaign, as planned and executed, relied on a very thin thread, where individuals were far more important in determining the result of the campaign than line diagrams related to the prescribed organisational structures. It furthermore emphasises how a few key individuals managed to maintain a strategic focus, as envisioned in the Instant Thunder concept, throughout the planning in an environment dominated by operational and tactical concepts of warfare. The chapter determines to what degree the initial concept with its radical revision of air power theory was kept, and as the perceptions of the participants are taken into account the military–political interplay will be identified. It is therefore also an attempt to disclose how political, inter-service and operational concerns played important parts in forming the overall campaign plan.

FROM INSTANT THUNDER TO DESERT STORM

Horner's decision on 20 August 1990 to leave Warden out of the war-planning was a great disappointment to Warden personally and to the rest of Checkmate.[1] Warden realised that Horner saw another 'armchair colonel' from Washington, using academic terms such as 'strategic' and 'centre of gravity', but he also felt that he had not been given a fair hearing.[2] The planners' confidence was shaken, it was perceived as a reversal and a tactical defeat, but although discouraged they did not feel beaten. Warden recognised that he had not been able to communicate with Horner, but he came to the conclusion that there was still a good chance that Instant Thunder as a concept could survive.[3] After all, Horner had not only chosen to keep his three subordinates: Lieutenant Colonels David Deptula, Ronnie Stanfill and Bernard Harvey, but he had decided also to establish an organisation that would develop an offensive air plan that should be ready for execution by early September.[4] When Warden returned to Washington he decided to keep Checkmate at work as a supportive agency for the newly established Special Planning Group in Riyadh. Although Warden had to retreat from the centre stage of the air campaign planning, he was determined to see his mission through. His controversial contribution to the air campaign was far from over.

Brigadier General Buster C. Glosson was an electrical engineer by education with a personal interest in military history. He had recently held the position of Deputy Assistant Secretary of Defense for Legislative Affairs. He was well connected in Congress, and he was on first name terms with Secretary of Defense Richard Cheney and General Colin Powell.[5] Just prior to the invasion of Kuwait he had been commanding Exercise Ivory Justice and fostering good relations with the Persian Gulf states.[6] Shortly after Iraq invaded Kuwait, Glosson called Horner, whom he had known for years, and asked if there was anything he could do for him in Riyadh, as he was desperate to get 'off this ship' and into action.[7] They discussed the importance of putting together an air plan on 16 August, and Glosson insisted that he would be 'ready to come to Riyadh at a moment's notice'.[8] Glosson did not find himself in the command structure that was to be involved with the crisis management, but he was determined to make his presence felt. On 22 August, 48 hours after Horner received the Instant Thunder briefing, he appointed Glosson as Director of a highly secret ad hoc CENTAF Special Planning Group, giving him five days to come up with an ATO ready for implementation.[9]

The first thing Glosson did as Director of the offensive planning was to ask the JCS, the CENTCOM and the CENTAF planners if there was any offensive option available. He was told that nothing existed beyond the defence of Saudi Arabia, with the exception of Instant Thunder.[10] Horner had instructed him to provide an offensive option, something Horner perceived as a retaliation option at the time, ready for execution within days if necessary.[11] Beyond that it was up to him whether he wanted to build on the Checkmate effort or 'start with a blank sheet of paper'.[12] Deptula briefed Glosson on Instant Thunder when he arrived in theatre, and although Glosson argued that it was 'a bit naive', 'too optimistic' and 'too narrow a focus', he felt it was a good starting point as a 'conceptual plan of a strategic air campaign against Iraq'.[13] Glosson argued that the concept did not focus adequately on attacking the Iraqi chemical capability, and he noted that they needed an 'air campaign for fifteen rounds not three; six days is dumb'.[14] Glosson was furthermore critical about only attacking at night, but he agreed with the Checkmate group that air power could win this war short of ground operations,[15] or at least those operations would be nothing more than a 'police action', but he also knew that this argument was unacceptable to army officers who believed in the classic counterforce battle.[16] However, air campaign planning is not only about the theory and practice of air power, but how people get along with each other. After a few days in theatre it became clear that Glosson had a different focus from Harvey and Stanfill, who both returned to Washington by the end of the month. Glosson 'hit it off' immediately with the amiable personality of Deptula and turned him into his key planner.

Although Glosson was well aware of the theories of Douhet and Mitchell, and was a strong believer in air power capabilities, he had not spent much time on air power doctrine. In late August 1990 he was not particularly comfortable with the term 'strategic', although he believed in going after the enemy's high-value target-sets.[17] In Glosson's mind such long-distance targeting was 'interdiction', while 'strategic' meant 'nuclear', and consequently there was no such thing as a 'conventional strategic air campaign'.[18] Nevertheless, by late August, Deptula had convinced Glosson that 'conventional strategic air power' was the right term. The distinction between 'interdiction' and 'strategic' operations is important: although there might be considerable overlap in the minds of some, interdiction focuses on contributing to victory on the battlefield, while strategic focuses on pressuring the political leadership directly. The significance of Glosson fully accepting the concept articulated in Instant Thunder was that from the day he entered the planning scene the air planners could not have asked for a better proponent of the strategic air campaign plan. In the words of Deptula, from late August the air planners had 'a 500-pound locomotive going in the right direction'.[19]

By the end of the month Glosson had succeeded in getting some 20 officers to the Special Planning Group, and as the planning continued Deptula would do the actual planning, ensuring a strategic orientation, while Glosson would present this strategic air campaign proposal to wing-commanders, Horner, Schwarzkopf, Powell, Cheney and ultimately President Bush. Glosson's forte was his ability to carry out the concept and convince Horner and Schwarzkopf of air power's validity in meeting the President's objectives. Glosson was given the authorisation to get the people he needed to do the job, a clear sign of commitment on Horner's behalf, and as Glosson took action people and information seemed to go into the top-secret Special Planning Group, but never come out again. Thus, early on, the Special Planning Group was simply referred to as the Black Hole.[20] There were both operational and political considerations for keeping the planning secret at the time, but importantly, as there was no political mandate to liberate Kuwait with force, it was simply not considered wise to disclose that the United

States was planning an extensive bombing campaign against the heart of an Arab state.[21]

Glosson and Warden had briefly met in the mid 1980s when they were both assigned to Germany, but the relationship was not easy.[22] Glosson knew about Warden's Bitburg assignment, and believed he had a tendency to promise too much,[23] while Warden was concerned that Glosson did not appreciate the potential of conventional strategic air power.[24] Still, they were both men of great energy and more than ready to circumvent bureaucratic obstacles for the cause in which they believed. Deptula was aware of Glosson's and Horner's antipathy to Warden, but, on the other hand, Checkmate had intelligence and information necessary for completing the plan that was not available in theatre. Thus, Deptula chose to keep his continued contact with Warden a secret,[25] but by late August he had gradually convinced Glosson of the necessity of Checkmate as a supporting agency. By early September Glosson and Warden had overcome pervious tensions and the two would frequently talk on the telephone, discussing how to develop a sustainable air campaign.[26] The trio was, however, careful not to reveal their contacts to Horner, and whenever faxes were sent between the two agencies the products had as little identification of address as possible.[27] Warden and Deptula agreed that it was necessary to make the Black Hole staff get the feeling that it was their plan, because only then would the planners and commanders be fully dedicated to it.[28] Deptula termed this the CENTAFisation of the plan. Indeed, Lieutenant General Adams, who was oftentimes less than happy with Warden's efforts, told Glosson that he could treat Checkmate as part of his team, asking them to do whatever he needed. Although there was no official commitment 'to go offensive' in late August, the planners were directed by Horner to work as if an air campaign would have to be executed on 48 hours notice within the next few days.[29] Deptula saw this as a once in a lifetime opportunity to demonstrate the utility of Global Reach Global Power, and Glosson for his part called a former colleague in the White House who confirmed that the President was thinking of execution sooner rather than later.[30] Warden was of course 100 per cent dedicated, and in essence the three main planners were extremely well motivated and committed to the task.

On 25 August, Schwarzkopf flew from his headquarters at MacDill AFB, Florida, to Washington, DC, and presented the Secretary of Defense and the Chairman of the JCS with a four-phased offensive plan based on the following intent:

> We will offset the imbalance of ground combat power by using our strength against his weakness. Initially execute deception operations to focus his attention on defense and cause incorrect organization of forces.

We will initially attack into the Iraqi homeland using air power to decapitate his leadership, command and control, and eliminate his ability to reinforce Iraqi forces in Kuwait and southern Iraq. We will then gain undisputed air superiority over Kuwait so that we can subsequently and selectively attack Iraqi ground forces with air power in order to reduce his combat power and destroy reinforcing units. Finally, we will fix Iraqi forces in place by feints and limited objective attacks followed by armoured force penetration and exploitation to seize key lines of communication nodes, which will put us in a position to interdict resupply and remaining reinforcement from Iraq and eliminate forces in Kuwait.[31]

Phase I was the strategic air campaign, which was based on Instant Thunder and sought to paralyse the Iraqi leadership. The intensity and mass bombing suggested by Warden was upheld, but after four to six days it would continue at a 'reduced level until conflict termination'.[32] Phase II was to ensure air superiority over the Kuwaiti Theatre of Operations (KTO), and Phase III was ground combat attrition to 'reduce Iraqi ground force capability, soften ground forces to assure successful penetration and exploitation, reduce ability to lay down chemicals, and destroy Republican Guard capability to reinforce into Kuwait'.[33] Phase IV was the ground attack to eject Iraqi forces from Kuwait. Schwarzkopf argued that air power would accomplish the first three, while ground and air power together would complete the last phase. Although Cheney directed Schwarzkopf to include the Republican Guard in Phase I, these four phases were to remain as a framework for the planners throughout the crisis:

Phase I: Strategic Air Campaign Against Iraq;
Phase II: Air Campaign Against Iraqi Air Forces in Kuwait;
Phase III: Ground Combat Power Attrition to Neutralize the Republican Guard and Isolate the Kuwait Battlefield;
Phase IV: Ground Attack to Eject Iraqi Forces from Kuwait.[34]

Schwarzkopf returned to the Saudi Arabian theatre of operations on 26 August. Horner consequently went back to his job as JFACC and the commander of CENTAF. He reacted strongly to the sequence of the four phases, and in particular Phase II did not make much sense to Horner. In his mind, creating air superiority was the essential first step, and separating Phases I and II was unhealthy and confusing. Horner viewed it as shifting levels of effort rather than a sequence. Still, it would not make much practical difference, as they believed air superiority over the Kuwaiti theatre would implicitly be achieved through Phase I.[35] Horner's reasoning was that in order to get the complex ideas on air power through, he had to present the plan in such a fashion that

Schwarzkopf understood it. Since Schwarzkopf had defined his strategy in four phases Horner reasoned that it was imperative to stay with that design.[36] Although Glosson tried to merge the first two phases on some of the briefings the air planners agreed that if it made Schwarzkopf happy they had no objections, and thus Phase II was accepted. Although it made little difference in the end, as the air phases were executed simultaneously, it represented Schwarzkopf's intuitive vision of using air power in support of ground forces. He gave himself the role of joint force land component commander (JFLACC) and always perceived it as necessary to use ground forces to liberate Kuwait.[37] The mere fact that two-thirds of the sorties flown in the air war were against Phase III targets is a reflection of Schwarzkopf's belief that the war would culminate with a ground offensive. This partly explains why he insisted on Phase II: in order for Apaches and B-52s to operate freely in suppressing Iraqi forces in Kuwait, distinct air superiority was required. This would further enable close air support and added fire-power from the air to complement light ground forces. In such a context Phase I was a prelude to Schwarzkopf: he would not rely on it being successful, but if it was successful that would be a nice bonus. In contrast to many Army, Navy and Marine Corps commanders, who developed tense relationships with the CINC, Horner and Glosson developed cordial relations and gained unique personal access to Schwarzkopf.

As it happened, Schwarzkopf trusted Horner fully, and did not involve himself with the details of the Master Attack Plan (MAP) or the ATO. While Schwarzkopf should be acknowledged for a good intuitive understanding of air power's potential, it is indicative of Horner's pragmatic approach not to challenge what apparently contradicted the fundamental dictum of air power, namely to ensure air superiority prior to other engagements.

Glosson and Deptula continued to improve Phase I, and the original CENTAF staff continued to develop plans for defending Saudi Arabia (D-Day Plan). While the military and political leadership was thinking of offensive retaliation against Iraq as early as late August, the official objective remained the defence of Saudi Arabia, and General Horner's priority was consequently the D-Day Plan. The following month would witness, however, four key briefings that set the stage for the future of Phase I.

It took Deptula and Glosson, with considerable support from Checkmate, only four days to prepare a reworked plan in which the number of strategic targets had increased from 84 to 127. On 26 August Glosson briefed Horner on Instant Thunder: Concept of Operation and Execution. According to Glosson he was almost thrown out of the office after a briefing he characterised as 'ill-prepared, poorly presented, and violently received'.[38] Horner did not like the way it was presented: to him it should be a retaliation option, or a first step in a larger effort, and not a grand move for air power to fix the problem on its own.[39] The briefing basically reminded him too much of 'that crazy colonel', and consequently he ordered Glosson to drop the title 'Instant Thunder' and stop using the terms 'strategic' and 'centre of gravity' all the time.[40] According to Glosson, who again had been persuaded by Deptula, 'strategic' was the best term whether Horner liked it or not. After a while pragmatism got the better of Horner: 'All right. Just don't use it very often.' At the time the planners had not actually been given the official name of Special Planning Group so they simply pinned the sign 'Det 1, Instant Thunder' on the door, but the sign did not survive Horner's first sight of it.[41] The term 'Instant Thunder' just gave him all the wrong associations. After having been thrown out of Horner's office Glosson and Deptula worked on improving the layout concept for execution within the next 24 hours.

Horner informed Glosson that this would be part of a four-phase campaign plan, something the air planners did not know at the time, and in Horner's mind the briefing had to be presented on maps with a 'story-flow', because that was the way army officers could relate to it.[42] Although Horner realised the importance of an offensive campaign, he was not comfortable with the concept of bombing for strategic effects. At the time he suggested that a target list should be identified in order to prioritise the targets and take them out one by one.[43] After further iterations on the form and content Horner agreed to present the new air campaign plan to Schwarzkopf.

When Warden returned to the Pentagon he kept pushing for more target information, and Checkmate managed to serve as a nucleus for intelligence gathering.[44] Since Instant Thunder had been planned outside the intelligence community that was established in Riyadh, the intelligence officers were really never integrated with the planners, and this unfortunate state of affairs led to planners in the Black Hole continuing to approach Checkmate in Washington for information.[45] As USAF historian Richard G. Davis has observed:

> Security compartmentalization kept intelligence personnel in their own stove-piped career patterns, separate from the service as a whole. If the Warden group had immersed itself in intelligence, it would have become enmeshed in security restrictions, which would have defeated its *raison d'être*: the promulgation of new thought and ideas ... Neither party could speak the other's language fluently, and during the crisis in the Gulf, they would lose much time in asking the wrong questions or in preparing the wrong answers.[46]

Whether it was the intelligence community or Checkmate that asked the wrong questions could be debated, but the latter had professional intelligence officers assigned to it, and Checkmate seems to have been the only place in Washington where intelligence agencies could meet with the operations people to discuss issues in the context of a plan. Much flowed as mentioned from Rich Stimer and his Concept Division, but importantly, Checkmate established a very close relationship with the Navy's Strike Projection Evaluation Anti-Air Warfare Research (SPEAR). Ben Harvey also played a huge role in pulling intelligence people together in an attempt to teach the intelligence community how to do strategic level bomb damage assessment. In the process, indivi- duals from the National Intelligence Council (NIC), the Central Intelligence Agency (CIA) and the Defence Intelligence Agency (DIA) were of immense importance.[47] On 31 August Warden gave the first comprehensive briefing of the Instant Thunder concept to the NIC, of which Charlie Allen was the National Intelligence Officer for Warning. They were enthusiastic about the plan and agreed that the offensive use of air power would seriously challenge the Iraqi regime, and if Saddam Hussein managed to stay in power they would at least have prevented Iraq from having offensive capabilities. The intelligence officials suggested that one could not guarantee getting the Iraqi leader, but concluded that it was worthwhile trying, and that by isolating the regime electronically and physically from the rest of its society, the regime could be prevented from running the war effectively. The successful contacts formed at this point were not part of a mandate, but an informal networking through personal channels that probably never would have found acceptance through the chain of command.

Warden made sure that part of the Checkmate team was committed to feeding plans and information to Deptula. Sometimes the Black Hole received different information from that which was available to the intelligence officers in the theatre, other times they received the same intelligence but one or two days earlier. Although the information was of immense importance to the Black Hole in the crucial early days, the price was tension between the Black Hole and the intelligence community in Riyadh.[48]

These practical, conceptual and bureaucratic problems with the air plan were a direct result of it having been developed in isolation in the basement of the Pentagon. In addition, the intelligence agencies found that they were working with air planners who viewed the conduct of war rather differently from what was described in the existing doctrine.

The networking of intelligence that Warden managed to orchestrate seems to have been extraordinarily effective during both the planning and the war itself. In talking to Arab experts and other contacts, Checkmate's knowledge of Iraq improved rapidly, and they would constantly make sure that Glosson and Deptula were updated in the Black Hole. Glosson, for his part, further explored his contacts in the Arab world, and when he asked a member of the Saudi Arabian royal family whether he thought it would be prudent to bomb Saddam Hussein's working and living quarters, the reply was 'Yes, you should hit the palaces right in the middle of the lake, because the Iraqis will understand that he's not invincible and that he has to suffer with every-body else. That's loss of face to him.'[49] On the other hand, Glosson was told to avoid encouraging Shia independence, because the Saudis had such a large Shia population in their eastern province.[50]

The September briefings

On 2 September, Horner embraced CENTAF operational order (OPORD) Offensive Campaign – Phase I, which Glosson and Deptula had prepared.[51] According to the operational order the planners sought attacks against 12 inter-related target-sets to 'result in disruption of Iraqi command and control, loss of confidence in the government, and significant degradation of Iraqi military capabilities'.[52] Command of the skies was to be gained by targeting the strategic air defence system and airfields, while the fourth political objective, promoting the security and stability of the Persian Gulf, was to be achieved by eliminating Iraqi nuclear, biological, chemical and missile prospects. The campaign focused on the leadership and its command and communication systems, with the intent of isolating the regime from its people and armed forces.[53] The plan reflected the President's wish from the Camp David meeting, on 4 August, that casualties on both sides should be as low as possible, and that the Coalition did not object to the Iraqi people, only the leadership. On the one hand, the objective was to 'cripple production' and 'complicate movement of goods and services',[54] but on the other, there was an 'intent to convince the Iraqi populace that a bright economic and political future will result from the replacement of the Saddam Hussein regime'.[55] Moreover, 'anything which could be considered as terror attacks or attacks on the Iraqi people will be avoided'.[56] 'When taken in total, the result of Phase I will be the progressive and systematic collapse of Saddam Hussein's entire war machine and regime.'[57] Glosson's overview chart, prepared by Deptula, reflected the Instant Thunder concept of focusing on the Iraqi leadership.

Although the target-list had increased from 84 to 195, the Republican Guard, by no means an insignificant target, was the only addition and the concept was clearly founded on the Five Rings Model. Although the bombing strategy was perceived by its architects to have a high degree of psychological coercion by nature, Instant Thunder had further

Figure 2: Strategy for Phase 1

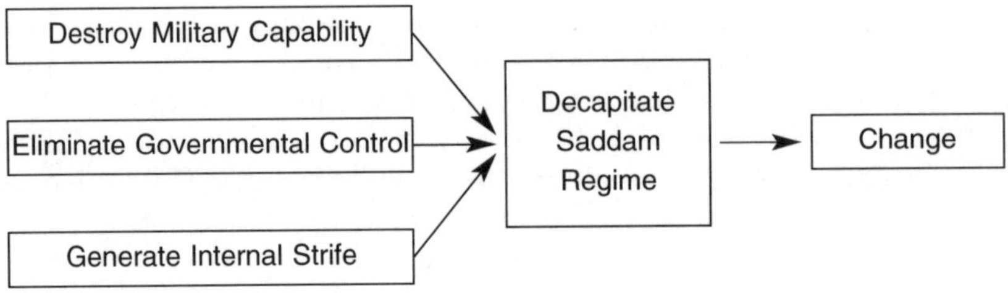

Source: Cohen *et al.*, *Gulf War Air Power Survey: Effects and Effectiveness*, p. 276, Gordon and Trainor, *The General's War*, p. 99.

stressed separate psychological operations as a critical element of the campaign. Warden and Deptula especially emphasised taking advantage of the media to separate the leadership from its people and the military,[58] and this idea remained at the centre of the 2 September proposal: 'Psychological operations are inherent to this operation and will be as important as strike operations. Every mission will have critical political and psychological overtones; every bomb will have a psychological impact as well.'[59] Schwarzkopf received the briefing the next day, and Glosson could not have hoped for a better reception: 'That's the most impressive planning effort that I have ever received in my military career.'[60] According to Glosson 'He stood up and put his arms around me, and tears swelled up in his eyes.'[61] Schwarzkopf called Powell shortly after and stated that 'If you want to execute an air attack by itself, we're ready.'[62] Schwarzkopf recognised that 'It gave us a broad range of attack options and could be conducted as a stand-alone operation or as part of a larger war.'[63] While in Riyadh on 11 September, General Michael Dugan and Lieutenant General James Adams also received the briefing.

As the rationale for a strategic air campaign as part of an overall military campaign was taking form, Cheney and Powell appeared before Congress. The potential of air power was one of the debated themes, and Senator William S. Cohen among others urged

> a measure of caution to those who are looking for quick, surgical strikes against the Iraqis. This notion that somehow we are going to go in and just simply wipe out the Iraqis within a matter of a couple of days with air power I think is sadly mistaken.[64]

Senator John McCain pointed out that although surgical strikes would probably not work, air assets could 'be used primarily to gain the objectives' rather than start with a ground war.[65] Cohen's and McCain's views reflected the traditional air power debate as to whether air power alone could be decisive.[66] The Black Hole and Checkmate planners were now realising that Powell was not as positive to what air power could do to the Iraqi leadership as expressed during the 11 August Instant Thunder briefing.[67] When the Chairman discussed air power matters with Glosson he was reflecting profound concerns:

> Buster, don't let this bullet-head air thinking get you headed down the wrong path. This is eventually going to have some sort of land component in it or else it's not gonna happen. Airplanes don't occupy land and don't drive people out of cities ... When you put this air campaign together, you make sure you don't let the work of these guys have done back here in the [Pentagon] influence the way you go. You make sure this is a theatre effort – use everyone's strength, and I'm sure it will come out right.[68]

The comments were revealing larger concerns on Powell's part. Consequently, when Glosson briefed Powell on 13 September he emphasised Phase I, briefly outlined Phases II and III, and although he believed this was sufficient to win the war, he ended the briefing by arguing that there was also a Phase IV, 'if you decide to launch a ground campaign'.[69] After the briefing Powell seemed more at ease: 'Buster, that's exactly what I expected ... I'm happy to tell you that I'm going to go tell the President that he has some options, and up until now he's had none.'[70] Powell's comments clearly suggested that he was impressed with Phase I, the strategic air campaign, but both he and Schwarzkopf still thought of it in terms of retaliation, and they genuinely believed that if it came to war, then ground forces would be needed to ensure victory. The briefing was, nevertheless, a milestone in the offensive planning: General Powell and General Schwarzkopf not only approved the plan as ready for execution, they made the important decision that the offensive air campaign plan would be their primary response if Iraq took further offensive action.[71] On 15 September Powell informed President Bush that they were ready 'to execute and sustain an offensive strategic air campaign against Iraq, should he order one'.[72]

In the meantime, General Dugan revealed to the press that 'If push comes to shove, the cutting edge would be in downtown Baghdad ... We're looking for the centers of gravity where airpower could make a difference early on ... He [Saddam Hussein] ought to be at the focus of our effort.'[73] The *Washington Post* headline on 16 September read 'Dugan Says Air Force Can Do It Alone'.[74] Dugan had recently talked to an Israeli general who told him that he was concerned that the United States did not know how to deal with Saddam Hussein. The Israeli officer argued that he thought they would go after military targets and nuclear facilities, while the things the Iraqi leader really cared about were his tight circle of friends, advisors, 'mistresses, wives and children'.[75] Warden sensed trouble from the moment he read the story, and called Dugan immediately to inform him that they were preparing a paper for his defence in case it was needed.[76] It seems as if Warden was the only one who grasped the importance of the disclosure at the time. He consulted Brigadier General Hallie E. Robertson, the head of the Public Affairs Group, and others in senior positions in the USAF, but he was basically told that there was nothing to worry about.[77] Dugan for his part found that his candid remarks were right on target, but the next day Secretary Cheney asked for his resignation.[78] The immediate effect was that the Air Staff kept a lower profile for some time, but Checkmate support to the Black Hole did not lose momentum despite losing its 'top cover', because General Loh held the position as Chief of Staff until General Merrill A. McPeak was confirmed by the Senate on 30 October 1990.

In the latter half of August and the early part of September, the offensive plan had undergone two substantial changes: the Republican Guard had been added as a target-set and a 'centre of gravity', and the initial stand-alone strategic air campaign was now part of an overall CENTCOM plan. In addition to this, Horner, who at first did not appear interested in employing air power beyond battlefield support for the army,[79] had become a strong advocate for the offensive use of air power against Baghdad. Horner avoided the term 'strategic', preferring 'deep-interdiction' and 'high-value' targets, but by September he supported the idea of going after leadership targets in Baghdad, as long as that was part of an overall strategy. Although the planning that took place in the Black Hole remained highly secret, the hearings in Congress, the Dugan debacle and articles in journals produced a high degree of public debate on the potential of conventional strategic air power.[80] Looking back to early August when the notion of conventional strategic air power was almost unknown, Warden and Deptula had come a long way in promoting their ideas to the military and political leadership.

The significance of Powell's and Schwarzkopf's acceptance of the direction of the air campaign planning was that air power applied independently from ground operations would be given a chance prior to ground engagement, as opposed to a conventional scenario where the first line of defence would be suppressed with successive attacks on deeper lines, and only after such a success would a switch to interdiction or strategic bombing be made. Not everybody in the theatre of operations agreed, however. Major General Royal N. Moore, the Marine Corps air wing commander, was not ready to abandon the AirLand Battle theory: 'We have a theory along with the Air Force and others, that we could roll back those guys, and I think we could do it very, very effectively. I'm not going to predict a cakewalk, but if we do it right, the casualties will be light, we hope.'[81] Moore further stated that

'The first bomb that falls in Iraq ought to be only after the first Marine crosses the border with his bayonet fixed.'[82] Despite these internal differences on strategy, the air campaign was approved by Schwarzkopf and Powell and declared ready for execution should the President give the order. By mid September it had further become clear that the Iraqis would not invade Saudi Arabia, and consequently the objectives of Operation Desert Shield were within reach. As the defensive mission of Desert Shield was about to be accomplished, the Bush administration increasingly focused on the liberation of Kuwait. On 6 October, Powell ordered Schwarzkopf to send somebody to Washington to brief the White House on an offensive strategy, in case they had 'to drive the Iraqis out of Kuwait'. Schwarzkopf replied that he had no such plan 'because I haven't got the ground forces'.[83] Powell's response was indicative of both commanders' view of the necessity to use ground forces to liberate Kuwait: 'Well, your air offensive plan is so good that I want these people to hear it, but you can't just brief the air plan. You have to brief the ground plan too.'[84]

The October Briefings

Schwarzkopf decided to send CENTCOM Chief of Staff Major General Robert Johnson from the Marine Corps and Lieutenant Colonel Joseph Purvis from the Army together with Glosson to brief the decision-makers in Washington. While Johnson and Purvis were to present the ground strategy, Glosson was to present the first three phases. Glosson was convinced that they could achieve the President's objectives without a ground campaign, but he also knew that in order to get acceptance for air power he needed to argue that the logical path led from an air campaign to a ground campaign.[85] On 10 October 1990 they briefed Secretary Cheney, his assistant Paul Wolfowitz and the Chiefs of Staff in the Pentagon. In 90 minutes Glosson presented the various facets of Phase I in some detail and a brief and concise description of Phases II and III. Both Cheney and Powell felt reassured regarding air power capabilities,[86] but the ground strategy gave rise to much concern. The basic plan was to attack the Iraqi forces straight on rather than encircle, with an estimated US casualty figure of some 10,000–20,000 soldiers.[87] The proposed strategy was surprisingly unimaginative, and hardly compatible with the manoeuvre warfare concept on which so much effort had been lavished since the mid 1980s. Schwarzkopf was not comfortable with the plan himself, but felt it was the best he could do with the 18th Airborne Corps that he had available in the theatre.[88] In all fairness, there was more to it than running straight into the Iraqi strength: at the time it was not realistic to do a grand Left Hook operation and they sought gaps through tactical manoeuvring within the Iraqi front. There were logistical problems with a Left Hook and there was great concern at the time that the Iraqis had laid the desert open as a trap for chemical and biological detonations. Moreover, Glosson and Purvis had worked together on targeting Iraqi troops in the Kuwaiti Theatre of Operations, and consequently the select group of Army planners who developed the ground operation, the so-called Jedi Knights, relied on the Iraqi troops' combat effectiveness being severely reduced prior to a ground attack. Thus, the option ridiculed later made some sense at the time, and for those who strongly believed in air power it was the right way to go about it.

Although Powell was deeply concerned about the ground strategy, he cautioned Glosson on the briefing that was to be held at the White House the following day: 'Buster, absolutely great. It's almost too good. It's too easy to grab onto. Be careful over at the White House tomorrow. I don't want the President to grab onto that air campaign as a solution to everything. I know it is going to be tempting for you to do that.'[89] Schwarzkopf, too, told Glosson after the briefing on the telephone that 'The chairman is afraid that if the brief goes to the president like this, the president will execute the air campaign . . . just stick to the facts. Let's not be too enthusiastic.'[90]

On 11 October Glosson gave a 30-minute long presentation to President Bush, Vice President Quayle, Secretary Cheney, Secretary Baker, National Security Advisor Scowcroft, White House Chief of Staff Sununu, General Powell and a few others.[91] Again Glosson focused on the first phase and gave a brief outline of the next two. He went through how they were going to obtain air superiority and the essence of the target strategy. The number of targets had by now reached 218 as intelligence on Iraq improved, but the target-sets remained the same as in the September briefings. One of Bush's immediate concerns was that as leadership targets, such as the Royal Palace, were attacked, other targets of historic and religious significance might be damaged. Glosson remarked that they would do everything they could to avoid such damage, and next assured the President of the accuracy of precision guided weapons.[92] After having graphically illustrated the plan for the first 24 hours of operations, Glosson described Phase II, Air Supremacy in Kuwait, and Phase III: attacks against the Republican Guard stationed in southern Iraq and the conscripts at the border between Kuwait and Saudi Arabia. After having commented on some of the logistical matters Bush wanted to know if Saddam Hussein could rise from the rubble on national television and state his continued presence. Glosson admitted that it could happen, but only if Saddam received outside help, because the television and radio network would be destroyed. Both Powell and Cheney commented that one had to be careful not to lead the public to expect that the Iraqi leader would be eliminated personally in Phase I.[93] After Glosson had finished his briefing Purvis presented the ground strategy. The ground attack plan once again resulted in controversy,[94] and towards the end of the overall briefing Bush asked, 'Why not do Phase I, II, and III, then stop?'[95] Glosson replied 'It's just like a grape on the end of a vine. If it doesn't have food and water, it will shrivel up.'[96] While Cheney agreed that one needed to think of such an option, Powell injected 'But he [Glosson] cannot guarantee you [Bush] that he [Saddam Hussein] will remove the Iraqi Army from Kuwait.'[97] Powell next summed up his concerns:

> Phase I will devastate him, it will be massive, and I don't know how he will deal with it. Phase II will make it more difficult for him, and Phase III will be additive, but you will have no assurance or guarantee we would get him out of Kuwait. Because we can't guarantee he'll leave Kuwait, we must be prepared to do Phase IV.[98]

The ground option faced much criticism, and Cheney even established his own special planning unit in the Pentagon, led by a retired Army lieutenant general, to develop an option.[99] Schwarzkopf hated Cheney's intrusion and developed an option in parallel that would eventually become the preferred strategy.

The 11 October briefing was another milestone in preparations for Desert Storm. While the White House was comfortable with the air plan,[100] it felt the ground plan was far from complete.[101] Bush later asked Powell, 'How many more people will you need',[102] in order to liberate Kuwait? Powell replied that Schwarzkopf needed an additional heavy corps and 90 days of preparation. Although Bush seems to have been ready to accept an offensive operation based on air power alone, he chose to listen to his military advisor who clearly recommended a doubling of forces in order to prepare for ground operations. The administration decided, however, not to make the decision public until early November, after the congressional elections, but to the military commanders it was a welcome sign of political determination.[103] The air planners in the Black Hole and Checkmate could take great satisfaction in the outcome: there was now political commitment for an offensive air campaign if it came to war, and the expansion of forces would also double the air resources.[104] The briefing was the point at which the strategic air campaign was given full acceptance, and in the following weeks the air planners would turn their attention to Phase III. In their minds – using a quote from Deptula – they would not be 'preparing the battlefield' for ground operations: they would be 'destroying it' to ensure victory through the air.[105]

Although the concept behind the strategic air campaign was deeply imbedded in Phase I, the Washington briefings also witnessed an element of lost opportunity. Prior to the presentation Horner had decided to take out issues that were related to war-termination and strategic psychological operations, because he felt he would be interfering with the business of the Department of State.[106] Warden and the Checkmate team argued that the psychological campaign should go hand in hand with the bombing campaign, and that it had to be developed at the national level. Moreover, they initiated the writing of a peace treaty, in which they suggested that the conditions for a ceasefire should be advertised in advance, but General Horner argued that these things should be conducted by politicians. Warden on the other hand argued that it was a tight iterative process in which one 'erroneously tried to separate the political and the military'.[107]

Scowcroft, in his memoirs, stated that his impression was that by mid October Bush had become calmer and had come to the conclusion that he had to do whatever was necessary to liberate Kuwait, and that probably meant using force.[108] The briefing made Bush feel confident that if they had to go sooner rather than later, air power could do much of the job. Bush told Prime Minister Thatcher that if sufficient provocation came about, 'We could then launch a huge air strike.'[109] By mid October Bush felt that 'We could simply devastate Iraq's military and strategic facilities with all our air power after a provocation', but Scowcroft disagreed:

> Brent [Scowcroft] warned that we might eventually have to follow through with ground troops to liberate Kuwait, and if we pounded from the air too soon, before our forces were ready, there could be public pressure to stop all fighting and turn opinion against ever launching a ground campaign. That might leave Saddam in Kuwait – and us without a military option.[110]

Throughout Desert Shield, Glosson, Warden and Deptula predicted that the bombing could change the political regime in Iraq, eliminate its strategic offensive and defensive capabilities and disrupt the internal economy and control. The bombing would nevertheless leave Iraq's ability to export oil intact, and enable the nations of the Persian Gulf to deal effectively with Iraq's residual forces.[111] Powell and the political leadership did not publicly approve of eliminating the Iraqi leader as an official objective, although Scowcroft admitted after the war 'We would have preferred a coup'.[112] After the 11 October briefing, the expression 'Decapitate Saddam Regime' was changed, however, to *destroying* its command and control and *disrupting* its ability to communicate with the Iraqi people and troops in Kuwait.[113] Secretary Baker was particularly concerned about the wording, preferring 'incapacitate' to 'decapitate', to avoid problems with the US law on assassination. Rather

1. Colonel John A. Warden in Checkmate, Pentagon, 15 August 1990.

2. The core of the Checkmate team stopping in Greece en route to Saudi Arabia on 18 August 1990. Colonel John Warden, Lieutenant-Colonel Ben Harvey, Lieutenant-Colonel David Deptula and Lieutenant-Colonel Ronnie Stanfill (left to right).

3. Lieutenant-Colonel Ben Harvey, Colonel John Warden, Lieutenant-Colonel David Deptula and Lieutenant-Colonel Ronnie Stanfill (left to right) going over the Instant Thunder plan during a refuelling stop in Greece en route to Riyadh on 18 August 1990.

4. Lieutenant-Colonel Ben Harvey, Colonel John Warden, Lieutenant-Colonel David Deptula and Lieutenant Colonel Ronnie Stanfill (left to right) in the Royal Saudi Air Force HQ taken after their arrival in Riyadh 19 August 1990.

5. Part of the Checkmate team standing in the front of an open source SPOT satellite photo on which targets in Baghdad were plotted. The USAF historian Wayne Thompson, Lieutenant-Colonel Ben Harvey, Major Buck Rogers, Lieutenant-Colonel David Deptula and Colonel John Warden (left to right).

6. Lieutenant-General Charles Horner and Lieutenant-Colonel David Deptula discussing a daily update on the status of the planning effort.

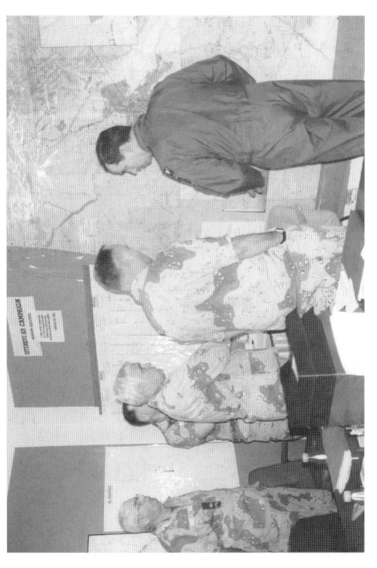

7. Lieutenant-Colonel Deptula briefing General Norman Schwarpkopf on the initial attack hours before its launch. From left to right: Major-General Tom Olsen, 9th Air Force Vice Commander; Lieutenant-General Charles Horner; Brigadier-General Buster Glosson; General Norman Schwarpkopf and Lieutenant-Colonel David Deptula.

8. Discussing targeting options on 28 January 1991 in the 'Black Hole'.

9. A typical day in the planning cell known as the 'Black Hole', 8 February 1991. Lieutenant-Colonel San Baptiste and Lieutenant-Colonel David Deptula confer over the master attack plan for next day.

10. Key planners of the Gulf War Air Campaign in the Black Hole just after its conclusion.

11. Colonel John Warden (front row, centre) and a fair number of people who participated in the Checkmate planning process before and during the war. (The picture is taken on the steps of the River Entrance to the Pentagon, early March 1991.)

than 'eliminate', air power was to 'facilitate' conditions that might lead to Saddam Hussein's overthrow. Despite the modifications, Warden, Deptula and Glosson still believed a ground campaign would not be necessary, and Air Secretary Rice agreed: one could do Phase III over and over again until Saddam Hussein withdrew.[114]

Although Executive Order 12333, first signed by President Gerald Ford in 1977, prohibits assassination of foreign heads of state as a matter of foreign policy, the military planners saw it differently. Saddam Hussein was, as far as they were concerned, the cause of the crisis. From a basic military point of view the logic was that if you killed the supreme commander you improved your own position. Moreover, Saddam Hussein was the military Commander-in-Chief, and consequently, they believed it was no less legitimate to go after him than after conscripts in the field. Indeed, from a military point of view it would be immoral *not* to try to kill the military leader if you had the means, as that would shorten the war and thereby save lives. But the political dimension to that reasoning is different, as a case could be made that deliberate 'assassination' is contrary to international law. It does however, come, down to interpretations, as the whole notion of 'assassination' is a peacetime term, and that issue does not form part of this research.[115] The point to be made, however, is that the air planners believed Saddam Hussein was a legitimate target, and although the White House never opposed such attacks there was considerable unease about making the killing of an official head of state a declared objective. In the end the change of wording after the October briefing had no real impact on the air campaign: they still sought to hit the Iraqi leader as hard as they could. Reservations continued to be expressed in Cheney's office about targeting the Iraqi leader, but nothing was actively done to discourage such action.

The air planners were, on the one hand, up against the argument that air power could fail in achieving the national objectives on its own, but, on the other, were up against the argument that even if the Iraqi leader chose to withdraw short of 'boots on the ground', then that too was unacceptable. Syria's President Hafiz al-Assad told Secretary Baker that if Saddam Hussein withdrew short of a ground war, however devastating the air war was, he would be able to claim victory on the basis that it was not a fight man-to-man, and that such an argument would have reasonable appeal in the region. Scowcroft and Baker argued that even if air power could succeed on its own, it was politically important to defeat the Iraqi Army in the field. Without pictures on world television showing the Iraqi soldiers surrendering, the Iraqi leader would claim victory. He could state that he had remained bloodied but unbeaten, and that his army had been too formidable for the United States to meet face-to-face. Deptula strongly disagreed in an interview on 1 November 1990: 'If *he* surrenders *we* dictate the terms of surrender.'[116] In Deptula's mind, the Iraqi leader was the root of the problem, and if he chose to surrender after the application of air power then the Coalition could prevent the Iraqis from taking the tanks home through the terms of surrender. The air planners did consequently find that there was a void in Washington's reasoning: the official objective was to liberate Kuwait with as few casualties as possible; air power was the best tool but it could not do it on its own; but even if it could that was not politically and institutionally acceptable.

In addition to presenting the air campaign on 11 October, Glosson shared some of his concerns regarding lack of intelligence in the theatre with Secretary Cheney in private. Although not a supporter of informal networking, Cheney allowed Glosson to engage in direct dialogues with Rear Admiral J. M. McConnell, the deputy director of DIA, who he knew personally from earlier assignments. As the planning progressed, Glosson and McConnell spoke frequently on secure telephones.[117] Although there were all kinds of concerns, by mid October the importance of conventional strategic air power was not questioned, and the fact that it would play a leading role was recognised: it was a question of timing and scope. Bush felt they were 'ready for the air campaign', and that 'our overwhelming air power would smash Saddam's military threat and wipe out Iraq's nuclear, chemical and biological weapons facilities'.[118] But he also believed that Scowcroft was right that there were further military and political preparations that needed to be considered. The newly appointed Air Force Chief of Staff, General McPeak, did not have the same belief in conventional strategic air power as his predecessor, General Dugan, but he certainly felt confident about air power as a dominating military instrument. On 24 October he told Powell that air power combat advantages would start to deteriorate steadily after 1 November as the Iraqis would dig into their defensive positions in Kuwait, and consequently an air war should start as soon as possible.[119] On 30 October in the White House, Bush asked Powell once again if he was sure that air power 'won't do it?', and again Powell responded that it might, but they could not depend on it.[120] Powell argued that one could not rely on air power alone, and that more troops were required if the President chose to go on the offensive.[121] On that day, 30 October 1990, Bush told Powell that he would give him the troop reinforcements that Schwarzkopf found necessary to eject Iraq from Kuwait. The decision was to have a major impact on the conflict: while the military mission changed from being defensive to offensive, the implication was that if it came to war the objective would not only be withdrawal, but the destruction of the Iraqi armed forces.[122] While Warden disagreed with any focus on the battlefield, Deptula was less dogmatic. Both argued, however, that tanks and artillery were not the linchpin to strategic success, but they were not in a position to influence such a high-level decision. Nevertheless, in accepting that decision, they would make sure the air campaign was as effective as possible on both the strategic and operational levels. Additionally, Deptula was pragmatic and believed that as time became available attacks against fielded military forces *should* be included in the plan, and he began incorporating attacks against fielded forces shortly after his arrival in Riyadh. He told Checkmate of the evolution in planning, and as a result Warden and Checkmate gradually turned their attention to Phase III.

The Final Refinements

At some point Phase III planning became concerned with how much bombing of Iraqi tanks, anti-personnel carriers and artillery within the KTO was required to reduce Iraqi combat effectiveness by 50 per cent. The number was considered well beyond the point where armies would lose operational coherence and thus would no longer be combat effective. According to Diane T. Putney, 'the specific 50 per cent attrition requirement stemmed not from doctrine, but from computer simulations and calculations that the CENTCOM Combat Analysis Group (CAG) produced to answer two questions during DESERT SHIELD'.[123] First, if the Iraqis were to attack Saudi Arabia, how effective did air power have to be to avoid 'heavy casualties'? Second, how long should an air campaign run if the objective was minimal casualties on the ground? Colonel Gary Ware, head of CAG, answered 50 per cent on both accounts.

The '50 per cent' attrition figure also showed up in an early Checkmate draft on Phase III, without knowledge of the earlier CENTCOM effort. Warden's team had originally not given the subject much thought since they were preoccupied with improving the strategic air campaign, but after the 11 October briefing the subject received increased attention. Warden had, in the meantime, been slightly upset by a RAND report which questioned some of his basic assumptions. The report, conducted by Project Air Force and titled 'Gulf Crisis Analysis', observed that 'the political leadership should not resort to force without a commitment to victory on the ground', basically because 'prompt destruction of Iraq's "strategic" assets is necessary but probably not sufficient'.[124] Still, RAND had also come to the conclusion that the 50 per cent attrition level could be achieved with B-52s bombing Iraqi ground forces over a period of one month. Air Secretary Rice and General Loh next directed Warden to make his own assessment, and although reluctant in the beginning, he soon reasoned that if he could convince the Bush administration that air power in Phase III could destroy the

Iraqi army, then a ground war would not be required.[125] It was during the latter part of October that Warden realised what precision bombing could do to ground forces, and this period represents a shift in Checkmate's contribution to the Black Hole: from having focused on targeting intelligence they now focused on planning to destroy the Iraqi ground forces. Indeed, by 16 October Warden was so excited about the project that he told his staff that their Phase III study was 'the most important work in Washington now'.[126] Within the next few days Checkmate faxed the Black Hole simulation results of how one could produce 50–90 per cent attrition levels.

Warden informed Glosson that their analysis concluded that they could achieve 50 per cent destruction of the Iraqi troops in Kuwait in only nine days, but Glosson pointed out that he could not take the analysis to Schwarzkopf if they did not include the destruction of the Republican Guard. Glosson felt that Warden's assumptions for the modelling were accurate, but since he was going to brief Schwarzkopf and Powell he decided to be extremely conservative. The result of the Checkmate simulation with the new input was that the Iraqi armour, artillery and manpower would be reduced by 50 per cent within 16 to 20 days, given good weather and 1,000 sorties a day. Thus, based on an 'unbelievably conservative' assumption about air power efficiency, Glosson assured General Schwarzkopf and General Powell that they could achieve the 50 per cent destruction within 21 days, and the latter replied 'I think those assumptions are about right.'[127] Glosson's November briefing to Schwarzkopf was basically on how they were going to conduct Phases II and III, what the effects were going to be, how many sorties were required, what the targets were, and how many days it would take to reduce the Iraqi tanks, artillery and personnel in theatre by 50 per cent.

In early November the Black Hole planners focused on improving Phase III. Glosson and Major Buck Rogers, who Deptula had personally arranged to be sent from Checkmate to the Black Hole as reinforcement, hand-carrying hard copies of Checkmate's latest iteration on Phase III, briefed Horner several times and when he was satisfied with both the content and the layout he presented it to General Schwarzkopf. Phase III was divided into two sections, attacking both the Republican Guard and the conscript-dominated Iraqi Army. The Black Hole planners were still convinced that they could do without a large-scale ground campaign, discussing the fact that the actual liberation could be conducted by Arab forces only, but Horner was careful not to present it that way. His job was to develop a plan for Schwarzkopf, and he trusted the CINC to make the right decisions as far as implementation was concerned. Horner, for his part, used to talk to Lieutenant General John Yeosock, the ARCENT, before he presented Schwarzkopf with options.

Schwarzkopf chose to allocate only eight days for Phase III, and importantly, he had come to the conclusion that he would not engage in a ground war until the 50 per cent attrition rate had been accomplished. There was immense confidence in the Black Hole and in Checkmate that air power would be extremely successful. Glosson even told each of the squadrons that 'The No. 1 risk is shooting each other down. The No. 2 risk is having a mid-air. The No. 3 risk is the Iraqis ... The outcome of this war is not in question. The only question is how many people will die before we reach our objectives.'[128] Paradoxically, therefore, Glosson argued that it was not all positive to perform at an extreme intensity level, because the likelihood of short-term failures, because of traffic congestion, increased as well. As the evolution of the operational phases was taking form, however, other aspects of the planning were of greater concern.

During the latter part of November, as Schwarzkopf had approved the concept of all three air power phases, the Black Hole planners briefed several Saudi Arabian generals, including Khalid bin Sultan. In late November and early December there was another series of Hearings before the Committee on Armed Services in the Senate. Senator McCain repeated his argument from September: 'We have the capability to carry out not *surgical* strikes, but strikes which would be concentrated on military, air defense, command and control communications, which I think would go a long, long way in carrying out the mission which we seek.'[129] Edward Luttwak had by that time become an advocate of air power, pointing to both potentials and limitations:

> If the use of force is nevertheless deemed inevitable, that leaves only the much-maligned Air Option. Much has been heard of the past failures of airpower from assorted pundits and retired military officers. True enough, airpower has always disappointed whenever more than a purely mechanical effect was expected. Airpower cannot break morale of a rigidly controlled population ... it cannot destroy regimes ... it cannot kill rulers except by mere chance ... On the other hand, bombardment can reliably destroy buildings, including those that contain stored weapons and weapon assembly lines ... an air offensive could literally demolish Saddam Hussein's military ambitions within a week or so ... Moreover, airpower can also force Iraqi troops to evacuate Kuwait ...[130]

Powell, who had no problem accepting the first part of Luttwak's assessment, advised Congress that air power was clearly not a quick, cheap and definite way to force the Iraqi leader out of Kuwait:

> Many experts, amateurs and others in this town believe that this can be accomplished by such things as surgical air strikes or perhaps a sustained air strike. There are a variety of other, nice, tidy, alleged low-cost incre-

mental, may-work options that were floated around with regularity in this town. The fundamental fatal flaw in all such strategies is that it leaves the initiative in Saddam Hussein's hands. He makes the decision as to whether or not he will or will not withdraw. He decides whether he has been punished enough so that it is now necessary for him to reverse direction and take a new political track. Those strategies may work. But they also may not. The initiative is left in Saddam Hussein's hands.[131]

Powell's statement upset Glosson, Warden and Deptula so much that they sent a memorandum to Secretary Rice.[132] Rice was already concerned, and he told Secretary Cheney in private discussions that the decision to launch an air campaign did not imply that a ground campaign would follow. Rice argued that Checkmate had done some analysis which concluded that US air power could be employed overwhelmingly against Iraqi ground forces, and it might very well be that if an actual ground intervention was needed in the end, then it could be carried out by the Arabs themselves. The expected results of Phase III, which were:

- Iraqi Army in Kuwait is effectively destroyed
- Re-occupation should meet minimal resistance
  Would be desirable (and maybe possible) by Kuwaiti/Arab ground forces
  U.S. ground forces could be held in reserve as a 'cocked fist'
- Near certain achievement of presidential objectives
  Without significant casualties of U.S. ground forces[133]

Warden stressed that the strategic air campaign would have an over-whelming affect on the Iraqi leadership, but he insisted that if it did not prove sufficient they could use air power to shatter Iraqi ground forces. Warden argued that no more than 30–40 airmen were likely to be killed: air power could win the war short of ground operations, and that would reduce US casualties that were inevitable if field forces clashed. Secretary Cheney seemed receptive, but in his usual manner he did not reveal his thoughts.[134] Warden's main concern at the time was that the military and political leadership would not give the air campaign enough time to succeed.

Warden saw the air campaign planning in two parts: the political Washington-based campaign, which sought to convince the policy-makers of air power's potential, and the operational Riyadh-based effort, which sought to translate concepts into execution. While he was running the first campaign, Glosson and Deptula were running the second, and as such they were all part of the same team however separated by distance.[135] In developing the master attack plans, and thereby the

ATOs, for each and every day of Operation Desert Storm, Deptula not only gave practical leverage to many of Warden's original ideas, but expanded beyond them in large part by introducing the concept of 'parallel warfare' – near-simultaneous attacks upon the strategic centres of gravity throughout the entire theatre of war.[136]

THE POLITICAL CAMPAIGN FOR THE AIR CAMPAIGN

From mid September to mid October, the USAF acting Chief of Staff, General Loh, had become convinced that the United States had sufficient capability in theatre to launch a strategic air campaign, and then complete the liberation of Kuwait with the corps that was in place.[137] While large parts of the senior leadership in Washington viewed a strategic option as 'bombing the enemy into the stone age', General Loh argued that although air power alone could 'control events' and 'continue to erode the Iraqi position over time', it could not dictate the outcome.[138] Although this was the official USAF line, Loh felt that his position was somewhat compromised: on the one hand General Powell kept repeating in meetings that there were not sufficient ground forces in theatre to start a war, and on the other hand there was an undercurrent in Washington arguing that 'air could do it alone'.[139] The latter, to a large degree, was a result of the actions of Warden, who genuinely believed that the political decision-makers did not know enough about the potential of air power and took it upon himself to promote these ideas to the leadership. Since the first Instant Thunder briefing Warden viewed every single issue as an individual and bureaucratic battle,[140] but by early September he became convinced that Powell, for 'parochial reasons', was making a 'concerted effort to control ideas going to the Secretary of Defense, to the Under Secretary of Defense for Policy, to the White House, and to the President'.[141]

Although Warden's sense of foreboding was extreme, there was a general concern within the Air Force that their institution was not adequately represented at the senior decision-making level. By early August General Loh had already made sure that Lieutenant General Adams became a representative of the Joint Staff because he was afraid the director of operations, Lieutenant General Tom Kelly, would dominate the process and diminish the contribution of air to the overall planning.[142] When Schwarzkopf decided in November that he needed a deputy in theatre, Secretary Donald Rice argued that it should not be an army officer, but Powell was successful in pushing through his candidate, Lieutenant General Calvin E. Waller.[143] General McPeak for his part argued that decision-making in Washington was dominated by Colin Powell and Vice Chairman Admiral David Jeremiah.[144] Glosson, furthermore, stated after the war that 'There's reluctance in some cases for JCS to present options to the White House because of concern that a wrong option might be selected. I think that's insulting to the President.'[145]

While most people accepted the chain of command and did their best to get their ideas pushed through the organisation, Warden went around that system to get his ideas to the highest level and thus ensure that they would not be diluted in the process. Although most airmen appreciated Warden's dedication to air power concepts, some of his superiors had become increasingly irritated with him during his Pentagon tenure.[146] He earned himself the nickname 'Right Turn', according to David Halberstam,

> because if he had a compelling idea and a superior rejected it, he simply took a right turn and went to the next higher level. Failing there, he would take yet another right turn and go to the next higher level, infuriating in the process a long line of his superiors. Predictably, the system hated him, although isolated, young iconoclastic officers working inside the system and often frustrated by it thought he was one of the most original thinkers in the service.[147]

Warden would never take 'no' for an answer, and as a result of his persistence he was seen by some as pursuing his own agenda and thus not to be fully trusted. The fact that he was very articulate and good at presenting and selling concepts only strengthened that concern. Many disapproved of his work-around methods in promoting his ideas, and according to Lieutenant General James Adams he was simply 'uncontrollable'.[148] Warden simply believed that in order to make major changes one had to take major steps, and as far as the ideas were concerned he would operate in the twilight of the feasible as a matter of principle:

> Real exploitation of air power's potential can only come through making assumptions that it can do something we thought it couldn't do ... We must start our thinking by assuming we can do everything with air power, not by assuming that it can only do what it did in the past.[149]

Convinced that Powell was 'squashing the air campaign', he decided to sell the plan to the decision-makers himself. Since briefing President Bush was unrealistic and they knew little about Secretary Cheney's opinion on air power at the time, Warden decided to aim for Under Secretary Paul Wolfowitz.[150] Warden knew that Wolfowitz had a long-standing friendship with the President, and he also had been at the important Camp David meetings in early August. Warden discussed the matter with Secretary Rice, who knew Wolfowitz personally, and they arranged for Wolfowitz to come down to Checkmate in early September, emphasising 'this is a non-briefing'.[151]

In early October Warden argued 'We've got to get the story out, because if we don't get it out in the right way, it ain't gonna go. It's going to be pushed off by the parochial interests that don't want it to go because they want to get tanks and all the rest of the stuff involved in it.'[152] With a vague consent from Loh and Alexander, Warden would play the game of informal networking to the fullest. While some would criticise him for going beyond his legitimate mandate, others would argue that this was his very strength: the ability to always look forward, thinking of the next step.

By early November it was becoming increasingly difficult to get Wolfowitz updated on the latest developments of the air campaign plan, but in a characteristic sub rosa fashion it had been arranged for him to come down to Checkmate. In the meantime, the director of the Joint Staff, Lieutenant General Michael Carns, became aware of this 'Air Force briefing on war',[153] and he next informed Powell, who strongly opposed such an unofficial agency briefing that was not even theirs. Warden, insisting on pushing the matter, as one would expect, talked to Secretary Rice, who talked to Secretary Cheney, who agreed to the idea of briefing Wolfowitz. After the presentation Powell conveyed to McPeak that this was not the way one was supposed to work, and consequently McPeak was angry with Lieutenant General Adams for not being able to control his own staff. Adams, once again witnessing Warden 'getting out in front of [him]' wanted to fire Warden and shut down Checkmate.[154] Although the incident resulted in much frustration among military commanders, the ultimate outcome was that Warden managed not only to brief Wolfowitz, but also to get the attention of Secretary Cheney, who was subsequently briefed on 6 November.[155] In Warden's mind:

> part of the fascination of this whole business is that military plans have little to do with military ... only five per cent of it is getting military people convinced and selling them on that. The other ninety-five per cent is getting the civilians to sign on to it.[156]

Powell, who had the official role as the military–political interface, felt uncomfortable about all these independent USAF networks: Checkmate provided separate access to the top echelon of the Department of Defense, Secretary Rice would frequently talk to Lieutenant Colonel Deptula in the Black Hole, Brigadier General Glosson talked directly to members of the White House and the DIA, and finally, Warden briefed every politician he could get access to in Washington. It should be noted, however, that Warden did not always succeed: although he managed to get the attention of the Director of the CIA, William Webster, Secretary Cheney never gave a green light for such a briefing.[157] Warden, of course, did not have a mandate for briefing politicians, and technically speaking he did not have the War Plan. He was, according to General Loh's recollection, 'overly zealous in trying to market what he called his plan, or the Air Force plan, and that is where you have to go through the operating commanders'.[158] Much of the antagonism towards, and criticism of, Warden resides therefore just as much in his methods of operating as with his actual thinking on air power. This was for Warden, however, the essence of making it all happen, and he received reasonable political coverage from Secretary Rice:

> That is not to say that they couldn't have planned some level of strategic air campaign plan out there, but a lot of the details about how the telephone system worked that we got from AT&T and other contractors; a lot of details that we got on the actual construction and layout of the buried bunkers, command and control centres, special facilities in the key Iraqi buildings and palaces; the way the Yugoslav shelters were constructed, and various other things; the Checkmate operation, through intelligence sources and working through diplomatic sources to access foreign companies, as well as our own; [so] we got a tremendous amount of information, sometimes down to the detailed architectural plans for some of the structures that ended up being targets in the attack. I don't see how that level of stuff ever could have been done out in Riyadh.[159]

Although Warden's briefings were well received by both Cheney and Wolfowitz, it is difficult to assess how much difference the increased air power awareness made to the decision-makers beyond establishing a higher degree of confidence in the military plan. Throughout the war, assistant executives from the Department of Defense and the Office of the Secretary of the Air Force would come down to get an update on air power accomplishments, and Checkmate briefed among others Ambassador April Glaspie, Chargé d'Affaires Joe Wilson and Iraqi expert Phebe Marr.[160] Glaspie, in particular turned out to be very useful in intelligence gathering, as she had insight not found within the intelligence community.[161]

Iraqi defectors were moreover explored in order to improve HUMINT, and a former station chief in Baghdad, 'Mr Smith', provided knowledge of which rooms within the Iraqi intelligence compounds were most critical.[162] Whenever Checkmate prepared briefings for Secretary Rice or General McPeak, they would also make sure that copies found their way to Cheney's office through his military assistant, hoping to get the Secretary's attention.[163] General McPeak, who openly admitted to Warden that he was more comfortable with the tactical aspects of an air campaign, soon became a strong advocate of conventional strategic air power.[164] He spent hours at Checkmate preparing briefings for the political leadership and the press,[165] and he made an extremely good impression on the President when they first met in early December.

Little is known about how this meeting came about in the first place. In late November Warden and Edward Luttwak discussed how they could sell the idea of air power. By that time Luttwak had already written some controversial articles, and he agreed with Warden that the Bush administration was not given all the information about air power capabilities. One of the affects of the 1986 Goldwater–Nichols Act was that the Chiefs of Staff did not meet the President in person unless the Chairman or the President suggested it. Luttwak called Senator John Warner, a ranking member of the Committee of Armed Services, and suggested that there were ideas on the war that Powell was holding back. Senator Warner supposedly called the White House,[166] and shortly after, on 1 December, General McPeak was invited to Camp David together with the other chiefs of staff: General Carl Vuono, General Alfred Gray and Admiral Frank Kelso.

At Camp David, General McPeak seems to have been the only Chief of Staff who felt confident about victory if they had to go to war. McPeak argued that the war would be over in 37 days at the cost of a maximum of 2,000 Iraqi civilians and 100 aircraft. Bush was impressed and asked Scowcroft 'Who is this guy McPeak? Does he know what he is talking about?'[167] McPeak was also invited in early January 1991 to the White House, and at a lunch with Scowcroft, Cheney and Bush he argued that he felt they had better act sooner rather than later. By that time, on 11 December 1990, Cheney had been given a briefing by the Checkmate group, and he seems to have agreed that there was much air power could achieve in the opening phase through stealth and precision.[168] Warden had further taken the opportunity to brief Les Aspin's staff, and Ike Skelton on the request of Alexander. Deptula, who was in Washington at the time, was also particularly concerned about Powell's statement in the Senate on 3 December. He helped Eliot Cohen and General Russell E. Dougherty prepare their testimonies before the Senate on 10 December,[169] and also prepared more arguments for Secretary Rice to take to Wolfowitz and Cheney. One should be careful with speculation, but it might be that one of the important factors in President Bush's decision to go to war was his team's accumulated confidence in air power.

Powell did not believe that war termination could be accomplished by 'surgical air strikes or perhaps a sustained air strike' for two reasons: it would leave the initiative on when to withdraw in the hands of Saddam Hussein, and it would allow him to concentrate on the air threat only.[170] This would enable the Iraqi leader to 'hunker down' and to disperse resources. Powell concluded that 'such strategies are designed to hope to win; they are not designed to win'.[171] Paradoxically, what was now defined as the strategic air campaign had been accepted by the air commander and several senior politicians in the Bush administration, while Powell and Schwarzkopf, the two who had decided to call the Air Staff and made the planning possible in the first place, were the ones most strongly identifying its limitations. Still, Warden made it his personal objective throughout the war to prevent a ground war because he felt it was unnecessary, suggesting that ground engagements would increase US casualties. As the war progressed, much of Checkmate's effort was directed towards convincing Secretary Cheney that the air campaign had such an impact on the ground forces that the start of the ground attack should be postponed.[172]

Loh, who seems to have given Warden a carte blanche to talk to anybody he wanted, and deeply respected Warden's enthusiasm and intentions, argued after the war that Warden went too far:

> It is improper for an Air Force officer to try and brief the Under Secretary of Defense for Policy on the air campaign when technically that is not the War Plan … Warden had no right and clearly no responsibility and authority to go around town briefing other people on this air campaign … If Wolfowitz wanted a briefing on the campaign plan, he could have called Colin Powell.[173]

It is an interesting statement, as Loh and Warden talked on a daily basis during the war, and Loh for sure must have been aware of Warden's actions. Major General Alexander, who also came to Warden's defence throughout the crisis, argued that Warden was one of the most gifted strategists in the USAF, but that he constantly had to assess Warden's liabilities versus contributions, and at times that balance was only marginally in his favour.[174] Secretary Rice supported that view, arguing that although he was indispensable he was hard to restrain.[175] According to Colonel Richard T. Reynolds part of the problem with John Warden was that he was so convinced that his idea was the right one, that he used this 'go-around method to extract decisions out of the leadership that he feels will benefit the plan', rather than opt for letting the leadership make the actual decision.[176] Thus, Warden was not only persistent in getting the ideas to the top, he was also persistent in selling them to the people he felt would be supportive and have an influence. He pushed hard, not simply to give the senior leadership a range of options, but to convince them that strategic air power could really make a difference. Consequently, he was so convinced of his own ideas that he was sure that as long as President Bush and Secretary Cheney were briefed on the concept they would appreciate it and implement it. Although President Bush became convinced that 'We could devastate Iraq's military and strategic facilities with all our air power after a provocation', such a provocation never materialised, and he was not ready to act against the advice of Scowcroft, Powell and Schwarzkopf.

Warden received, at the end of the day, far more promotion for his ideas than he had ever dreamed of. When the war started, CNN appointed Major General (ret.) Perry Smith as their air power analyst. Smith and Warden had known each other for years, and Smith had helped edit and promote Warden's book, *The Air Campaign*.[177] As the war progressed, Smith called Warden three to four times a day to get an update, stating that 'He became my primary source, the No. 1 source, for information and insight during the period I worked for CNN ... I wouldn't have been able to pull off the CNN job without John Warden.'[178] Warden's intention was first to help an old friend and to bounce ideas off each other, but it also gave him the opportunity to argue his air power concept indirectly to a wider audience.[179] It should be noted that the discussions with Perry Smith were blessed in advance by General McPeak and were no secret.

THE FINAL SCRIPT OF THE OFFENSIVE AIR CAMPAIGN PLAN

On 17 December, after Cheney and Powell had visited the theatre and approved the final air plan, General Horner decided to abandon the defensive planning completely by merging the planning effort into an 'Iraqi Cell' and a 'KTO Cell'. The Black Hole, which originally started as an ad hoc outcast organisation with no official power, ended up with an incredible level of control over the prosecution of the air war. The planning as called for in mission Operation Desert Shield had resulted in a defensive plan published by the Joint Directorate of Planning, Combined OPLAN for Defense of Saudi Arabia, on 29 November 1990. The D-Day ATO culminated in an exercise code-named Imminent Thunder. The exercise focused on close air support and served as an attempt to deceive Iraqi intelligence.[180] The Combined OPLAN focused on administrative command and control procedures, Coalition inter-relations and a defensive strategy envisioned in OPLAN 1002-90. In essence, based on a defensive posture as it was, it reflected the AirLand Battle Doctrine: 'support the land campaign ... air forces provide counter-air, interdiction, and close air support to land forces throughout the area of operations'.[181]

Horner appointed Glosson as director of plans for the new planning organisation, while General John Corder became director of operations. Glosson made sure Deptula became head of the 'Iraqi Cell', focusing on Phases I and II, while Lieutenant Colonel Samuel J. Baptista, who had been strongly influential in the D-Day planning, was appointed head of the 'KTO Cell', focusing on Phases III and IV. With the vast amount of air power assets available, Horner and Glosson decided that they should execute the first three phases simultaneously. Herein lies one of the unique features of Desert Storm: the Coalition had so many resources available that they did not have to make hard choices.

In National Security Directive (NSD) 54, signed 15 January 1991, President George Bush 'authorized military actions designed to bring about Iraq's withdrawal from Kuwait'.[182] The authorisation was for the following purposes:

- to effect the immediate, complete and unconditional withdrawal of all Iraqi forces from Kuwait;
- to restore Kuwait's legitimate government;
- to protect the lives of American citizens abroad; and
- to promote the security and the stability of the Persian Gulf.[183]

These national security objectives were the same as the ones announced on 8 August, but to achieve the above purposes the US and Coalition forces should seek to:

- defend Saudi Arabia and the other GCC [Gulf Co-operation Council] states against attack;
- preclude Iraqi launch of ballistic missiles against neighbouring states and friendly forces;
- destroy Iraq's chemical, biological, and nuclear capabilities;
- destroy Iraq's command, control and communication capabilities;
- eliminate the Republican Guard as an effective fighting force; and
- conduct operations designed to drive Iraq's forces from Kuwait, break the will of the Iraqi forces, discourage Iraqi use of chemical, biological or nuclear weapons, encourage defection of Iraqi forces, and weaken Iraqi popular support for the current government.[184]

The presumption was to give conventional strategic air power against the Iraqi regime a chance to work. Importantly, the necessity to use ground forces to liberate Kuwait was not mentioned. The final operational orders manifested the influence of Warden's and Deptula's initiatives back in early August. Phase I – the strategic air campaign – would start the offensive and was estimated to require six to nine days to meet its objectives. The Operational Order (OPORD) stated that the:

> strategic air campaign will be initiated to attack Iraq's strategic air defenses; aircraft/airfields; strategic chemical, biological and nuclear capability; leadership targets; command and control systems; RGFC [Republican Guard Forces Command]; telecommunications facilities; and key elements of the national infrastructure, such as critical LOCs [Lines

of Communication], electric grids, petroleum storage, and military production facilities.[185] ... [Additionally,] cut key bridges, roads and rail lines immediately south of Basra to block withdrawal of RGFC forces. Cut bridges, roads and rail lines in the vicinity of An Nasiriyah to block reinforcement and/or resupply of Iraqi forces from the west and isolate Iraqi forces in the KTO.[186]

Although the above paragraph reflects much of Instant Thunder, it should be noted that Phase I was increasingly concerned with interdiction. Phase II – the attainment of air superiority in the KTO – was estimated to begin between days seven and ten, and require two to four days, ending no later than 13 days after the bombing had started. The OPORD stated that:

> air superiority in the Kuwaiti theater of operations will be established by attacking aircraft/airfields, air defence weapons and command and control systems in order to roll back enemy air defenses ... The ultimate goal of the phase is to achieve air supremacy through the KTO.[187]

Phase III – battlefield preparations – was estimated to start sometime between the ninth and fourteenth day, and require six to eight days. The OPORD stated that Phase III would involve:

> attacking Iraqi ground combat forces (particularly RGFC units) and supporting missile/rocket/artillery units; interdicting supply lines; and destroying command, control and communications systems in southern Iraq and Kuwait with B-52s, tactical air, and naval surface fire ... The desired effect is to sever Iraqi supply lines, destroy Iraqi chemical, biological, and nuclear capability, and reduce Iraqi combat effectiveness in the KTO by at least 50 per cent, particularly the RGFC ... [Moreover,] the purpose ... is to open the window of opportunity for initiating ground offensive operations by confusing and terrorising Iraqi forces in the KTO and shifting combat force ratios in favor of friendly force.[188]

Phase IV – the ground offensive – had no estimated start or finish day, but in December Glosson estimated that the ground offensive would require 18 days, resulting in the total campaign taking no more than 32 days. Air power was tasked to accomplish the traditional missions of close air support and interdiction.

The operational orders for Phase I reflected the offensive, aggressive and intense application of air power, as was suggested in Global Reach Global Power and Instant Thunder. Although the number of targets had grown substantially over the months as more intelligence and information on Iraq became available, the target categories, which reflected the philosophical construct of the Five Rings, remained the same. While the focus on the strategic realm survived to a large extent, one should note that the two categories that witnessed the highest percentage increase were Military Support (MS) and Railroad and Bridges (RR). This reflected the increased attention given to traditional interdiction targets as more resources became available. In the end the number of targets in the RR category was the same as the number of leadership (L) targets. While it represented a compromise on the part of the key air planners, it also reflected the lack of intelligence on how the Iraqi regime worked. One might suggest that had it not been for the continued effort by Deptula to keep the plan's focus on the 'inner ring', the initial strategic air campaign would probably have been reduced to one focusing on air superiority over Iraq and interdiction. Table 2 encompasses the growth of targets from Instant Thunder to the final plan ready for execution on 15 January 1991. As it shows, the target-sets remained much the same. Instant Thunder was further emphasising 'bombing for effect' rather than destruction per se, and as Table 3 shows,

Table 2: The Growth of Targets: From Instant Thunder to Phase I

Target-Set	Instant Thunder 21 Aug. 90	CENTAF OPLAN 2 Sept. 90	Briefing CJCS 13 Sept. 90	Briefing President 11 Oct. 90	Briefing Sec. Def. 20 Dec. 90	START Air Camp 15 Jan. 91
L	5	15	15	15	27	33
CCC	19	27	26	27	30	56
E	10	17	14	18	16	17
O	6	9	8	10	8	12
C	8	15	15	15	20	23
MS	15	35	41	43	46	73
RR	3	12	12	12	21	33
SAD	10	39	21	40	27	56
A	7	19	13	27	25	31
SC	–	–	5	5	13	48
RG	–	7	–	–	–	37
N	1	–	4	6	4	17
BR	–	–	–	–	–	–
SAM	–	–	–	–	–	45
Total No.	84	195	174	218	237	481

Source: Cohen *et al.*, *Gulf War Air Power Survey: Planning*, pp. 145, 185. Chart originally prepared by Deptula to show the evolution of target development. Leadership (L), Command, Control and Communication (CCC), Electricity (E), Oil (O), Nuclear Biological and Chemical Weapons (C), Military Support/Production and Storage (MS), Railroads and Bridges (RR), Strategic Air Defense (SAD), Airfields (A), Scuds (S), Republican Guard (RG), Naval Ports (N), breaching (BR) and Surface-to-Air Missiles (SAM).

that concept remained throughout the planning. Although the Five Rings Model was taken out of the briefings after 16 August, it remained the basis for the planning philosophy, particularly for Phase I, and although the code-name Instant Thunder was dropped, its substance was largely projected into what became the first phase of Operation Desert Storm. In Warden's 17 August briefing to Schwarzkopf there were four centres of gravity: Saddam's political and military leadership and internal control network; Saddam's strategic chemical warfare capability; the telecommunication, industrial and transportation systems that supported his rule; and, critical military systems such as the Iraqi air defence

Table 3: Desired Effects: From Instant Thunder to Phase I

Target Identification	Desired effects Instant Thunder	Desired effects Phase I of Desert Storm
Hussein Regime (L)	Isolate and incapacitate	Isolate, incapacitate and reduce public trust
Telecommunications and C3 (CCC)	Rupture Hussein's link to people and military	Rupture Hussein's link to military population and outside world
Electricity (E)	Cripple production (60% in Baghdad & 35% in country)	Leveraged target affecting all target-sets
Oil (refined products) (O)	Paralyse domestic and internal movement	Paralyse internal military mobility
NBC (C)	Reduce long-term international threat	Reduce offensive threat to regional states and friendly forces
Mil. support/prod. storage (MS)	Limit offensive capability	Reduce offensive capability, long and short term
Railroads and bridges (RR)	Complicate movements of goods and services	Restrict escape avenue of RG and complicate resupply of KTO
Strategic Air Defense (SAD)	Render Iraq defenceless	Render Iraq defenceless and minimise threat to allied force
Airfields (A)	Reduce threat to adjacent states, now and in the future	Achieve control in the air to enable friendly force operations
Strategic Offensive capability, Scud (SC)	Reduce threat to adjacent states now and in the future	Reduce offensive threat to regional states and friendly force
Republican Guard (RG)	–	Destroy the Republican Guard by 50%
Naval Ports (N)	Reduce threat to friendly forces	Reduce threat to friendly forces
KTO armour, artillery personnel	–	Destroy 50% of enemy ground forces in KTO

Source: Deptula, 'Reflections on Desert Storm: The Air Campaign Planning Process', presentation to author, Incirlik (Turkey), 14 August 1999.

network. By 13 September Glosson had compressed these to three: leadership, infrastructure and military forces. These three were to stay throughout in the main, and on the eve of the execution they had been termed: National Command Authority, NBC capability and Forces of the Republican Guard.[189]

Although there was much of Instant Thunder in the final air campaign plan, one should note that Instant Thunder was technically never executed as intended by the Checkmate group. In early August the planners were trying to come up with a plan that could make as much impact as possible on the Iraqi leadership in a short period of time (days not weeks), and it was planned as if execution would be in early September. The latter part is often forgotten when critiquing the concept: within the first six weeks after the Iraqi invasion, the Checkmate and Black Hole planners were working on the concept while understanding that it might have to be executed within days, if ordered to. Instant Thunder was devised as the best possible response. One should not forget, therefore, that through this initiative, the military and political leadership had an option to retaliate with decisive force against the heart of the Iraqi regime by early September if it chose to do so, and there was no other conventional military alternative at the time.[190] As the planners were given more time, the initial strategic air-alone option was turned into a four-phased combined strategy.

In early September Schwarzkopf argued that the Republican Guard should not only be a separate target-set for Phase I, but one out of three 'centres of gravity'. Deptula and Warden opposed the idea at the time, arguing that it would divert resources from the 'inner ring'.[191] Warden and Deptula agreed that conceptually the Republican Guard was extremely important to Saddam Hussein, but they argued that it was not a practical target in the sense that taking out tanks and dispersed ground forces was not the best way to apply air power at the time. However, since Schwarzkopf was 'obsessed' with the Iraqi elite military forces, they had to follow instructions. When Deptula asked Horner just prior to the execution what he honestly thought about the strategic air campaign plan he said:

> Well, Dave, quite frankly, it's too precise. It requires too many things to happen before something else happens. I have talked this over with Schwarzkopf. You know, we would be happy if we just achieved 50 per cent of what you're trying to do here. We know what you are trying to do, but it's just not going to work out that way.[192]

The significance of Instant Thunder in contributing to the final plan does not reside, however, in the correlation between the two, but in the fact that it provided the air planners with a 'foot in the door'.[193] Instant Thunder suggested a strategic response to the occupation of Kuwait that did not exist at the time, and by convincing Schwarzkopf and Powell in early August of air capabilities the strategic direction of planning was ensured. The significance of Instant Thunder lies in the direction it gave at the time: it focused on certain target-sets and associated individual targets, relied on functional measures of degradation rather than physical destruction to evaluate the campaign's progress, and it planned attacks against a large number of targets over each 24-hour period.[194] Thus, the air campaign focused on the Iraqi state as a system rather than a military entity – the foundation of 'effects-based operations'. Although Warden was the principal architect of this approach, it was Deptula who managed to develop his own ideas to ensure that this strategic orientation prevailed in the theatre, and who actually constructed a plan ready for execution. Finally, although the execution would not witness the emphasis of effort originally called for on the 'inner ring', among other things a consequence of not accepting the suggested importance of strategic psychological operations, Figure 3 shows the relationship between the Five Rings Model and the target-sets defined in the final plan.

CONCLUSIONS

This chapter has examined the evolution of the strategic air campaign, from the initial Instant Thunder concept to the final plan. Although Warden orchestrated the early stages of the planning, it was Deptula who managed to translate Warden's innovative ideas into a format that was politically acceptable and capable of execution. While Deptula did the actual planning, and maintained the strategic focus called for in Instant Thunder,[195] Glosson managed to sell these ideas to the military commanders and political decision-makers. Without Deptula and Glosson, Warden's ideas and tireless effort would therefore most likely never have been put into practice. Horner's decision to send Warden back to Washington on 20 August proved to be rather fortunate: Glosson and Deptula established a relationship with their commander that Warden most likely could not have developed, and with Warden facilitating support from Washington one could not have hoped for a better combination.[196] With Horner establishing the *ad hoc* Special Planning Group in Riyadh, and Warden providing unofficial support from Checkmate in the Pentagon, the strategic air campaign plan was developed completely outside the pre-defined war-planning organisation. Each of the three key planners – Glosson, Warden and Deptula – managed to influence the process by virtue of personal initiative and dedication. Had these three not inserted themselves into the planning process, the offensive air campaign would most likely have developed in accordance with

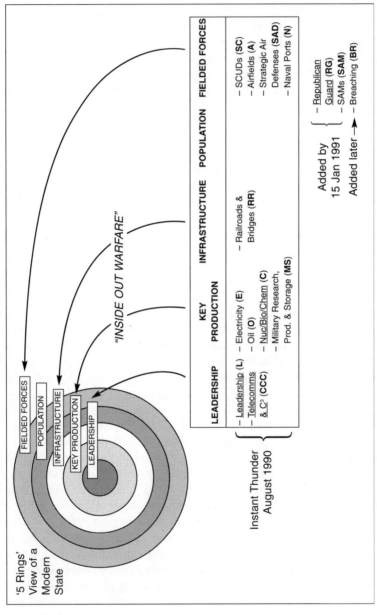

Figure 3: The Five Rings Model and Phase I

Source: Barry Watts, 'The Effectiveness of Coalition Air Power Against Iraq's Nuclear Weapons Program & Modified "Scud" Missiles during Desert Storm', OSD Counterforce Workshop, RDA Logicon Arlington, USA, 19 July 1995. Permission granted to use this chart.

the plans for ground operations as envisioned in the AirLand Battle Doctrine.

Horner for his part contributed to the planning by letting it unfold without interference from the military leadership, and importantly he was able to present the concept in a manner that Schwarzkopf found acceptable.[197] Although sceptical towards any idea of the strategic use of air power in the beginning, Horner was by late September a strong advocate of conventional air power used in an independent fashion. In retrospect it seems likely that Horner was more opposed to the term 'strategic' than the actual substance of a 'strategic air campaign'. But Instant Thunder suggested going after strategic targets as the only option, and at the time Horner believed that Warden failed to acknowledge that 'sometimes there are legitimate higher priorities than your master air campaign plan'.[198] Although there was indirect pressure from Schwarzkopf and Powell, it was Horner who acted on the idea of a strategic air campaign plan. Little did he know, however, of the continued influence from Warden's Checkmate, and when he found out he acknowledged the contribution and saw no reason to interfere. As soon as it was recognised that the strategic air campaign would become one of several phases, Horner's acceptance grew, but the fact that so much of Instant Thunder's conceptual focus on the Iraqi leadership survived all the planning iterations was the result of Deptula's dedication to the concept, his persistence and vision more than anything else. The combination of Horner, Glosson, Warden and Deptula is basically one of happenstance.

It is worth noting that Warden in many ways presented a concept that most likely would not have been politically acceptable during the Cold War. While TAC's thinking maintained a Cold War mentality, Warden managed to take advantage of the grand strategic changes that were about to manifest themselves. Thus, the 'man and the moment met and jumped as one' also in geo-political terms.

It has further been established that the development of the operational air campaign plan that resulted in Phases I, II and III of Operation Desert Storm witnessed several key briefings. On 21 August Glosson was convinced that Instant Thunder was a good starting point, and thus the ideas of Warden and Deptula prevailed at a crucial stage. On 2 September Horner signed the first operational order of a strategic air campaign, and by mid September the plan was accepted by Schwarzkopf and Powell as the sole retaliation option at the time. Glosson argued after the war that 'We never changed the plan after the 13th day of September, the only thing we did ... was more of the plan, simultaneously.'[199] By mid October Secretary Cheney and President Bush accepted that if it came to war it would start with the bombing of the Iraqi leadership and communication systems. By late November

Schwarzkopf came to the conclusion that he would not engage in ground operations until air power had succeeded in achieving 50 per cent attrition of the Iraqi armed forces in Kuwait, stressing the importance of Phase III. The period between late August and late November therefore witnessed a gradual acceptance of the potential of air power working independently from the ground engagements, and the strategic dimension that Warden and Deptula had started promoting in 1988 and 1989 came to fruition. The process was nevertheless not without inter-service tension. Waller, Schwarzkopf's CENTCOM deputy commander, found that Glosson appeared too confident about air power's capability. While it may well be that senior Army officers misunderstood Glosson, he became, 'perhaps, the most despised senior officer in the theater to some Third Army commanders'.[200]

The contribution of Checkmate to the final war-script and the war itself is difficult to measure. It provided intelligence and made things easier for the planners, but one cannot conclude that the planning would have failed without it. By October the intelligence community in theatre had replaced Checkmate as the major source, and Checkmate's contribution shifted to become one of analysis. Checkmate gave significant evaluation with regard to Phase III, especially attrition modelling, but there was also much information that Glosson and Deptula did not use.[201] Nevertheless, much of the information that Checkmate gathered could only have come from Washington, and as long as they were supporting the war effort, being a sort of 'reach-back' for strategy, targeting intelligence and analysis, a concept that is now accepted, it is hard to argue against it. One might criticise them for conducting informal networking that went far beyond their legitimate mandate, but what else should one do when the official organisational charts were inadequate? Checkmate did not sever formal links – they complemented them. While it is easy to underestimate Checkmate's contribution, one should not overestimate it. It helped cut corners, and the continued intellectual exchanges were no doubt significant, but again one cannot conclude that the planning would have failed without it.[202] Warden deserves much credit for his contribution to Phase III, but again, it was the interaction with the Black Hole that made it happen. After the war Brigadier General Buster Glosson acknowledged that Checkmate was the single most important agency outside the theatre, while Schwarzkopf stated that

> the Air Force [in Washington] jumped right in and came up with a very rudimentary essence of what started out to be the air campaign plan. Very quickly Chuck Horner made it clear to me that this was not the desired way of doing it, and we took the skeletal plan that was started in Washington and I shifted the whole thing … By the middle of October,

early November, we had a completely robust strategic air campaign that was very executable right down to the gnat's eyelash.[203]

In addition to Checkmate, TAC established a command, CENTAF Rear, under the leadership of Major General Ryan, which contributed significantly to deployment and other logistical matters. Although the Black Hole planners found the Checkmate contribution indeed valuable, Horner argued that it was the same old story when it comes to credit: 'There are 10,000 ants on a log going down the Potomac River, each of them thinking they are steering the log.'[204] As so often is the case, victory has many fathers.

Although Warden and Deptula were indispensable in initiating and carrying through a strategic air campaign, it should also be acknowledged that without CENTAF's insistence one would probably not have added the operational and tactical levels of the plan that were so important in convincing the military commanders and the political leadership of air power's overall capability. There was therefore a shift in Warden's and Deptula's thinking as the planning evolved. In the early days of the crisis Deptula thought of the Five Rings Model as a conceptual framework where the focus should be on the leadership, but importantly, as the planning unfolded he realised that an effort should also be made against the Iraqi ground forces. Warden was slower in accepting this, but the shift was also governed by the fact that they had more resources in November than in August. Thus, with the overwhelming air power available no hard choices would have to be made: they could do it all and see what worked best.

As the planning reached its final stages and the war commenced, Checkmate would serve as an information centre, facilitating an exchange of ideas among officers, politicians and academics hardly witnessed in the United States Armed Services. Checkmate therefore did serve as an important link between the Black Hole and the Washington community, ensuring a higher degree of awareness of air power in the minds of civilians. This again was an arrangement that caused much controversy, but in Warden's mind one could not separate politics from military planning at a strategic level.[205] In retrospect there seem to have been two motives behind Warden's 'campaign for the air campaign': he feared that the strategic air campaign would not be executed if left to CENTAF alone, and next he wanted to make sure it stayed focused on the things he thought were important.[206] Warden was entirely committed, however, to the cause, and even his opponents argued that he was not seeking personal aggrandisement. One should not forget that both Loh and Alexander played an important part in ensuring that Warden was allowed to continue his controversial effort of promoting air power.[207] It was Loh who told Schwarzkopf in the first place that he would provide an air option on 8 August 1990, and he made sure that the planning was allowed to unfold. As Acting Chief of Staff he continued to shelter Warden's behind-the-scene manipulations, and so did Alexander, who took a lot of criticism from his superior, Adams, who time and again wanted to shut down Checkmate. Interestingly, when Schwarzkopf needed an air campaign plan in early August the Joint Staff was unable to deliver. Warden filled a crucial void in a crisis that no one else seemed able to fill, and yet he would be resented for doing so even though he was largely successful. Warden's role in 1991, according to strategist Edward N. Luttwak, 'was absolutely central therefore in rescuing the USAF from its tactical mentality'.[208]

Some of these parochial struggles within the services have been illustrated. As Warden became convinced that Powell was pushing for the employment of ground forces, his personal objective was to convince the politicians that such operations were not necessary. In mid October Powell simply was not convinced that the air power advocates would be able to deliver on their promises, and concerned about American lives he was not ready to recommend a strategy to President Bush that was short of ground operations. However, as the second corps deployed from Germany, there was a political concern that not employing them would send a counter-productive message about the United States, determination to see the job through, even if air power alone could have ensured an Iraqi withdrawal.[209]

In retrospect, the point in time when the strategic air campaign was accepted by the military and political leadership was during Glosson's presentation on 11 October 1990. Since that briefing did not include strategic psychological operations, or war-termination issues, it also proved to be the point in time when a significant part of Warden's initial ideas lost important momentum. On the surface, the approval of the plan was a great success for Glosson, Warden and Deptula, but it was also the point at which General Schwarzkopf and General Powell received acceptance for ground reinforcement. Consequently, from a political standpoint, once the war started it would be unacceptable not to engage in ground operations for political and parochial, if not military and operational, reasons.

General (ret.) Merrill A. McPeak argued after the war that 'any three fighter pilots in a bar' could have come up with the Instant Thunder concept,[210] but the fact of the matter is that only Checkmate did come up with what he also referred to as a 'straightforward no-brainer'.[211] Perhaps Horner, by no means a supporter of the Five Rings Model, said it best when he was asked how the final script differed from Instant Thunder: 'How does a butterfly differ from a larva?'[212]

Now that the planning contributions from Checkmate and Black Hole planners have been established, it has to be determined whether they correctly identified Iraqi centres of gravity. Furthermore, acknowledging that only 740 out of 43,123 strikes were directly engaged with the 'central nervous system',[213] one has to question whether the planners were given a sufficient chance to achieve their mission and whether or not that effort was worthwhile. Such a task requires an understanding of the inner working of the Iraqi regime.

NOTES

1. Wayne Thompson, interview with author, tape-recording, Washington, DC, 1 March 1999; Allan W. Howey, telephone interview with author, notes, 6 April 1999; Warden, interview, *Desert Story Collection*, 22 October 1991, pp. 110–15;. Warden, interview, *Desert Story Collection*, 10 December 1991, p. 1; and Reynolds, *Heart of the Storm*, p. 133.
2. Ben Harvey, cited in Deptula, *Desert Story Collection*, 22 May 1991, pp. 56–7; Mark B. Rogers, interview, *Desert Story Collection*, 3 June 1991, p. 8; and Warden, interview, Tom Clancy, *Fighter Wing*, p. 47.
3. Major Mark B. Rogers, interview, *Desert Story Collection*, 3 June 1991, p. 8.
4. Deptula, interview with author, tape-recording, Incirlik (Turkey), 14 August 1999; Deptula, interview, *Desert Story Collection*, 10 December 1991, p. 4; and Horner, interview with author, notes, London, 20 July 1999.
5. Glosson, interview, *Desert Story Collection*, 29 May 1991, p. 39; 31 May 1991, p. 114.
6. Davis, 'The Offensive Air Campaign Plan', p. 33; Clancy with Horner, *Every Man a Tiger*, pp. 265–7; and Glosson, interview, *Desert Story Collection*, 29 May 1991, pp. 23–5.
7. Horner, interview with author, notes, London, 20 August 1999; Horner, interview, *Desert Story Collection*, 4 March 1992, p. 15; Glosson, interview, *Desert Story Collection*, 4 June 1992, p. 31.
8. Glosson, interview, *Desert Story Collection*, 29 May 1991, p. 27.
9. Deptula, interview, *Desert Story Collection*, 10 December 1991, p. 4.
10. Glosson, interview, *Desert Story Collection*, 4 June 1992, pp. 5–9. Glosson did know of the TAC alternative, which stayed in a vault from 9 August 1990 until after the war.
11. Cohen *et al.*, *Gulf War Air Power Survey: Operations*, p. 29.
12. Glosson, interview, *Desert Story Collection*, 29 May 1991, pp. 29–38; and Robert M. Alexander, interview, *Desert Story Collection*, 3 June 1992, p. 55.
13. Deptula, interview, *Desert Story Collection*, 22 May 1991, p. 91; Glosson, interview, *Desert Story Collection*, 4 June 1992, p. 6; and Glosson, interview, *Desert Story Collection*, 29 May 1991, p. 47.
14. Glosson, personal journal, 23 August 1990, cited in Cohen *et al.*, *Gulf War Air Power Survey: Operations*, p. 28.
15. Michael A. Palmer, 'The Storm in the Air: One Plan, Two Air Wars?', *Air Power History* 39, No. 4 (Winter 1992), p. 27.
16. Gordon and Trainor, *The Generals' War*, p. 99, and James A. Winnefeld, Dana J. Johnson and Preston Niblack, *A League of Airmen: U.S. Air Power in the Gulf War* (Santa Monica, CA: RAND, 1994), p. 68.
17. Deptula, interview with author, tape-recording, Incirlik (Turkey), 14 August 1999; and Warden, *Desert Story Collection*, 10 December 1991, pp. 44–5.
18. Deptula, interview, *Desert Story Collection*, 22 May 1991, pp. 38–40.

19. Deptula, interview with author, tape-recording, Incirlik (Turkey), 14 August 1999.
20. Commander Daniel J. Muir, USN, 'A View from the Black Hole', *Proceedings* (October 1991), pp. 85–6.
21. Mandeles, Hone and Sanford, *Managing 'Command and Control' in the Persian Gulf War*, p. 123; Horner, interview with author, notes, London, 20 July 1999; and Deptula, interview with author, tape-recording, Incirlik (Turkey), 14 August 1999.
22. Warden, interview, *Desert Story Collection*, 10 December 1991, p. 8.
23. Glosson, interview, *Desert Story Collection*, 4 June 1992, p. 44.
24. Warden, interview, *Desert Story Collection*, 10 December 1991, p. 8.
25. Deptula, interview with author, tape-recording, Incirlik (Turkey), 14 August 1999; James V. Adams, interview, *Desert Story Collection*, 3 February 1992, p. 28; and Robert M. Alexander, interview, *Desert Story Collection*, 30 May 1991, p. 46.
26. Glosson, interview, *Desert Story Collection*, 29 May 1991, p. 40.
27. Ibid., p. 43; Warden, interview, *Desert Story Collection*, 30 May 1991; and Warden, interview, Tom Clancy, *Fighter Wing*, p. 49. During the early days of planning in the Black Hole Deptula would make sure that messages sent to, or received from, Checkmate, would not reveal Checkmate's role. Deptula, interview with author, tape-recording, Incirlik (Turkey), 14 August 1999.
28. Warden, interview, *Desert Story Collection*, 22 October 1991, p. 33.
29. Horner, interview with author, notes, London, 20 July 1999; and Deptula, interview with author, tape-recording, Incirlik (Turkey), 14 August 1999.
30. Glosson, interview, *Desert Story Collection*, 4 June 1992, p. 32.
31. Schwarzkopf to Secretary of Defense Richard Cheney, '*CINCENT'S INTENT*', briefing, 25 August 1990, cited in United States Department of Defense, *Conduct of the Persian Gulf War* (1992), p. 66.
32. Davis, 'The Offensive Air Campaign Plan', p. 45.
33. Putney, 'From Instant Thunder to Desert Storm', p. 44.
34. Davis, *Decisive Force*, p. 20.
35. Horner, interview with author, notes, London, 20 July 1999; and Deptula, interview with author, tape-recording, Incirlik (Turkey), 14 August 1999.
36. Horner, correspondence with author, transcript, 5 January 2000.
37. Putney, 'Planning the Air Campaign – the Washington Perspective', draft manuscript, p. 2.
38. Horner, interview, *Desert Story Collection*, 4 March 1992, p. 16; and Glosson, interview, *Desert Story Collection*, 29 May 1991, p. 51.
39. Horner, interview with author, notes, London, 20 July 1999; and Davis, 'The Offensive Air Campaign Plan', p. 37.
40. Gordon and Trainor, *The Generals' War*, p. 96; and Deptula, interview, *Desert Story Collection*, 22 May 1991, p. 148. See Glosson, interview, *Desert Story Collection*, 29 May 1991, p. 55.
41. Deptula, interview, *Desert Story Collection*, 10 December 1991, p. 10.
42. Horner, interview with author, notes, London, 20 July 1999; and Deptula, interview with author, tape-recording, Incirlik (Turkey), 14 August 1999.
43. Deptula, interview, *Desert Story Collection*, 22 May 1991, p. 137; and Horner, *Desert Story Collection*, 2 December 1991, p. 53.
44. Deptula, interview with author, tape-recording, Washington, DC, 11 March 1998; and Davis, interview with author, tape-recording, Washington, DC, 10 March 1998.
45. Cohen *et al.*, *Gulf War Air Power Survey: Planning*, p. 231.
46. Davis, 'The Offensive Air Campaign Plan', p. 5.
47. Warden, interview, *Desert Story Collection*, 30 May 1991, pp. 105–6; and Atkinson, *Crusade*, p. 276.

48. Deptula, 'Linking Strategy to Tactics in Air Campaign Planning: Perspective and Process', essay at National Defense University, National War College, 1994.
49. Glosson, interview, *Desert Story Collection*, 29 May 1991, p. 82.
50. Ibid., p. 82.
51. Ibid., 4 June 1992, pp. 67, 70; and Horner, 'The Air Campaign', *Military Review* 71, No. 9 (September 1991), p. 22.
52. OPORD 91-001, paragraph 3C, cited in Keaney and Cohen, *Gulf War Air Power Survey: Summary Report*, p. 40.
53. Ben Harvey, interview with James P. Coyne, 9 May 1991, cited in Coyne, *Airpower in the Gulf*, p. 44.
54. Warden to Schwarzkopf, 'Iraqi Air Campaign Instant Thunder', briefing, 17 August, p. 10.
55. COMUSCENTAF, Operations Order (OPORD), Offensive Campaign – Phase I, 2 Sept. 1990, pp. 3–4, cited in Keaney and Cohen, *Gulf War Air Power Survey: Summary Report*, p. 44.
56. Ibid., p. 46.
57. Ibid., p. 45.
58. Warden to Schwarzkopf, 'Iraqi Air Campaign Instant Thunder', briefing, 17 August, p. 23.
59. COMUSCENTAF, OPORD Offensive Campaign, 2 September, 1990, cited in Davis, 'The Offensive Air Campaign Plan', p. 1.
60. Glosson, interview, *Desert Story Collection*, 29 May 1991, pp. 54–6.
61. Ibid.
62. Schwarzkopf with Petre, *It Doesn't Take a Hero*, pp. 411–12; and Warden, interview, *Desert Story Collection*, 10 December 1991, p. 30. Note that Schwarzkopf still at this point referred to this as Instant Thunder, and that he referred to it as an expansion of the retaliatory scheme developed earlier.
63. Schwarzkopf with Petre, *It Doesn't Take a Hero*, p. 412.
64. Congress, Senate, Senator William S. Cohen speaking on the Crisis in the Persian Gulf Region: United States Policy Options and Implications to the Committee on Armed Services, S. Hrg. 101–1071, 101st Cong., 2nd sess., *Congressional Record*, pt. 44–5 (11 September 1990).
65. Ibid., pt. 52.
66. The debate received renewed attention with Dugan's September statement and would be the subject in the media throughout the crisis. See for example, H.D.S. Greenway, 'The Case For Airpower', *Boston Globe*, 16 December 1990; and Patrick Boyle and Richard C. Gross, 'Air vs. ground power: Debate continues', *Washington Times*, 18 January 1991.
67. Warden, telephone-interview with author, notes, 12 April 1999; and Deptula, interview with author, tape-recording, Incirlik (Turkey), 14 August 1999.
68. Glosson, interview, *Desert Story Collection*, 29 May 1991, p. 102.
69. Ibid., p. 57.
70. Ibid., p. 56.
71. Keaney and Cohen, *Revolution in Warfare?*, p. 5; and Les Aspin and William Dickinson, *Defense for a New Era: Lessons of the Persian Gulf War*, House of Armed Services Committee (New York: Brassey's, 1992), p. 90.
72. United States Department of Defense, *Conduct of the Persian Gulf War* (1992), p. 94; and Horner, interview, *Desert Story Collection*, 4 March 1992, p. 20.
73. General Michael Dugan, interviews in the *Washington Post* and the *Los Angeles Times*, 16 September 1990.
74. Melinda Beck, 'For the Air Force, It's the Big One', *Newsweek*, 1 October 1990, p. 11.

75. James V. Adams, interview, *Desert Story Collection*, 3 February 1992, p. 34.
76. Michael J. Dugan, interview, *Desert Story Collection*, 15 August 1991, pp. 24–5; Wayne Thompson, interview with author, tape-recording, Washington, DC, 1 March 1999; and Allan W. Howey, telephone interview with author, notes, 6 April 1999.
77. Warden, interview, *Desert Story Collection*, 10 December 1991, pp. 22–6.
78. Woodward, *The Commanders*, pp. 293–6; and Davis, 'The Offensive Air Campaign Plan', pp. 53–4.
79. Cohen *et al.*, *Gulf War Air Power Survey: Operations*, p. 27.
80. Les Aspin, *The Aspin Papers: Sanctions, Diplomacy, and War in the Persian Gulf* (Washington, DC: Centre for Strategic and International Studies, 1991), pp. 68–77; and John Barry, 'A Second Look at an Air War', *Newsweek*, 7 January 1991, p. 18.
81. Major General Royal N. Moore, *Los Angeles Times*, 17 September 1990. See also Colonel Norman G. Ewers, USMC (ret.), 'A Conversation With Lt Gen Royal N. Moore Jr.', *Marine Corps Gazette* (October 1991), pp. 44–9.
82. Deptula, interview, *Desert Story Collection*, 10 December 1991, p. 31.
83. Powell with Persico, *My American Journey*, p. 470.
84. Schwarzkopf with Petre, *It Doesn't Take a Hero*, p. 416. Powell told Schwarzkopf: 'Look, your air plan is coming together nicely, and the White House needs to be briefed on it. I also need to show the bosses what the ground plan looks like, even if it isn't complete.' See Powell with Persico, *My American Journey*, p. 470.
85. Glosson, interview, *Desert Story Collection*, 29 May 1991, p. 44.
86. Powell with Persico, *My American Journey*, p. 470.
87. Glosson, interview, *Desert Story Collection*, 29 May 1991, pp. 61–6.
88. Davis, 'The Offensive Air Campaign Plan', p. 55; and Scales, *Certain Victory*, pp. 127–8.
89. Glosson, interview, *Desert Story Collection*, 29 May 1991, p. 72; John M. Loh, interview, *Desert Story Collection*, 26 September 1991, pp. 41–2; and Horner, interview, *Desert Story Collection*, 4 March 1992, p. 16.
90. Gordon and Trainor, *The Generals' War*, p. 138; and Warden, interview, *Desert Story Collection*, 10 December 1991, p. 29.
91. Gordon and Trainor, *The Generals' War*, pp. 135–41.
92. Davis, 'The Offensive Air Campaign Plan', pp. 58–9.
93. Cohen *et al.*, *Gulf War Air Power Survey: Operations*, p. 29; and Davis, 'The Offensive Air Campaign Plan', p. 60.
94. Scales, *Certain Victory*, p. 128.
95. Putney, 'From Instant Thunder to Desert Storm', p. 48; and John M. Loh, interview, *Desert Story Collection*, 16 October 1991, pp. 75–6.
96. Glosson, interview, *Desert Story Collection*, 29 May 1991, p. 73.
97. Ibid.
98. Putney, 'From Instant Thunder to Desert Storm', p. 48; and Bush and Scowcroft, *A World Transformed*, p. 381.
99. Putney, 'Planning the Air Campaign – The Washington Perspective', pp. 6–7.
100. Powell with Persico, *My American Journey*, p. 471; and Schwarzkopf with Petre, *It Doesn't Take a Hero*, p. 419.
101. United States Department of Defense, *Conduct of the Persian Gulf War*, p. 67.
102. Davis, 'The Offensive Air Campaign Plan', p. 62.
103. Cohen *et al.*, *Gulf War Air Power Survey: Operations*, p. 45.
104. Horner, 'Desert Shield/Desert Storm', p. 6.
105. Allan W. Howey, telephone interview with author, notes, 6 April 1999.
106. Warden, interview, *Desert Story Collection*, 10 December 1991, p. 54.

107. Ibid., p. 56.
108. Bush and Scowcroft, *A World Transformed*, p. 382.
109. Ibid., p. 384.
110. Ibid.
111. Warden to Schwarzkopf, 'Iraqi Air Campaign Instant Thunder', briefing, 17 August, p. 13.
112. Kanan Makiya, *Republic of Fear: The Politics of Modern Iraq*, updated version with a new introduction (Berkeley, CA: University Press of California, 1998), p. xx.
113. Cohen *et al.*, *Gulf War Air Power Survey: Effects and Effectiveness*, p. 276; and Gordon and Trainor, *The Generals' War*, p. 99.
114. Putney, 'From Instant Thunder to Desert Storm', p. 48.
115. For an overview, see Lieutenant Commander Bruce A. Ross, United States Navy, 'The Case for Targeting Leadership in War', *Naval War College Review* 46, No. 4 (Winter 1993), pp. 73–93; and Ken Matthews, *The Gulf Conflict and International Relations* (London: Routledge, 1993), pp. 149–69.
116. Deptula, interview, *Desert Story Collection*, 1 November 1990, p. 2. (emphasis in original text).
117. Ibid., 12 December 1991, pp. 101–4.
118. Bush and Scowcroft, *A World Transformed*, pp. 386–7.
119. Woodward, *The Commanders*, pp. 313–14.
120. Powell with Persico, *My American Journey*, p. 475. When asked in Riyadh about air power on 19 December, Powell replied, 'airpower will be overwhelming, but in every war, it's the infantrymen who have to raise the flag of victory on the battlefield'. See Powell with Persico, *My American Journey*, p. 484.
121. George Bush allegedly replied: 'Okay, do it.' Bush and Scowcroft, *A World Transformed*, pp. 393–5; and Powell with Persico, *My American Journey*, p. 476.
122. United States Department of Defense, *Conduct of the Persian Gulf War* (1992), p. 19; Freedman and Karsh, *The Gulf Conflict 1990–1991*, pp. 201–4; and Gordon and Trainor, *The Generals' War*, p. 66.
123. Putney, 'Planning the Air Campaign – the Washington Perspective', draft manuscript, p.11.
124. RAND, Project Air Force, 'Gulf Crisis Analysis', 6 October 1990 (the unpublished report has been declassified and made available to the author).
125. Putney, interview with author, tape-recording, Washington, DC, 1 March 1998.
126. Wayne Thompson, discussion with author, notes, Washington, DC, 1 March 1999; and Cohen *et al.*, *Gulf War Air Power Survey: Planning*, p. 172.
127. Glosson, interview, *Desert Story Collection*, 29 May 1991, p. 69.
128. Ibid., p. 76.
129. Congress, Senate, Senator John McCain speaking on the Crisis in the Persian Gulf Region: United States Policy Options and Implications to the Committee on Armed Services, S. Hrg. 101–1071, 101st Cong., 2nd sess., *Congressional Record*, pt. 287 (28 November 1990).
130. Edward N. Luttwak, ibid. (28 November 1990), pt. 319.
131. Powell, ibid. (3 December 1990), pt. 663.
132. Deptula, interview, *Desert Story Collection*, 10 December 1991, p. 39.
133. Warden to Secretary of Defense Richard Cheney, briefing, 11 December 1990 (the slide has been made available to the author, and the substance – with slightly different wording, is reprinted in Gordon and Trainor, *The Generals' War*, p. 178).
134. Donald B. Rice, interview with author, tape-recording, Birmingham (England), 17 July 1999.
135. Mark B. Rogers, interview, *Desert Story Collection*, 3 June 1991, p. 100.
136. Deptula, 'Parallel Warfare', pp. 127–56. Note that the term was apparently

first used in March 1991 in a briefing Warden gave to Andy Marshall in Checkmate.

137. John M. Loh, interview, *Desert Story Collection*, 26 September 1991, pp. 41–2.
138. Ibid., 16 October 1991, pp. 49–51.
139. Ibid. and 26 September 1991, pp. 29–30.
140. Deptula, interview, *Desert Story Collection*, 23 May 1991, p. 2; and Edward C. Mann, correspondence with author, transcript, 19 September 1999.
141. Warden, interview, *Desert Story Collection*, 30 May 1991, pp. 88, 101–2; and Deptula, interview, *Desert Story Collection*, 23 May 1991, p. 81.
142. General John M. Loh, interview, *Desert Story Collection*, 26 September 1991, pp. 22–5. See also John Miller and Fred Shultz, interview with Lieutenant General (ret.) Thomas W. Kelly, *Proceedings* (September 1991), pp. 76–80.
143. Gordon and Trainor, *The Generals' War*, p. 187; and Donald B. Rice, interview with author, tape-recording, Birmingham (England), 17 July 1999.
144. General Merrill A. McPeak, USAF (ret.), 'Desert Storm: A Personal Memoir', *Aviation Week & Space Technology* 146, No. 15 (16 April 1997), p. 64.
145. David A. Fulghum, 'Glosson: U.S. Gulf War Shortfalls Linger', *Aviation and Week Technology* 144, No. 5 (29 January 1996), p. 61.
146. James V. Adams, interview, *Desert Story Collection*, 3 February 1992, pp. 22, 41.
147. Halberstam, *War in a Time of Peace*, p. 49.
148. James V. Adams, interview, *Desert Story Collection*, 3 February 1992, p. 19.
149. Warden, interview with Major David S. Fadok, cited in Fadok, *John Boyd and John A. Warden: Air Power's Quest for Strategic Paralysis* (Maxwell Air Force Base, AL: Air University Press, 1995), p. 23.
150. Warden, interview, *Desert Story Collection*, 30 May 1991, p. 103; Robert M. Alexander, interview, *Desert Story Collection*, 3 June 1992, p. 61; and John M. Loh, interview, *Desert Story Collection*, 16 October 1991, p. 62.
151. Warden, interview, *Desert Story Collection*, 30 May 1991, p. 103.
152. Ibid., p. 108.
153. Ibid., p. 91.
154. Robert M. Alexander, interview, *Desert Story Collection*, 3 June 1992, p. 60; and Lieutenant Colonel Allan W. Howey, 'Checkmate Journal: The Gulf War Air Campaign From Inside the Pentagon', CAFH Working Papers, Center for Air Force History Air Staff Division, p. 63.
155. John M. Loh, interview, *Desert Story Collection*, 16 October 1991, p. 52; and Robert M. Alexander, interview, *Desert Story Collection*, 3 June 1992, p. 59.
156. Warden, interview, *Desert Story Collection*, 10 December 1991, p. 14.
157. Ibid., 30 May 1991, p. 94.
158. John M. Loh, interview, *Desert Story Collection*, 16 October 1991, p. 63.
159. Donald B. Rice, interview, *Desert Story Collection, Desert Story Collection*, 11 December 1991, p. 9.
160. Allan W. Howey, 'Checkmate Journal', pp. 25, 35; and Warden, correspondence with author, transcript, 15 September 1999.
161. Warden, interview with author, 4 June 2002.
162. William M. Arkin, www.thestarsandstrips.com/arkin/secret/weekseven.shtml
163. Allan W. Howey, 'Checkmate Journal', p. 24.
164. Warden, correspondence with author, transcript, 15 September 1999.
165. Robert M. Alexander, interview, *Desert Story Collection*, 30 May 1991, pp. 53, 63; Warden, telephone interview with author, notes, 12 April 1999; Warden, interview, *Desert Story Collection*, 30 May 1991, p. 89; and Allan W. Howey, telephone interview with author, notes, 6 April 1999.
166. Warden, interview, *Desert Story Collection*, 30 May 1991, pp. 88–9; Warden,

interview, *Desert Story Collection*, 10 December 1991, p. 20; and Warden, telephone interview with author, notes, 12 April 1999.

167. James W. Canan, 'Lesson Number One', *Air Force Magazine* 74, No. 10 (October 1991), p. 26.
168. Warden, 'Airpower in the Gulf', p. 15.
169. Deptula, interview, *Desert Story Collection*, 10 December 1991, p. 36.
170. Congress, Senate, General Colin Powell speaking on the Crisis in the Persian Gulf Region (3 December 1990), pt. 662.
171. Ibid.
172. Allan W. Howey, 'Checkmate Journal', p. 33.
173. John M. Loh, interview, *Desert Story Collection*, 16 October 1991, pp. 64–5.
174. Robert M. Alexander, interview, *Desert Story Collection*, 3 June 1992, pp. 61–2.
175. Donald B. Rice, interview with author, tape-recording, Birmingham (England), 17 July 1999.
176. Reynolds in Perry Smith, interview, *Desert Story Collection*, 18 June 1992, p. 17.
177. Perry Smith, interview, *Desert Story Collection*, 18 June 1992, pp. 5–6.
178. Ibid., pp. 4–5, 36, 44.
179. Warden, interview, *Desert Story Collection*, 10 December 1991, p. 87.
180. Cohen *et al.*, *Gulf War Air Power Survey: Operations*, p. 47.
181. 'Combined OPLAN for Defense of Saudi Arabia', 29 November 1990, p. 6, cited in Cohen *et al.*, *Gulf War Air Power Survey: Planning*, p. 134.
182. George Bush, 'Responding to Iraqi Aggression in the Gulf', National Security Directive (NSD) 54, 17 January 1991, paragraph 2. The document is available on the internet: www.washingtonpost.com under 'war goals'.
183. Ibid.
184. Ibid., paragraph 3.
185. OPORD 91-001, p. 9, cited in General Accounting Office (GAO), 'Operation Desert Storm: Evaluation of the Air Campaign', *GAO/NSIAD-97-134*, Appendix 5; and Cohen *et al.*, *Gulf War Air Power Survey: Effect and Effectiveness*, p. 93.
186. OPORD 91-001, cited in Cohen *et al.*, *Gulf War Air Power Survey: Effect and Effectiveness*, p. 94.
187. OPORD 91-001, p. 9, cited in GAO, 'Operation Desert Storm', Appendix 5.
188. Ibid.
189. Cohen *et al.*, *Gulf War Air Power Survey: Planning*, p. 145.
190. Glosson, interview, *Desert Story Collection*, 4 June 1992, p. 28.
191. Deptula, interview with author, tape-recording, Incirlik (Turkey) 14 August 1999.
192. Deptula, interview, *Desert Story Collection*, 11 December 1991, p. 25.
193. Deptula, interview with author, tape-recording, Incirlik (Turkey) 14 August 1999.
194. Mandeles, Hone and Sanford, *Managing 'Command and Control' in the Persian Gulf War*, p. 151.
195. The plan underwent no 'philosophical or conceptual' changes. See Deptula, interview, *Desert Story Collection*, 22 May 1991, pp. 36–8.
196. There is consensus on this point among Horner, Deptula and Warden: Deptula, interview with author, tape-recording, Washington, DC, 11 March 1998; Horner, interview with author, notes, London, 20 July 1999; and Warden, interview, *Desert Story Collection*, 30 May 1991, p. 110.
197. Deptula, interview, *Desert Story Collection*, 10 December 1991, pp. 45–7.
198. Horner, interview, *Desert Story Collection*, 4 March 1992, p. 21.
199. Glosson, interview 23 July 1991, cited in Michael A. Palmer, 'The Storm in the Air: One Plan, Two Air Wars?', p. 30.

200. Swain, *'Lucky War': Third Army in Desert Storm*, pp. 182, 214.
201. Warden, interview, *Desert Story Collection*, 10 December 1991, p. 102.
202. Ibid., 22 October 1991, pp. 116–17.
203. 'Schwarzkopf: 'I Got a Lot of Guff'', *Newsweek*, 11 March 1991, p. 20.
204. Horner, interview, *Desert Story Collection*, 10 December 1991, pp. 45–7.
205. Deptula, interview with author, tape-recording, Incirlik (Turkey) 14 August 1999.
206. Edward C. Mann, correspondence with author, transcript, 19 September 1999.
207. Robert M. Alexander, interview, *Desert Story Collection*, 2 December 1991, p. 61.
208. Edward N. Luttwak, correspondence with author, 15 November 2000.
209. Robert D. Russ, interview, *Desert Story Collection*, 9 December 1991, p. 48.
210. General Merrill McPeak stated this in 1991 according to Colonel Richard T. Reynolds, correspondence with author, transcript, 10 September 1999. See also Lieutenant Colonel Suzanne B. Gehri in Major General (ret.) Perry Smith, transcript of interview with Lieutenant Colonels Suzanne B. Gehri and Richard T. Reynolds, *Desert Story Collection*, 18 June 1992, p. 99. See also Lieutenant Colonel (ret.) Barry Watts 'Doctrine, Technology and Air Warfare', in Hallion (ed.), *Air Power Confronts an Unstable World*, p. 41.
211. Mann, *Thunder and Lightning*, p. 19.
212. Horner, interview, in *Desert Story Collection*, 4 March 1992, p. 31.
213. Keaney and Cohen, *Gulf War Air Power Survey: Summary Report*, pp. 66, 70.

4

The Target State:
The Iraqi Regime's Political
Power Structure

In order to gauge the effectiveness of the strategic air campaign one has to examine the inner workings of the Iraqi regime, which the air planners sought to paralyse. Herein lie a number of related problems. The mission of the campaign was to 'isolate and incapacitate', but key members of the Black Hole and Checkmate teams believed that intense and focused air operations against the Baghdad leadership and its ability to communicate would facilitate Saddam Hussein's departure from power by either coup or popular revolt.[1] This unofficial objective, once revealed after the war, invited obvious criticism and accusation of failure that was impossible to brush aside. The strategic air campaign presented, nevertheless, an opportunity to overthrow a compromised and detested regime, but for a number of reasons this opportunity was not used by Coalition forces. In the meantime, Iraqi opposition that rose in the revolt, enabled in part by the air campaign, was massacred in the tens of thousands by a vengeful regime.

In part such a situation came about because of limited knowledge regarding the political power structure of Iraq, and its vulnerability to either coup d'état or uprising. The Coalition did not understand how the Iraqi regime functioned, and importantly, as will be demonstrated, the structure of the regime did not lend itself to collapse through the use of air power. Military studies have devoted little attention to this matter, while studies on orders of battle and main force operations are plentiful.[2] In this case there is also another factor at work: the secret nature of the Iraqi regime. There was the state system, which was duplicated at every level by a party organisation, while within both, but also separated from both at different levels, was a system of personal, family, clan and regional loyalties that provided the lubricant of the system. This ensured Saddam's personal power base. The combination of formal and informal structures renders any attempt to analyse the air offensive fraught with difficulty, but a proper understanding of the subversive potential of air power in this conflict cannot be attained unless there is an examination, in some detail, of the system that the strategic air campaign sought to dissect.

The first challenge in understanding the Iraqi system is to set aside Western ideas of democratic form and practice, in particular the idea of the separation of power, which do not apply in this case. Saddam's reliance upon violence, both personal and institutional, had reached an unprecedented dimension by the late 1980s. The basis for understanding the strategic air campaign and its effectiveness resides in an examination first of the personality of Saddam Hussein and then the political power which was the basis of his personal authority and rule in 1990–91. Rather than dealing with the latter in successive layers, one would identify five pillars of establishment – instruments of personal power. These were the formal state or government structure and organisation; the state security and intelligence networks that stood apart from the formal state structure; the military, which again was separated from the state system; the Ba'ath Party structure and organisation; and what may be termed an informal kinship system. These institutions and arrangements, which collectively amounted to the Iraqi leader's 'centre of gravity', overlapped, and in their various layers provided the system with redundancy and unprecedented powers of endurance. This explains, in part, the personal and institutional survival of Saddam and his regime in 1991 (see Figure 4).[3]

Figure 4: Saddam Hussein's Five Instruments of Power

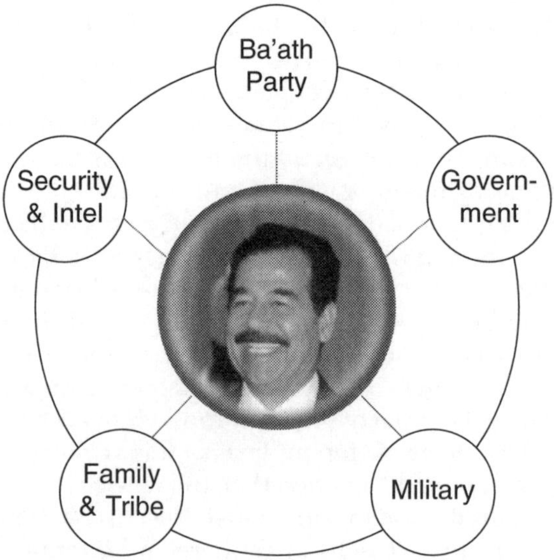

Drawn by Christian Wattengård.

A PROFILE OF SADDAM HUSSEIN

Efraim Karsh and Inari Rautsi have argued that Saddam Hussein, much like Thomas Hobbes in *Leviathan*, perceived the world as a fierce and hostile place in which self-preservation ruled:

> In the permanently beleaguered mind of Saddam Hussein, politics is a ceaseless struggle for survival. The ultimate goal of staying alive, and in power, justifies all means. Plots lurk around every corner. Nobody is trustworthy. Everybody is an actual or potential enemy. One must remain constantly on alert, making others cower so that they do not attack, always ready to kill before being killed ... he made his way to the premier position by purging actual and potential rivals for the leadership, and forging *ad hoc* alliances only to break them at the most suitable moment, betraying friends and foes alike.[4]

Within this Hobbesian framework, several mutually reinforcing features amount to the alleged characteristics of Saddam Hussein's conspiratorial and analytical mindset.[5] They also reflect the negative and demonised image of Saddam, which has become so popular in the Western world.[6] At the other end of the spectrum there are a couple of official biographies that more or less glorify the Iraqi leader,[7] as do to a large extent the Iraqi state-controlled media. It is, consequently, difficult to find the middle ground as the man has become increasingly surrounded by myths.[8] This study suggests that Saddam trusted nobody, that he always gave priority to internal security matters, and that although he miscalculated his adversaries several times in pursuing grand strategic gambits, he was both a rational and calculating decision-maker.

Saddam was born to Subha Tulfah al-Masallat and her second cousin Hussein al-Majid Abd al-Ghafur on 28 April 1937 in a poor family of al-Bu Nasir in the Ouja village, 5 kilometres outside Tikrit, a historic albeit impoverished town on the Tigris River, 100 miles north of Baghdad. Saddam literally means someone who confronts or clashes, and the mere connotation of physical strength and violence indicates that he belonged to the lower echelons of tribal society. The family had to settle for a confined and unsanitary mud-brick dwelling, which was basically one room with an attached shed that they had to share with their animals, most likely a donkey and a couple of sheep.[9] The people of Tikrit and the tribe of al-Bu Nasir were, according to Said K. Aburish 'known as a difficult lot of people, cunning and secretive, whose poverty drove most of them to pervert the Bedouins' legendary qualities of being warlike and fearless into dishonesty, theft and violence'.[10] Allegedly, the Tikritis upheld the tradition of nomadic Arab societies where they eliminated their enemies to demonstrate resolve. The tribal bonds and affiliations were strong and further strengthened through intermarriage. Saddam's father, Hussein al-Majid, died before Saddam was born, and Subha married a distant relative from the same sub-tribal unit, Ibrahim Hasan, an illiterate peasant. Saddam lived with his maternal uncle, Khair Allah Tulfah, in Tikrit, until he turned three, possibly because his mother tried to abort him, but thereafter he returned to her in Ouja. Used by his stepfather as a shepherd rather than being sent to school, Saddam grew up in the violent surroundings of Ouja and Tikrit. Teased persistently for not growing up with a biological father and cursed with an ambivalent relationship with Ibrahim Hasan, Saddam, not altogether surprisingly, developed a somewhat bitter and introvert personality. The only strong emotional bond that he developed seems to have been with his mother. She was allegedly an outspoken woman who attended family meetings normally reserved for men and refused to 'keep herself under lock and key'.[11]

Determined to improve his life, Saddam at the age of 10 moved back to Khair Allah Tulfah, a nationalist who had fought the British during the Second World War and spent time in prison for those actions. Khair Allah was a schoolteacher with a keen interest in history and politics, two themes that greatly inspired Saddam. Khair Allah believed that pan-Arabism could only materialise through a strong Iraq,[12] and his selection of historical heroes can hardly have been coincidental: Nebuchadnezzar was the King of Babylon who conquered Jerusalem in 586 BC,[13] and Saladin was a Tikriti who conquered the same historic city in 1187 by defeating the Crusaders. The new household took care of Saddam, and as they moved from Tikrit to Baghdad's working-class district of al-Kharkh in the early 1950s he quickly developed a considerable drive for politics and power.[14] The district was a mixture of Sunni and Shia Muslims, and it seems as if this was Saddam's first contact with the latter. Khair Allah's hatred for Shia Muslims, whom he considered not to be true Arabs, probably influenced Saddam's young mind. Although some 60 per cent of the Iraqis were Shia Muslims, the country's political life was to a large extent governed by Sunni Arabs located in the fertile triangle between Baghdad, Ar-Ramadi and Samarra. At the heart of this Sunni Triangle lay Greater Tikrit and the area to which Saddam was disposed in his childhood and youth.

The 1950s were turbulent years in Iraq as they were in the Middle East in general, and Saddam increasingly participated in demonstrations and riots against the pro-British government. Having been turned down at the Military Academy, possibly because of his uncle's political past, but more likely because of an insufficient academic background, he was determined to gain rank in the Ba'ath Party, identifying with the pan-Arab cause of Gamal Abd al-Nasser.[15] By the second half of the decade he was a student leader, carrying a handgun and organising riots. The popular 14 July 1958 coup turned Iraq into a republic, and although the Ba'ath Party appreciated the fall of King Faysal II and his regime, it would soon try to replace its new leader, Abd al-Karim Qassem. The rise of Brigadier Qassem, who became Prime Minister and Minister of Defence, but never President, marked the end of the Arab Hashemite Federation of Iraq and Jordan. Qassem genuinely rejected the idea of the United Arab Republic of Egypt and Syria, finding himself in opposition to Ba'ath Party members who believed in the pan-Arab plans of Nasser. Qassem explored the notion of Iraqi patriotism (*wataniya Iraqiya*), and for the time it seemed to be at the expense of Arab nationalism (*qawmiya Arabiya*).[16] As the two parties were unable to reconcile, the 22-year-old Saddam participated in a poorly organised attempt to assassinate Qassem on 7 October 1959. The coup failed, and as Saddam was wounded, taking a bullet in his leg, he fled to Syria. During a three-month period in Damascus he met Michel Aflaq, the Christian co-founder of the Ba'ath Party, who thought highly of the determined and persistent Tikriti. By the end of the year, thanks to Aflaq's contacts and his own Tikriti family affiliations, Saddam became a full member (*aduw'amil*) of the Party.

He spent the next three years in Cairo as an exile, partly supported by President Abd al-Nasser, and in 1963 he returned to Iraq, following the Ba'ath coup that toppled Qassem. Between 1963 and 1968 Saddam proved himself as an efficient organiser within the Party: he worked late hours, had an eye for detail and an immense ability to get things done. He rose quickly to an influential position, and at the age of 31 he had a prominent role in the July coup of 1968, when the Ba'ath Party managed to topple the Aref regime that had come to power on 8 February 1963.[17] Khair Allah Tulfah, Saddam's uncle, foster father and mentor, convinced the new President, Ahmad Hasan al-Bakr, his own distant relative, that in order to stay in power one needed to be supported by one's own family. Khair Allah pointed out that the Kuwaiti, Saudi Arabian and Iranian monarchies had remained strong because the sovereigns had brought their own families to government and power. This furthermore, had been, the strength of the Arefs and the weakness of Qassem. Since Saddam was al-Bakr's relative from the same region and tribe, and a devoted Party supporter, the choice for a deputy was easy.[18] According to Salah Umar al-Ali, a Tikriti and former senior party member, Ahmed Hasan al-Bakr followed this advice and selected his hard-working relative as his closest aid.[19]

Saddam became known as 'Lord Deputy' (*al-Sayyed al-Na'eb*), a reference that has a connotation of being a descendant of the Prophet, but within three years he was recognised as the de facto number one man in the country.[20] The Iraqi Petroleum Company was nationalised in June 1972 and as oil revenues skyrocketed following the 1973 Arab–Israeli

War, the new Ba'ath regime was associated with economic prosperity, providing for a considerable degree of political viability. Most Iraqis witnessed improved living standards as some 4,000 villages were equipped with electricity, and even poor regions received access to commodities such as refrigerators and television sets, on which they could see President Bakr and his young and energetic Deputy.[21] Saddam went further by paying close attention to economic development in general, preferring a market economy to collectivisation, and providing women with education. Major programmes for social welfare were issued and the infrastructure improved with impressive speed. In essence, the 1970s proved to be a stabilising period for a country that previously had seemed tormented with chronic economic difficulties and problems of internal stability. Saddam used television cleverly for propaganda purposes, emphasising what he had done for the people, and what he would do for them in the future. He soon appeared everywhere, spending time in villages to which he came unannounced, presenting himself as a caring leader who understood the common Iraqi. He was quickly perceived as an intelligent man, quoting from Arab poets, discussing all kinds of issues with journalists and academics alike in a relaxed manner, and with a dose of good humour.[22] 'Lord Deputy' became the Ba'ath Party's representative for negotiations and he soon showed considerable diplomatic talent, as he signed treaties with the Kurds in March 1970, with Moscow in 1972, and with Iran in March 1975 (the Algiers Accord).[23] The latter settled for the moment the dispute over Shat al-Arab, the 60-mile waterway formed by the confluence of the Tigris and the Euphrates as they flow into the Gulf. The 1970s was indeed a prosperous period for the Iraqi state, and Saddam Hussein became the very symbol of a dynamic and modern leadership.

Saddam's ability to work patiently and methodically, combined with an extraordinary memory, perhaps a photographic one, gave him a strong platform on which to realise his quest for power and recognition. The new regime, with al-Bakr as the front-figure and Saddam working behind the scenes, managed to gain strict control of intractable political and economic matters that beset the country. While other regimes in the region gave priority to palaces and luxury, Saddam spent most of his resources on developing security forces in the early 1970s, constituting a domestic power base. He also assumed responsibility for the state security system, and within a decade he made it the means whereby he was able to consolidate absolute personal power within the Iraqi political system.

The reason for such a development, specifically the switch from seeking to secure the power base through economic reform and programmes to a policy of ensuring personal rule and security through the police state system, was not hard to find. Saddam had witnessed the brutal overthrow of the monarchy, the successor, Qassem, being un-mercifully ousted, and next the Aref regime being toppled. These events served to convince Saddam that the ultimate purpose of political power was personal survival. To Saddam there was no substitute for personal security. In order to survive he relied on the strategy of divide-and-rule, combined with terror and repression, and therein commitment and loyalty were matters of circumstance, and circumstances changed. In order to strengthen his own position he made concessions when he was weak only to break them when he was strong, be it on an individual or institutional basis. In less than two weeks after having seized power in 1968 he managed to get rid of two of the officers who had made the coup possible in the first place (General Ibrahim Abd al-Rahman al-Daud and Colonel Abd al-Razzaq al-Nayif). The 1970 agreement with the Kurds has still to be implemented, and the critical Algiers Accord was announced as invalid immediately before the invasion of Iran, only to be acknowledged again on 15 August 1990 in order to transfer troops from the Iranian border to Kuwait. As for the subject of democracy in Iraq, Saddam Hussein stated that 'nowhere in the region did the regime come to power by way of democracy and Iraq is no exception'.[24] In an interview with Diane Sawyer, on 24 June 1990, he retrospectively revealed that he was surprised that no measures were taken against those who insulted the US President.[25] Moreover, according to Mohamed Heikal, the Iraqi leader showed a peculiar ruthlessness and almost calculated cruelty when he argued that 'we don't need proof' in order to execute, 'suspicion is enough'.[26] Saddam for his part defended his autocratic style of leadership by arguing that nothing else could keep such a vast and diverse nation united. By 1979 Saddam felt ready for the presidency, and the popular Ahmed al-Bakr announced his resig-nation quietly, supposedly for health reasons.

Saddam's thirst for power was undoubtedly driven by the glory that would necessarily follow. In a rare interview given to Fuad Matar he compared himself not only to leaders such as V. I. Lenin, Gamal Abd al-Nasser, Charles de Gaulle, Mao Tse Tung, Ho Chi Minh and Josef Tito, but also with Nebuchadnezzar, Saladin and the Arab conqueror Saad Ibn al-Waqqas.[27] Although Nebuchadnezzar was not an Arab, but a Babylonian king, Saddam 'Arabised' him, and thus by the late 1970s he was regarded as both an Iraqi and an Arab.[28] Inspired by his foster-father the Iraqi leader adhered to the Orwellian dictum of 'Who controls the past controls the future: who controls the present controls the past.' An example of the regime fabricating its identity into history is the 1988 restoration of the ruins of the ancient city of Babylon. New layers of bricks were built *over* the foundations and the inscription now reads that these are the ancient ruins of Babylon 'restored during the time of Saddam Hussayn of Iraq'.[29] Saddam developed an obsession for history, or at least a very selective historical view that stressed past Arab glories, and within this context he convinced himself that foreign imperialism, whether Persian, Zionist or generally from the Western world, was the constant and implacable enemy of pan-Arab aspirations.[30] There is little doubt that in starting the war with Iran in 1980 Saddam saw himself as the defender of the Arab nations against their historic enemy from the plateau, and thus in a direct line of succession that reached back through time from Nasser to Nebuchadnezzar. Authors and artists were given prizes for comparing him to great Arab leaders of the past,[31] and by the end of the war with Iran Saddam Hussein was convinced that he was on a messianic mission. At the Arab Summit in May 1990, General Khaled bin Sultan noted that 'Saddam Hussein behaved as the master, addressing other Arab leaders as if they were his inferiors. He was condescending. You could see that he did not consider the assembled Kings and Presidents to be his equal.'[32]

Apparently by the late 1980s Saddam Hussein had come to believe that he was in close contact with God. After the invasion of Kuwait he declared that it had been God's decision, and his mission was only to carry through God's wishes.[33] He even inscribed the Iraqi flag with 'Allah is Great' one day before the bombing commenced, supposedly a duplicate of his own handwriting. The propaganda aspect of such statements is obvious, but it is difficult to resist the idea that, at least in part, there was more than an element of self-fulfilment in them and that they also reflected years of self-inflicted isolation from reality at the top of the Iraqi political system. Although Saddam identified himself with the poor Iraqis in the early 1970s, as he became ever more successful he seems to have become increasingly dismissive of their wishes, and throughout the 1980s he became even more inclined to use his security apparatus against the Iraqi people. Horrific events that bring such matters to mind were the gassing of some 5,000 Kurds and the killing of another 100,000 throughout 1988. In addition to 'the Anfal campaigns' large 'resettling programmes' had affected Kurds for more than a decade. Shias, too, painfully witnessed systematic mass deportations to Iran.

Certainly, after the early 1980s Saddam surrounded himself with sycophants who were cowed by the Iraqi leader's reputation for brutality.[34] In 1982 the Minister of Health, Riyadh Ibrahim, was shot by Saddam during a Cabinet meeting for having failed in his duties.[35] While there are many stories of the Iraqi leader as the judge, jury and executioner, it forms a popular image of the Iraqi leader that he does not seem to mind. Indeed, he seemed to relish the Machiavellian view that if one cannot rule through popularity, then one must rule through fear. To Saddam, criticism of his leadership equalled disloyalty, and with his notorious reputation for ruthlessness nobody had the courage to contradict him. Although he often consulted individuals and members of the more important state and party organisations, as soon as he had made up his mind there were few who dared oppose him.[36] Within the elite, Saddam's decisions were therefore either endorsed in public, or members took a more extreme stand to be on the safe side.[37] In other words, the officers carefully refrained from providing him with their professional advice, and at the same time, to avoid looking tedious in front of their comrades, their replies were borrowed from the world of mythology and pretended faith in the leader's omnipotence and omniscience. According to a former lecturer at the Iraqi Military Academy, Ghassan Attiya, when Saddam Hussein asked his council what it believed he should do regarding the UN ultimatum on 'immediate and unconditional withdrawal from Kuwait', one member stated: 'I can see victory, it is written in your eyes', while another said 'Mr. President, I saw you in my dream. You were victorious on your white horse.'[38]

Over the years Saddam came to believe in many of the myths he had created and consequently he perceived himself as a modern day prophet. More importantly, he came to believe that he was the saviour of the Iraqis and the Arabs, and, moreover, destined to rule. The effect was that decision-making in Iraq was in the hands of a leader who received selective and distorted information. This manifested itself during the occupation of Kuwait, where he did not comprehend the consequences of the invasion, and he did not know how bad the situation was during the air campaign until the Russian envoy, Yevgeny Primakov, showed him pictures of the bombing in mid February 1991.[39] Neither did Saddam realise that morale was extremely low in the military ranks, as any commander admitting to that would be held responsible and punishment would follow.[40] The low morale never turned into a forceful opposition, however. Part of the explanation resides in the fact that he was successful in methodically combining terror with inducement – what the Arabs call *tarhib* and *targhib*: those who chose to commit themselves to his cause were rewarded by positions within the party or financial incentives, while those who opposed him were often imprisoned, tortured or killed for 'treason'.[41]

Although a brilliant manipulator and organiser of domestic politics, and not without a considerable amount of charisma, diplomatic skill and genuine popular support at the time, Saddam clearly had a limited understanding of politics outside the Arab world. According to Saudi Arabian Ambassador Ghazi A. Algosaibi, Saddam believed that in terms of effectiveness and resolution, President Bush was to be found somewhere between Carter and Reagan.[42] Carter was deemed to have been reluctant to impose even economic sanctions on perceived belligerents, while even the hawkish Reagan did not go beyond the dispatching of warships or possibly air raids in reprisal – as had been the case with

Libya in 1986. Since even the latter would withdraw when faced with casualties, as was the case with Lebanon in 1983, Saddam Hussein and his Arab counterparts believed Washington was a 'paper tiger' that would not be able to sustain a war.[43] Consequently, surrounded by flattery and self-abasement, Saddam came to suffer from a flawed perception of political realities. Additionally, according to Saad al-Bazzaz, a former editor-in-chief of *al-Jumhuriya*, much of the Iraqi leader's decision-making was based on political instinct rather than 'political knowledge, expertise and reasoning'. He refers to this as 'instinctracy' – 'a certain feeling of instinct in which hopes mingle with expectations and the attempt to personify figures of old times or repeat events as they were hundreds or thousands of years ago'.[44]

Moreover, coupled with this instinct, Saddam had a profound feeling of being persecuted, to the extent that he had a strongly suspicious mindset. Not altogether surprisingly, such views of history and instincts went hand in hand with acute suspicion and a sense of persecution which seems to have developed over time. The immediate manifestation of such developments was obvious: he personalised domestic and foreign issues. As such, Kuwait's indifference to Iraq's desperate economic situation amounted to personal hostility and humiliation that justified self-defence.[45] Saddam was convinced that the United States, Britain, Iran and Israel were involved in a conspiracy to overthrow the Iraqi regime and eliminate him. Kuwait's economic policy of overproduction and low oil prices was to Saddam an untimely provocation that was encouraged, or at least supported, by other countries. These ideas were published in a pamphlet preceding the invasion of Kuwait.[46] The paper cited the Irangate documents as evidence that the alleged conspiracy was orchestrated by then Vice President George Bush. According to the paper, when Iraq emerged victorious against Iran the conspiracy shifted from military to economic warfare: British Prime Minister Margaret Thatcher joined Bush, and in seeking the economic destruction of Iraq they allegedly recruited various Gulf states. Thus, Bush and Thatcher seized upon the invasion of Kuwait as an excuse to implement sanctions which had already been agreed upon. According to Tariq Aziz, perhaps the most famous mouthpiece of Saddam:

> The decision we took in August 1990 was a defensive decision ... We were pushed into a fatal struggle in the sense of a struggle in which your fate will be decided. You will either be hit inside your house and destroyed, economically and militarily. Or you go outside and attack the enemy in one of his bases [Kuwait]. We had to do that, we had no choice, we had no other choice. Iraq was designated by George Bush for destruction, with or without Kuwait. Inside Kuwait or outside. Before the 2nd of August or after the 2nd of August.[47]

One may question the credibility of such comments, but it should be recognised that Saddam and his leadership strongly believed in conspiracy theories. The Iraqi leader personally knew the art almost to perfection as it had been his means to power in the first place, and when the regional and international communities condemned the Iraqi invasion without hesitation such belief was strengthened. As mentioned earlier, the polarisation of the Middle East after the June 1967 War undermined Arab beliefs in diplomatic solutions, and especially after eight years of war with Iran and two decades of domestic brutality, an invasion of Kuwait with the intention of installing a puppet regime was not perceived as too extreme from Saddam's point of view.

Although Saddam was driven by dreams of glory, and his political perspective was narrow and distorted, he was a shrewd tactician with the ability to adapt.[48] It is not by chance that the Iraqi leader remains in power as one enters a new century. Most importantly, Saddam has never possessed a Masada complex; as he remains the quintessential survivor.[49] He has always given priority to one day at a time, and over the years he developed excellent skills for immediate domestic problems, albeit at the expense of long-term planning. Saddam has always been a first-rate *tactician*, but his *strategic* vision has sometimes been called into question.[50] According to former Iraqi Colonel Hamed Salem al-Zyadi, Saddam Hussein neither had a long-term strategy for defeating Iran in 1980 nor had he thought through the question of what might happen after the occupation of Kuwait.[51] One should not, however, underestimate Saddam's ability to think and act strategically. It could be argued that his strategic plan on Iran was rather clear: he intended to overrun the Khuzestan lowlands, specifically the coastal areas behind Abadan and Khorramshahr, before moving against Dezful. The strategic goal was unrealistic, partly because Saddam had limited knowledge of his own army's capability,[52] but failure of strategy does not equal lack of strategic goals. The Iraqi leader, nevertheless, clearly had limitations as a military strategist, but as a propagandist, viewed from the Iraqi and Arab masses, he was indeed successful. He showed great political creativity when he allowed Iraqi women to take an important part in the labour force during the war with Iran in order to maintain the appearance of a peace-time economy, and next, non-Iraqis were given considerable accommodation as foreign workers, another act that secured popularity among the Arab masses. He opened the door for non-Iraqis to join his armed forces and explored the latent need among Arabs to realise their Arab identity. By developing slogans and gradually superimposing himself onto the notion of Arabness, he came to identify himself as the reincarnation of the great Arab cause. By the end of the 1980s pictures, posters and symbols of Saddam were omnipresent: he was the war-fighting general, the Bedouin sheikh and the statesman who discussed politics in an expensive suit. Billboards, posters and statues of the Iraqi President adorn Baghdad's street corners, traffic circles, hotel lobbies and restaurants. However hypocritical, such propaganda worked for the time being, at least on non-Iraqi Arabs only too willing to see him as a knight in shining armour riding in the distance on his white Arab stallion, promising them the world. In the months that led up to the war of 1991, Saddam did in fact display qualities that still make him adored in parts of the Arab world. On the streets of Arab cities he is admired as a leader who dared to defy and challenge Israel and the West, a symbol of Arab steadfastness in the face of Western aggression. It is all the more important to realise, therefore, that Saddam was never possessed of principle or policy: he was concerned only with power and his personal security.[53] In such a context, defeat in a foreign war, even in a war with the United States, was probably of less account than loss of face before his own Iraqi people.[54]

One might conclude that in addition to a thirst for personal power, the Iraqi leader had an obsession with symbolic greatness combined with a selective reading of history. Saddam Hussein clearly had a persecution complex and a suspicious mind, founded in a strongly held Anglo-American–Zionist conspiracy theory. As a result, suspicion governed his agenda, but although willing to gamble on the destiny of the Iraqi people he would never jeopardise his personal security. As a quintessential survivor with extraordinary tactical skills, he had a notorious reputation for killing the bearer of bad news. Consequently, surrounded by 'yes-men', he came to believe that he was on a messianic mission, and his narrow and distorted view of the outside world would transcend the wider decision-making process.

The Black Hole and Checkmate air planners were therefore correct in identifying Saddam as the heart of the problem presented by the occupation of Kuwait. Saddam had complete control and he was the only one who could make concessions. Indeed, Saddam Hussein's cousin, Ali Hasan al-Majid, summarised a general perception when he proclaimed in October 1991 that 'Iraq is Saddam; Saddam is Iraq',[55] reminding his countrymen of Ludwig XIV's '*L'Etat c'est moi.*' At least since 1979 the personality cult of the leader has influenced most aspects of Iraqi life, and decision-making has been highly centralised in the person of Saddam. It was the Iraqi leader alone who took the decision to invade Iran in 1980 and Kuwait a decade later, leading Iraq into two disastrous wars.[56] Thus, the leadership in Iraq was extremely centralised, making it both an attractive and feasible target on paper, but Saddam had developed an impressive party apparatus that ultimately served to protect him.

THE IRAQI BA'ATH PARTY

By expanding the number of Ba'ath Party members and registered supporters, from less than 1,000 in 1968 to almost 2 million in 1990,[57] Saddam managed to use the Party to create and sustain his own personal power base. The Iraqi leader had by the early 1980s succeeded in turning Iraq into a one-party state, which in principle reflected George Orwell's *Oceania*, where everybody felt watched, nobody could be trusted, and truth was decreed by Big Brother and the Thought Police.

The Ba'ath Party in Iraq, like its counterparts in other Arab states, derived from the official founding congress in Damascus in 1947.[58] One of the most distinctive features of Ba'athism was its pan-Arab ideology,[59] and its belief that the individual Arab states were all part of a single Arab nation, as expressed in the slogan 'One Arab Nation with an Eternal Mission', and its credo 'Unity, Freedom and Socialism.'[60] Details on religion and sect relations were not part of the doctrine, however, as that would imply a declaration of the Arab nation being divided along religious lines between Shia and Sunni.[61] The Ba'athists had gained some support in Syria by the late 1940s, but in Iraq they remained clandestine until 1958. When members participated in the failed coup attempt against Premier Qassem in 1959, many were sent to jail or fled the country, resulting in a temporary breakdown of what was nothing more than a fragile structure in the first place. Continuing as an underground movement, the Party's objective was to grasp power through a coup rather than elections, and in its search for allies to topple Qassem it found pan-Arab nationalists in the army who for their part were looking for political validation of their intention to seize power.[62] The partnership succeeded in February 1963, but within nine months the new nationalist government removed the Ba'ath branch of the alliance from power, including Prime Minister Ahmad Hasan al-Bakr and Minister of Defence Hardan al-Tikriti Abd al-Ghafur. The main concern of the new President, Abd al-Salam Aref, was to secure his own position against future coups. He managed to achieve this by establishing a loyal elite within the army, the Republican Guard, and putting friends and relatives from his own Jumalia tribe in key positions. Giving such priority to constituting a personal power base was at the expense of growing social and economic problems. By 1965 the war between Baghdad and the Kurds had began in earnest once more after a brief cease-fire.[63] Moreover, Abd al-Salam Aref died in April 1966 and his brother, General Abd al-Rahman Aref, was appointed President. The failure to participate effectively in the Arab–Israeli war of June 1967, the continuing conflict with the Kurds and concessions made to the Iraqi Communist Party, all resulted in a weakened leadership. Thus, when the growing Ba'ath Party decided to overthrow

Abd al-Rahman Aref on 17 July 1968, again in alliance with factions in the military, the coup was arranged professionally without substantial opposition and with little bloodshed.[64]

The Ba'ath Party learned much from Iraq's various coups and the example of the Aref experience: alliances are temporary by nature; the protection of the regime must be the first priority; clan and family connections strengthen the regime; and, finally, domestic issues must be kept in check at the same time as nationalism is promoted. Thus, when Ahmad Hasan al-Bakr and Saddam Hussein overthrew the Aref regime in 1968, they intended to provide for themselves in two crucial respects. First, they sought the active participation in their coup of three key individuals upon whom the security of the Aref security system rested: Colonel Abd al-Razzaq al-Nayif (director of military intelligence); General Ibrahim Abd al-Rahman al-Daud (commander of the Republican Guard); and General Sadoun Ghaydan (commander of 10th Armoured Brigade). After having been among the main participants in the coup that ousted Aref, the first two were removed in the second Ba'ath coup 13 days later, on 30 July 1968. Second, once in power the new leadership immediately sought to create a political power base within the state, and it fell upon Saddam to expand the party as the means of generating widespread support, and hence legitimacy, for the regime across society.

Immediately after the July coups of 1968 the Ba'ath Party drafted a constitution which set out legitimacy for the power-holders. The Revolutionary Command Council (RCC) was established as the 'supreme institution in the state',[65] consisting of Generals Ahmad Hasan al-Bakr, Salih Mahdi Ammash, Hardan al-Tikriti Abd al-Ghafur, Sadoun Ghaydan and Hammad Shihab. They were all career officers without any further education, Sunni Arabs from either Tikrit or Baghdad, born prior to 1930, and with the exception of Hardan al-Tikriti they were all urban lower middle class.[66] The much younger Saddam, who did not have a military education, assumed responsibility for the Party's secret security apparatus, a position that allegedly was offered first to more senior members of the party, who declined it because they considered it unpromising. They may have regretted their decision, as their fate later would be in the hands of the 'Lord Deputy' who spent the year networking for the future. Already by November 1969 he was appointed Vice President, Deputy Chairman of the RCC and Deputy Secretary of the Regional Command – the highest decision-making organ within the party. From these positions, and by working behind the scenes through the infamous security apparatus, he enhanced his personal power by transforming the ruling political elite to his personal advantage.[67] The process ensured that the Party became a wider shield for a small inner circle.

By the mid-1980s Iraq was in effect ruled by a new generation of party activists. The average age of those in power compared to the previous regimes had decreased substantially. Career officers, who had held the leading political roles during the previous nationalistic regimes,[68] almost disappeared from the RCC, Regional Command and government. Shia Arabs gained considerable power, and although Sunni Arabs from the Sunni Triangle were clearly dominant, political positions were opened to Iraqis from all over the country. The ruling elite was now predominantly rural lower class.

The process provides an interesting illustration of the art of constituting personal power, and the methods are revealing of Saddam's operational mind-set. Four months after the coup Saddam made sure that his supporters, Izzat Ibrahim al-Duri and Samir Abd al-Aziz Najam, became members of the Regional Command. One year later Saddam made sure that all members of the Party's decision-making organ, including himself, became members of the elitist RCC (amounting to 15 in total). As Deputy Secretary General of the RCC he next made sure that prominent officers who opposed him, such as the Minister of Defence, Hardan al-Tikriti, and Minister of Interior, Salih Mahdi Ammash, lost their posts. Over the next decade, through systematic purges, RCC members were reduced in numbers, but most of those remaining were Saddam's placemen. Among those dismissed were Shafiq al-Kamali, Abd Allah Sallum, Salah Umar al-Ali, Murtada al-Hadithi, Izzat Mustafa and Abs al-Khaliq al-Samarra.[69]

In the meantime, he also ensured that there was a significant reshuffle in the Regional Command itself. By March 1977, Saddam was supported by 14 out of 21 Regional Command members, and Ahmad Hasan al-Bakr was the only career officer left. In the process Saddam formed an alliance with the men who would continue to serve him: Taha Yassin Ramadan, Tariq Aziz, Saadoun Shaker, Izzat Ibrahim and Ali Hasan al-Majid among others. In order to avoid conflicts of tribal seniority in decision-making, he typically made sure that new appointees were younger than he was.[70] Additionally, the new and younger regime marked out its distance from previous governments.

One now had to be a Regional Command member to become a new RCC member, and the Regional Command 'assumed its role of leading the revolution through the RCC'.[71] Saddam further ensured that important appointments, especially within the expanding security network, were given to members of his own tribe, or individuals who had proved their loyalty to him. Because of Saddam's background, and social affiliation, the process also meant that the Baghdad urban lower-middle classes, which had previously governed the state, were gradually replaced by the rural lower class, predominately from the region of Tikrit. Although this resulted in a Tikriti inner core, Saddam pursued a policy in which Shia Arabs were given considerable power.[72] The fact that two RCC Shia members were executed in 1979 indicates that they had had power beyond mere window-dressing.[73] By early 1987 some 25 per cent of the RCC membership, and 30 per cent of the Regional Command personnel, were Shia.[74] Saddam's appreciation of the ethnic-religious complexities of Iraq proved to be of immense value, as most Iraqi Shia decided to fight Iranian Shia during the war with Iran to preserve the Iraqi state, which was run by Sunnis. The mutlilayered divisions that are inherent in Iraq require a strong state, and the process ensured some degree of national unity. Saddam succeeded also in ensuring the self-serving imperative as he built an unprecedented social structure for his own protection.

Additionally, being well aware of the Army's prominent role in previous coups, Saddam made sure that promotions, assignments and reorganisations were controlled by the Party's Military Bureau.[75] Although he made sure that a certain degree of military professionalism was upheld, the Party's Military Bureau became much more influential in military affairs than was the case with its Arab counterparts. The Iraqi Army was by the late 1970s under civilian control, according to Iraqi analyst Faleh al-Jabber.[76] The process reflected not only Saddam's suspicion of the Army, but a rare mix of hate and respect for an organisation to which he was never admitted. The Army became less important in political life, and Saddam further relied on the security system rather than the armed forces as his key praetorian guard. One consequence was that with a party-controlled military system, officers would find it increasingly difficult to maintain a group identity separate from Party policy.[77] Thus, Saddam made sure that loyal civilian party workers gained a strong foothold within the military organisation, at the same time as generals were squeezed out of the political bodies of the RCC and Regional Command.

The overall effect was that by the late 1970s the ultimate power was in the hands of Saddam Hussein. Although Shia Arabs were provided with representation in the Party and the government, the people from the Tikrit area became the predominant group throughout the armed forces and the Party itself. On 16 July 1979, when Saddam replaced his relative as President, he ensured complete control by having five of the 22 senior RCC members executed together with some 50 senior Party officials. None of those executed was from Saddam's own tribe or town, and to further strengthen his grip he had the remaining RCC members perform the execution.[78] Herein lies the essence of ensuring absolute control, according to Kanan Makiya:

> The Ba'ath developed the politics of fear into an art form, one that ultimately served the purpose of legitimizing their rule by making large numbers of people complicit in the violence of the regime. The special problem of Ba'athi violence begins with the realization that hundreds of thousands of perfectly ordinary people were routinely implicated in it. In most cases they had no choice in the matter.[79]

The infamous executions left no doubt that there was only one man in charge. After 1979 Saddam made sure that both the RCC and the Regional Command lost real power: they existed in order to rubber-stamp his own personal decisions. Moreover, he also ensured that personal insecurity was a hallmark of his rule: execution or disappearance became synonymous with his rule, and were deliberately employed to cow possible opposition. In 1982, when the war with Iran was going badly, and some speculated that Ahmad al-Bakr should resume his position, Saddam apparently eliminated the threat by poisoning the man who had facilitated his rise to power.[80] Whenever somebody challenged the Iraqi leader's position, or became too popular, he would remove them from power, one way or another. Prominent officers faced the same consequences after the war with Iran, and although it weakened the military force's capability it also reduced the threat to Saddam's personal power.

Saddam Hussein's patience enabled him to strengthen the regime's narrow base of political legitimacy through a pan-Arab ideology, which was not practised in the real world, but through fear – the barrel of the gun. This in turn became the foundation for political survival and for realising the ambition of absolute power. Much of his stranglehold was made possible through the security apparatus, which was structured along military lines, but, importantly, not held under army control. Saddam Hussein's security apparatus had started by protecting the Party from sabotage and preventing military coups, but it gradually developed control over all aspects of Iraqi life.[81] The organisational structure of the Party consisted, in the main, of small secretive cells, and combined with priority on security it turned the Party apparatus into a civilian militia.[82] Although the cell system was not Saddam's creation, he managed to exploit it to the full.

In the 1980s 'cells' of new recruits became, in fact, large groups and were not clandestine any more, but low level members would still know very little of what was happening at the higher levels. At the baseline there was the Party/circle cell (*halaqah/khalia*) composed of three to seven members. It was the lowest level of official membership, but in addition to discussing Party directives it had the important mission of recruiting new members and ensuring that daily activities in their geographical area did not contradict Ba'athist ideas. Each of these members was responsible for several *Naseers*. These *Naseers* strongly supported Ba'ath ideas and aspired to become official Party members, but not everybody was fortunate enough to have the right background for such an advancement, even after a lifetime of loyalty. They were given various assignments and directives, typically being responsible for arranging staged demonstrations. Each *Naseer* had further several *Muaids*, but the *Muaids* and the *Naseers* were defined as 'supporters' rather than formal members of the Ba'ath Party. A minimum of two and a maximum of seven cells formed the second level, the Party division (*firqah*), which often operated in urban areas, larger villages, offices, factories, schools and other organisations. Two to five divisions composed the third level, the section (*shubah*). The next level was the branch (*far*) which included at least two sections and operated at a provincial level. There were 21 branches in Iraq, one for each of the 18 provinces and three in Baghdad. Then there was the union of all the branches formed into the Party Congress, which elected the Regional Iraqi Command, the fifth level of the Ba'ath Party. The sixth level was the National pan-Arab Command, the highest policy-making body, consisting of representatives from all Regional country commands, which next was responsible to the National Congress. However, because of rivalry and cross-country disputes, this level has never been influential, leaving the Regional Command as the de facto highest authority within the Ba'ath Party.[83] One of the most important tasks for the Regional Command was to coordinate the secret bureaux. The two most powerful were the Interior Bureau and the Military Bureau, but other influential bureaux in domestic politics were the Farmer's Bureau, the Student's Bureau, the Worker's Bureau, the Education Bureau, the Women's Bureau, the Foreign Affairs Bureau and the Bureau of Arab Affairs.[84] The latter was headed by Naim Haddad until 1986 and later by Tariq Aziz.

One distinctive feature of the Regional Command was that the members tended to stay for a considerable period of time. By 1990 some two-thirds had been members since the mid-1970s. The 10th Congress of the Arab Socialist Ba'ath Party (the Congress of Jihad and Construction) was held in September 1991, and with 42 candidates on paper, Saddam was unanimously re-elected as prearranged by the 257 members.[85] The members were given strong guidance from the presidential office, and with a need to present the regime as legitimate they presented an ethno-religious combination that was supposed to look representative of society, but the number of Shia was still far lower than their proportion in the population. As Party affiliation became increasingly compulsory in schools and organisations, loyalty rather than ideological belief or professional skill became the key determinant of social mobility. The Ba'ath Party cells, where full membership remained semi-secret, made sure that a large area outside Baghdad remained loyal to the leader, and with pictures and symbols everywhere, and a Party-controlled media, the Iraqi citizen was truly watched.[86]

The result of this massive Party system was that when Saddam took over the presidency on 16 July 1979, he had established a unique power system, and those in prominent political positions were appointed first and foremost for their loyalty to Saddam. A small group of trusted people ran the Party and the Party ran the Army, the government and the population. Although these institutions entrusted Saddam with extensive personal power, it was the Party that provided him with an institutional and ideological framework that allowed the regime to reach deep into society. Although ideology was a means rather than an end, it also provided the Iraqi leader with the basis for an ambitious pan-Arab vision. The combination of military forces, governmental institutions and an extensive security apparatus, orchestrated through the Party's Regional Command and led by Saddam's family and tribe, became the instrument of both domestic and regional rule.

The many years of membership and Party discipline played a crucial role in keeping a lid on discontent. To some extent, the importance relates not to the power of the Party, but the power of the Party relative to possible opposition. One effect of the increased Ba'ath membership was that strong, organised opposition became extremely difficult, and by the 1980s almost all of it had been driven abroad. Those who remained were clandestine and weak, and therefore one may suggest that the leadership was in fact better prepared to outlast the 1991 air campaign than the opposition was to capitalise on its opportunities. The leadership was most vulnerable in the early days of the campaign, but with no pressure from within the capital, or the country at large, there was nobody who was ready to take advantage of the air campaign's effort to overthrow Saddam Hussein. Moreover, Saddam's venture of letting the Party run the military certainly weakened the Iraqi combat performance of January and February 1991, but it also reduced the chances of influential Iraqi officers taking the opportunity to turn against him. It seems unlikely, given the imbalance in terms of technical and professional capability between Iraqi and Coalition forces, that the outcome of Desert Storm would have been much affected had the Iraqi military establishment not been so affected by the domestic requirements of the incumbent Saddam regime. But it seems likely, however, that the latter's priorities in the organisation of its military formations and personnel ensured Saddam's personal survival during the uprising that followed. The Western world may find it strange that Saddam was willing to let Party bureaucrats more or less run the military, but there should be no doubt that this played an important part in Saddam's surviving 'the Mother of all Battles' and the decade that followed.

It should be clear that bombing a regime such as the Iraqi one into submission is an immense undertaking. While buildings, headquarters and technological equipment can be identified, the less tangible party apparatus is far less quantifiable. Additionally, if the objective is to change the regime, one needs a strong group for succession, and in the Iraqi case the Party ensured that there was no credible opposition. By the late 1980s the Ba'athist regime had become undeniably strong, enjoying immense oil revenues that it used to develop a massive authoritarian bureaucracy, which in turn was used to control the population. So Saddam used the Party to develop his own power base, which ultimately helped deter internal opposition from taking an organised form during Desert Storm, and that control was further strengthened by the state's governmental structure.

THE IRAQI GOVERNMENT

The present Iraqi Interim Constitution was formed in 1970, but ever since then the political system has been officially characterised as being in a 'transitional' phase,[87] and consequently it has operated with little reference to constitutional provisions. Paradoxically, in the country where Hammurabi set down the first legislation of the world, its people some 6,000 years later are without a permanent constitution that guarantees their rights and freedoms.

As already established, the RCC (*Majliss Qiyadat al-Thawra*) was the top executive and legislative organ of the state. During most of Ahmad Hasan al-Bakr's presidency his wide-ranging power was shared with Saddam, and discussions among RCC members were often on significant political and economic matters, but after Saddam assumed the presidency he took complete control, leaving many of the substantial decisions to an informal inner circle.[88] Although the RCC derived their actual authority from Saddam, the members enjoyed his trust, and some had considerable personal power because of their government portfolios, position within the Party, daily contact with the upper echelon and long association with internal security measures.

The Constitution nevertheless provided for a governmental system that, in appearance, was divided into three mutually checking branches: the executive (Council of Ministers), the legislative (National Assembly) and the judiciary (Court of Cassation). The RCC should accordingly act on advice from the three branches. Although the government was symbolic in terms of real influence in national politics, by serving as a counterbalance to the Party, with close control of the media, it was one of the instruments Saddam relied on to keep him in power. It was also partly responsible for carrying out the RCC resolutions. According to Amatzia Baram, 'Although the government is officially subordinate to the RCC, and its prestige is not equal to that of the RL [Regional Command], it is of major importance as the highest purely executive institution in the country.'[89]

According to Article 43 of the Constitution, the RCC was responsible for ordering mobilisation, declaring war, accepting truce, ratifying treaties and international agreements, concluding peace, and approving the state's general budget among other things.[90]

The Revolutionary Command Council is the supreme institution in the State, which on 17 July 1968, assumed the responsibility to realize the public will of the people, by removing the authority from the reactionary, individual, and corruptive regime, and returning it to the people.[91]

Figure 5: The Iraqi Governmental System

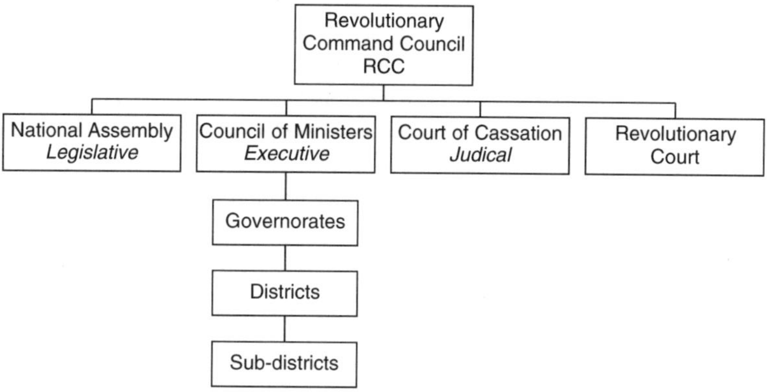

```
                    ┌──────────────────┐
                    │   Revolutionary  │
                    │ Command Council  │
                    │       RCC        │
                    └──────────────────┘
        ┌───────────────┬──────────┴──────────┬───────────────┐
┌───────────────┐ ┌───────────────────┐ ┌──────────────┐ ┌──────────────┐
│National Assembly│ │Council of Ministers│ │Court of Cassation│ │ Revolutionary │
│   Legislative  │ │     Executive     │ │    Judical    │ │    Court     │
└───────────────┘ └───────────────────┘ └──────────────┘ └──────────────┘
                          │
                   ┌──────────────┐
                   │ Governorates │
                   └──────────────┘
                          │
                   ┌──────────────┐
                   │  Districts   │
                   └──────────────┘
                          │
                   ┌──────────────┐
                   │ Sub-districts│
                   └──────────────┘
```

Source: Derived from Metz *et al.*, *Iraq*, p. 180.

On paper, however, the Council of Ministers was the executive organ: 'composed of the People's representatives from various political, economic and social sectors', and when giving advice its members were not 'censured for opinions or suggestions expressed by them in the performance of their task'.[92] Although some meetings were held, the Council of Ministers was for all practical purposes reduced to a collection of bureaucratic technocrats as long as they were not senior Party members. Moreover, during the 1980s, the percentage of ministers possessing post-graduate degrees decreased considerably.[93] As was the case with the RCC and Regional Command, government members were increasingly recruited from the rural lower class, and both Shia and Kurds were given representation. The Party's Military Bureau nevertheless dominated over the Ministry of Defence, the Public Relations Bureau took precedence over the Secretary of Foreign Affairs, and the Culture and Information Bureau took precedence over the Secretary of Culture and Information.[94] Still, service in these positions provided some officials with a foot in the door, and if they proved themselves loyal, and showed diplomatic aptitude, they could be selected to serve at foreign embassies.

Through good diplomats and papers that indicated a democratic constitution, the effort of presenting the Iraqi regime as legitimate worked well with the Western world throughout the 1980s, and it ensured Iraq the much-needed support during its war with Iran. This was not because Iraq was perceived as democratic in any form or fashion, but because it was fighting against Khomeini's Iran. Also, foreign policy in the 1980s was flexible and effective, all formulated by Saddam. States express themselves not only in their own territories through domestic policy, but also externally through foreign policy,[95] and again, during the 1980s Iraq was extremely successful. Adding to this general rule, the importance of ministers depended on the individual. For example, when Saadoun Hammadi was the Minister of Foreign Affairs in the early 1980s he was the most important foreign policy formulator, immensely trusted especially in negotiations with the Americans. The most powerful position within the formal government system was perhaps the Ministry of Interior, because it was entirely devoted to matters of policing and national security, and in a police state almost everything concerns national security.[96] When Saadoun Shaker held the position he was no less important than Saddam's half-brother, Barzan, who was heading the intelligence service, al-Mukhabarat. It is a complex picture, but on the whole one should recognise the RCC, the Regional Command and the Cabinet members as separate and complementary advisors to Saddam.

In theory, the National Assembly (Parliament) represented the electorate and through the Council of Ministers it recommended political actions to the RCC. The National Assembly was elected for the first time in 1980, and 40 per cent of the delegates were Shia: presumably an outcome desired by the regime.[97] Although it consisted of 250 members from 250 electoral districts, each member had to be acknowledged by the governmentally appointed election commission.[98] It functioned, however, as a channel for upward mobility and recruitment for other positions within the regime. There was some prestige in holding these positions: it required moving to the capital, it ensured some media coverage, and all in all, it amounted to a good starting point for further promotion. Sometimes the RCC decided to translate a specific programme into action through the relevant minister in the Cabinet, which again trickled down to groups in the National Assembly and civil servants, but at other times the President chose to overlook the RCC, and exercise his authority directly. Certain portfolios have always been held by RCC members, indicating their importance, while others seem to contribute indirectly to policy-making by 'forming an integral part of the ruling elite'.[99] Although not a real seat of power, the Assembly played its part in presenting the Iraqi leader's views. Saddam was, however, very critical of bureaucrats:

> A bureaucrat is a person who looks at the world through a flow of paper across his desk. He has no knowledge of the real world except what he reads ... But do I get anything realistic from these reports? No. Most of the time I don't. They are the reports of a bureaucrat, totally disengaged from what is really going on.[100]

The third branch, the judiciary, came under the jurisdiction of the Ministry of Justice, but the President appointed all judges. The Court of Cassation was divided into four sub-divisions: administrative court, courts of appeal, courts of sessions and religious courts. In addition there was the Revolutionary Court which dealt with security matters under the jurisdiction of the secret security police. The members of the RCC were, according to the Constitution, only accountable to the RCC itself since it was 'the supreme institution of the State and all members enjoy full immunity. No measures could be taken against any of them without permission of the Council.'[101] Again, with such a system, and closed sessions, the only information the people received was that presented in the news, and without being able to hear both sides of the story the reprisals were not contested. The official version became the truth, and over time a sense of complete helplessness descended upon the people.

The importance of the Iraqi government as far as Saddam's power is concerned is first and foremost in the RCC, which controls the media, and the media serve as his mouthpiece. It has been fully controlled by Saddam since the late 1970s and the amalgamation of a controlled government system and media network linked him directly to the people, at the same time as it gave him an avenue outside the Party organisation, and thus control of both regime and state. For example, the RCC endorsed the Iraqi leader's determination to fight the Coalition on 14 January 1991 by giving their commander-in-chief 'full constitutional authority'.[102] The point to be made is that for a country that had little knowledge of the Western notion of democracy, this was the way it had worked in the past, and so, such 'independent' support for Saddam Hussein might have had some credibility, or at least a unifying effect.

The media played an important part in ensuring domestic and regional support during the invasion of Kuwait. On 3 August 1991, the *Baghdad Observer* reported that 'An RCC communiqué said the new government in Kuwait has asked Iraq for help and aid against any possible foreign invasion of Kuwait with the aim of occupying the country and toppling the new popular system of government.'[103] It went on to state that the RCC 'has therefore decided to respond to the request of the Interim Free Government of Kuwait and cooperate with it on this basis'.[104] The National Assembly followed up these statements, but they merely re-emphasised the RCC statements, and never contradicted them.[105] The power of a state-controlled media should not be disregarded in any society, and the RCC, being part and parcel of the Party, made sure that continuous television statements, newspaper stories and radio broadcasts supported the Iraqi leader, which in turn ensured that the people knew that the system was working effectively.

As explored previously, in 1968 the RCC was the real seat of power, and at the time it included only military officers. In November 1969

Saddam managed to increase the power of the Party's Regional Command at the expense of the previous RCC members, and by the mid-1970s elements of the new system had come together so that civilians replaced officers.[106] By the late 1980s the RCC was again the most important formal institutional decision-making body. Thus, Saddam Hussein, thanks to previous groundwork ruled by decree and presented his views as collective decisions made by the RCC.

The clearest indication of the *limited* power of the RCC prior to the invasion of Kuwait resided in the fact that most of Saddam Hussein's inner circle was not represented. His half-brothers were not members, nor were his two oldest sons, Uday and Qussay. Significantly, his personal secretary, Abd Hamid Hmoud, was not part of the body, and his most trusted executive during the late 1980s and early 1990s, Hussein Kamel al-Majid, was not a member.[107] This alone suggests that the RCC did not exert real power, but merely represented it. Key individuals such as Defence Minister Abd al-Jabber Shanshal, Foreign Minister Tariq Aziz and the Chief of Staff for the Armed Forces, Nizar Khasraji, heard about the invasion of Kuwait on the radio, according to Saad al-Bazzaz.[108] They were not consulted, and not even informed, as was the case with the military commanders but for a few in the Republican Guard who were informed only hours in advance.[109] Arguably, by mid July 1990, only three were involved in the planning of a complete invasion besides Saddam himself: his son-in-law and nephew Hussein Kamil, his cousin Ali Hasan al-Majid and the Commander of the Republican Guard, General Iyad al-Rawi. None of the members of the RCC, according to the Constitution the highest decision-making authority in Iraq, or the Regional Command, the highest decision-making authority of the Ba'ath Party, was informed of the decision to occupy the whole of Kuwait. The bottom line is that neither the Party apparatus nor the government system was even informed of a decision that would ultimately bring the entire country to war.

The organisational complexity that ensured complete control by the Iraqi leader can be illustrated by looking into the military related institutions. The Military Bureau was the Ba'ath Party's military branch and it operated separately from the governmental Ministry of Defence. Its main role was to feed all military units with party ideas and monitor their loyalty to the party doctrine. It was responsible for all party activity in the military forces and reported both to the Regional Command and directly to Saddam Hussein's centre – the Office of the Presidential Palace. It was deeply involved in military affairs and responsible for promotions and postings, reducing the Ministry of Defence to administrative and logistical affairs. While the Military Bureau was tasked with ensuring party loyalty in the ranks, party security concentrated on party loyalty throughout the society and reported separately to the Regional

Command and the Office of the Presidential Palace. Added to this, the Special Security Organisation was in charge of the loyalty of all army officers as well as the chiefs and officers of the internal security branches. Since military service was compulsory for all male adults, both agencies were selected to target virtually all of the regime's potential opponents, and therefore the two organisations overlapped in nature and by intent. In addition to these military–Party-related security issues, there were agencies in the security and intelligence network that dealt with other security issues, most notably the Military Intelligence Service and the Military Security Service. Thus, several officials were watching each other and reported independently and directly to Saddam Hussein's office. Both Party and security individuals were assigned to every military unit, reporting on all decisions taken by their commanders, reflecting the wider social system where all households had to report on their neighbours' activities and school-children were encouraged to inform on their parents.[110] Although until 1989 the Secretary of Defence tended to be a Tikriti, and therefore the holder of one of the most important governmental portfolios, he had little real influence on the military apparatus, for which, according to the constitution, he was responsible. His main responsibility, however, was to coordinate military operations with the presidential palace in times of war; to plan and supervise training; to serve as a buffer that would absorb the shocks and frustrations of the officers; and to manage relations between them and Saddam.[111] Saddam's cousin, General Adnan Khayr Allah, who was Minister of Defence from 1977 to 1989, performed well in all these positions.

In essence, the RCC was used by Saddam Hussein to legitimise his own actions with an appearance of consensus, but for all practical purposes it was the organ he used to address the people on personal decisions. One may conclude that the party apparatus and the government were of more or less equal weight, depending on the individuals' standing within the party and Saddam's family and tribe. It was the dual existence that created a balance, and the equaliser was always Saddam. Although somewhat disassociated from the government, the Iraqi military apparatus was another dimension of the Iraqi leader's main instruments of power. It provided the state with the means for regional ambitions and it strengthened the security of the regime against internal and external threats.

THE IRAQI MILITARY APPARATUS

The third of Saddam's overarching pillars of power, the Iraqi military system, was similar to its political counterpart in the sense that there was a formal and an informal structure. The Iraqi military organisation, reflecting the society at large, was based on divide-and-rule with the power vested in Saddam, and although Iraqi military officers had reasonable social status, especially after the perceived victory over Iran, the depoliticisation of the armed forces had resulted in their detachment from real political influence.[112] Consequently, generals had little say in policy-making and threat assessments. The military system was also hierarchical in the extreme, but with some officers having influential positions in the Party, and others coming from specific tribes, the real power did not relate to the rigidity of the command structure. Thus, through a rigid command structure and crosscutting patterns that only Saddam knew, the centralisation of the military was complete. For example, the Iraqi leader conducted much of the war against Iran from a bunker underneath the presidential palace, getting involved in details from platoon level action to the bombing of concrete targets. High-ranking generals had to defer to the President on even the smallest matters.[113] All three military services were heavily infiltrated by Party officials and members of the security and intelligence apparatus to the degree that even small military exercises had to be approved by the Military Bureau.[114] According to former Iraqi army officer Colonel Hasan Khafaji, whenever large military movements were to take place, they had to be approved by the Military Bureau, the Ministry of Defence and Military Intelligence.[115]

Under Saddam Hussein Iraq developed the largest military force in the Arab Middle East: two-and-a-half times the size of the second largest, the Egyptian force. Such size reflected the demands of the war with Iran after 1980, but also at work were the regional aspirations of Saddam Hussein and his predecessor, both of whom recognised that regional preponderance necessitated armed forces to match. The attendant problem, however, was obvious: powerful armed forces presented a threat to the President and his regime. The solution they found was to bring the military under civilian control, by relying on tribe and family members in elite military forces, commanding divisions and army groups, and establishing the Republican Guard and internal security forces. They also feared that a military threat might just as easily come from within, from either Kurds in the north or Shia in the south. Consequently, the security element became predominant in the Iraqi armed forces,[116] and the command highly centralised in the person of the President and his ruling clan. At first glance, nevertheless, the Iraqi military structure reflected the traditional tri-service system: the Army, the Air Force and the Navy.[117] The Army was by far the most important, but it was complemented by the Republican Guard and the Ba'ath Party's para-military army, the Popular Army.[118] Only the Army, Navy and Air Force reported to the Ministry of Defence: the Popular Army reported to the Military Bureau of the Regional

Command and, since 1988, the Republican Guard reported directly to the Office of the Presidential Palace.

Operational planning was governed by a defensive strategy where limited offensive operations were conducted only to recover critical terrain or counterattack. The defence line included flooded ditches, minefields and barbed wire, and by the end of the war with Iran the Iraqis had gained considerable skill in defensive and chemical warfare. Indeed, in early 1988 the Iraqi leader planned to stop the war by using al-Hussein missiles with chemical warheads. The strategy was to bomb Teheran with conventional bombs and missiles in order to shatter the windows, and then follow up the attacks with chemical warheads that would result in poison gas spreading around into homes.[119]

Apart from the chemical aspect, the organisation of the Army remained somewhat British-inspired with the lowest unit being a section and the highest a corps, a direct reflection of Iraq's historic association with them. The corps could frequently have responsibility for as many as eight divisions and during the occupation of Kuwait the Iraqi Army added up to seven or eight corps. There were also three types of divisions, the equipment being overwhelmingly Soviet: armoured, mechanised and infantry. Typically, a mechanised division had two mechanised brigades and one armoured brigade, while an armoured division had two armoured brigades and one mechanised brigade. The infantry division had three infantry brigades and a single organic tank battalion.[120]

The now infamous Republican Guard was merely two brigades in 1983, and was totally dependent on Saddam Hussein for its existence. The soldiers' social background was predominantly Sunni lower class, and recruits were expected to join the Ba'ath Party. Saddam personally oversaw the training and indoctrination scheme in his methodical and systematic fashion. The commander, General Abd al-Sattar al-Tikriti, furthermore, bypassed the military service when reporting to the President. It was the unquestionable elite armed force in Iraq, but not even the Republican Guard after its augmentation in the mid 1980s was allowed passage through Baghdad, despite closely controlled security zones throughout the city. Its officers furthermore, were not allowed to carry side-arms except when ordered into battle.[121] It was originally created to prevent army attacks upon the regime,[122] but as it expanded in the course of the war with Iran it became a genuine fighting force. When it suffered heavy casualties in an unsuccessful counterattack following the Iranian capture of the Faw Peninsula in February 1986, the defeat convinced the leadership that it needed major improvement.[123] It basically developed into a strategic reserve, and in April 1988 it acted as an offensive force in liberating the Faw Peninsula in less than two days.[124] From that moment, the Republican Guard enjoyed much respect in the region as a force with considerable offensive capability,

and it was the obvious choice for Saddam in spearheading the invasion
of Kuwait. By the time of the invasion the Republican Guard had
grown to eight divisions, which amounted to a total of some 30 to 35
brigades.[125] Unlike the Iraqi Army, which was based on conscripts, the
Republican Guard was an all-volunteer force. Its members were originally drawn mostly from regions known for their loyalty to Saddam, but
with the need for expansion volunteers from all over the country were
admitted, including Shia Arabs and Kurds. By the time of the occupation of Kuwait all military officers were, however, members of the
Ba'ath Party, and naturally continuously under the surveillance of the
Military Bureau.[126] The force, which enjoyed far better facilities and
weapons than the Iraqi Army, was by 1988 self-reliant: it could support
itself without external means.[127] The Republican Guard had therefore
undergone a considerable change during the decade. Prior to the war
with Iran it was a rather small force known for its political loyalty and
it was not necessarily better at fighting than the Army proper, but the
demands of the war had resulted in a considerable expansion and
improvement in fighting skills. Thus, that expansion made it less
politically reliable, and therein lie the reasons for the establishment of
a new core – the Special Republican Guard. Still, the Republican Guard
stood behind the regime in the crucial uprising that followed the end
of Desert Storm, and although size may have made it less politically
reliable, it was by most standards extremely loyal to the regime, simply
because it was an important part of it. As far as the Iraqi armed forces
were concerned, the Republican Guard was the linchpin on which the
occupation depended, and the very link between the Iraqi leader and
his military might.

While the Republican Guard represented the elite, the Popular Army
(*Al-Jaysh ash Shaabi*) ensured added mass. It was formed originally in
1970 with responsibility for local defence, but over the years the force
grew dramatically and its role and mission changed under Taha Yasin
Ramadan.[128] It was established as a popular militia composed of civilian
volunteers, including women, and was regarded initially as a means of
ensuring the survival of the Ba'ath regime against internal opposition,[129]
and of acting as a counterweight against any attempted coups by the
regular armed forces.[130] Its members received a minimum level of training,
primarily with rifle, grenade and anti-tank rockets,[131] but the organisation developed with a headquarters in Baghdad and a commander in
each of the 18 administrative districts. Each district consisted of a
number of sectors, and each sector had some ten bases led by platoon
commanders.[132] By duplicating the army's system of organisation and
establishing the Popular Army on a national basis, the regime thus created
a counterweight in numbers to the Iraqi Army. During the war with
Iran, however, the Popular Army and its relationship with the regular

army changed. The former remained a militia and was primarily political rather than military in nature, but it ceased to be a volunteer force and, with all males obliged to register for military service,[133] it quickly became the manpower reserve for the army in the field.[134] With relatively few exemptions from service allowed by the authorities, the Popular Army therefore acquired both numbers and military experience, and some 15,000 of its members served in units that entered Kuwait after the Republican Guard had occupied the country, and thereafter conducted security operations inside and outside Kuwait City.[135]

While the composition of the Iraqi Army looked formidable on paper one could argue that to some extent the force was also the Iraqi leader's Achilles Heel. Saddam was determined to build a massive war machine, but he was afraid it would get so powerful that it might turn against him. Thus, the armed forces lacked the leadership, training and motivation that is required in order to have an effective force. Any military force needs extensive peacetime training to function in real action, but rather than give his army free rein to develop its professionalism the Iraqi leader was content to emasculate it. For example, on 10 December 1990, the Iraqi leader apparently feared his military leadership more than the impending result as he ordered the dismissal of 12 senior officers and some 16 executions for allegedly 'plotting against the regime'.[136] During a period when most Western countries encouraged the manoeuverist approach to warfare, the Iraqi leader showed little appreciation for initiative and creativity as that challenged his own close control. In such an environment the combat intelligence proved to be non-existent for the Iraqi Army during the air campaign, because Saddam Hussein feared 'that too much information in the hands of his subordinates posed a danger to him'.[137] The Iraqi Army proper, which occupied Kuwait after the Republican Guard withdrew in mid August 1990, was far less capable than Western assessments indicated.

It has previously been established that one of the most important elements of any military strategy is to ensure air superiority over the battlefield prior to engagement. The Iraqi regime was under no illusion that it could compete with the Coalition in the air if war came about, but it strongly believed the air defence system would give them some protection and destroy attacking aircraft. The Iraqi Air Force (IQAF) was ranked as the sixth largest in the world and had 24 main operating bases, 30 dispersal bases, and some 1,000 fixed-wing combat and support aircraft.[138] A French-built command and control network of modern radar, military communication equipment, computers and anti-aircraft missiles further integrated these bases.[139]

In 1990 the Iraqi Air Force consisted of 40,000 men of whom 10,000 were attached to its subordinate Air Defence Command. The headquarters was in Baghdad and the major bases were located at Basra,

H-3, Kirkuk, Mosul, Rashid and Ash Shuaybah. It had more than 500 combat aircraft formed into two bomber squadrons, 11 fighter ground attack squadrons, five interceptor squadrons, and one counter-insurgency squadron (10 to 30 aircraft each). In addition, support aircraft included two transport squadrons. As many as ten helicopter squadrons were also operational, although these formed the Army Air Corps.

Although the Iraqi Air Force had conducted piecemeal strategic bombing of Iran, targeting mostly the population and oil installations, its doctrine reflected a defensive orientation. Saddam was aware of the prominent role Air Force officers had previously played in Iraqi politics, as they had been strongly involved in several coup attempts, particularly throughout the 1960s. In a state where military professionalism was second to political loyalty, the demilitarisation of the Air Force, as well as the rest of the armed forces, would be at the expense of military effectiveness. Although perceived as a strategic reserve, the Iraqi Air Force was in effect designed not for winning wars, or even for fighting them, but for coup prevention.[140] Saddam Hussein's subordination of military planning to political factors manifested itself early in the war with Iran: while having a numerically superior air force, he did not allow it to exploit the situation because of fear of not being able to replace lost aircraft for logistical and financial reasons. The Iraqi Air Force was therefore, like the rest of the regime, characterised by a rigid command structure with centralised decision-making and execution. Thus, within the defensive strategy ground-based air defence was considered the key.

The heart of the air defence network, KARI, included vast numbers of surface-to-air missiles (SAMs) and anti-aircraft artillery (AAA).[141] KARI had a hierarchical structure based on some 400 observation posts and 73 radar reporting stations spread all over the country. These stations were connected to 17 Intercept Operational Centres (IOC). These regional command centres were either located in hardened shelters or mounted on vehicles for mobility. Their purpose was to direct interception and inform batteries of anti-aircraft artillery. They also reported to the next level of command, the four regional Sector Operations Centres (SOCs). Located in hardened buildings, these controlled the regions around, and monitored any threats to Baghdad. They gave orders to IOCs and reported to the overall centre, the National Air Defence Operations Centre (ADOC) in Baghdad. The Iraqi high command had a nation-wide picture of the situation with terminals in strategic places, such as the presidential bunkers and palaces in addition to certain hideaways and hotels that were used for intelligence purposes.[142]

The communication network was built on lines buried under land and rivers, on microwave relay stations, on field radio frequencies, telephone lines and fibre optic cables. Despite this redundancy, much of the system depended on civilian telephone lines, and if those were cut KARI's effectiveness would be substantially reduced. There were essentially four other limitations to KARI. First, under optimal conditions each command centre could only track 120 planes. Second, it did not pick up signals from low-level flights, although other systems partly compensated for this. Third, it was a mixture of technology from different nations giving it an uncertain integration. For example, if one took out the ADOC, the SOCs could not communicate effectively with each other, and further, if one took out an SOC, its respective IOCs were isolated, leaving the whole sector open to attack.[143] Fourth, the system was oriented towards the east (Iran) and the west (Israel) rather than the south (Saudi Arabia). One should note, however, that although there were technological limitations to the system, the main weakness, in terms of operational effectiveness, was the rigid command structure that did not allow for delegating tasks. The system was nevertheless impressive on paper and it was only in the course of events that these flaws manifested themselves. Naturally, the first air power objective in Operation Desert Storm was to disrupt this network in order to obtain air superiority.

In addition to the conventional arsenal, Iraq held the most advanced and ambitious non-conventional weapons programme in the Arab world. Moreover, it developed missiles, rockets and superguns to deliver them. By the end of the 1980s Iraq had a considerable chemical weapons production capability; the most important site was located near Samarra, some 70 kilometres northwest of Baghdad.[144] Iraq reportedly used chemical weapons both defensively and during pre-assault preparations of Iranian positions, and by the end of the war authority for employment was delegated to the divisional commander, indicating that the tactical use of chemical weapons had become almost routine.[145] Iraq had also developed considerable skills with its biological weapons programme, using Salman Pak about 35 kilometres southwest of Baghdad as its principle centre for research. Stockpiles of botulin toxin in militarily significant quantities were reported prior to the invasion of Kuwait, and research into anthrax, typhoid and cholera was expanding, but press reports on actual use remained unverified. While chemical weapons constituted the backbone of Iraq's strategic weapons capability, and biological weapons added to that feature, it was the nuclear programme which the Iraqi leader held dearest. Iraq embarked on a serious programme in the early 1970s, and although it had signed the Non-Proliferation Treaty in 1968, it cynically took advantage of the opportunity to develop nuclear weapons. Since 1973 the centre for nuclear research was located in Tuwaitha, a complex approximately 30 kilometres southeast of Baghdad. The weapons were originally meant for deterrence, but within a few years the Iraqi leader grew confident that these weapons could be used to 're-shape the map of the Middle East', through nuclear threats.[146] In order to succeed he needed money and expertise. The first was ensured through oil, and to achieve the second Saddam systematically educated Iraqis abroad and hired scientists from all over the world. According to Khidhir Hamza, who was responsible for developing the first Arab bomb, his team was only a few months away from having a bomb equivalent to the one dropped on Hiroshima when Iraq invaded Kuwait.[147] Other reports speculate that it might have been two or three years, but the Iraqi leader initiated a crash programme during the occupation, desperately hoping to have a bomb ready by early January 1991. The fact remains that Saddam Hussein wholeheartedly believed that he would be able to acquire nuclear weapons, and that would give him the opportunity through threats to become the undisputed pan-Arab leader. The non-conventional weapons, and the long-range strike systems to deliver them, were part of his vision for regional domination.

Although weaknesses in the Iraqi armed forces have been identified, there is no doubt that Saddam was confident that his military apparatus would be able to cause the Coalition a reasonable amount of concern. As will be detailed later, he believed he could sustain the air campaign, and then, by sheer mass, inflict a serious number of casualties on US troops. Moreover, as he was convinced that a nuclear bomb would become reality before the war against the Coalition commenced, he saw no reason to withdraw under the humiliating conditions provided for by the United Nations. He was to realise in the event of war the gap between his military capacity and that of the Coalition, but for all his misconceptions he never miscalculated the power of the security apparatus that ensured his survival.

THE IRAQI SECURITY AND INTELLIGENCE NETWORK

Throughout the 1970s and 1980s the Iraqi leader developed an authoritarian system charged with a wide variety of security and intelligence functions. Despite the already mentioned pillars of power, this highly secretive and faceless network was the structural foundation of the regime's power base.[148] With the overall objective of protecting the Iraqi leader and his closest family from internal and external enemies, the means was a detailed network built on wide-ranging agencies and informers (*mu'taman*).[149] Many of these agencies were created or expanded during the Iran–Iraq War, providing the Iraqi leader with unparalleled levers of power. In analysing the different agencies it is worth noting, however, that it was Saddam's personal commitment and appreciation of details that made all the difference.[150]

The key agencies reported to Saddam Hussein's nerve centre, the Office of the Presidential Palace, rather than to the Ministry of Interior or the Ministry of Defence.[151] Saddam and his personal secretary, Abd Hamid Hmoud, ran the security apparatus on a day-to-day basis, getting reports from highly trusted individuals.[152] The latter were normally from either Saddam Hussein's native region or related to him, either directly or through marriage. Recruitment was built on personal loyalty rather than ideological commitment, and with the inner family holding the most important positions, recruitment was based on discipline, loyalty and ruthlessness, rather than formal education. The areas of responsibility for the different agencies were duplicated in order to ensure competition among the services. Each agency had a security branch that watched over its own and it reported directly to the agency chief. Other agencies focused on the perceived threat from abroad, watching potential dissidents. For example, Iraqi diplomatic missions usually included representatives from at least three security and intelligence agencies: Mukhabarat (General Intelligence Service), Estikhbarat (Military Intelligence Service) and Amn al-Khass (Special Security Service). There were seven agencies altogether that reported to the Office of the Presidential Palace, as shown in Figure 6.

The Office of the Presidential Palace consisted of a coterie of loyal and discreet bureaucrats and was the most important decision-making body within the security and intelligence network. The executive

Figure 6: The Iraqi Security and Intelligence Network

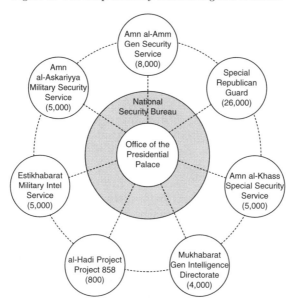

agencies usually reported directly to the Office of the Presidential Palace and received most of their orders directly from there. The Office of the Presidential Palace also had direct links to the Revolutionary Court judge on trial matters, and for all practical purposes it was the crux of power in Iraq and the personal instrument of Saddam Hussein. The government, the Party and the military in effect received their orders from the Office of the Presidential Palace, one way or the other, often through one of the agencies. While the inner core remained rather constant over the years, as was the case with the RCC and Regional Command, Saddam made sure that no one stayed too long in a position that was critical for his personal protection. As such he reduced the likelihood of any single individual developing his own power base to possibly challenge him as the absolute leader.

The National Security Bureau (*Maktab al-Amn al-Qawmi*), located in the Presidential Palace, took care of the day-to-day affairs on issues concerning the national security of Iraq and any perceived threat, internally and externally. The National Security Bureau (NSB) was designed to oversee and coordinate the work of the agencies, but the internal rivalry rendered it ineffective as an entity. In the agencies' attempt to bring exclusive information to the top for incentives they also sabotaged each other. It was also quite common for Saddam Hussein to go directly to the agencies, omitting or overriding the NSB. The NSB was therefore reduced to a think-tank and advisory group, although it was quite powerful in arranging the execution of coup suspects.[153]

The NSB included, however, an extensive computer network: the Joint Operations Room (JOR). It was one of the NSB's most important instruments in controlling the regime's activities, since it coordinated the various security forces that kept order in Baghdad. It was situated in the Presidential Palace and the officers assigned to the JOR were drawn selectively from the Amn al-Khass. The JOR was connected to a wide area computer network (WAN), which was again linked to the rapid brigade and technical department of the Mukhabarat. Additionally, the JOR was linked to both a rapid intervention battalion and a rapid security battalion from the Estikhbarat, and finally a rapid intervention brigade from the Special Republican Guard. Among other things, it had access to the records of everybody detained for political reasons in Iraq and it made sure that all international calls were recorded. It played as such an important part in the surveillance and monitoring of the people and the Party. Finally, the NSB was organised into different areas of responsibility: military and security, economic, foreign affairs, tribal relations and a department dealing only with economic agreements.

The role of the Mukhabarat was to collect intelligence at home and abroad on matters that had to do with the security of the state, and to carry out operations at home and abroad against those considered to be a threat to state security.[154] It was developed in the mid-1960s to ensure party loyalty, then called the Jihaz al-Khass (Special Apparatus) – code-named Jihaz al-Haneen (Instrument of Yearning) – but after the Ba'ath Party came to power in 1968 it was expanded to include the security (Amn) of the state. It was led by Nazim Kazzar, Saddoun Shakir and Saddam Hussein's half-brother Barzan, but it was not until Fadil Barak Hussein took over in the early 1980s that the agency really expanded to become arguably the most important arm of the state security system. Under the auspices of Barzan security was tightened, and a mobile headquarters was introduced in order to avoid assassination attempts. Fadil Barak Hussein, who was also born in Tikrit, next developed the agency beyond the family core of Saddam Hussein, and by the late 1980s its strength was some 4,000 full-time employees. The headquarters consisted of three main bureaux; the Special Bureau (M1), the Administration Bureau (M2) and the Political Bureau (M3).[155] The first was concerned with extremely sensitive matters and internal security, while the latter collected information from all around the world. Each country or region had its own office that conducted research and reported to the main office. These offices had personnel that were fluent in the relevant foreign language and some had influential business positions abroad. One of the offices, according to Major Harbi al-Jubburi, ran a very popular six-week course on how to make letter bombs and car bombs, while another, according to Scott Ritter, was responsible for educating terrorists.[156] This 'Long Arm of Saddam' played a leading role in suppressing discontent around Baghdad during the air campaign, and in seeking to deter would-be deserters from the Army it arranged highly publicised summary executions.[157] As a key intelligence agency it was critically important in installing fear among the Iraqi people.

Unlike the Mukhabarat, which was concerned with state security, Amn al-Khass provided the President with personal protection. It was the single most powerful agency, the most feared organ of domestic repression and may be regarded as a 5,000-man strong bodyguard for Saddam Hussein and his immediate family.[158] The Amn al-Khass was at the top of the pecking order, had the right to investigate members of all other agencies and enjoyed great power and prestige. It was set up at the end of the Iran–Iraq War and led by the late Hussein Kamel, Saddam Hussein's son-in-law and nephew. Their ranks were filled with the most loyal troops from the Republican Guard, Mukhabarat and Estikhbarat.[159] Again, the recruits came from reliable backgrounds, the Sunni lower class loyal to, and dependent on, Saddam Hussein. The feeling of unbound loyalty to their leader was reflected in the fact that they did not use formal titles for Saddam, they often refered to him as Ammna al-Chebiri (our Great Parental Uncle).[160] These people were further trained in explosives, assassination and protecting strategic sites such as palaces, in addition to electronic personnel surveillance. To qualify for the agency one normally had to be either a Tikriti or from the tribe of al-Bu Nasir, although exceptions were made. The employees were usually not well educated, but enjoyed good salaries and apartments in special quarters of Baghdad. According to Aras Habib, a member of the Iraqi National Congress, the Amn al-Khass soldiers often operated in plain clothes, and typically secured the palaces, while the Special Republican Guard secured the wider gardens of the palaces.[161] These two organisations had separate commands and no communication between them was accepted. Additionally, the inner circles of the palaces were supervised and guarded by the Himayat al-Ra'is and the Murafiqoun, both being somewhat separate from al-Amn al-Khass. Hussein Kamel had an important role in coordinating the Himayat, which was by the late 1980s a fairly large force of a few thousand in its own right. The Amn al-Khass provided teams, some specialised in static protection, guarding Saddam when he was present in one of his many palaces, while other teams specialised in protecting Saddam Hussein and his entourage when they were on the move. In addition to these bodyguard services they took great care in detecting dissidents, both in Iraq and abroad. The Amn al-Khass was further divided into three branches, much like the Mukhabarat. The first was the Security Branch (M1), which ensured internal security by watching members and ordering operations against suspects among its own staff. The second was the Administration Branch (M2), which dealt with general administration, food, supplies, salaries, driving and cleaning and so forth. The third was the Political Branch (M3), which gathered and analysed information and formulated scenarios for dealing with enemies of the regime. There were files on all citizens who had ever come to the attention of the authorities as possible dissidents, and these were further compared and incorporated into the JOR of the NSB. Hussein Kamel, as Minister of Military Industrialisation in the late 1980s, also used the Amn al-Khass to run an extensive arms and technology procurement network, operating through a host of some 52 companies world-wide.[162]

While Amn al-Khass provided the inner protection of the ruling family of the regime, the Special Republican Guard served as a second shield and the Republican Guard as a third concentric circle around Baghdad. Unlike the Army and the Republican Guard, which were military forces, the Special Republican Guard was predominately a security force, albeit with military capabilities. Its stated mission was fourfold: to protect the President, conduct any other duty that may be ordered, protect presidential facilities and prepare for combat duties.[163]

In order to carry out its role it was organised into two basic structures: the combat brigade and the security brigade. The members of this elite force were drawn from areas and clans noted for their loyalty to the Iraqi leader.[164] It was established in 1983 with only three battalions to take care of matters around Saddam Hussein, but over the years it had gradually increased both in size and quality. By 1990 it amounted to a possible strength of some 26,000.[165] As with the Amn al-Khass, the units contained 'static' and 'dynamic' elements. One part of the security force surrounded Saddam Hussein's palaces and his immediate family while another part followed him wherever he went. Among the latter some always stayed with the Iraqi leader, while the others dispersed, so that only a very limited number of people would know his exact whereabouts. An area of 5 square miles around the place he intended to visit would furthermore typically be checked for mines and snipers.[166] Other parts of the Special Republican Guard were further concerned with administration, while some constituted the intervention (emergency) force, ready to deploy whenever and wherever needed. This was known as the fighter unit, consisting of some 9,000 members. Although administrative, logistical and general military matters were sometimes coordinated with the Republican Guard, the Special Republican Guard reported separately to the Office of the Presidential Palace. By 1984, to further confuse his potential enemies about his whereabouts, Saddam Hussein relied on 'doubles', a practice copied by his son, Uday.[167] The Iraqi leader often arranged fake attacks against himself, or one of his doubles, in order to see who would sacrifice their lives for him,[168] constantly testing the loyalty of the forces designed to protect him.

Another important element of the security and intelligence network was the military intelligence service, al-Istikhbarat al-Askariya. Its main role was to deal with military threats abroad and from within Iraq, such as those posed by the Kurdish forces in the north. Its heavily guarded complex was like a small town, including its own supermarket, prison, interrogation centre and car park, making it totally independent of the military institutions. It used to report to the Ministry of Defence, but with the outbreak of the Iran–Iraq war it was brought under the command of the Office of the Presidential Palace.[169] Isatikhbarat was divided into four regional headquarters. The Kirkuk base was responsible for the northern sector, particularly the Kurdish region and the north-east border with Iran. The Mosul base handled intelligence regarding Turkey and Syria, while the Basra base covered intelligence on the Gulf states and the south-east border with Iran. The fourth base was in Baghdad, but separate from the main headquarters, and dealt with intelligence related to Jordan, Syria, Saudi Arabia, Iran and opposition groups. While al-Amn al-Khass was predominately responsible for general state security, the Estikhbarat handled the military threats. The single largest unit in the Estikhbarat was al-Amn al-Askariyya (military security service), which was established as an independent agency in 1992. Al-Amn al-Askariyya was responsible for detecting dissent and corruption within the Iraqi armed forces, including the Republican Guard, and by the late 1980s it operated as if it were an independent agency. Although theoretically part of the special branch (M1), it often reported directly to the Office of the Presidential Palace, and its role went far beyond the traditional Military Police that one finds in US and European services. One section ensured also that the watchers were being watched, and Unity 999 dealt with deep penetration and infiltration in clandestine operations at home and abroad. Al-Amn al-Askariyya was responsible for the sabotage of oil installations in Iran and later Kuwait, and they also tried to kidnap General Norman Schwarzkopf during Operation Desert Shield.[170] Unlike the special branch, the political branch did not involve itself with combat operations, but ensured a network of intelligence gathering on all military and strategic affairs.[171]

While Estikbarat was concerned with military security and loyalty within the armed forces, the Amn al-Amm (General Security Service) dealt with detecting dissidents among the civilian population of Iraq. The Amn al-Amm was the notorious secret police, and although it reported to the Ministry of Interior during the 1970s, by the time the Iran–Iraq war was under way it reported directly to the Office of the Presidential Palace. By the late 1980s a number of directives were transferred to this branch from the anti-crime section of the civilian police, expanding its authority further. There was typically an Amn al-Amm branch in every police station providing the regime with eyes and ears throughout the society with its mere presence in every town and village. It included a security branch, which checked internal affairs, and a military brigade, which provided for rapid intervention, amounting in total to more than 8,000 members. In the insurgency campaigns against the Kurds in the 1980s the Amn al-Amm would hunt down members of the Kurdish parties in towns or the urban underground, infiltrating organisations, while Estikhbarat would gather information of a military nature, often fighting armed guerrillas in the countryside or in neighbouring Iran. Its most important role was to make sure that no dissent occurred in every-day life. For example, some teachers had to give a report on their colleges, and this was to be sent directly to an agency. The agency then decided whether a copy should go to the Ba'ath Party organisation or not. Others had to report to the Party itself, and in both cases the immediate superiors in the school were bypassed. In addition to the core of 8,000 members in the Amm, the informers, who were placed throughout the country, often guided by the Ministry of Interior, may have added up to some 260,000, according to Kanan Makiya, by the late 1980s.[172] One should, however, be very careful in accepting such numbers. There were certainly many, most of them unpaid, and the system was roughly similar to the one that prevailed in East Germany before the collapse of the Soviet bloc.[173] The East Germans were instructing the Iraqis on matters of internal security, but it is simply too difficult to provide an estimate of how many Iraqis were involved.

The final agency that deserves mentioning is al-Hadi Project (Project 858). It was not well known in 1990, but it included some 800 full-time employees operating around the clock, gathering signals intelligence (SIGINT) and electronic intelligence (ELINT) both inside and outside Iraq. Its sophisticated computer equipment was acquired via Japan in 1983–84, and it monitored military and civilian communications in the Kurdish region and the neighbouring countries throughout the latter half of the decade. The headquarters was at al-Rashedia, about 2 kilometres north of Baghdad, but it maintained five other ground stations, or listening posts, around Iraq. The members of al-Hadi decoded messages that were related to sensitive information, and sent them to the relevant agency for evaluation. For example, if the information was of a military nature it might go to the Estikhbarat, and if it was of a civilian nature it might go to al-Amm or al-Khass. Project 858 was a technical agency as opposed to the others, but it was responsible directly to the Office of the Presidential Palace and thus enjoyed considerable status in the Iraqi intelligence community. This electronic network naturally became an attractive target for the US strategic air power planners in their attempt to isolate the regime.

When taken altogether the elaborate security system reminds one of Franz Kafka's novels wherein he demonstrates man's fear, isolation and bewilderment in a nightmarish dehumanised world. While these agencies were all-important in preventing people from getting close to the Iraqi leader, there was always that added security dimension: he did not stay long in one place; he had many doubles; dinner was prepared for him in five or six places; the food-taster was closely related to the cook; and he normally wore a bullet-proof vest and hat. The whole business of getting to him was made almost impossible, and allegedly visitors were x-rayed in case they had swallowed some kind of explosive that would detonate in a suicide mission. According to Khidhir Hamza:

> Saddam had a terrible fear, perhaps paranoia, about germs. A physician was always stationed outside his office to look over visitors ... Although he was a nominal Muslim, Saddam permitted only Christians to work on his housekeeping staff, convinced they were cleaner than his own people.[174]

The purpose and design of the security and intelligence network, which reflected the Iraqi leader's suspicious nature, was the basis for the regime's power as it managed to control the Ba'ath Party and provide the leadership with personal security. While the perceived omnipresence of the Party prevented demonstrations, riots and uprisings from taking an organised form inside Iraq during the air campaign, the security and intelligence network prevented coups and plots against the regime from succeeding during the Intifada. The regime's brutal revenge on those who were merely suspected of being associated with such attempts further discouraged expressions of discontent. Saddam's success in surviving both the air strikes in Desert Storm and the subsequent turmoil was no small achievement, and although many factors contributed, his survival demonstrated first and foremost the extraordinary efficiency of the described network. The structure of Saddam's political power base made sure that the opposition was totally unprepared when their moment arrived in March 1991. The conditions for a coup or an uprising simply did not exist. Although the Black Hole and Checkmate planners received some information about the Iraqi regime through 'Iraqi experts', the Cockburns argue that not a single analyst from the Department of State, CIA, DIA or NSA 'had ever set foot inside Iraq'.[175] This was to some extent a result of former Secretary of State George Shultz's 1988 memorandum, which forbade any US official from having contact with Iraqi opposition groups.[176] It was also a reflection of US military doctrine, where the order of battle was the focus rather than the construction of the regime itself. While the air planners sought to isolate the regime from its own people, the military forces and the outside world, they also intended to disrupt the core itself: the security and intelligence network which was intertwined with a unique tribal kinship system. However, because of the rigid focus of the US military intelligence system, very little information was available to the air campaign planners on the subject of the Iraqi intelligence network and the inner workings of the Saddam regime.

THE IRAQI TRIBAL KINSHIP SYSTEM

However important the aforementioned institutions were to Saddam's hold on power, comprehending the inner workings of the Iraqi regime requires that one goes beyond this extraordinary organisational design and discusses how the ruling elite was linked by tribe, clan and family ties. It was a social network of both formal and informal structures, in which connectivity between individuals and clans, and social closeness with the leader, determined power. These ties amounted to an informal kinship network which included extensive configurations through mutual residence, intermarriage, common lineage and other links.[177] Saddam modelled himself and his system partly on Stalin and the security system of Eastern Europe, but he merged these features with his instinct for tribalism (*al-qabaliyya*). Family and tribal connection were supreme to him, because such ties were stronger than individual commitment to the state and ideology. Saddam intuitively considered these tribal soldiers of primarily rural Bedouin roots to be more 'Arab', placing a greater emphasis on honour and ferocity in war than non-tribal urban ones.[178] It was often the case that the tribal and family proximity to Saddam personally was more important than the formal position. Thus, a junior officer or official could be responsible for issues completely unknown to his superior. In order to understand the workings of the Iraqi regime it becomes imperative to identify the 'ruling clan' and its relations to the more formal structure.

Saddam Hussein's tribal policy started when the Ba'ath Party came to power in 1968, but underwent a quantum leap in the late 1980s, according to Amatzia Baram:

> First, rather than eliminating the tribal shaykh as a socio-political power, as dictated by party doctrine, he endeavoured to manipulate the shaykhs, and through a process of socialization (or 'Ba'thization'), turn them into docile tools in the service of the regime. Second, and a far sharper departure from party tradition, he turned the tribal shaykhs into legitimate partners of power-sharing; he tribalized the regime's Praetorian Guard, and he worked to reawaken long-suppressed and often forgotten tribal affinities in that part of Iraqi society which is no longer tribal and to graft onto the tribal values, or what he considered to be such values.[179]

In the early 1970s the Iraqi sociology expert Hanna Batatu observed that 'the Takritis rule through the Ba'th party, rather than the Ba'th party through the Takritis'.[180] Thus:

> to depend on a tribe is a thousand times safer than depending on the government, for while the latter defers or neglects oppression, the tribe, no matter how feeble it may be, as soon as it learns that an injustice has been committed against one of its members, readies itself to exact vengeance on its behalf.[181]

By the early 1970s Tikrit had provided leading members of the RCC: the President, the Vice President, Secretary of Defence and Foreign Affairs, the Mayor of Baghdad, the commander of the Baghdad garrison and the commander of the Republican Guard. Since the Ba'ath Party came to power in 1968, Iraq has more or less been run as an extended family business, and supreme power rested in the hands of the tribe of al-Bu Nasir, which predominately resided in the environs of Tikrit and Beiji. It is difficult to get a complete picture of al-Bu Nasir, but Figure 7, which is developed by Amatzia Baram, is rather comprehensive.

Figure 7: al-Bu Nasir: Saddam Hussein's Tribe.
Source: Baram, *Building Toward Crisis.*

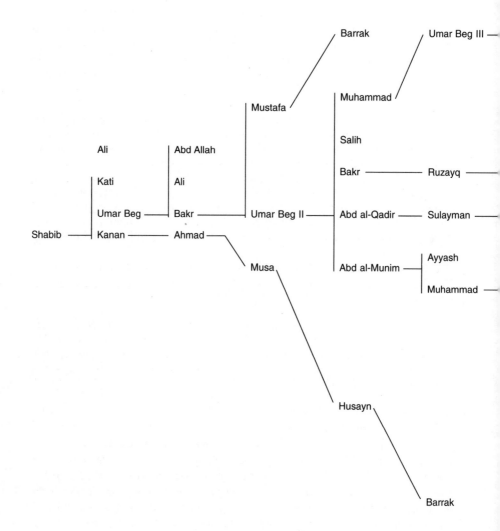

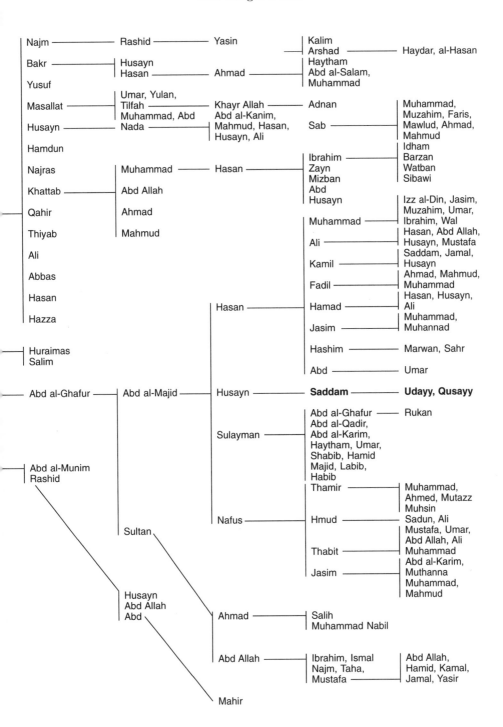

Within the tribe of al-Bu Nasir, Umar Beg III played an important role in Saddam's power base, as it provided for al-Masallat (the origins of al-Tilfah, Saddam's foster-father and uncle), al-Bakr (the origins of Ahamd Hasan, the former President and Saddam's relative) and al-Khattab (the origins of Abd Hamid Hmoud, Saddam's personal secretary, and Ibrahim Hasan Muhammad, Saddam's step-father and thus his three half-brothers). These parts of Saddam's family tree held extremely important positions during the late 1980s and early 1990s, but the key line of power nevertheless went through Abd al-Ghafur, who gave rise to the Majid family. Within this family branch there were his cousin, Ali Hasan al-Majid, and his nephews, Hussein and Saddam Kamil Hasan al-Majid. One of Saddam's key bodyguards, Rukan abd al-Ghafur Sulayman, was also one of the Majids, given the responsibility of overseeing Saddam's relationship within his own clan.

The area where the Majid tribe resided, together with their allies, had been given its own governorate status: the Salah al-Din governorate. It was one of 18 governates in Iraq, and it encompassed some 800,000 citizens. The urban centres were Samarra, Tikrit, Door and Beiji, but the medium-sized al-Bu Nasir included no more than 25,000.[182] Furthermore, if one concentrated on Umar Beg III and Abd al-Ghafur, the number amounted to perhaps a little more than 1,000 in 1990, of whom half were women who were more or less excluded from public life. Thus, the active core of individuals engaged in political, military or security affairs ran to a few hundred. Al-Bu Nasir was indeed a small tribe compared to huge federations such as Shammar, Dulaym and Jubbur. This may well be the source of their power, in addition to good organisation and social cohesion: the tribe is too small to threaten the larger federations, and can therefore serve as mediator, moderator and coordinator without becoming a serious menace.

The Sunni Triangle was the underpinning of the Iraqi leader's power base, and tribal structure permeated the Iraqi society. Rather than eliminate the tribal sheikhs as a sociopolitical power, as decreed by the 1968 Ba'ath Party manifesto, which saw tribalism as a symbol of backwardness and a threat to the social elite, Saddam Hussein managed to turn the sheikhs into instruments that served his regime.[183] He allowed the sheikhs to govern rural regions, and in return they would support him as their national leader. Families and relatives of the sheikhs were given advantages in social life and education, officers from the right tribal background were promoted most rapidly and Saddam Hussein rewarded the villages of the tribes in which recruitment had taken place with electricity, roads and water. The young men who were recruited were proud to serve their leader, and, knowing that their tribe relied on them, Saddam Hussein received the most loyal force one could imagine. In a typical *divide et impere* fashion the Iraqi leader would furthermore distribute land areas among the tribes so that the smaller were strengthened at the expense of the larger, avoiding monopoly in local power and maintaining a certain 'balance of power'. Saddam Hussein had by the late 1980s been successful in securing tribal support in the countryside, as he persuaded tribal chiefs to betray members of their own tribes who posed a threat to his regime. Consequently he relied on the tribal leaders themselves, not on his internal security soldiers, to police within the tribe. The power invested in these sheikhs provided the President with a certain leverage against the Ba'ath Party becoming too strong.[184] Using kinship relations as an instrument of power was truly an art in creating and maintaining personal power and the Iraqi leader had almost tuned this to perfection. Still, these were all manifestations of power that ultimately were conditioned by the Iraqi leader. While great power was invested in family connections they too were only acting on delegated authority, and their power was completely in the hands of Saddam Hussein.

In essence, the inner core of the family network was based on two rival wings: the Majids, progeny of his father and his parental uncle, and the Ibrahims, progeny of Saddam Hussein's step-father. From the former family there were personalities like Ali Hasan al-Majid, Hussein Kamel al-Majid, Saddam Kamel al-Majid and Rokan Abd al-Ghafur Suleiman al-Majid. The Ibrahims was dominated by Saddam's three half brothers: Barzan, Sabawi and Wathban. Both family branches realised that if Saddam were overthrown, they too would meet their destiny. The Iraqi leader's policy over the years had been to balance the two against each other. A typical intrigue arose in 1983 when Saddam Hussein approved of Hussein Kamel al-Majid marrying his eldest daughter, Raghab, instead of Barzan Hasan al-Ibrahim's nephew. Barzan Hasan protested, knowing that the Majid side would increase its power-share at the expense of the Ibrahims, with the result that he was fired as chief of Mukhabarat. Finally, Saddam relied on his two sons, Uday and Qussay, of whom the latter proved himself the most able in terms of regime security matters. By the late 1980s people from al-Majid's extended family controlled the Ministry of Defence, the Military Bureau, Ministry of Military Industries, the Mukhabarat, the internal security organisations and other agencies. While the members who belonged to the administrative chain, the Party chain and the security chain were part of an organisation that set certain restraints on their authority, members of the clan enjoyed a wider reach of power only controlled by the President. This was therefore a vast informal network that served as a counterbalance to the Ba'ath Party at the same time as complementing it, ensuring a formidable cohesion which kept the ruling elite in power, outliving massive challenges such as the 1991 Gulf War and the civil war that followed. By the late 1980s, Hussein

Kamel al-Majid, Saddam Hussein's nephew and son-in-law, was the second most powerful man in Iraq. But even he was under supervision by Saddam Hussein's personal secretary, a member of the Khattab family branch, Brigadier General Abd Hamid Hmoud of the Office of the Presidential Palace.

Saddam Hussein, however, from the outset realised that basing his power on his own tribe and family was both his strength and his weakness. Occasionally tribal loyalty took precedence over regime loyalty, and with too many from his own tribe in powerful places they would also have the required levels of power to overthrow him. This narrow base was therefore compensated by liaisons to other clans and tribes within the Sunni Arab configuration. Most importantly they included the Jubbur, Ubayd and Dulaym tribe federations, all located in the Sunni Triangle. The part of Jubbur that resided in the Tikrit area was typically closer to Saddam's tribe than the areas south of Baghdad. To complicate the matter further al-Bu Nasir had Shia branches in the south, and other predominantly Shia tribes, such as the Banu Hisan tribe, had been long-time supporters of both the Party and the regime. Saddam Hussein managed to play these groups off against each other, and shielded by the Iran–Iraq war he obtained strong support throughout the 1980s. There was, however, the Jubbur-led coup attempt in January 1990, but Saddam Hussein exposed it and executed scores of Jubburi officers in the Army and the Republican Guard. Others were retired, according to Colonel Muhammed Ali, but their positions were partly restored after the invasion of Kuwait when Saddam Hussein needed as many able officers as possible.[185] Lieutenant General Sadi Tuma Abbas al-Jubburi was made Minister of Defence, being considered one of Iraq's greatest practitioners of defensive warfare – a reputation he obtained while skilfully defending Basra from Iranian offensives in 1982.[186] Table 4 provides a summary of the tribes and clans on which Saddam relied in addition to his own al-Bu Nasir tribe.[187] Although tribal relations were important to the Aref regimes and Ahmad al-Bakr, it was during Saddam's period that it became almost an art of statecraft, and therein lie many of the secrets regarding the absolutism of the regime.

The present leadership did not invent the ethnic, religious, sectarian and tribal diversities in Iraqi society, but it perpetuated and exacerbated these divisions rather than work to overcome them, and all for the purpose of strengthening the regime.[188] For example, the rank and file of the armed forces were Shia and a substantial number in the secret police were Shia.[189] Some tribes, most notably the Jubburi, had both Shia and Sunni clans. About 10 per cent of the Republican Guard were Shia, but typically there were less as one moved upwards in the system. Among the 60 generals, including the Iraqi Army, who received most

Table 4: Al-Bu Nasir's Closest Allies

Al-Bu Nasir tribe and clan allies	Location
Jubbur	In the Tikrit area, and immediately south of Baghdad
Ubayd	Immediately north of Baghdad
Dulaym	West of Baghdad – the Anbar province
Saddoun	Deep south around Nasiriyya
Harb	Dur-area
Adayat	South-west of Mosul
Khazraji	West of the Tigris, between Baghdad and Samarra
Mushahada	South of Khazraji
Azza	Between Tigris and Iranian border north of Baghdad
(Shammar Jarbah)	Jazirah, west and north-west of Baghdad and Samarra

media attention during the war with Iran, at least 20 per cent were Shia.[190] The Popular Army, once a small group of the Party militia, was by the late 1980s recruited from all over Iraq.

Saddam Hussein's bodyguards, however, almost to a man came from the same tribe and same geographical area, being housed in special compounds in Baghdad (al-Radwaniyya, Havyy al-Salam and al-Qasr al-Jumhuri) rather isolated from the rest of the population. While this was the inner circle, he further recruited extensively from al-Bu Nasir, al-Jubbur and al-Ubayd for other security positions, and again these officials tended to live in the same quarters of Baghdad. One of the characteristics of the Iraqi political structure was that the avenue of social mobility was either through the Ba'ath Party or through tribal inheritance. Iraq was not a *military* dictatorship, despite the size of its armed forces. The regime had a stronghold within civilian society through special agencies, party organisations and internal competition.[191] The system was not cost-effective compared to US and European democratic standards, but it served its major goals: it ensured the President's personal power through promoting a sense of helplessness among the population.[192] It was, in one sense, not the Ba'ath Party or its military forces that held the system together on the eve of Desert Storm, nor even the security and intelligence system itself, but the Tikritis and the tribe of al-Bu Nasir, who in their total permeation of these official institutions became an unofficial but crucial power source in their own right. It was the members of these tribes, clans and families that in effect ran the country through the security and intelligence network. Although Shia Arabs had been given a certain degree of representation, Saddam Hussein relied on members of his own tribe for the most influential posts. Saddam Hussein, by the time he became President, had orchestrated a change that might be referred to as a depoliticisation of the military, coupled with a Ba'athistisation of society and a selective reintroduction of tribalism into politics.[193] While headquarters and bunkers make easy targets, the ruling clan of Iraq was far less tangible and definable. On the eve of Desert Storm, Tikrit, some 1,000 kilometres from the front line, was a fortress, leaving no doubt that Iraq's pre-war security arrangements were mostly concerned with internal matters.[194]

Importantly, while these family connections were powerful they were not directly involved in high politics. Such matters were left to Tariq Aziz (Christian), Saadoun Hammadi (Shia), Taha Ramadan (Sunni with Kurdish ancestry) and Izzat Ibrahim al-Duri. One group was concerned with regime security, while the other was concerned with domestic and foreign policy – all controlled by Saddam. Thus, a hierarchical ranking of power would not make sense, and what determined the 'inner circle' depended on the issue. It is the overall combination and interaction of 'powers' that put Saddam in such a unique position. This was a system of checks and balances where everyone was vulnerable, one way or the other.[195]

The complexity of the Iraqi political power structure has been illustrated. The combination of military forces, governmental institutions and an extensive security apparatus, orchestrated through the Party and led by the tribe and family, were the instruments Saddam Hussein al-Majid Abd al-Ghafur developed to sustain personal, domestic and regional power. Although each of the five identified 'pillars' contributed to the power of the man at the centre, the synergy of the 'parallel hierarchies' amounted to an extremely resilient regime. The whole structure was founded on security precautions taken by the Iraqi leader, who surrounded himself with coalition tribes, relatives and supporters in order to minimise the risk of assassination. Although such a rigid and centralised command structure has weaknesses, it presented the regime with an enormous durability and survivability.

On the eve of 'the Mother of all Battles', the Iraqi leader had established a bifurcation in the armed forces. The Ministry of Defence and the Republican Guard were entrusted to loyal non-Tikritis, while the positions of Chief of Staff, Air Force Commander and Minister of Military Industries remained in the hands of Tikritis. Saddam Hussein's own half-brothers controlled the security and intelligence, with other close family members in counterweight positions. This arrangement made any attempt to seize power dependent on cooperation between groups that did not work closely together.[196] While Ba'ath Party membership was a precondition for social prestige, the significance was not so much that a one-party state secured the Iraqi leader popularity, but that it prevented powerful opposition. While the security and intelligence network protected the regime against coups, the Ba'ath Party's perceived omnipresence prevented organised opposition from getting a foothold inside Iraq. Although life in Iraq is beyond what outsiders can comprehend, one may suggest that it is an environment of fear, suspicion and secrecy, and therein all problems of organising an effective opposition reside. It seems as though the Iraqi people, however closely connected to the regime, were more afraid of Saddam Hussein than of the bombers. As long as Saddam was on the ground close by and with a lot of sensors and tentacles everywhere he was perceived as much more dangerous than the precision-guided missiles.

When an institution such as the RCC is presented as the collective decision- and policy-making organ for over 20 years with a state controlled media, one may suspect that it eventually carries with it some degree of perceived legitimacy. For a people fond of reading newspapers and listening to news on the radio, the multilayer endorsement of the Iraqi leader may have had the desired effect of ensuring some support for the regime, or at least ensuring passivity in the wide masses. When combined with violent suppression of internal opposition, there are further incentives to accept the status quo rather than protest. On one level, the media was Saddam's mouthpiece, but on another, by coming out regularly even during wars, it gave the impression that the regime was functioning rather smoothly. Thus, any attempt to challenge it could be fatal. Indeed, the Shia Intifada gained momentum in the south only after Iraqi radio broadcasts were disrupted and replaced by the BBC's psychological warfare pieces.[197]

By the end of the 1980s, the Kurdish separatists and the communists presented no significant threat to the Ba'ath regime. Any operation against the regime would require weeks of planning, and the conspirators would need to seize key instruments of executive power. The Iraqi system was, however, good at detecting such efforts at an early stage and with deadly consequences for the participants and their families such attempts were discouraged. Moreover, to physically seize control of the instruments of power was extremely difficult, as clan-based rule was less definable than traditional parliamentary systems. Security and control were furthermore tighter the closer one came to the inner circle. Additionally, minority rule had the prerogative that most people in powerful positions realised that they would face trouble if the Iraqi leader were overthrown. Large parts of Iraqi society were dependent on Saddam in order to retain their own positions. Support of the regime, therefore, was more of a necessity than a choice for some. The political power structure enabled Saddam Hussein to maintain micro-management of population and staff, which ultimately ensured that the regime was extremely resistant to coup and revolt. While the Party and the state institutions provided a facade of legitimacy with a political platform and collective policy-making in the name of the RCC, a relatively small unaccountable group held the real power. As such, the combination of having the largest military apparatus in the Arab world in a tightly knit one-party state provided the Iraqi leader with considerable domestic power.

Any examination of the Iraqi political power structure should question the air planners' assumption that a strategic air campaign could change the Iraqi regime. While one may understand that the air planners had limited knowledge of the inner workings of the Iraqi regime in the early days of the crisis, the Five Rings Model has been suggested as a generic concept, and therein one must question the understanding of foreign political cultures. Even if classified details of the Iraqi regime were not made available to the planners at the time, there is nothing new about the regime's overall political architecture. Whether one goes back to the Praetorian Guard or the then existing structure of the Soviet Union or Eastern European states, one will understand that the Iraqi regime was an extensive bodyguard system. When Instant Thunder was put together there was no mention of the Republican Guard, the Special Republican Guard, Amn al-Khass or the extensive security and intelligence network, which collectively, in effect, linked the outer and inner ring of the Five Ring Model. Nor did the model account for the complexities inside the inner ring itself, and its reliance on tribal networks. In sum, while the air planners introduced a new air power concept, which suggested going to the heart of the problem with lethal force from the outset, they had very limited understanding of the true centres of gravity. In order to examine the political validity of the air planners' strategy, Chapter 5 will discuss the showdown between the strategic air campaign and what proved to be an extremely resilient regime.

NOTES

1. United States Department of Defense, *Conduct of the Persian Gulf War*, 1992, pp. 95–6.
2. United States Army, *The Iraqi Army: Organization and Tactics* (Boulder, CO: Paladin Press, 1991); Peter Gilchrist, *Sea Power: the Coalition and Iraqi Navies*, Desert Storm Special 1 (London: Osprey Publishing, 1991); Roy Braybrook, *Air Power: the Coalition and Iraqi Air Forces*, Desert Storm Special 2 (London: Osprey Publishing, 1991); Tim Ripley, *Land Power: the Coalition and Iraqi Armies*, Desert Storm Special 3 (London: Osprey Publishing, 1991); United States Department of Defense, *Conduct of the Persian Gulf War 1992*, pp. 95–6; Cohen *et al.*, *Gulf War Air Power Survey: Operations*, pp. 53–82; Cordesman and Wagner, *The Lessons of Modern War*, Vol. IV, pp. 113–36; Blackwell, *Thunder in the Desert*, pp. 29–73; James F. Dunnigan and Austin Bay, *From Shield to Storm: High-Tech Weapons, Military Strategy, and Coalition Warfare in the Persian Gulf* (New York: William Morrow and Company, 1992), pp. 74–91.

3. Figure 4 was developed from talks with Amatzia Baram, Michael Eisenstadt, Faleh al-Jabbar and Saleh Umar al-Ali: Amatzia Baram, interview with author, tape-recording, Washington, DC, 19 February 1999; Michael Eisenstadt, interview with author, tape-recording, Washington, DC, 25 February 1999; Faleh al-Jabbar, interviews with author, tape-recordings, London, 4 and 19 August 1998; and Salah Umar al-Ali, interviews with author, tape-recordings, London, 11 July 1998 and 13 May 1999. A note of appreciation to Christian Wattengård for drawing the figure.

4. Karsh and Rautsi, *Saddam Hussein*, p. 2. See also Musallam Ali Musallam, *The Iraqi Invasion of Kuwait: Saddam Hussein, his State and International Power Politics* (London: British Academic Press, 1996), pp. 14, 27 and 59.

5. Algosaibi, *The Gulf Crisis*, pp. 5–14; Jerold M. Post, 'The Defining Moment of Saddam's Life: A Political Psychology Perspective on the Leadership and Decision Making of Saddam Hussein During the Gulf Crisis', in Stanley A. Renshon (ed.), *The Political Psychology of the Gulf War: Leaders, Publics, and the Process of Conflict* (London: University of Pittsburg Press, 1993), pp. 49–66; Musallam, *The Iraqi Invasion of Kuwait*, pp. 33–61; Khaled Bin Sultan with Seale, *Desert Warrior*, pp. 153–72; Alan Munro, *An Arabian Affair: Politics and Diplomacy behind the Gulf War* (London: Brassey's, 1996), pp. 1–14; Paul Gray, 'The Man Behind the Demonic Image', *Time Magazine*, 11 February 1991, pp. 28–9; Ofra Bengio, 'Saddam Husayn's Quest for Power and Survival', *Asian and African Studies* 15 (1981), pp. 323–41; and Amatzia Baram, 'Saddam Husayn: a Political Profile', *Jerusalem Quarterly* 17, No. 3 (Fall 1980), pp. 115–44.

6. Otto Friedrich, 'Master of His Universe', *Time Magazine*, 13 August 1990, pp. 15–16; and Peter McGrath *et al.*, 'More Than a Madman', *Newsweek*, 14 January 1991, pp. 16–19.

7. For two accounts favourable to Saddam Hussein available in English: Faud Matar, *Saddam Hussein: the Man, the Cause and the Future* (London: Third World Centre, 1981); and Amir Iskander, *Saddam Hussein: The Fighter, the Thinker and the Man*, transl. Hasan Selim (Paris: Hachette Realities, 1980). Note that both deal with Saddam Hussein's rise to the presidency and not beyond.

8. According to an Arab Press Service profile of Saddam Hussein in 1987, he was 'fearless, ruthless, calculating, fair, conscientious, extremely intelligent, analytical, extremely shrewd, efficient, consistent, organized, generous, elegant, polite, and cautious', as cited in Simon Henderson, *Instant Empire: Saddam Hussein's Ambition for Iraq* (San Francisco: Mercury House, 1991), p. 232.

9. Aburish, *Saddam Hussein*, p. 15.

10. Ibid., p. 13.

11. Ibid., p. 12.

12. Karsh and Rautsi, *Saddam Hussein*, p. 15; and Laith Kubba, interview with author, tape-recording, London, 3 August 1998.

13. Henderson, *Instant Empire*, p. 3.

14. Iskander, *Saddam Hussein*, pp. 17–29.

15. Saddam Hussein, interview with Matar, *Saddam Hussein*, p. 236; Post, 'The Defining Moment of Saddam's Life', p. 51; and Musallam, *The Iraqi Invasion of Kuwait*, pp. 40, 43.

16. Mohamedou, *Iraq and the Second Gulf War*, p. 91.

17. Iskander, *Saddam Hussein*, pp. 112–19.

18. Salah Umar al-Ali, interview with author, tape-recording, London, 10 July 1998.

19. Ibid.

20. Iskander, *Saddam Hussein*, pp. 112–19; Ranim Hampton, interview with author, tape-recording, London, 5 August 1998; Laith Kubba, interview with author, tape-recording, London, 3 August 1998; Habib Karim, interview with author,

tape-recording, London, 17 May 1999; and Colonel Hamed Salem al-Zyadi, inter-view with author, tape-recording, London, 27 January 1999. See also Adel Darwish and Gregory Alexander, *Unholy Babylon: The Secret History of Saddam's War* (New York: St. Martin's Press, 1991), p. 205.

21. Hanna Batatu, *The Old Social Classes and the Revolutionary Movements of Iraq: A Study of Iraq's Old Landed and Commercial Classes and of its Communities, Ba'thists and Free Officers* (Princeton, NJ: Princeton University Press, 1978), p. 1095.
22. Robert Fisk, 'Saddam Hussein: The Last Great Tyrant', *The Independent*, 30 December 2000.
23. 'The Algiers Accord on 6 March 1975', full text in A. G. Noorani, *The Gulf Wars: Documents and Analysis* (New Delhi: Konark Publishers Pvt, 1991), pp. 7–9.
24. Saad al-Bazzaz, *The Ashes of Wars: Post Gulf War Secrets* (London: Dor at-Hikma, 1995), p. 53.
25. Saddam Hussein, interview with Diane Sawyer, *ABC Television*, 24 June 1990, cited in Karsh and Rautsi, *Saddam Hussein*, p. 179. See also Henderson, *Instant Empire*, p. 237.
26. Fisk, 'Saddam Hussein'.
27. Matar, *Saddam Hussein*, pp. 235–6. See also General Wafiq Samarrai, interview with BBC Frontline, p. 13.
28. Amatzia Baram, *Culture, History and Ideology in the Formation of Ba'thist Iraq: 1968–1969* (London: Macmillan, 1991), pp. 101–8.
29. Mohamedou, *Iraq and the Second Gulf War*, p. 79.
30. John Bullock and Harvey Morris, *Saddam's War: The Origins of the Kuwait Conflict and the International Response* (London: Faber and Faber, 1991), pp. 26–7.
31. Zoheir al-Yasarei, interview with author, tape-recording, London, 19 August 1998; Ofra Bengio, *Saddam's Word: Political Discourse in Iraq* (New York: Oxford University Press, 1998), pp. 11, 41; and Henderson, *Instant Empire*, pp. 78–9.
32. Khaled Bin Sultan with Seale, *Desert Warrior*, p. 156.
33. Faleh al-Jabbar, 'Saddam Says He Was Just Following God's Order into War', *The Guardian* (London), 11 June 1990.
34. Yevgeni Primakov, 'The Inside Story of Moscow's Quest for a Deal', *Time Magazine*, 4 April 1991, pp. 32–8; General Wafiq Samarrai, interview with BBC Frontline, transcript, p. 22; Jerold M. Post, 'The Defining Moment of Saddam's Life', p. 50; and Norman Cigar, 'Iraq's Strategic Mindset and the Gulf War', p. 1.
35. Aburish, *Saddam Hussein*, pp. 208–9. Ghassan Attiya, interview with author, tape-recording, London, 4 December 1998; and Aras Habib, interview with author, tape-recording, London, 2 April 1998.
36. Julian Walker, former Ambassador to Iraq, interview with author, tape-recording, London, 3 August 1998; Tashin Mualla, interview with author, tape-recording, London, 14 August 1998; Aras Habib, interview with author, tape-recording, London, 2 April 1998; Ghasan Attiya, interview with author, tape-recording, 4 February 1999; and Salah Umar al-Ali, interview with author, tape-recording, London, 13 May 1999.
37. Amatzia Baram, interview with author, tape-recording, Washington, DC, 19 February 1999.
38. Ghassan Attiya, interview with author, tape-recording, London, 4 December 1998.
39. Yevgeni Primakov, 'The Inside Story of Moscow's Quest for a Deal', *Time Magazine*, 4 April 1991, pp. 32–8.
40. Tashin Mualla, interview with author, tape-recording, London, 14 August 1998; Brigadier General Tawfiq al-Yasiri, interview with author, notes, London, 6 August 1998; and Colonel Hasan Khafaji, interview with author, notes, London, 3 August 1998.

41. Aburish, *Saddam Hussein*, p. 199.
42. Algosaibi, *The Gulf Crisis*, pp. 14–15.
43. *Al-Jumhuriyya* (Baghdad), 2 August 1990, p. 3, cited in Cigar, 'Iraq's Strategic Mindset and the Gulf War', p. 3.
44. Saad al-Bazzaz, *The Ashes of Wars*, 1995, p. 6.
45. Karsh and Rautsi, *Saddam Hussein*, p. 211; and Algosaibi, *The Gulf Crisis*, p. 7.
46. Post, 'The Defining Moment of Saddam's Life', p. 64; Ranim Hampton, interview with author, tape-recording, London, 5 August 1998; and Hiro, *Desert Shield to Desert Storm*, p. 85.
47. Tariq Aziz, interview with BBC Frontline, transcript, pp. 4, 9.
48. Post, 'The Defining Moment of Saddam's Life', p. 55.
49. Ibid., pp. 55–6; Iraqi National Accord, interview with author, tape-recording, London, 14 May 1998; and Kanan Makiya, interview with author, tape-recording, London, 2 July 1998. (The term Masada complex originates with the siege of the Jewish fortress of Masada in 73 AD, whose inhabitants committed mass suicide rather than surrender.)
50. Algosaibi, *The Gulf Crisis*, p. 14.
51. Colonel Hamed Salem al-Zyadi, interview with author, tape-recording, London, 27 January 1999. See also Cordesman and Wagner, *The Lessons of Modern War*, Vol. 2, p. 591.
52. Amatzia Baram, correspondence with author, 14 April 2002.
53. Aburish, 'Secrets of His Life and Leadership', interview with Frontline, pp. 1–2.
54. Makiya, *Republic of Fear*, p. xx.
55. Post, 'The Defining Moment of Saddam's Life', p. 49. See also, Michael Hedges, 'In Iraq, if Saddam Says it, it's True', *Washington Times*, 26 October 1990; and George Lardner Jr, 'Saddam's Inner Circle Seen as Unquestioning', *Washington Post*, 3 December 1990.
56. Salah Umar al-Ali, interview with author, tape-recording, London, 11 July 1998. Salah was with Saddam Hussein at the time and was allegedly the first person to be informed on the decision. Amatzia Baram confirmed this view: Baram, interview with author, tape-recording, Washington, DC, 19 February 1999. For confirmation on Saddam Hussein taking the decision to invade Kuwait: Tariq Aziz, interview with Milton Viorst, *The New Yorker*, 30 May 1991, pp. 64–7; Tahsin Mualla, interview with author, tape-recording, 14 August 1998; Ahmad Cheleby, interview with author, notes, London, 24 January 1999; and Hamed al-Joubouri, interview with author, tape-recording, London, 15 August 1998.
57. Faleh al-Jabbar, 'The State, Society, Clan, Party and Army in Iraq: A Totalitarian State in the Twilight of Totalitarianism', in Faleh A. Jabbar, Ahmad Shikara and Keiko Sakai, *From Storm to Thunder: Unfinished Showdown Between Iraq and the U.S.* (Tokyo: Institute of Developing Economics, 1998), pp. 16, 27.
58. On the origins of Ba'athism, see for example, Marion Farouk-Sluglett and Peter Sluglett, *Iraq Since 1958: From Revolution to Dictatorship*, 2nd edn (London: I.B. Tauris and Co., 1990), pp. 85–106; and Bengio, *Saddam's Word*, pp. 24–39. For further background on Iraq, see for example, Phebe Marr, *A Modern History of Iraq* (Boulder, CO: Westview Press, 1988); and Geoff Simons, *Iraq: from Sumer to Saddam* (Basingstoke: Macmillan, 1994).
59. According to Zuhair al-Jazairi 'The Ba'th Party is a single Arab party led by a single leadership, the Pan-Arab Command, and its division into regional organizations is due to the partition of the Arab nation into the many states and the practical requirements of revolutionary struggle.' See Zuhair al-Jazairi, 'Ba'thist Ideology and Practice', in Fran Hazelton (ed.) for The Committee Against Repression and for Democratic Rights (CARDRI), *Iraq Since the Gulf War: Prospects for*

Democracy (London: Zed Books Ltd, 1989), p. 32: The founder of the Ba'ath Party is Michael Aflaq who developed a close relationship with Saddam Hussein. For a brief profile of the man, see Mark Grossman, *Encyclopaedia of the Persian Gulf War* (Santa Barbara, CA: ABC-CLIO, 1995), pp. 6–7.

60. Laurie Mylroie, 'The Future of Iraq', *The Washington Institute For Near East Policy* 24 (1991), p. 4; Hamed al-Jubburi, interview with author, tape-recording, London, 15 August 1998; Zuhair al-Jazairi, interview with author, tape-recording, London, 19 August 1998; Laith Kubba, interview with author, tape-recording, London, 3 August 1998; and Qasem Karim, interview with author, tape-recording, London, 10 September 1998.

61. Amatzia Baram, 'The Ruling Political Elite in Ba'thi Iraq, 1968–1986: The Changing Features of a Collective Profile', *International Journal of Middle East Studies* 21, No. 4 (November 1989), p. 448; and Salah Umar al-Ali, interview with author, tape-recording, London, 11 July 1998 and 13 May 1999.

62. For background, see Aburish, *A Brutal Friendship*, pp. 109–42; and Makiya, *Republic of Fear*, pp. 47–50. For more specific information, see Farouk-Sluglett and Sluglett, *Iraq Since 1958*, pp. 85–107.

63. Farouk-Sluglett and Sluglett, *Iraq Since 1958*, p. 103.

64. Abd al-Rahman Aref lived in Ankara for many years as a hotel manager, an indication of his honesty and integrity. He stole nothing from the Iraqi state and smuggled no resources abroad. He was allowed back during the war with Iran and lived in Baghdad, drawing on a four-star army general retirement pension.

65. Fouad Fahmy Shafik (trans.), *The Iraqi Interim Constitution* (Dobbs Ferry, NY: Oceana Publication, 1990), Article 37, p. 28.

66. Baram, 'The Ruling Political Elite in Ba'thi Iraq, 1968–1986', p. 450.

67. Ibid.

68. Mohamedou, *Iraq and the Second Gulf War*, p. 3.

69. Baram, 'The Ruling Political Elite in Ba'thi Iraq, 1968–1986', p. 452.

70. Amatzia Baram, *Building Toward Crisis: Saddam Husayn's Strategy for Survival* (Washington, DC: The Washington Institute for Near East Policy, 1988), p. 43.

71. For an expanded version of the four level change, see Baram, 'The Ruling Political Elite in Ba'thi Iraq, 1968–1986', p. 449.

72. Amatzia Baram, interview with author, tape-recording, Washington, DC, 19 February 1999; Salah Umar al-Ali, interview with author, tape-recording, London, 11 July 1998 and 13 May 1999; Laith Kubba, interview with author, tape-recording, London, 3 August 1998; and Faleh al-Jabbar, interview with author, tape-recording, London, 4 and 19 August 1998.

73. Baram, 'The Ruling Political Elite in Ba'thi Iraq, 1968–1986', p. 455.

74. Ibid., p. 467.

75. Aras Habib, interviews with author, tape-recordings, London, 27 June and 19 August 1998; Faleh al-Jabbar, interviews with author, tape-recordings, London, 4 and 19 August 1998; and Tashin Mualla, interview with author, tape-recording, London, 14 August 1998.

76. Faleh Abdul al-Jabbar, 'The State, Society, Clan, Party and Army in Iraq', p. 17; and interview with author, tape-recording, London, 4 August 1998.

77. Makiya, *Republic of Fear*, p. 26.

78. Salah Umar al-Ali, interview with author, notes, London, 27 May 1999.

79. Makiya, *Republic of Fear*, p. xi.

80. Hamid al-Bayati, interview with author, tape-recording, London, 26 June 1998; and Aras Habib, interview with author, tape-recording, London, 4 April 1998.

81. Makiya, *Republic of Fear*, p. 5; and 'The House Saddam built', *The Economist*, 29 September 1990, pp. 73–4.

82. Zuhair al-Jazairi, 'Ba'thist Ideology and Practice', p. 43; interview with author, tape-recording, London, 19 August 1998; Hamed al-Jabouri, interview with author, tape-recording, London, 15 August 1998; and Aras Habib, interview with author, tape-recording, London, 27 June and 19 August 1998.
83. Metz *et al.*, *Iraq*, p. 193.
84. Salah Umar al-Ali, interview with author, tape-recording, London, 10 July 1998.
85. According to Latif Yahia, reports from those meetings became textbooks that they had to memorise in elementary school. See Latif Yahia and Karl Wendel, *I Was Saddam's Son* (New York: Arcade Publishing, 1997), p. 21.
86. Yahia and Wendel, *I Was Saddam's Son*, pp. 16–17.
87. Metz *et al.*, *Iraq*, p. 175. Note that the first official election of the President in Iraq was conducted in December 1995.
88. Baram, 'The Ruling Political Elite in Ba'thi Iraq, 1968–1986', pp. 449–50.
89. Ibid.
90. Shafik, *The Iraqi Interim Constitution*, Article 37, p. 28.
91. Ibid.
92. Ibid., Article 46 and 49, p. 31.
93. Baram, 'The Ruling Political Elite in Ba'thi Iraq, 1968–1986', p. 460.
94. Zuhair al-Jazairi; 'Ba'thist Ideology and Practice', p. 42.
95. Mohamedou, *Iraq and the Second Gulf War*, p. 46.
96. Makiya, *Republic of Fear*, pp. 36–7.
97. Amatzia Baram, 'The June 1980 Elections to the National Assembly', *Orient* (September 1981).
98. See for example Deborah Cobbett, 'Women in Iraq', in CADRI, *Saddam's Iraq*, p. 132.
99. Baram, 'The Ruling Political Elite in Ba'thi Iraq, 1968–1986', pp. 449–50.
100. Khidhir Hamza with Jeff Stein, *Saddam's Bombmaker* (London: Simon & Schuster, 2000), p. 91.
101. Shafik, *The Iraqi Interim Constitution*, Article 37, p. 28 and Article 43, p. 30.
102. *Iraqi News Agency*, 14 January 1991, cited in Freedman and Karsh, *The Gulf Conflict 1990–1991*, p. 278.
103. *Baghdad Observer*, 3 August 1990, p. 1.
104. Ibid.
105. Ibid.; and 15 January 1991, p. 1.
106. Farouk-Sluglett and Sluglett, *Iraq Since 1958*, p. 121; Faleh Abdul al-Jabbar, interview with author, tape-recording, London, 4 August 1998; Amatzia Baram, interview with author, tape-recording, Washington, DC, 19 February 1999; and Hamed al-Jabouri, interview with author, tape-recording, London, 15 August 1998.
107. Aras Habib, interview with author, tape-recording, London, 17 May 1999; Aras Habib, telephone conversation, notes, London, 7 May 1999; Habib Karim, interview with author, tape-recording, London, 17 May 1999; and Farouk-Sluglett and Sluglett, *Iraq Since 1958*, pp. 142–4.
108. Amatzia Baram, interview with author, tape-recording, Washington, DC, 19 February 1999. This is confirmed by Nabeel Musawi, Iraqi National Congress, telephone interview with author, notes, 8 March 1999.
109. Saad al-Bazzaz, 'An Insider's View of Iraq', p. 67; and al-Bazzaz, *The Ashes of Wars*, p. 8.
110. Ritter, *Endgame*, p. 124; and Makiya, *Republic of Fear*, pp. 61–3.
111. Amatzia Baram, correspondence with author, 14 April 2002.
112. Ranim Hampton, interview with author, tape-recording, London, 5 August 1998; and Faleh al-Jabbar, interview with author, tape-recording, London, 19 August 1998.
113. Aburish, *Saddam Hussein*, p. 196.

114. James Bruce, 'Saddam Buying Time?', *Jane's Defence Weekly* 16, No. 2 (13 July 1991), p. 63; Sean Boyne, 'Qusay Considers a Reshuffle for Iraq's Command Structure, *Jane's Intelligence Review* 9, No. 9 (September 1997), p. 416.
115. Colonel Hasan Khafaji, interview with author, tape-recording, London, 3 August 1998.
116. Mark A. Heller, 'Iraq's Army: Military Weakness, Political Utility', in Baram and Rubin, *Iraq's Road to War*, pp. 37–50.
117. Cordesman and Wagner, *The Lessons of Modern War*, Vol. IV, pp. 113–25.
118. Ibid., pp. 135–36.
119. Wafiq Samarrai, interview with Patrick Cockburn, *The Independent*, 13 March 1998, cited in Baram, 'An Analysis of Iraq's WMD Strategy', pp. 25–39.
120. United States Army, *The Iraqi Army*, p. 12.
121. Aburish, *Saddam Hussein*, p. 232.
122. United States Army, *The Iraqi Army*, pp. 25–7; Darwish and Alexander, *Unholy Babylon*, p. 27; and Blackwell, *Thunder in the Desert*, pp 52–5.
123. Major General Edward Fursdon, 'The Republican Guards, Elite, Tough and Highly Professional', *Asia-Pacific Defence Reporter* (March 1991), p. 11; and United States Army, *The Iraqi Army*, p. 25.
124. Colonel Muhammed Ali, interview with author, tape-recording, London, 23 August 1998.
125. United States Army, *The Iraqi Army*, p. 25.
126. Salah Umar al-Ali, interview with author, tape-recording, London, 10 July 1998.
127. Norman Friedman, *Desert Victory: The War for Kuwait* (Annapolis, MD: The Naval Institute Press, 1993), p. 25; Makiya, *Republic of Fear*, p. 31; and Karsh and Rautsi, *Saddam Hussein*, p. 190.
128. See for example, Makiya, *Republic of Fear*, pp. 32–3, and 44.
129. United States Army, *The Iraqi Army*, p. 33.
130. Metz *et al.*, *Iraq*, p. 225.
131. Ibid.
132. United States Army, *The Iraqi Army*, pp. 137–41.
133. Colonel Hamed Salem al-Zyadi, interview with author, tape-recording, London, 25 January 1999; and Aras Habib, interview with author, tape-recording, London, 27 June 1998.
134. Colonel Hasan Khafaji, interview with author, tape-recording, London, 3 August 1998.
135. Colonel Hamed Salem al-Zyadi, interview with author, tape-recording, London, 25 January 1999; and Aras Habib, interview with author, 27 June 1998.
136. Staff Writer, 'Command Purged', *Jane's Defence Weekly* 15, No. 1 (5 January 1991), p. 10.
137. James Zumwalt, 'The Iraqi Military's Achilles' Heel Is Saddam Hussein', *Los Angeles Times*, 26 December 2001.
138. David Eshel, 'The Iraqi Air Force – How Effective Is It?', *Military Technology* 91, No. 2 (February 1991), pp. 72–6.
139. Winnefeld, Johnson and Niblack *A League of Airmen*, p. 118.
140. Matthew M. Hurley, 'Saddam Hussein and Iraqi Air Power: Just Having an Air Force Isn't Enough', *Airpower Journal* 6, No. 4 (Winter 1992), pp. 4–16; Darwish and Alexander, *Unholy Babylon*, pp. 21–5. See also Bergquist, *The Role of Air Power in the Iran–Iraq War*.
141. The code-name KARI is Iraq spelled backwards in French.
142. Gordon and Trainor, *The Generals' War*, pp. 102–22.
143. Cordesman and Wagner; *The Lessons of Modern War*, Vol. IV, p. 133.
144. Michael Eisenstadt, 'The Sword for the Arabs: Iraq's Strategic Weapons', *The*

Washington Institute Police Paper, No. 21, 1990, p. 6.
145. Ibid.
146. Amatzia Baram, 'An Analysis of Iraq's WMD Strategy', pp. 25–39.
147. Khidir Hamaza, *60 Minutes*, 27 January 1999, CBS News Transcripts.
148. Ahmad Cheleby, interview with author, notes, London, 24 January 1999. Ahmad Cheleby contends that the structure of the Iraqi security and intelligence network was known in 1990–91 by the opposition. See for example 'The House Saddam Built', *The Economist*, 29 September 1990, pp. 73–74. In addition to Makiya's *Republic of Fear*, first printed in 1989, the first account in book form was Hussein Sumaida with Carole Jerome, *Circle of Fear: A Renegade's Journey from the Mossad to the Iraqi Secret Service* (Toronto: Stoddart, 1991).
149. Boyne, 'Inside Iraq's Security Network: Part One', *Jane's Intelligence Review* 9, No. 7 (July 1997), pp. 312–14; and 'Inside Iraq's Security Network: Part Two', *Jane's Intelligence Review* 9, No. 8 (August 1997), pp. 365–7. See also Yahia and Wendel, *I Was Saddam's Son*, pp. 250–1.
150. Aburish, *Saddam Hussein*, p. 240.
151. Colonel Hasan Khafaji, interview with author, tape-recording, London, 3 August 1998; Julian Walker, interview with author, tape-recording, London, 3 August 1998; and Hamid al-Bayati, interview with author, tape-recording, London, 26 June 1998.
152. Boyne, 'Inside Iraq's Security Network', p. 313; Ritter, *Endgame*, pp. 18–19, 129; Amatzia Baram, interview with author, tape-recording, 19 February 1999; and Kenneth Pollack, interview with author, tape-recording, Washington, 24 February 1999.
153. Aras Habib, interview with author, tape-recording, London, 2 April 1998.
154. Sumaida with Jerome, *Circle of Fear*, pp. 152–68; and Colonel Hamed Salem al-Zyadi, interview with author, tape-recording, London, 25 January 1999.
155. United States warships fired Tomahawk missiles at the complex on 27 June 1994 in retaliation against Mukhabarat's plot to assassinate Bush on his visit to Kuwait two months earlier.
156. Boyne, 'Inside Iraq's Security Network', p. 366: and Scott Ritter, *Endgame*, p. 121.
157. Tashin Mualla, interview with author, tape-recording, London, 14 August 1998.
158. Boyne, 'Inside Iraq's Security Network', p. 365.
159. Ritter, *Endgame*, p. 77.
160. Isam al-Khafji, 'State Terror and the Degradation of Politics in Iraq', *Middle East Report* (May–June 1992), p. 18.
161. Aras Habib, interview with author, tape-recording, London, 2 April 1998. For insight into one of these bunker facilities, see 'Sanctuary Underground: The Hussein Hilton', *Newsweek* (4 February 1991), pp. 26–7.
162. Andrew Rathmell, in *International Defense Review* 25, No. 5 (May 1991), p. 394 and Boyne, 'Inside Iraq's Security Network', p. 314.
163. Ritter, *Endgame*, pp. 124–5.
164. Boyne, 'Saddam's Shield: The Role of the Special Republican Guard', *Jane's Intelligence Review* 11, No. 1 (January 1999), pp. 29–32.
165. Ibid.
166. Aburish, *Saddam Hussein*, p. 234.
167. For two accounts on 'doubles', see Mikhael Ramadan, *In the Shadow of Saddam: Saddam Hussein's Former Double* (Auckland: GreeNZone, 1999); and Yahia and Wendel, *I Was Saddam's Son*.
168. Saad Salah Jabour, Free Iraqi Council, interview with author, notes, London, 14 July 2001.
169. Boyne, 'Inside Iraq's Security Network', p. 314.
170. 'Factors which lead [*sic*] to failure in the interior center for military unit 999: the

abduction or assassination of the American forces' leader Norman Schwarzkopf.'
This Iraqi document was captured after the war regarding the operational orders
to kidnap General Schwarzkopf (the document has been translated and given to
the author).

171. For insight into the role of some of the agencies in the battle with UNSCOM,
see Boyne, 'Iraqis Perfect the Art of Evading UNSCOM', *Jane's Intelligence
Review* 10, No. 2 (February 1998), pp. 27–30; and Boyne, 'Iraq's MIO: Ministry
of Missing Weapons', *Jane's Intelligence Review* 10, No. 3 (March 1998), pp. 23–5.

172. Makiya, *Republic of Fear*, p. 36.

173. Amatzia Baram, correspondence with author, transcript, 22 March 2001.

174. Hamza with Stein, *Saddam's Bombmaker*, p. 87.

175. Cockburn and Cockburn, *Out of the Ashes*, p. 37.

176. *Senate Foreign Relations Committee Report*, 'Civil War in Iraq' (5 January 1991),
cited in Cockburn and Cockburn, *Out of the Ashes*, p. 36; and confirmed by
Nabeel Musawi, discussion with author, notes, London, 27 June 1998.

177. Ahmed Hashim, 'Iraq: Fin de Régime?', *Current History* 95, No. 577 (January
1996), pp. 14–15; Faleh al-Jabbar, 'The State, Society, Clan, Party and Army in
Iraq', p. 4; Faleh al-Jabbar, interview with author, tape-recording, London,
19 August 1998; Amatzia Baram, interview with author, tape-recording,
Washington, DC, 19 February 1999; and Kenneth Pollack, interview with author,
tape-recording, Washington, DC, 24 February 1999.

178. Baram, 'Neo-Tribalism in Iraq', p. 5.

179. Ibid., p. 1.

180. Hanna Batatu, *The Old Social Classes and the Revolutionary Movements of Iraq*,
p. 1088.

181. Ibid., p. 21.

182. Baram, *Building Toward Crisis*, p. 21; Amatzia Baram, correspondence with
author, transcript, 20 May 1999; and Salah Umar al-Ali, interview with author,
notes, London, 10 July 1998.

183. Baram, 'Neo-Tribalism in Iraq', pp. 1–2.

184. Ibid.

185. Colonel Muhammed Ali, interview with author, tape-recording, London, 23
August 1998.

186. Baram, *Building Toward Crisis*, p. 35; and Kenneth Pollack, interview with
author, tape-recording, Washington, DC, 24 February 1999.

187. Amatzia Baram, interview with author, tape-recording, Washington, DC, 19
February 1999; Salah Umar al-Ali, interview with author, tape-recording, London,
11 July 1998; Faleh al-Jabbar, interview with author, tape-recording, London,
19 August 1998; and Habib Karim, interview with author, tape-recording, London,
17 May 1999.

188. Isam al-Khafji, 'State Terror and the Degradation of Politics in Iraq', p. 26.

189. Salah Umar al-Ali, interview with author, tape-recording, London, 13 May 1999.

190. Baram, 'The Ruling Political Elite in Ba'thi Iraq, 1968–1986', p. 466.

191. Marr, *A Modern History of Iraq*, pp. 232–3.

192. Isam al-Khafji, 'State Terror and the Degradation of Politics in Iraq', pp. 15–21.

193. Laith Kubba, interview with author, tape-recording, London, 3 August 1998.

194. Faleh al-Jabbar, 'Why the Intifada Failed', in Hazelton (ed.), *Iraq Since the Gulf
War*, p. 112.

195. Amatzia Baram, correspondence with author, 11 April 2002.

196. Faleh al-Jabbar, 'Why the Intifada Failed', p. 117; and interviews with author,
tape-recordings, London, 4 and 19 August 1998.

197. Amatzia Baram, correspondence with author, 11 April 2002.

5

An Examination of the Strategic Air Campaign

According to General Norman Schwarzkopf's mission statement, the objective of the Coalition attacks on the Iraqi political–military leadership was to 'neutralise' the Iraqi National Command Authority.[1] To achieve neutralisation, the air campaign plan aimed to 'incapacitate' and 'isolate' the Iraqi senior decision-making authorities.[2] The more ambitious objective of instituting a change in the Iraqi regime by destroying the Iraqi leader was at the heart of Instant Thunder, but it was never a declared aim of the air campaign. Nevertheless, unofficially Washington blessed the pursuit of targeting the Iraqi leadership and the plan was implemented albeit under certain restraints and constraints.[3] The Black Hole planners, by expanding the Instant Thunder philosophy, came to the conclusion that strategic bombing had an unprecedented leverage through the combination of stealth, precision and stand-off capability. Such a synthesis provided for information dominance, and in the process of developing a master attack plan Lieutenant Colonel David Deptula articulated the importance of near-simultaneous attacks upon the strategic centres of gravity throughout the entire theatre of war – an approach that would later be termed 'parallel warfare'.[4] In examining the strategic attacks against the Iraqi National Command Authority, the following will focus on the validity of the Warden–Deptula theory of 'strategic paralysis' by examining it against the structure, mind-set and connections identified as the Iraqi political power structure.

THE IRAQI STRATEGIC FRAMEWORK

It has previously been argued that Saddam Hussein ordered the invasion of Kuwait with the objective of installing an Iraqi puppet regime.[5] He did not believe the United States would go to war over Kuwait since negotiations and compromises could be arranged,[6] but when Iraqi forces failed to capture the Emir, and the immediate regional and international response was far more determined than expected, the Iraqi leadership moved to a policy of brinkmanship. Iraqi strategy was one of pressing an already dangerous situation to the limits, at the same time as it prepared for a ground war, all accompanied by various attempts to engage in protracted processes of negotiation with Washington, hoping to trap the United States in endless mediations.

At the forefront, Iraqi crisis management sought to weaken Coalition resolve and strengthen Iraqi morale. Through the radio and state controlled newspapers – *al-Thawrah*, *al-Jumhuriyah* and *al-Qadisiyah* – the leadership tried to convince the domestic, regional and international organisations that the Iraqis had no choice but to fight, and in the event of war the Coalition would suffer severe consequences. These consequences were huge casualties through a prolonged ground war, retaliation through terrorism, the destruction of Kuwaiti oilfields and Scud attacks against Israel. According to the former Iraqi Ambassador to Switzerland and Tunisia, Hamed al-Jabouri, there was a widespread belief among Arab leaders and the Arab population that the Coalition could not survive an actual war. Although large portions of the Arab masses opposed the invasion and occupation of Kuwait, they disagreed with the proposition of using military force against Iraq.[7]

The propaganda apparatus presented the Iraqis as martyrs willing to die for the cause,[8] and to emphasise the seriousness of Iraqi threats the regime called for large-scale mobilisation of reserves. Kuwait was furthermore turned into a fortress and military forces deployed chemical weapons throughout Kuwait.[9] The Iraqi regime argued consistently that any military conflict would be prolonged and lead to high casualties, and with the regime's ability to sacrifice lives it would prevail.[10] The Iraqi Vice President, Izzat Ibrahim al-Duri, promised in mid December 1990 that the United States would not be able to win a war 'in [a] matter of days or weeks', but that Iraq would drag it out for 'long years'.[11]

The Iraqi leadership was fully aware of the public debate that had questioned US military professionalism in the wake of operations against Grenada (1983), Libya (1986) and Panama (1989). Saddam knew that the United States had pulled out of Lebanon in 1983 when faced with casualties, and that Vietnam had cast a long shadow that governed Washington's thinking. 'We know that Washington's threats are those of a paper tiger. America is still nursing the disasters from the Vietnam War, and no American official, be it even George Bush, would dare to do anything serious against the Arab nation.'[12] Saddam had also made it clear to the US Ambassador in Iraq, April Glaspie, that American society could not accept 10,000 dead in one battle. The Iraqi policy was therefore focusing on the American national *will* to use military force, rather than the capability itself. Vietnam and casualties were repeated themes throughout the crisis, coupled with the prediction that if push came to shove, Syria and Egypt would not fight their Iraqi Arab brothers.[13]

The Iraqi regime, with the support of the Palestinian Liberation Organisation (PLO), predicted world-wide terrorism,[14] but George Habash was a single voice when he promised: 'We have our finger on the trigger to shoot American and Western interests the moment America launches any attack on Baghdad or Iraq.'[15] By threatening to set alight the Kuwaiti oilfields,[16] the Iraqi regime seemed to believe that the United States would be reluctant to react forcefully if faced with an oil crisis: 'There is no doubt that those who will bear this vast expense are the citizens who are taxpayers in all 51 [*sic*] states in the USA.'[17] Although world-wide terrorism and burning oilfields were the Iraqi leader's weapons of terror, his trump card was missile attacks against Israel.[18] By provoking Israeli retaliation the Iraqi leader hoped to redeem Iraq's military honour, re-establish Iraqi deterrence credibility and split the Coalition.[19] Israeli attacks against Iraq would be militarily marginal compared to US attacks, but from a pan-Arab political view, strikes against Israel would strengthen Iraqi morale immensely. In early November 1990, just prior to the vote on a UN resolution to allow the use of military force to remove Iraqi forces from Kuwait, statements came from the Iraqi leadership, promising that if Iraq were attacked, both Saudi Arabia and Israel would be turned into battle-zones.[20]

Saddam Hussein seems never to have been fully convinced that the United States would use extensive military force. In late October President Bush's personal popularity was at an all-time low,[21] and a *New York Times* poll shortly after suggested that more than 50 per cent of the American people believed Bush had not explained the goals 'clearly enough'. Only 21 per cent argued that military action should be initiated.[22] Giving priority to such reports, and perhaps misled by his own propaganda, Saddam calculated that he would be in a better position by holding on to Kuwait than accepting US demands for an unconditional withdrawal. The Iraqi leadership was updated on American anti-war demonstrations and newspaper articles criticising the war option, concluding that this uncertainty indicated lack of national *will*.[23] The Iraqi media reported on every aspect that was favourable to it, from individual remarks to the paper signed by 81 members of the US Congress who opposed military action.[24] The passing of Resolution 678 on 29 November 1990, authorising the use of all necessary means to force Iraq out of Kuwait, was the clearest signal to the Iraqi leadership of US determination, but the following announcement by President Bush that the two parties should meet, in order to go 'an extra mile for peace', might well have reinforced the Iraqi perception that Washington lacked resolve.

The decision seems to have given the Iraqi leadership new confidence, as it restated publicly that there would be no compromise on Kuwait. On 6 December the Iraqi leader argued 'Iraq will never yield to pressure, threats and blackmail',[25] and five days later Latif Nusseif Jasim, a member of the Regional Command, stressed 'Iraq will not relinquish any part of the Kuwaiti province.'[26] On 18 December the RCC made clear 'We are ready for the decisive showdown, if thus God wants. Then, many heads will roll and many thrones of tyrants will fall.'[27] On Christmas Eve, Saddam reaffirmed that there would be no withdrawal from Kuwait,[28] and three days later civil defence exercises took place in Baghdad, including blackout and evacuation drills.[29] The leadership continued to stress that in the event of war Tel Aviv would witness the first retaliation.[30] To avoid any doubt on the Iraqi position, the RCC stated on 31 December that any discussion of withdrawal was 'sick thinking that exists only in the minds of the planners of evil and their dubious circles'.[31] Even as late as 9 January 1991 the Iraqi President's half brother, Barzan Ibrahim, reported that 'The Americans don't want to fight ... They want to talk their way out. They are weak.'[32] 'An extra mile for peace' may have signalled US weakness to the Iraqi leader, but Bush's initiative may have been all-important for domestic reasons: the US Congress authorised the use of force as late as 12 January, and then only with the narrow margin of 53 to 47 in the Senate.[33]

Although many of the Iraqi statements were directed at a regional rather than a Western audience, and the Iraqi leader tried to pursue alternative solutions in an unofficial manner, there seems to have been an awareness in Saddam's mind that war was a possibility. By mid-December the Chief of Armed Forces, General Nazir al-Khazzraji, and the Secretary of Defence, General Abd al-Jabbar Shansal, were both replaced by the more aggressive Lieutenant General Hussein Rashid and Lieutenant General Said Tuma Abbas.[34] The Iraqi leader stated with the passing of Resolution 678 that the likelihood of war had increased to 'fifty-fifty',[35] and according to Wafiq Samarrai, Saddam kept saying in private 'perhaps they [would] fight, perhaps they would not'.[36] In hindsight, the writing was on the wall, but there was a hope at the time that a diplomatic face-saving option would prevent the United States from using military force beyond limited air strikes. Both the French and the Soviets, who had long-standing ties with the Ba'ath regime, engaged in dialogues throughout the crisis.[37] Revealingly, after the war the Iraqi leader stated: 'We believed that everything would be rectified at the last minute [without war]. Mitterand and Gorbashev [*sic*] misled me.'[38] He also emphasised that his biggest mistake was not to attack US positions in Saudi Arabia in the early days of the crisis.[39] The Iraqi leader's decision not to attack at that point, despite being aware of the scale of US deployment,[40] indicates that he believed a diplomatic solution was possible as long as he did not threaten Saudi Arabia. According to Colonel Muhammed Ali, who was a member of a team that wrote a 65-page field report in early January 1991, Iraqi forces would not stand a chance against the Coalition, but the Iraqi leader chose to disregard the findings. The Iraqi officer suggests that the flaw resided not in the information given to Saddam, but in his determination: he had decided to 'cross the sea', but did not know 'how to swim'.[41] General Wafiq Samarrai contended that the Iraqi leader had close to perfect knowledge of the military balance throughout the crisis.[42] He met Saddam on 13 January and provided him with a comprehensive report:

> We showed in detail information about the allied build-up and that we thought they had serious intention to launch an air attack and a land attack later on ... We were quite specific about the targets that would be hit ... He [Saddam Hussein] spoke about the Turkish threat. He said he would fight Turkey, the Iraqi women would be his soldiers ... What happened matched our expectations ... we had a sufficient amount of information produced by our work. That is why Saddam did not kill us. Had we provided him with wrong information, we would have been killed and blamed.[43]

While military officers were not in the position to tell the Iraqi leader what to do, inaccuracy in reporting was punishable by death, and executions within the Iraqi intelligence community did not take place during the 1991 Gulf War. Thus, Saddam's knowledge of the situation seems to have been reasonably good, but he believed he would prevail, one way or another. He seems, however, to have overestimated his own leadership: Iraq had 'a unified, experienced political leadership, forged over a span of many years in an environment of struggle and jihad, which has endowed it with experience in governing and directing combat operations'.[44] In the final analysis, Saddam badly underestimated US resolve, and the limited influence France and the Soviet Union had on the Bush administration. He also underestimated the leverage of air power, but with the exception of a few airmen, so did most of the world prior to the Instant Thunder proposal.

As the UN deadline for Iraqi withdrawal from Kuwait passed on 15 January 1991, the Ba'ath Party arranged huge demonstrations throughout the country in support of the Iraqi leader.[45] When Saddam visited troops at the battlefront, he stated that the Iraqis were ready for military confrontation.[46] On 16 January 1991 he published a letter to George Bush, emphasising that the only diplomatic solution would be to review the Iraqi 12 August 1990 initiative of linkage and if that was not acceptable, the Iraqis were ready for war. In the letter the Iraqi leader argued that air power alone could not defeat his country:

I want to say to you that you might be planning air strikes to achieve lightning war, thinking that Iraq will yield. You are deluding yourself. Your calculations may have led you to believe that this alone will fulfill the slogan of the lightning war you are talking about. If this is what you are thinking of, hoping that Iraq will yield to you after the air strikes and the emergence of the brokers and merchants of politics who will call for a cease-fire of bargains, and if you believe that the ground forces can be neutralized, then you are deluding yourself, and this delusion will place you in great trouble ... You will find that the Air Force, on which you base your explanation of the lightning war, will not be alone in the battle. The battle will be prolonged and heavy blood will be shed.[47]

When the United States deployed aircraft to Saudi Arabia on 8 August 1990 the Iraqi military leadership started preparing for both air strikes and full-blown war.[48] According to General Wafiq Samarrai, the leadership was prepared for air strikes throughout the country, including central Baghdad from mid August, and Saddam took General Dugan's September statement about going after the inner circles of the Iraqi leader seriously.[49] While Wafiq Samarrai contended that the air war 'matched our expectations' and that they knew which targets would be hit, Brigadier General Fehed Abdul Baki Mohammed, who was head of the Iraqi air operations, stated that the Iraqi military predicted that 'the theatre of battle would be located in the South of Iraq, near Kuwait'.[50] Although Iraqi accounts differ on the expected air attacks, Saddam seems to have felt reasonably safe in Baghdad, as he believed his regime was strong enough to sustain the bombing. Although sleeping in different houses every few nights, he stayed mostly in the middle-class al-Taifya district of the city, which was partly vacant since many had fled the capital during the war. Additionally, Soviet and French officials assured him that the Coalition would not destroy the capital, nor pursue its capture or occupy any part of Iraq.[51] To be sure, he nevertheless had key members of the regime relocate their offices,[52] sensitive equipment removed from facilities that were expected to be bombed,[53] and alternative places to conduct meetings in the event of war were arranged in the outskirts of Baghdad.[54]

Saddam surely expected some kind of air power retaliation, but air strikes did not amount to a war in his mind, and he remained confident that such strikes could not alter his regime. The Iraqi leader assured his ground forces that 'air power alone will not decide the battle', justifying it by claiming that 'in Vietnam, the US's air superiority was undisputed. However, [the United States] lost the war and departed from South Vietnam, while North Vietnam won.'[55] The Iraqi leader further dismissed US stealth aircraft, arguing that it 'will be seen even by a shepherd in the desert as well as by Iraqi technology, and [the Americans] will see how their Stealth falls just like ... any [other] aggressor aircraft'.[56]

Although some of the Iraqi leader's statements served propaganda purposes, they also reflected perceptions on the nature of war. Saddam believed that air power alone could not force him to withdraw from Kuwait. He strongly believed that even extensive bombing and command of the skies were insufficient to defeat his well-organised and durable regime.[57] He therefore instructed his commanders to 'stay motionless' during the air operations, because 'if you do this, their [bombing] will be in vain ... On the ground the battle will be another story.'[58] The Iraqi leadership, as was the case with Colin Powell, Norman Schwarzkopf and most of the Coalition military establishment, were convinced that at the end of the day it would all be decided on the battlefield.

By mid January 1991 the Iraqis had an impressive number of ground forces in Kuwait: when President Bush announced the increase of US armed forces to the region on 8 November 1990, the Iraqi leader promptly responded by announcing that he would send another 250,000 Iraqi troops to Kuwait, bringing the total number to a nominal 680,000.[59] Some 500,000 troops were allegedly transferred from the Iran–Iraq border in late August, and by mid October some 2 million volunteers, including women, were presented as the determined para-military Popular Army.[60] According to the DIA the number did not exceed 360,000 Iraqi troops in theatre on the eve of the war, but the Iraqi order of battle was still formidable.[61] In essence, the Iraqi troops formed three defensive lines. The front line, which was closest to the Saudi–Kuwaiti border, was the first line of defence comprising infantry divisions, intended to slow a Coalition ground offensive, allowing the Iraqi leadership to determine the shape and form of the attack. The second Iraqi echelon included armoured and mechanised divisions deployed in depth throughout the KTO. Its mission was to reinforce other formations and block Coalition penetrations of the first line. The Republican Guard, deployed in southern Iraq and northern Kuwait, formed the third echelon. These divisions, including heavy ones such as the Tawakalna, Hammurabi and Madina, were the strategic reserve. Their mission was to protect the coast, reinforce the other two echelons and defend against possible airborne attacks in central Kuwait. The Iraqi defence comprised 42 divisions in total,[62] and the two front echelons were strengthened with vast oil trenches, minefields and barbed wire. Added to this, elements of the security and police forces were dispatched throughout Kuwait. There should be no doubt about the fact that the Kuwaiti theatre of operation was deeply entrenched with Iraqi forces.

The fortress reflected the Iraqi leadership's perception of the impending war according to the 'official' Iraqi account, *A War Gives Birth to Another*:

The Iraqi mind is overwhelmed by a military conviction that believes in the priority of the infantry corps over the other types of warfare, because the soldiers crossing on the ground are the only ones in control and they alone can determine any military conflict whatever the adversary's supremacy in modern weaponry may be. The Iraqi forces were ready to wage a war with light and medium weapons in the manner of popular liberation wars.[63]

In a unique article after the war Saddam acknowledged that the Iraqi strategy anticipated a huge infantry battle in which the United States' superiority in weapons and military technology would come to nothing. Prior to the war he had told Iraqi commanders that 'If we are able to prevail over their weapons and their technical superiority, then we should be superior in our mentality and through our jihad [holy war].'[64] Saddam stressed that the Iraqi strategy was one of prolonging the war 'to force them [the US-led Coalition] to fight us face to face and not just fire from a distance. Although long-range firing may harm our people and economy, it cannot end a battle decisively in their favour and eventually they will be forced to return home in failure.'[65] These perceptions were probably a result of air power being unable to influence the ground battle in the war with Iran, despite considerable investment. According to Anthony H. Cordesman and Abraham R. Wagner, either side's air power in that war did little more than prevent the other side from using it efficiently.[66]

The Iraqi armed forces had furthermore demonstrated an impressive defence record in that war, and Saddam genuinely believed they were strong enough to inflict sufficient damage on the Coalition to claim political victory. The rationale was based on two assumptions, namely, that a war could not be won by the Coalition without a land battle and that the sheer size of the Iraqi forces, and the preparation of a defence in depth, ensured that any ground offensive would not be swift in execution and would thus be costly in terms of casualties.[67] Given these beliefs, Saddam could not foresee certain defeat. Iraqi preparations at the tactical level blinded the Iraqi leader to strategic weakness, and convinced that air power could not play a decisive role, Saddam could not anticipate either the scale or intensity of an air offensive, which in effect changed the whole setting.[68] Indeed, conventional strategic air power offered a way around the whole Iraqi concept of prolonged battle and high casualties, but such realisation only came about after the event.

THE COURSE OF THE STRATEGIC AIR CAMPAIGN

In order to establish the utility of the philosophy behind the strategic air campaign plan one cannot merely examine what was expected and what was accomplished. One must also determine to what degree the execution differed from the final plan. There were several such changes that need to be taken into account when examining the effectiveness of the air campaign.

The First 24 Hours of Operations

According to Operational Order 91-001, the military objectives were to attack the Iraqi political–military leadership and command facilities; gain and maintain air superiority; sever Iraqi supply lines; destroy known nuclear, biological and chemical production, storage and delivery capabilities; destroy Republican Guard forces in the Kuwaiti Theatre of Operations; and liberate Kuwait City.[69] The air campaign, which was to play the crucial role in achieving the first five objectives, was given the following missions: gain and maintain air supremacy to permit unhindered air and ground operations; isolate and incapacitate the Iraqi regime; destroy Iraq's known NBC warfare capability; eliminate Iraq's offensive military capability by destroying key military production, infrastructure, and power capabilities; and render the Iraqi army and its mechanised equipment in Kuwait ineffective in order to cause its collapse.[70]

In order to isolate and incapacitate the Iraqi regime, the disruption of the command and control system was essential. In the process the Coalition needed to neutralise Iraq's integrated air defence system, which consisted of some 7,000 radar-guided and 9,000 infrared SAMs and 7,000 anti-aircraft AAA pieces.[71] The first night's objective was therefore to disable the Iraqi air defence system, the regime's communication network and the electrical power system on which the war effort was dependent.[72] The newly developed F-117s conducted two-thirds of the strikes against leadership targets, and one-third of the strikes against command, control and communication targets.[73]

While the F-117 was the only aircraft to attack central Baghdad, with the exception of a few F-16 sorties on the third day of the war, its attacks were supplemented by Tomahawk land attack missiles (TLAMs).[74] The latter was not expected to achieve much in the view of Colin Powell, who told Glosson in October 1990: 'I don't [care] if you shoot every TLAM the Navy's got, they're still not worth [anything]. Any target you intend to destroy with the TLAM, put a fighter on it to make sure the target's destroyed.'[75] The Tomahawks, costing $1.1 million each, had never been used in conflict before. Moreover, the missiles were planned to be launched from carriers in the Mediterranean, the Red Sea and the Persian Gulf, but since landmarks were needed for navigation, which the flat desert of Iraq did not provide, they would be flying over Turkey, Syria, Saudi Arabia and Iran in order next to turn towards Baghdad. Since neither Turkey nor Syria accepted flights over their territory, all launches from the Mediterranean were cancelled just prior to the war. While launches from the Red Sea were programmed along mountains in Saudi Arabia, the launches from the Persian Gulf went over the Iranian mountains without Teheran being informed of their intrusion.[76] Fortunately for the Coalition, the missiles performed well,[77] and nothing was made of transgressing Iranian airspace. In the end a total of 282 Tomahawk missiles were launched during the war, but 64 per cent in the first two days, and none after 1 February.[78]

Operation Desert Storm officially commenced at 03:00 Baghdad time on 17 January 1991. While US Army helicopters led by Air Force helicopters destroyed two Iraqi early warning outposts, opening a corridor for a flight of F-15E aircraft that would destroy fixed Scud launchers, USAF F-117A Nighthawks and US Navy Tomahawk cruise missiles attacked central Baghdad. In a span of 20 minutes the Nighthawks dropped precision guided bombs on several intercept and sector operation centres, one command bunker, two telecommunication centres and the Presidential Palace of Abu Guryahb. Tomahawks hit the national Ba'ath Party Headquarters, the Presidential Office Complex (the Republican Palace) and parts of the Iraqi national power grid. Within the next few hours Iraqi radar screens detected several dozen flights that appeared to be heavy bombers, but in reality they were 13 foot-long unmanned decoys. SAM and AAA batteries filled the air with missiles, while high-speed anti-radiation missiles (HARMs) that followed behind the drones locked on to the radar beams and destroyed the heart of the Iraqi defence network. Known as 'Puba's Party', the idea, which originated with Israeli attacks on Syrian air defence systems in 1982, was put forward by the Checkmate team.[79] It achieved the desired functional effect: for the rest of the war the Iraqis remained reluctant to use radars, preferring to launch SAMs without guidance.[80] Within three days the Iraqi air defence radar activity level fell by over 90 per cent.[81]

The air planners sought to degrade key elements of the electric power system during the war's opening moment because of the impact it would have on the communication apparatus and the air defence network. Although the physical destruction would leave large parts of Iraq vulnerable to Coalition air power, the air planners also believed 'turning off the lights' in Baghdad would degrade the regime's morale and resolve.[82] During the first two days of the war 11 power plants and seven transformers were attacked.[83] The result was that within the first hours of operations Baghdad lost commercial power, and with large parts of the national grid disrupted, military equipment was forced to rely on less satisfactory back-up systems. Again the desired functional effect was beyond physical damage: the Iraqis remained reluctant to generate electrical power throughout the war to avoid being targeted. The destruction of the so-called 'AT&T building' alone ensured the disruption of 60 per cent of Iraq's military landline communications.[84]

The air planners could take great satisfaction in the first night's operations. The Iraqi air defence system was substantially degraded, the Iraqi aircraft did not challenge Coalition control of the skies, the national power grid was severely disrupted, Baghdad's ability to communicate with the outside world was reduced and there was little collateral damage.[85] From the early moments of war, the Iraqis possessed no effective defence against attacks on their military and civil infrastructure. Reports in the Iraqi media that Iraqi 'valiant hawks' had destroyed 44 allied aircraft and 33 cruise missiles were unfounded.[86] Saddam's decision to execute air defence and air force officers in the middle of the war suggests that he genuinely believed Iraqi defences were better prepared than they were.[87] The initial allied success established preconditions for the rest of the air campaign: the Coalition could bomb unhindered, and the US ground forces could re-deploy for the Left Hook at their own convenience. The air supremacy might have reduced Iraqi intelligence considerably, but according to General Wafiq Samarrai, such intelligence was available through other sources – the real problem being that if Iraqi troops moved then they would be targeted. Thus, if that observation is correct, the significance of air power was that it prevented Iraqi movements on the ground and enabled Coalition disposition.

As far as the strategic attacks on Baghdad were concerned,[88] the F-117s would strike at night while Tomahawks would strike during daylight, keeping pressure on the regime around the clock.[89] Within the first 24 hours, 122 missiles were fired from nine ships, and F-117s conducted 61 strikes.[90] Among these, 32 missiles and 16 F-117 strikes struck leadership targets. During the first 24 hours of the war, the Coalition struck the following 'inner ring' target-sets, adhering to the Instant Thunder philosophy: Directorate of Military Intelligence, Ministry of Defence National Computer Complex, Ministry of Defence Headquarters, Air Force Headquarters, Iraqi Intelligence Service, Secret Police Complex, Republican Guard Headquarters, New Presidential Palace, Ba'ath Party Headquarters, Government Conference Centre, Ministry of Industry and Military Production, Ministry of Propaganda, TV transmitter, Communication Relay Station, Government Control Centre South, Presidential Palace Command Centre, Presidential Palace Command Bunker, Secret Police Headquarters, Iraqi Intelligence Service Regional Headquarters and National Air Defence Regional Headquarters. Despite intense bombardment, the raw data was rather modest: F-117s hit 14 targets in the centre of Baghdad within the first

24 hours and only one in the second, while Tomahawks struck 39 targets in the first 24 hours and 18 in the second.[91] The Iraqi regime was nevertheless subject to *inside-out warfare*, wherein the 'central nervous system' of Iraq was attacked at the same time as Iraqi air defences were suppressed. The ability to target high-value targets systematically, without any separate sustained preliminary battle for air supremacy, was a crucial advantage in the overall conduct of the war.

In order to keep the pressure on the Iraqi regime the air planners depended on battle damage assessment in order to decide whether a target needed to be reattacked the following day. As argued previously, the relationship between the air planners in the Black Hole and the intelligence community in Riyadh improved gradually throughout the planning period, but there was still a high degree of tension when the war started. While Glosson and Deptula wanted a brief bomb damage assessment immediately, the intelligence agency wanted to process and analyse the data first. From the air planners' point of view they only needed to know whether the designated targets were hit or not, in order to plan for reattack, and then get a more detailed assessment later, but the intelligence community was not willing to give the planners raw data. The result was that the Black Hole obtained alternative sources: Glosson talked to his contact in the DIA in Washington, Deptula talked to Checkmate, they used video-recordings from aircraft and they explored an informal relationship with the Navy's Strike Projection Evaluation Anti-Air Warfare Research (SPEAR) in Suitland, Maryland.[92] Some of the friction between the two parties was a result of the reintroduction of strategic air power: the whole notion of *effects-based operations* and *inside-out warfare* was not incorporated by US intelligence organisations into bomb damage assessment methods. The intelligence community was geared to battlefield assessment: the idea of assessing regime vulnerability was simply not part of its terms of reference. While there is no evidence to suggest that the friction had a major impact on air power results, it is important to note that those who introduced a new concept expected the intelligence community to adapt and provide the appropriate feedback. Thus, the air planners had not dealt with provisions for measuring their own effectiveness.

The Scud Diversion

Although the first crucial hours of bombing had been more successful than even the most optimistic planners in the Black Hole and Checkmate had dared to hope,[93] the Iraqi leader responded by ordering the firing of eight Scud missiles against Israel the following night, 'avenging the suffering of the Arab and Islamic people'.[94] President Bush, after having talked to Israeli Prime Minister Yitzhak Shamir, stated in a press conference that they were determined to destroy these Scuds to avoid Israeli retaliation.[95] Secretary Cheney, concerned about the political ramifications of Israeli engagement, ordered Schwarzkopf to undertake an extensive 'Scud hunt'. Schwarzkopf and the air planners strongly opposed diversions from the strategic air plan at such an early stage, knowing that these missiles were militarily insignificant, but Cheney overruled his commander. The planners had reasonable knowledge of the *fixed* Scud launchers, and the assessment was that the stationary launchers were not an immediate problem as most were facing Iran rather than Israel and Saudi Arabia.[96] The planners were also quite confident that cutting the command and communication chain, including fibre optic cables sending signals to the Scuds, would undermine Iraqi capability.[97] They had not anticipated however, the vast number of mobile Scud launchers that the Iraqis were able to hide before and immediately after use. While the Black Hole partly underestimated the Scud threat, and were deeply concerned about derailing the strategic air campaign, they adhered to their own principle of giving priority to political concerns over operational effectiveness. The Scud-hunt was, however, the first direct impediment from Washington in the conduct of the air campaign, and it was an example of the politicians not conforming to the air planner's view of events. The operations continued throughout the war, in cooperation with special forces inside Iraq, and in the end only airfields and the Republican Guard absorbed more strikes on the strategic target list.

The commander of Iraqi surface-to-surface missile corps, Brigadier General Hazim Abd al-Razzaq al-Ayyubi, provides insight into how Saddam took a personal interest in the development of Scuds from August 1987.[98] He supposedly received 'final directives' on 12 January 1991 from the Iraqi leader:

> conventional weaponry was to be the first response if and when an attack was launched against Iraq. Besides the president, those authorized to order an attack were members of the regional command and the defense minister and a requirement added afterward, the chief of staff of the armed forces so that military operations would be sustained in the case [that] the president's headquarters came under attack.[99]

On 17 January, as the Coalition started bombing the Iraqi capital, Saddam ordered the missile commander to use 'ordinary conventional ammunition' against Israel 'with the heaviest fire possible ... until further notice'.[100] Although some of the Scud missiles were loaded with chemical warheads,[101] they were not used because the Iraqi leadership feared either nuclear retaliation or US determination to make the destruction of the regime an official objective.[102] This perception all but certainly stemmed from the letter Secretary Baker gave his counterpart

Tariq Aziz in Geneva on 9 January 1991. Although the term 'nuclear' was never used, it was implicit in the letter. As the military forces were unable to neutralise the Scud threat, and Israelis grew increasingly worried, the United States deployed Patriot missiles to Israel. Contrary to television reports at the time, the precision of the Patriot was highly exaggerated, but since the Israeli government managed to keep the physical damage a secret, the Iraqi perception was that the interception was successful.[103] The Iraqis launched 39 Scuds during the last 32 days of the war, as opposed to 49 over the first ten. Nevertheless, 28 US Army reservists were killed in one attack,[104] and another nearly hit the USS *Tarawa*, which was loaded with ammunition. Although a terror-weapon that proved to be inaccurate, it was the single most effective weapon in the Iraqi inventory: it drew some resources away from the scripted strategic air campaign and it caused political and psychological repercussions. It may be that the Scud launches convinced the Turkish authorities to grant permission for air operations from their Incirlik base on 18 January. Whether influential or not, the decision resulted in Iraq facing attacks on two fronts from the air, and although precision guided weapons were not available, that operation, code-named Operation Proven Force, concentrated on military targets throughout northern Iraq.

Despite the Scud problem, the opening of the war had gone well for the air planners.[105] All over the world reporters were already referring to the massive application of air power as 'a new kind of warfare' and a *Newsweek* poll taken just after the fighting began showed that Bush's approval rating reached an all-time high of 83 per cent.[106] Other reports, such as an article by former Secretary of State Henry Kissinger, warned that one should be careful not to leave Iraq too weak as Iran might seek to fill the vacuum.[107] Saddam must have realised one week into the war that things were not going his way: Israel was not sufficiently provoked to enter the war and the Coalition seemed strong and united. After one week of war hundreds of Iraqis were returning to their capital, actions that were rather indicative of the Iraqi people's confidence in the bombs' precision and intent of targeting regime targets rather than the people.

Paradoxically, however, if the people felt safe one would assume that the leadership also felt reasonably safe.[108] As such the first week offered the Iraqi leader some comfort. The bombing pattern in Baghdad was predictable and more important the populace was not threatening his personal survival. All the major opposition groups not only had declared they were against the war, but even the Kurdish low-intensity military action in northern Iraq was halted in mid January so as not to 'stab the [Iraqi] army in the back'.[109] With close to 1 million of the capital's inhabitants evacuated and no active opposition from within the country, the Iraqi leadership was allowed to concentrate fully on reducing the effects of the bombing. While the air planners aimed to create conditions so that the people and the military would take advantage of the situation and oppose the leadership, they underestimated the force of Iraqi patriotism in addition to the regime's grip on power. Although the air campaign brought the war home to the Iraqis in a way that the war with Iran had not done, years of suppression had ensured that those who dared take action did not have the means. In fact, the Iraqi people and the armed forces were taken more by surprise by the air campaign than the leadership. Although the strategic air campaign as a whole provided air superiority and degraded the Iraqi war-making capability, there seemed not to be an imminent threat to Saddam's survival.

The Friction of Bad Weather and al-Khafji

During the first week of the war, the number of sortie cancellations amounted to some 1,700.[110] Although quite a few were caused by coordination problems, the lion's share was because of the bad weather. Operation Desert Storm air operations encountered the worst January and February weather reported in the theatre for 14 years and these conditions reduced the effectiveness of the bombing considerably.[111] Poor weather particularly hampered the early days of operations, and while Tomahawks performed relatively independent of weather, laser-guided bombs could not perform if the targets lay under fog or clouds. Consequently, it hampered operations at the crucial point where 'shock and awe' was a huge part of the strategy to achieve strategic paralysis. On 28 January, Glosson noted in his journal 'bad weather again. Fourteen days on the calendar ... Due to the weather [we] have flown fewer than 100 sorties on Baghdad. Supposed to have flown 300. Whole pace of the campaign disastrously affected.'[112] When Secretary Cheney came down to Checkmate on 6 February he was told that after three weeks of war, approximately half of the attack sorties into Iraq had either been diverted to other targets or cancelled because of weather-related problems.[113] Although Operations Desert One, Urgent Fury and Just Cause all witnessed unexpected bad weather, it was frustrating for the Black Hole planners who had not seen a single cloud from August to November.[114]

It would be unfair to argue that the diversions caused by the Scud Hunt combined with the bad weather witnessed during the early days of the campaign reduced the impact of air power per se, because the Iraqis could not take advantage of the situation either. Moreover, the Coalition had plenty of resources available, and so it was merely a matter of bombing for a longer period of time. Still, the intended high pressure on the regime from the opening moment of war was in part compromised, since the strategic air campaign effort was scripted to shift to the preparation of the battlefield (Phase III) after seven days. One might suggest therefore that the first phase was given less chance of succeeding than the plan envisaged. It was, nevertheless, sufficient to provoke Iraqi reactions. The Iraqi regime, realising that it could not challenge the control of the skies and that the Scuds had limited impact, opted for two alternative moves near the KTO. On 22 January Iraq torched two oil-refineries and one oilfield on the Saudi–Kuwaiti border, allowing crude oil to flow into the Gulf. Whether the action was an attempt to provoke a ground war, to make an amphibious assault more difficult,[115] precipitate negotiations to prevent ecological disaster or merely an attempt to destroy Saudi Arabian distillation terminals, is not known,[116] but two F-111Fs, using precision bombs on selected oil manifolds stopped that oil-flow five days later.

Powell was concerned, however: the opening moments of the air war had been so impressive that the public did not understand why it was not all over.[117] After one week it was obvious that the air campaign had ensured control in the air, shut down the capital's electricity, reduced the Scud threat and damaged much of the military and communication infrastructure.[118] Still, there was no sign that the Iraqis were about to give up Kuwait. Powell decided to give a high-profile briefing, stating on 23 January: 'Our strategy to go after this army is very, very simple. First we're going to cut if off and then we're going to kill it.'[119] Powell was essentially preparing the public for the ground campaign that was in the making, and his appearance seemed to have a good effect on the American public.

In the meantime, Saddam seems to have concluded that sitting out the bombing was not working. Targets that he held dear were attacked with impunity and he was perceived as vulnerable and passive, two characteristics that did not go well with his image. While planning for some kind of retaliation he remained confident when talking to his own troops. When he visited the front on 23 January he stated that air power could only inflict limited damage on Iraqi forces. He argued that a ground war was inevitable: 'It is only a matter of time before the enemy becomes convinced that it has done all it can do'.[120] Saddam apparently came to the conclusion that he could not remain passive throughout the bombing, and as the air campaign had not yet shifted the main effort from Iraq proper to its armed forces, the Iraqi troops were still in reasonable shape. Saddam reasoned that if a ground war was inevitable at some point in the future, and morale and capability would be severely degraded in the process of bombing, the best option was to go for a pre-emptive ground attack. On 26 January the Iraqi leader met with key ministers and military commanders, exploring a 'ground offensive plan'.[121] The following day the Iraqi leader went to Basra and gave the field commanders the 'final instructions for the implementation of the ground offensive'.[122] *Al-Qadisiyah*, the military newspaper, reported the same day that 'the coming days will witness momentous events', and 'Bush will lose everything.'[123] According to the newspaper the Coalition was 'afraid of actual confrontation' since it had not already used its ground forces together with air power.[124]

On 29 January, Iraqi troops attacked the evacuated Saudi Arabian town al-Khafji. The mere fact that the Iraqis managed to get so far was an embarrassment to the Coalition, and Glosson admitted that it was 'not the Air Force's best day'.[125] As soon as the counterattack started, however, Coalition ground forces captured and ejected Iraqi troops in two days as air power prevented other Iraqi divisions from crossing the border and eliminated any means of Iraqi reinforcement.[126] Despite the clear defeat, the Iraqi media claimed that Iraqi troops had accomplished their mission and returned to previous positions as planned.[127] Iraqi National Assembly Speaker, Sadi Mahdi Salih, argued that al-Khafji was all part of an overall plan to win the war, and that the 'enemy forces ran away'.[128] The commander of the operation stressed that the objective had merely been to inflict damage, and then return to positions inside Iraq.[129] Although Iraqi reports stressed success and high morale among their soldiers, the commanders themselves had no doubt that overall military defeat was inevitable.[130] Indeed, the able Iraqi 3rd Corps commander, Lieutenant General Salah Abbud Mahmud al-Daghastani, asked for permission to withdraw in the middle of the fighting over al-Khafji. Saddam allegedly refused and told him to make it 'the mother of all battles', whereupon the ground commander replied, 'Sir, the mother is killing her children', before he ordered a retreat.[131] Saddam for his part seems not to have interpreted it as a battle lost at the time.[132] The Iraqi media made the most of the initial success and continued to argue that air strikes were not sufficient to win the war,[133] concluding that the Iraqis would be victorious when it came to ground operations.

The incident of al-Khafji is significant in several respects. Some analysts argue that the Iraqi defeat demonstrated that an invading army can be destroyed from the air.[134] There should be no doubt about the seriousness of the attack. The 3rd Corps, which included the 5th Mechanised Division, was highly regarded within the Iraqi armed forces. It was the only time during the war that Saddam took the initiative, and since the Coalition ground forces were still at a stage of redeploying they were not ready to fight. Although much has been written about the al-Khafji incident, it should be recognised that Saddam's decision on 26 January to prepare operations must have been governed by the overall impact of the strategic air campaign as the bombing of the Iraqi Army had not began in earnest. Saddam could not passively accept the destruction of his country by air attacks.[135] After only nine days of bombing Saddam was gradually becoming convinced that his strategy of merely sitting out the bombing was not working: the bombing was lasting longer than expected and there was no renewed diplomacy in sight. Within that framework, the leader must nevertheless have felt reasonably confident, as he did not suggest complying with UNSC Resolution 660. While Saddam realised the war was going badly, and even that he was losing in a military sense, he did not perceive it as a direct threat to his personal survival.

Shelter Busting

The objective of eliminating Iraqi offensive capability was defined in Instant Thunder and remained an objective throughout the planning. The presumption was that the Iraqi Air Force would fight back, but although ordered to engage Coalition aircraft in the air, they had little means of doing so with radars and electricity substantially degraded.[136] There was in total only one known attempt of Iraqi aircraft that acted offensively, but a Saudi Arabian pilot shot down the two planes on 24 January before they managed to reach their targets. To some extent the air planners had miscalculated the effect of blinding Iraq: the Iraqis kept their planes in the hardened air shelters.[137] Although the Black Hole planners had thought about the idea of attacking the shelters in October, the idea was never implemented until the Checkmate group took the initiative a week into the war. Colonel Warden was particularly concerned that this was part of an overall strategy on the part of Iraq, and that the Coalition might witness an 'Air Tet' – referring to the Tet Offensive in Vietnam.[138] On 23 January, Glosson came to the conclusion after consultation with Warden and Deptula, that Iraqi aircraft shelters rather than the airfields should be the main focus. The decision to use F-111Fs and F-117s dropping laser-guided bombs on some 600 hardened air-shelters was to ensure that the Iraqi Air Force could not be used at a later stage of the war.

Once more the Iraqi response was beyond the air planners' anticipation, however, as they chose to evacuate these combat aircraft to Iran.[139] Over a four-day period, beginning on 26 January, nearly 80 aircraft fled to their neighbour in the east. Although the Coalition established air patrols on the border, over 100 aircraft were interned by the Iranian government. It was a desperate act: although the Iranians had agreed to receive some transport and civilian aircraft prior to the war, these planes were never part of a prearranged agreement, but Saddam gave the order hoping to save as many aircraft as possible.[140] According to former Iraqi Prime Minister Muhammed Hamza al-Zubaidi the decision to send its aircraft to Iran was two-fold:

Firstly, the Iranian Government was the first friendly government to respond positively at the time of international crisis when Iraq was seeking assistance from states friendly to it; we reached an agreement, about it as between governments; secondly the distance from the principle airports in Iraq (in particular Baghdad and Basra) to the border with Iran is short, so that the Iraqi government envisaged a shuttling of aircraft to safety there with relative speed and safety.[141]

Zubaidi argued that an Iraqi delegation arrived in Teheran around 10 January 1991. Rafsanjani reportedly agreed to shelter civilian planes for both cargo and passengers, adding that he would be willing to take care of all Iraqi aircraft. In return, the Iraqis sent the agreed-upon civilian planes, the Iranians received them well and the Iraqi pilots returned without hesitation. Next, realising that Iraqi aircraft had been destroyed in their shelters during the intense air campaign, the leadership decided to send warplanes too, only to find that they had been double-crossed. The ill-fated decision was a result of the strategic air campaign putting immense pressure on the Iraqi leadership, forcing it to act prematurely. Again, the overall effect was beyond gaining air superiority: Iraqi combat aircraft were no longer a threat to Coalition forces on land, at sea or in the air. The Iraqis further chose to disperse aircraft, placing some in residential areas and near cultural sites, clearly taking advantage of American concern about collateral damage, but in such positions the aircraft of course did not pose a threat – another example of effects-based operations.

On 27 January Schwarzkopf declared that air supremacy had been secured, and by the end of the war the Coalition had destroyed 375 of Iraq's 594 hardened air shelters and the majority of its hardened maintenance buildings.[142] In total, Iran received 148 Iraqi aircraft and the fighters have still to be returned. The strategic air campaign subdued the Iraqi leadership, and with the declaration of air supremacy, the main air effort shifted to Phase III.[143] Horner noted that it was important to continue efforts to isolate the Iraqi leadership, and six more F-117s arrived in theatre to help compensate for lost missions.[144] On the tenth day of the war the main effort was thus 'preparation of the battlefield', including the objective of isolating and destroying the Republican Guard.[145]

Restrictions on Bombing Baghdad

In early February an operational challenge was overcome. The air planners had hoped to destroy some 20 to 30 tanks per day on the battlefield, but they had not succeeded in getting more than six to eight.[146] One reason was inaccuracy in bombing, another was that the Iraqis often dug them into the sand. Some of the F-111 pilots had discovered, however, that one could identify those tanks with heat-detectors, as the tank's temperature differed from the surrounding sand. On 5 February Glosson decided that they should start going after tanks with precision guided weapons. It became known as 'tank plinking', and was immensely successful. It had a devastating effect on the Iraqis: on one level, it destroyed their weapon, but on another it prevented them from using the tanks in the first place as they knew they would then be targeted. Although the operations had little to do with the strategic air campaign per se, the innovation diverted resources from it. Although the shelter busting and the 'tank plinking' were not in accord with the scripted strategic air campaign, it was the planners' own choice in adapting to changing circumstances and utilising windows of opportunity to better the overall outcome. It was the kind of flexibility in execution that one would expect. Although both events diverted resources from bombing the 'inner ring' in central Baghdad, one should note that with the resources available it did not amount to significantly hampering those operations. What were perceived as affecting operations, however, were Powell's instructions to stop bombing bridges in Baghdad on 6 February, and, most importantly, ordering the capital off limits altogether on 13 February. In both cases public relations concerns were at the expense of operational effectiveness, and the directions came from Powell rather than the White House.

In early February British daylight strikes against the bridge at Nasiriyah on the Euphrates, 150 miles south-east of Baghdad, caused collateral damage in a residential neighbourhood as a laser-guided bomb malfunctioned. The air planners wanted to neutralise the most important bridges in central Baghdad, dividing the city in two, but after having destroyed three, Schwarzkopf ordered the Black Hole to stop targeting bridges altogether.[147] The planners knew that the two remaining bridges held fibre-optic cables, but because of negative publicity on CNN and pressure from the UK government,[148] bridges were taken off the target list. This decision coincided with Powell's order to halt all Tomahawk cruise missile launches. During the first two weeks of the campaign the air planners had enjoyed full autonomy, but now Powell was giving direct orders for the first time in the actual execution, requesting Schwarzkopf to 'tell Buster that I don't want any more Tomahawks fired'.[149] Powell's concern was that they were flying close by the Rashid Hotel, which accommodated the CNN crew, live on television,[150] and if an accident occurred the media would be all over the commanders. By the seventeenth day of operations, 282 TLAM missiles had been launched,[151] performing better than the manufacturer had claimed, but Powell decided to terminate these operations for the rest of the war.[152]

As weather improved, the air planners started intensively reattacking strategic leadership targets in and around Baghdad, from 11 to 13

February, with stealth aircraft only. F-117s struck the Iraqi Intelligence Service Headquarters; the Ministry of Information (an organ of internal control); the Ba'ath Party Headquarters; the Ministry of Defence; the Abu Guryalib Presidential command, control and communication centre; Iraqi Air Force Headquarters; the Taji Government Command Bunker; the Baghdad Conference Centre; International Television and press buildings; Military Intelligence Headquarters; General Security Headquarters; Camp Taji Presidential Retreat; and the Firdos communication bunker.[153] The latter was the most controversial raid of the war. The planners had received information that military officers had activated the bunker's command and communication equipment, using it for intelligence purposes. What the planners did not know was that the shelter also accommodated civilians. It was a sad day for the Black Hole planners as some 300 were killed.[154] It was the incident they had tried to avoid and it gave the Iraqi leader the first chance of demonstrating substantial casualties.

Saddam played his cards well and CNN gave the incident much coverage. Although the political leadership in Washington could have placed the blame for collateral damage on Glosson, who indisputably was responsible for selecting targets, they stood collectively together.[155] President Bush, Secretary Cheney and Chairman Powell all defended the selection as a legitimate military target. At the same time, they acknowledged the sad loss of civilian lives. Behind closed doors there were, however, measures taken to prevent it from happening again: Powell and Schwarzkopf were to approve every single strike on Baghdad.[156] It was, for all practical purposes, a bombing halt on the capital and an introduction of micro-management in target selections that was to last for the next nine days. It was the single most frustrating decision imposed on the Black Hole planners during the war: in their minds such restrictions would play right into the hands of the Iraqi media campaign, and it would send the wrong signal to the Iraqi leadership.[157] Subsequently, 90 per cent of the air effort was against the KTO, and in that process precision bombing aircraft were further diverted from strategic target-sets. In the two weeks preceding the Firdos bunker incident, F-117s struck 25 targets in metropolitan Baghdad, but during the following two weeks they struck only five.[158] Once again Washington did not conform to the air planners' priority, as public relations concerns were considered more important at that point than the operational effect.

The Final Days of Operations

On the morning of 15 February, as Warden was informed that there would be no F-117 attacks on Baghdad for the first time since the beginning of the war, he took his complaints to the Secretary of the

Air Force, Donald Rice. Four days later, when Secretary Cheney came down to Checkmate, Warden had three issues on his agenda. He argued in favour of lifting the restrictions on bombing central Baghdad by striking internal security facilities in the capital with F-117s and Tomahawks. He next stressed that they should continue to bomb the Republican Guard rather than shift the effort to Iraqi conscripts on the Saudi–Kuwaiti border, and finally he argued that the start of the coming ground war should be postponed. In the meantime, Deptula drafted six key targets for Baghdad which Schwarzkopf was reluctant to accept.[159] Frustrated, the air planners tried a new tactic: to target symbols of the regime rather than facilities themselves. Their first choice was a 60-foot tall statue of Saddam and the second was an even more enormous pair of bronze victory arches commemorating the Iran–Iraq War.[160] Although Schwarzkopf liked both, military lawyers, who felt it would be violating international law, argued that the targets could be interpreted as cultural and historical monuments, and thus prohibited these targets from appearing on the target-list.[161] The air planners had discussed symbolic targets as part of a strategic psychological campaign in August and early September, but at that time there were more critical objectives to achieve, and they did not attempt to convince the theatre commander of such operations. During Desert Shield CENTCOM lawyers argued that psychological operations might be counterproductive, as they could possibly encourage an uprising in Saudi Arabia, as well as in Iraq. Additionally, there was uncertainty as to whether encouraging the collapse of an enemy government at war was somewhat illegal in the first place.[162] Ultimately the air planners did not find the symbolic targets important enough in the early stages of the war to push sufficiently for their acceptance, but in late February they wanted to emphasise the Iraqi leader's vulnerability.[163] On 21 February Cheney was convinced of the correctness of lifting the restrictions on Baghdad,[164] and Black Hole gradually started re-striking leadership targets, but the statues remained off limits.

The Republican Guard makes an interesting case for targeting philosophy. The Black Hole and Checkmate planners did not have any knowledge of the force in August, and included the troops in their planning upon Schwarzkopf's input. The CINC became almost obsessed with it, defining it as one of the three centres of gravity, and ensuring that it became targeted in both Phase I and Phase III. He ordered the Black Hole planners to put pressure on the elite Iraqi troops from the beginning of the air campaign, as it was a defined military objective to destroy their capacity as a fighting force. In learning about the nature of the Iraqi regime the air planners gradually became convinced that the Republican Guard was an extension of the regime itself. Thus, by early February, as Phase III was dominating the air campaign, they argued that the Republican Guard was the most important target, and not the Iraqi conscripts who held the two first lines of defence in Kuwait. In the minds of Glosson, Warden and Deptula these conscripts were the ones who could possibly rebel against the leadership that had sent them to war in the first place. The US Army division commanders may well have recognised that the Republican Guard was more important than the rest of the Iraqi Army, but since they were preparing to liberate Kuwait, these conscripts would be their first points of contact. By mid February the division commanders had put so much pressure on Schwarzkopf that he agreed to shift the bombing effort away from the Republican Guard to focus on the Iraqi conscripts. Thus, towards the end of the campaign it was the air planners who insisted on remaining focused on the Republican Guard.

The dispute was essentially founded in one group thinking strategically and the other being preoccupied with local considerations. The latter group relied on current tactical doctrine and experiences of senior ground commanders, who expected air assets would be available to them in quantity. Interestingly, Richard M. Swain, a ground commander himself, argued that 'senior Army leaders failed to anticipate or understand their relative position in the competition for air assets or to divest themselves of service parochialism in the name of the jointness so applauded at the war's end'.[165] One consequence was that the Republican Guard managed to escape largely intact, and by doing so they contributed significantly to quelling the uprising in southern Iraq which started immediately after the cease-fire. While responsibility for the attacks on the Republican Guard was passed from the Black Hole planners to those running the air campaign in the KTO, the consequent escape undermined the achievements of the strategic air campaign. Paradoxically, the Republican Guard, a defined strategic centre of gravity, was not targeted systematically as a result of the ground commanders insistence on targeting the front line troops, and as the war progressed Schwarzkopf ignored his own operational guidance for a successful military outcome.

As Cheney returned from Riyadh on 19 February, having accepted Schwarzkopf's recommendation for starting a ground war within a few days, Warden and the Checkmate group argued that ground operations should be postponed. They did, however, come to realise that Cheney was not willing to interfere in Schwarzkopf's dispositions in theatre,[166] or object to the President's wish to get the ground offensive started sooner rather than later in order to end the war. Since Powell had been able to convince the political leadership of the necessity of a ground war, the air planners' best attempt was to play for more time, but they did not succeed. Indeed, when Schwarzkopf called Powell on 19 February to suggest a few days delay on the ground war, Powell replied that 'this [Soviet] peace initiative may be for real ... *we need to get on with this* [ground war]'.[167] On 24 February the ground war commenced, and Saddam continued to give the impression of invincible strength. Only a few hours after Coalition tanks rolled into Kuwait, he announced 'The sophisticated weapons of the enemy will have no meaning ... victory will be ours.'[168] The ground operation ended, nevertheless, 100 hours later with a devastated Iraqi Army in theatre, and a Republican Guard that managed to retreat predominantly intact.

AN ANALYSIS OF THE STRATEGIC AIR CAMPAIGN

During the air war, the number of leadership targets grew from 33 to 44, while the number of command, control and communication targets grew from 56 to 146. The Coalition ended up carrying out 260 attacks on the former category and 580 on the latter.[169] Despite all the spectacular footage of surgical attacks on central Baghdad, as the war ended these two target-sets encompassed merely 2 per cent of the overall number of strikes, according to the Black Hole target list.[170] The leadership targets were predominantly military and political headquarters, and command and control bunkers which the air planners assumed to be critical to the regime's ability to control its people and armed forces. The various means of communication were coaxial and fibre-optic landlines of voice and data, television and radio stations, microwave radio relays, and associated switching facilities.[171] Acknowledging that the planners sought psychological and functional effects rather than the mere physical, the ultimate measure of effectiveness is not how much damage was done, but the degree to which these attacks weakened the Iraqi politico-military entity.

Targeting the 'inner ring'

Examining the effects of 'inner ring' targeting is a complicated task, as one must ideally take into account the interchanging effects of other target-sets and the other phases of the war, including economic and diplomatic pressure. The process is one of non-linear effects and intangibles that are open to multiple interpretations, but some observations seem to form at least part of the overall picture.

As far as the leadership targets were concerned, Tomahawks and F-117s carried out 89 per cent of the total number of strikes.[172] The number of strikes was highest during the first two days of the operation, then steadily declined for the next ten days and for the last two-thirds of the war the strategic air campaign was conducted at 'a minimum level'.[173] The latter period included the two strikes against

Table 5: Coalition Strikes by Target Category for Desert Storm

Target	Strikes	%
Leadership	260	0.7
Command, control and communications	580	1.7
Electric power	280	0.8
Oil	540	1.5
Nuclear, biological and chemical	990	2.8
Military industry (production/storage)	970	2.8
Lines of communication	1,170	3.3
Surface-to-air missiles	1,370	3.9
Scuds	1,460	4.2
Iraqi Air Defence System (KARI)	630	1.8
Airfields	2,990	8.5
Naval targets	370	1.1
Iraqi ground forces	23,430	66.9
Total	**35,040**	**100**

Source: Cohen et al., The Gulf War Air Power Survey: Effects and Effectiveness, p. 148

the bunker of al-Firdos on 13 February 1991, which precipitated a significant tightening of control on target selection. The incident deserves particular attention, as it has implications for the relationship between operational concerns and political calculation for public relations.

Prior to this event, the Coalition had managed to give the public the impression that Iraq was subject to almost surgical bombing. The casualties from al-Firdos seem to have brought home to the Western world that even a modern air war demands its civilian deaths. Powell, who in military terms believed the air planners should focus on the battlefield, had already questioned the purpose of hitting facilities over and over again. In his mind it merely made the 'rubble bounce',[174] and as casualties occurred he decided to review the Baghdad target list.[175] The rationale for bombing the same facility over again was three-fold. First, some of the equipment was sheltered in the basement, thus several strikes were needed for penetration. Next, most of the facilities included more than one building, thus several strikes were needed to ensure inoperability. Finally, the continued pressure would have psychological impact. Thus the strikes would keep the leadership under pressure and the people would see that the United States was committed to changing the regime. The Black Hole and Checkmate planners, who had recently intensified the bombing of these targets with the improved weather, believed that Powell's 'bombing pause' of the 'inner ring' gave the Iraqi leadership unnecessary breathing space.

Although the dispute about continued pressure on central Baghdad reflected different beliefs in the efficacy of strategic operations, it also illustrated that operational considerations were subordinated to public relation concerns. While the Black Hole and Checkmate air planners believed 'strategic paralysis' would make the difference, General Powell was not willing to risk support for the war effort over another al-Firdos incident. The air planners, although saddened by the accident, argued that it brought the war home to the Iraqi leadership in ways that previous attacks on the regime had not. Thus, it was a question of maintaining momentum at a critical point in time. It may be that al-Firdos speeded up the war-termination process, either because it presented the Iraqi regime with a more imminent danger,[176] or because it made it easier for the regime to talk publicly about withdrawal,[177] but Powell's direct orders were not in harmony with the Black Hole and Checkmate perception. There is also another dimension to it: the incident was, according to the late King Hassan of Morocco,

> [not] viewed in Iraq in the way you in the West view it as the terrible, awful thing it is, but, rather, it is a demonstration ... to an awful lot of Iraqis as to how vulnerable they really are, and it is probably, in terms of the attitudes in Iraq towards Saddam Hussein, something that will lead to antagonism and criticism of him, not the reverse.[178]

Although the Iraqi leader managed to take advantage of propaganda related to the civilian casualties, there is little to indicate that the incident convinced the American public to change their minds about the war.[179] The incident illustrates, however, a dilemma in the relationship between targeting the regime and its armed forces. While 18-year-old conscripts from poor farming villages positioned at the front against their will were perceived as legitimate targets, the Ba'ath leadership, its families and the civilian elite who benefited from the regime, were not.[181] Although al-Firdos was particularly tragic as some 100 children died, Baghdad's hardened bunkers could host only 1 per cent of its population, and there is little doubt that only the families of high-ranking Ba'athists were given access.[181] Ironically, *because* of the precision witnessed in 1991 such collateral damage became unacceptable.

Interviews with Iraqi officers suggest that communications between Baghdad and the military forces occupying Kuwait were never completely severed.[182] Iraq had modern computerised equipment with high levels of redundancy, relying as it did on coaxial lines, multiple landlines, fibre-optic lines and microwave relays. The Iraqi leader furthermore relied on face-to-face meetings with his staff, couriers on motorcycles and pre-delegated orders.[183] Moreover, the Iraqis had to a large extent anticipated which buildings would be hit, thus relevant equipment had been transferred and many of the headquarters that were bombed were either relocated or evacuated prior to the air war. The Iraqi leadership avoided meeting in bunkers and headquarters that were potential targets and Saddam himself operated mainly from residential houses and regional ad hoc headquarters on the outskirts of Baghdad.[184] He allegedly met his military and political leaders on a regular basis throughout the war in farmhouses or ordinary homes – places they knew would provide them with safety.[185] When Peter Arnett interviewed the Iraqi leader on 27 January they met in a modest residential house. The same was the case when Yevgeni Primakov went to the capital. Indeed, Saddam could never have been completely isolated from the outside world, because he relied on a network of unofficial channels of diplomacy with regional state leaders.[186] Another measure was that the Ministry of Defence staff was moved to the Ministry of Youth building, parts of the Office of the Presidential Palace were moved to the Ministry of Central Planning and files and computers were placed in schools and hospitals.[187] The secret police were wearing civilian clothes rather than green uniforms, increasing insecurity among the citizens.[188]

Senior officers and officials also seemed to be safe. According to Robert A. Pape, 'All of the top forty-three Iraqi political and military leaders on 15 January 1991 were still alive after 1 March.'[189] All this information, when accounted for separately, may lead to the conclusion that the air campaign's focus on the national authority facilities was a waste of sorties, but a different interpretation surfaces when accounting for the aggregated effect. All these inconveniences ensured that the Iraqi leadership needed to spend a lot of time and energy on provisional and less effective solutions. Secondary and tertiary command posts are less suited for crisis management than the primary facilities per definition. The Iraqi elite was, for example, deterred from using cellular phones, depriving them of real-time and mobile communication. The bombing of a variety of communication links forced the Iraqi leadership to resort to far less secure means of communication, such as walkie-talkies, that could be monitored easily. While radio broadcasts continued throughout the war the transmission was on wavelengths that could not be received throughout the whole of Iraq. The reduced connectivity resulted in insecurity and passivity in the leadership and distribution problems within the theatre of operations. There was essentially enough food and clothes in Kuwait to provide for the Iraqi forces, but they were not able to distribute them effectively. Relocation to secondary command posts made it more difficult for the Iraqi leader to keep track of key personnel, which in turn loosened his otherwise tight control of the regime. Saddam was also more vulnerable to ambushes and personal attacks, as he often travelled incognito and alone, rather than with large escorts of bodyguards. The secret police seemed to be more occupied with staying alive than with protecting the regime, as some of its guards chose to abandon the jails and headquarters at night out of fear of being bombed.[190] Some were apathetic already by late January.[191] Witnesses claim that Baghdad was essentially a vacuum during the opening days of war, but since there was no organised opposition group with a base in Baghdad there was no serious thought of how to take advantage of the situation.[192] Saddam may not have feared continuously for his life during the opening days of the war, but he had to take extraordinary measures to protect himself, and thus his ability to direct the war-effort was hampered.

The bombing certainly left parts of Baghdad with an impression of precision targeting. Although there were collateral damage incidents, large parts of the population who had evacuated Baghdad in the early days of the bombing returned to the city after a week or two.[193] Children and adults of all ages could be seen running up to the rooftops to actually watch the bombing of military and political regime targets.[194] It has been claimed that the Battle of Britain and other strategic bombing campaigns strengthened the resolve of the people, but the opposite might be the case for Baghdad. In the Iraqi case the people did not share the leader's ambition, and the bombing seems to have widened the gap between them. Many Iraqis applauded the bombing of regime targets, and an Iraqi Foreign Ministry official stated after the war that the pinpoint accuracy reduced the fear of bombing.[195] After years of oppression many would have welcomed a change, and when the de facto bombing indicated that the regime rather than the people was the target, Tashin Mualla argues that the Iraqi people accepted even occasional collateral damage.[196] One should not conclude that this phenomenon is universally applicable, because in the Iraqi case there seems to have been a real distance between the leadership and the citizens. In addition, the Iraqi leadership, which did not depend on keeping Kuwait for survival, was able to avoid taking chances that would have jeopardised its ultimate power. The bombing provided pressure from the air, but again, without organised opposition on the ground, or any efforts from the Coalition's state departments to facilitate an overthrow, one-sided pressure would be inadequate to change an entire leadership. Moreover, the bombing halt gave the regime some days for reflection. Nevertheless, attacks on regime targets demonstrated that the leadership was unable to defend itself, and as it was at the mercy of its adversary there followed a certain loss of confidence in the leaders. The bombing of these targets showed determination on the Coalition's part, and sparing Baghdad would no doubt have increased Saddam's war-making and war-fighting capabilities. Not bombing regime targets when weapons allowed for precision attacks would definitely have indicated lack of resolve and commitment per se on the Coalition's part. Saddam lost considerable face during the war because of the Coalition's ability to bomb the Iraqi capital with impunity.

Communication on the tactical level was possible throughout the war, but the Iraqi leader was deprived of the strategic picture. According to Yevgeni Primakov the Iraqi leader was genuinely surprised at how bad his situation was when he received the satellite imagery on 12 February.[197] One may ask, however, whether that was a result of reduced communication or whether Saddam's men chose not to present their leader with 'bad news'. Saddam after all was known to shoot the messenger, but this perception should not be taken too far. According to General Wafiq Samarrai, former Chief of the Military Intelligence, the Iraqi leader was more likely to execute somebody who proved to be withholding important information. Thus, if bad news was kept from the Iraqi leader, and that information turned out to have been important for timely decision-making, the official stood no chance at all.[198] The mere fact that Samarrai was not replaced during the war or in its immediate aftermath indicates in itself that Saddam did not blame his own intelligence service.

Another example of problems created by the bombing of communication facilities is found in the memoirs of the Iraqi Missile Commander, Lieutenant General Hazim Abd al-Razzaq al-Ayyubi, who during the first three days of the air operations went without a single hour's sleep.[199] He argued that his Scud team had numerous technical problems because of reduced connectivity. The time and resources devoted to camouflage and concealment were additional burdens, resulting in far fewer launches being executed than requested by the Iraqi leader. Saddam placed great emphasis on launching Scuds against Israel, but after the first week his team was unable to launch more than 20 missiles against its 'arch enemy'.[200] Given the fact that Saddam had pre-delegated orders for continued and massive strikes, one might observe that the reduction in Scud launches had more to do with the second-order effect of communication links being destroyed and the Scud hunt inducing stress, than inadequate leadership on the Iraqi part.

As was the case for many other Iraqi generals, al-Ayyubi received the information about unconditional withdrawal on the commercial radio rather than through the military command system.[201] This was also the case for the Iraqi representative to the UN Security Council, Abdelamir al-Anbari.[202] Both cases indicate a rather isolated elite without the ability to communicate with key diplomatic and military players both inside and outside Iraq. It could of course be argued that the flip side of the coin is that if communication had been completely severed the Iraqi generals would have continued to fight after their leader had ordered a cease-fire. This raises a fundamental problem: if you manage to actually destroy the enemy leadership and its apparatus for command and control, with whom do you then discuss the terms of surrender? It is an interesting aspect that deserves attention, but suffice it here to suggest that with the multiple channels of information the chances of complete incapacitation are very small. In the pursuit of victory the benefits of complete strategic paralysis seem to outweigh the potential disadvantages by a large margin.

According to General Wafiq Samarrai, the Coalition attacks on communications, combined with attacks on electricity, substantially degraded efficiency in the Iraqi command system.[203] The bombing of Baghdad made rapid coordination of forces inside Iraq very difficult. The Department of Defense's report to Congress stated that the air strikes on the Iraqi leaders and national communication targets more or less paralysed Iraq's ability to direct battlefield operations,[204] and Saddam was genuinely surprised that air strikes could be so accurate and devastating.[205] Although the Iraqi leader was able to broadcast statements regularly on certain radio frequencies, he was prevented from using television, his favourite medium, to communicate with the Iraqi people. According to Saad al-Bazzaz, Saddam believed that persistent and flattering television coverage played an important role in keeping him in power. By executive order, his name and image had to be incorporated into every programme on the non-religious channel, with the exception of night movies and cartoons.[206] During Operation Desert Storm he was not able to use this medium, and combined with Western radio broadcasts from Saudi Arabia, the effort most likely undermined his power. Some of the Iraqi officers who eventually took part in the uprising against their leader argued that they did so partly because they believed he had been unseated.[207] In war it is exceptionally important to have a leader who motivates, encourages and gives hope. In the Iraqi case the people and the military forces were left without such comfort. Thus, reduced communication between the Iraqi leader and the forces in Kuwait might well have played an important part in demotivating and demoralising Iraqi troops who chose to surrender before or immediately after the ground war started.

One is reminded of Sun Tzu's dictum that the most successful strategy is to attack the enemy's plans. The strategic bombing played its part in making it difficult for Iraq to adapt adequately to changing circumstances as it weakened and confused its management.[208] Saddam stressed that the Iraqi strategy was one of prolonging the war 'to force them [the US led Coalition] to fight us face to face and not just fire from a distance'. He argued that 'long-range firing' could not 'end a battle decisively'.[209] Several aspects of the air campaign ensured that a bloody ground battle did not become necessary, but the fact that Saddam started preparing for the occupation of al-Khafji only a few days into the strategic air campaign indicates that he became convinced that his strategy of remaining passive during the bombing was not working. The decision to invade was taken before the bombing of Iraqi forces in Kuwait had started in earnest, and the attempt to jump-start the ground war by moving into Saudi Arabia in late January was a clear indication of the Iraqi leadership becoming ever more desperate.

Deprived of decisive offensive action the Iraqi leader was left only with the option of presenting himself as the victim. Rather than the action–reaction pattern that most wars witness, Iraqi decision-making was characterised by inaction. According to Phillip Meilinger

> air strikes against the Iraqi communications network, road and rail system, and electrical power grid made it extremely difficult, physically, for Saddam to control his military forces, but it also induced enormous confusion and uncertainty into his decision-making process. His OODA [Observation-Orientation-Decision-Action] loop was expanded dramatically and its cycle time was slowed accordingly.[210]

Borrowing from the thinking of John R. Boyd, one might talk about progressive chaotic dislocation wherein the offensive actions disrupted the capability of the Iraqi leadership to react and transmit relevant decisions. The Iraqi leader appealed, for example, to several terrorist organisations for support during the bombing, but the lack of dialogue made the effort futile.

The picture that emerges is one in which the Iraqi leader's *will* and *capacity* became irrelevant, because he was prevented from taking decisive action. The Iraqi leader's ability to communicate with his own population and military forces was considerably reduced and to make matters worse ordinary Iraqis started criticising their leader openly.[211] The omniscience and omnipresence of Saddam was shaken. The systematic and precise bombing of Ba'ath institutions seem to have changed the Iraqi people's perception of the Party as infallible: *hajiz al-khawf inkasar* ('the barrier of fear was broken').[212] Kanan Makiya describes one such incident:

> A column of Iraqi tanks fleeing from Kuwait happened to roll into Sa'ad Square, a huge rectangular open space in downtown Basra, Iraq's southernmost city. The commander at the head of the column positioned his vehicle in front of a gigantic mural of Saddam in military uniform located next to the Ba'ath Party headquarters in the middle of the square. Standing atop his vehicle and addressing the portrait, he denounced the dictator in a blistering speech: 'What has befallen us of defeat, shame, and humiliation, Saddam, is the result of your follies, your miscalculations, and your irresponsible actions!' A crowd assembled. The atmosphere became highly charged ... He blasted Saddam's face away with several shells, Saddam lost his face, literally, in a classic revolutionary moment, one that sparked the post-Gulf War Iraqi

Intifada. Within hours there was a meltdown of authority in Iraq, and Saddam Husain was confronted with the most serious threat ever to his power.[213]

After the war 'Saddam castigated the senior and middle-level membership for their helplessness and isolation from the masses in the face of the insurrection.'[214] The cumulative functional disruption, confusion and disorientation at the strategic level of command certainly undermined the effectiveness of the Ba'ath Party to collectively deter a spontaneous revolt. The actions taken by Saddam after the war makes a case for the effectiveness of the bombing of leadership targets. The Iraqi leader went out of his way to strengthen the sheikh system at the expense of the Ba'ath system, and the latter lost much of the prestige and power that it had enjoyed prior to the war. The Party was blamed for its inability to act coherently during the air war and membership dropped substantially in the immediate aftermath. The failure of the Ba'ath apparatus to prevent a popular and spontaneous uprising was nevertheless not sufficient to alter the regime. The previously mentioned sheikh system partly prevented the regime from having to spread its armed forces too thinly during the Intifada, and combined with the control of Baghdad through the security network, and repressive actions against the uprising, the regime managed to survive.

Although calibrating destruction is indeed difficult from the air, one might argue that less bombing should have been applied to the Iraqi Army and more on the Republican Guard and the Special Republican Guard. Parts of the Army participated in the Intifada, but some of the unorganised Shias killed revolutionary soldiers at the outset, preventing the large-scale cooperation that would have been required to defeat the regime. The destruction of regime targets seems to have had some symbolic effect, sending the message that Saddam could not protect what he holds dear, but destroying palaces and the Hamiya within would have increased that pressure. The Republican Palace in Karada, for example, was a purely military zone, the home of the Hamiya and the Special Security Service. Such actions would have been aimed at the heart of the regime with little chance of killing the civilian population. Moreover, water, electricity, telephones, bridges, factories and garages in Tikrit would also have had symbolic meaning. In examining the complex interactions of the social network on which the Iraqi leader depends to stay in power, one might suggest that destroying one or two parts would not make the change, but taken together, the combination of applying pressure throughout the system might have led to the overthrow of the Iraqi regime. Air strikes against the Special Republican Guard, the Special Security Service, wider internal security and the secret police might possibly have forced units to disperse and their communication links could have been interrupted. In total, their focus could temporarily have been on their own survival rather than on protection of the regime. As mentioned earlier, most of the tribes from which Saddam recruited lived in special compounds rather separate from the rest of the citizens in Baghdad, and thus targeting without high risk of collateral damage would have been possible.

The strategic air campaign, in conclusion, contributed strongly in rendering the Iraqi leadership largely ineffective as a strategic entity. Together with the bombing of the Iraqi ground forces and the subsequent ground operations it played an important part in achieving the stated military and political objectives. In total, there is circumstantial evidence supporting the claim that the bombing of Baghdad weakened the regime, but there is little to support the idea that the strategic air campaign came close to actually changing the regime on its own. The strategic air campaign did, however, contribute to establishing the conditions for the Shia and Kurdish uprising that attempted to change the Iraqi regime, and it contributed to putting so much pressure on the leadership that it decided to withdraw from Kuwait. Well-informed sources argue that the strategic air campaign would have had more leverage if the Special Republican Guard and the Special Security Service had been targeted. Additionally, one could have concentrated on Tikrit to a larger extent, but because of concerns with civilian collateral damage it escaped bombing to a degree, and a systematic targeting of the security network would surely have weakened the regime's grip on power even further. To suggest that a systematic air campaign against the de facto political power structure would have led to the replacement of the Iraqi leader would nevertheless be simplistic. The ability of human organisations to adapt to changing circumstances does not allow for such a direct cause-effect link. In total, the air planners were far from succeeding in getting Saddam, but on the level of attaining strategic incapacitation they were reasonably successful. How much the limited and restrained effort of targeting the inner ring target-sets influenced the overall outcome remains an open question, but with only 2 per cent of the overall air strikes committed to this aspect of the war one might suggest that it was worthwhile.

Coercing Saddam Hussein

In all fairness, once Saddam had committed his country to war he made a number of sound decisions. First, he kept the Republican Guard as a strategic reserve. Those armoured and mechanised divisions were used to defend southern Iraq, and they were not to be sacrificed in early clashes. Politically, they could be pulled back to Baghdad at any time to protect the capital, as indeed they were. Importantly, some divisions were kept in the north during the war and some stayed outside the capital. This deployment, enhancing regime security rather than war-fighting capability, may well have saved the regime in the uprising that followed the cease-fire. Forces in the north prevented the Kurdish revolt from getting a smooth start, and those sent back to the south crushed the Shia uprising. In the event of any new confrontation with Iran, too, the Republican Guard would have been indispensable.[215] Second, his decision not to challenge the Coalition in the air when he realised the Iraqi Air Force had no chance of success was sensible. Many helicopters and aircraft were saved by dispersion, and although one may question the decision to send aircraft to Iran, it made sense at the time as it was the only hope, and partial agreements with the Iranian government had been made. Third, the battle of al-Khafji was militarily and politically a clever initiative as the Iraqi Army had remained passive and was about to be destroyed from the air. It was, at the time, an opportunity to test the Coalition's resolve and perhaps get a ground war started while Iraqi forces were still intact. Fourth, Saddam decided not to use chemical or biological weapons, either of which might have provided the United States with an incentive to destroy the regime. To some extent the leadership was successful with decoys and deceptions: to this day, it has been successful in hiding its mobile Scud launchers. Finally, Saddam was successful in withdrawing his forces from Kuwait: both the Republican Guard and the Iraqi Army chose to defend the regime when challenged by large parts of the civilian population.

In examining the impact the strategic air campaign had on the Iraqi leadership, one may seek to find the exact point in time when that leadership changed its strategy or policy, and next determine what caused that change. Such an approach, although theoretically sound, does not work well in this case for two important reasons. One cannot treat strategic air power in terms of mechanical cause–effect links: one cannot easily determine what bombing certain targets did to the minds of the Iraqi leadership. The other factor is that the Iraqi regime did not have a clear-cut policy or strategy. For example, after only hours of bombing, the Iraqi ambassadors to France and Spain stated that Iraq was ready to negotiate since 'there were more civilian than military casualties'.[216] Four days later, Soviet President Michael Gorbachev sent a letter to Saddam, proposing that if the Iraqis announced withdrawal from Kuwait he would talk to Bush about suspending military operations.[217] The Iraqi leader replied that only the 12 August initiative could be the basis for a settlement and that 'Bush has committed aggression and must pay the price of his aggression if he continues to indulge in it.'[218]

When the Russian envoy Yevgeni Primakov met with Saddam in Baghdad on 11 February 1991, the Iraqi leader accepted withdrawal from Kuwait without economic or territorial compensation: 'Okay. I'm going to withdraw my troops from Kuwait. I just want to be sure that, as I retreat, they don't shoot me in the back.'[219] The first public statement to that effect came four days later, and although there were unacceptable conditions attached to the offer, it was a significant departure on the Iraqi part from the previous stand.[220] Until early February, the Iraqi leader believed he could sit out the bombing and then inflict substantial casualties on the Coalition, but by early February he started looking for a way out of the predicament.[221] The Black Hole and Checkmate planners could take pride in these developments: it suggested that air power alone could make a state withdraw its troops from occupied territory without ground engagement, at least when air power was applied against leadership targets *and* ground troops. The political objectives of liberating Kuwait and restoring the legitimate Kuwaiti government would have been achieved, but by the time Saddam proposed such concessions, Washington was demanding that the Iraqi Army should leave their tanks and artillery behind.[222] Saddam, not sufficiently subdued to accept the new terms, chose to bargain rather than withdraw without a fight. Warden may well have represented the American thinking when he observed that:

> The mistake of the Iraqis was that they were a victim of their culture. They were still trying to sell rugs. They were quite willing to sell their $1,000 rug for 10 bucks, but they were darned if they were going to come out with 10 bucks right from the beginning. They thought that there would be a process of negotiating, and maybe they would get $15 on the thing. They misinterpreted their enemy. If they had forgone their rug bartering right from the beginning, they could have brought the war to an instant halt ... and there is nothing that we could have done about it.[223]

On 21 February Moscow announced that the Iraqi leader had accepted a Soviet peace-plan that included 'full and unconditional withdrawal' from Kuwait.[224] As most Coalition demands were not met, the Bush administration denounced the plan for being too vague and lacking a timetable for the withdrawal.

What made the Iraqi leader change his mind in the first place, and why had Washington changed its terms of withdrawal? Saddam personally had become convinced that air power had been more effective than anticipated. Although his life was not in immediate danger, the magnitude of the air operations surprised him. Since he had visited the troops in Kuwait on 23 January and Basra four days later, he had seen for himself that the bombing, especially of military formations, was increasingly devastating. As the shelter-busting started to take effect, and he had to send fighters to Iran, he came to the conclusion that he needed to test US resolve and possibly get the ground war started. The invasion of al-Khafji convinced the military leadership that defeat on the ground was inevitable, but in Saddam's mind it was sufficient to claim success. The Iraqi leader seems to have believed that he had engaged in sufficient fighting to accept an unconditional withdrawal. Around the time of the defeat of al-Khafji, the first Iraqi indications that they preferred an overall withdrawal surfaced. The Soviet President approached Saddam several times and by mid February they had come to an agreement. In the meantime, the United States had already decided that they were determined to have their ground war, and they were not interested in a premature ending. An ending without using the large, massed ground forces that the United States had assembled might have put political pressure on the rationale for retaining a large active Army in the United States, and in addition, it would give the Soviet Union much credit.

When Primakov was in Baghdad, Cheney and Powell were in Riyadh reviewing the ground plan.[225] Saddam may have been affected by Bush's statement on 11 February that

> the air campaign has been very, very effective, and we will continue for a while. We are going to take whatever time is necessary to sort out when a next stage might begin ... We are not going to suit somebody else's timetable, whether it is in Baghdad or any place else.[226]

These statements may have convinced the Iraqi leader that the air campaign would continue until his troops would be unable to resist a ground assault.[227] Although Saddam may have changed his mind about holding on to Kuwait, he nevertheless felt secure enough to bargain rather than withdraw unconditionally. In the process Iraq lost several valuable days, but when an agreement with Moscow was reached on a cease-fire and the lifting of sanctions, Iraq was certain it would happen: celebrations took place in Baghdad and Iraqi forces set fire to Kuwaiti oilfields. It was probably the regime's way of demonstrating that there was a price to pay for taking on Iraq, or Saddam saying that 'If I cannot have it nobody should have it', but the action paradoxically helped the United States argue its case for ground engagement. While key units were ordered to withdraw as the ground war started, it took another two days for Saddam to accept immediate, complete and unconditional withdrawal.

By early February, as the Iraqi collapse did not seem imminent, there was escalation within the framework of Washington's stated political objectives. Despite repeated assurances from Washington that the allied military objective was limited to the liberation of Kuwait, defence analysts speculated that the momentum of battle had begun to escalate towards the destruction of Iraq's military capability in preparation for a ground assault.[228] Although Schwarzkopf and Powell advocated such destruction from the outset, it was evident on a political level when the Soviet peace proposals emerged.[229] There was no way that Washington would allow the war to end without engagements on the ground. Such an ending could be perceived as a compromised victory, both in military and political terms. The Soviet peace initiative suggests that the Iraqi leader was willing to withdraw by mid February, if given a little face-saving, but by that time it was not in Washington's interests to see the war end without ground forces 'seizing and holding' territory.

THE STRATEGIC AIR CAMPAIGN CONCEPT REVISITED

Operation Desert Storm did not succeed in overthrowing the Iraqi leader. However, it is important to recognise that overthrowing the Iraqi leader was never a declared objective of the war – it was not even an un-stated objective of the Coalition military leadership. Without being an objective, and therefore not having the benefit of the focus of the intelligence structure to determine what the key regime targets were, and not having the weight of the entire spectrum of resources to bear on that objective, it was unrealistic to expect that the air campaign would overthrow the Iraqi leader. Deptula recognised that reality and as a result crafted an air campaign using the resources available to him in the context of the stated Coalition objectives which were to achieve conditions that would increase the probability of an internal uprising by lessening Saddam's control over his people by attacking key leader-ship control targets. The result was that at the end of Coalition force application operations – both air and ground – the Shias in southern Iraq and the Kurds in northern Iraq rose up against Saddam's regime. Therefore, it appears that the internal objective of the key air campaign planners was accomplished. The conditions were set for the indigenous populations of Iraq to initiate a revolt to overthrow Saddam's regime. The primary reason they failed was because of the Coalition leader-ship decision not to support their revolt. That decision was made due to concern over leaving a political vacuum in Iraq, and is a subject worthy of a book of its own.

It has been argued that the survivability of the Iraqi regime resided in a complex state, societal and security system. The Iraqi leader sus-tained himself in power by creating and maintaining a persuasive and seemingly omnipotent internal security and intelligence network, strengthened by the wider control of the republic through the tribal linkages, the Ba'ath Party, the military and the government apparatuses. The resilience witnessed during the bombing was the result of two decades of systematic work by the Iraqi leadership. In such a context 'more of the same' in terms of bombing may not have provided for the added leverage which may have been needed to change the Iraqi regime on it own. There is in the end only so much that air power can do without being assigned regime overthrow as an objective, without inside information, without organised opposition on the ground, without political determination to see the job through and without timely human intelligence. Most importantly, it is imperative to understand the nature of the enemy regime in order to be able to change it. One must also go into the difficult business of thinking about an actual replacement, a matter that Washington was not ready to explore. The Iraqi people for their part knew that actions against their leader would result in revenge on their entire family, clan and tribe. Men might well move if their own lives are at stake, but passing such a threshold when the lives of wives and children are on the line is a different matter. Still, given that the objective of the strategic air campaign was not to kill the Iraqi leader but to 'incapacitate and isolate' the regime, the concept developed and implemented by Warden and Deptula proved reasonably successful. Its utility is evident in the high degree of fog and friction that was introduced into the Iraqi system at the strategic level of command. Although the leadership was not overthrown, the Iraqi decision-making capability and strategy were rendered largely inappropriate and ineffective. The strategic air campaign served as a facilitator for other operations, and it prevented Saddam from taking decisive action. A brief review of how the concept of 'strategic paralysis' can be improved is therefore in order.

Colonel Peter Faber provides a suitable framework for such a review. He argues that air power theory, from the 1920s to the 1990s, suffers from three 'pathologies': air theorists have sought to develop hoary maxims that would apply to all wars, regardless of time and circumstances; air theorists and planners have made a fetish of quantification and prediction in war; and air theorists have tended to rely on metaphors to buttress the 'logic' of their arguments.[230] Warden did to some extent fall neatly in line with his predecessors: he argued that the Five Rings Model could be applied to all countries and strategic entities; that six to nine days of strategic operations against 84 targets would influence the Iraqi leadership to change its position; and that modern industrialised societies are closed systems where loss of 'vital organs' would lead to 'strategic paralysis' and then the collapse of the regime.

Warden has a rather mechanistic view of war, as he believes that the strength of US air power can to a large extent control war through technological supremacy. Both he and Deptula acknowledge that war is always subject to friction and uncertainty, but argue that air power can 'inflict strategic and operational paralysis on any adversary by striking key nodes in his warmaking potential'.[231] In their minds, strategic air power has sufficient technological leverage to *reduce* friction and *optimise* control,[232] and 'general concepts', such as the Five Rings Model, are 'not dependent on a specific enemy'.[233] They have an extraordinary faith in air power solutions to political problems and in technological (stealth, stand-off and precision) solutions to air power problems. This knowledge, however, was not matched by a profound understanding of the complexities of the Iraqi regime on which they based many of their assumptions. One may criticise Warden's model for being static as he attempts an analytical approach to military strategy by perceiving the enemy as 'a passive collection of targets',[234] but the analogy is also what gives the model a high level of explanatory power and thus practical relevance in the short term. The model's weakness is its claim to be universal, but Warden and Deptula do not deny the need for a thorough examination of the enemy as a political, economic, military and socio-cultural system. In their minds the model is a starting point: it allows an immediate 'first order' analysis of any state, and with successive differentiation of the rings the dynamic inter-relations will be revealed, and consequently 'higher order' analysis should follow.[235] As such the model provides a theoretical framework which gives direction to the planning, as one tends to get lost in details and chaos, and consequently the model reflects a large degree of holism which undercuts some of the criticism for it being reductionist, rigid, schematic and formulaic. The model does assume, however, that the centres of gravity are material, that they are subject to attack and that the enemy state is reasonably modernised, but the fact that the model is not universally applicable does not erase its utility as a conceptual framework. The most important aspect of 'strategic paralysis' is beyond these issues, however. The over-arching significance of Warden's and Deptula's thinking, according to Edward N. Luttwak, is that they provided the planning with a strategic orientation that rescued 'the USAF from its tactical mentality'.[236] Alan Stephens makes a valid observation on the matter:

> Perhaps the main obstacle to the full development of new era warfare is the dogmatic attachment of many soldiers to the mantra of 'seize and hold ground', a doctrine which has been an article of faith in armies for thousands of years. There is no doubt that the imperative to take territory almost as an end in itself was valid for the majority of pre-21st century conflicts, and the concept retains considerable force today. But it is no longer necessarily the key to success. Two issues are paramount. First, modern warfare is concerned more with acceptable political out-comes than with seizing and holding ground. And second, while seizing and holding ground might still be a primary *objective* of many military actions, it is no longer the primary *means* for achieving that objective. Therefore, neither should it any longer be regarded as the primary *task* of surface forces.[237]

The model, because of its strategic orientation, when taken into the larger air power theory represented by Warden and Deptula, contains prospects for future planning when used flexibly and with a comprehensive appreciation of the adversary's power structure. Further potential resides in dissecting the inner ring target-sets in detail at the same time as looking beyond pure 'utility targeting' and moving into 'value targeting'.[238] When the target-group has been selected one has to assess the adversary's vulnerabilities and values, and Maslow's study of the 'Hierarchy of Needs' could provide a framework for the fundamental requirements of both individuals and societies.[239] In the words of Thomas Schelling 'One needs to know what an adversary treasures and what scares him.'[240] It is a matter of evaluating what the enemy leadership values rather than merely focusing on headquarters, command posts and communication centres, in an attempt to get a 'second-order change'. There are two types of change, according to Paul Watzlawick: one that occurs within a given system which itself remains unchanged, and one whose occurrence changes the system itself.[241] The first is referred to as a first-order change, while the latter is a second-order change. By nature, a first-order change allows continuity from start to end, and is part of the school of thought that believes in 'seizing and holding ground'. A second order change requires a logical jump, and herein strategic bombing provides possible leverage, if accompanied with a good understanding of how a regime works and what the enemy values. In order for a strategic air strike to be more effective it also requires additional measures, such as political commitment and active opposition seeking the overthrow of the regime from within the target country. To get a commitment to a second-order solution that is politically acceptable may be the biggest challenge to the strategy of strategic paralysis in limited and optional wars.

Warfare represents a highly complex reality, and the best way to ensure success is to hold several models and strategies simultaneously in our minds, rather than relying on any single, inevitably simplistic, paradigm. One has to explore different scenarios, expanding the Warden–Deptula thesis by combining it with other air power concepts into a synthesis on the one hand, and an analysis of the state's political construct on the other. In order to do so different professional and academic disciplines need to come together and discuss how each part helps in reaching the post-war objectives. This is not a blueprint for success in war, because there is no such thing, but it is a framework for thinking about air power in a socio-cultural context. The model provides the planners with an option that might prove decisive in certain situations when combined with other elements of force. In an era of precision weapons of high quality the challenge is to translate precise bombing into precise effect on the regime, which one seeks to deter,

Figure 8: Targeting Saddam Hussein's Regime

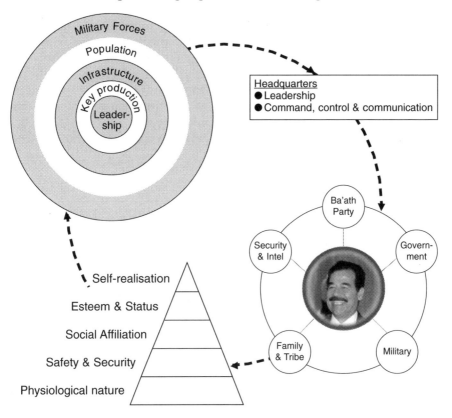

compel or even change. The strategy for concurrent attacks by stealth, stand-off and precision-guided weapons does not guarantee that an adversary will be defeated quickly and with a minimum of casualties, but a highly discriminate focus on its leadership can provide an air campaign with essential leverage in meeting political objectives. The results of the major applications of force in the last 12 years substantiate these conclusions – in Iraq, Bosnia-Herzogovinia, Kosovo and Afghanistan, air power was the dominant force used, and it did arguably result in Coalition objectives being achieved rapidly and with a minimum loss of life on both sides.

In the final analysis one cannot conclude with certainty why Saddam Hussein gave up Kuwait. It might have been a series of events: the strategic air campaign degrading electricity, command and communication, transport and power supply; the destruction of the Iraqi Army with the Republican Guard being next; failure to induce a ground war at al-Khafji; the Scuds not splitting the Coalition; the lack of world-wide

Muslim support; the realisation that the Soviet Union or France would not be able to interfere and halt the war; failure to induce world-wide terrorism; the feeling of the war becoming more personal with the targeting of al-Firdos; the realisation that the Iraqi Army would not be able to inflict sufficient damage on the Coalition in the approaching ground war; or the realisation after only hours of ground battle that he was facing a devastating defeat. Importantly, most of Saddam's avenues of escape were blocked, and within this context one may conclude that putting pressure on the leadership facilities contributed to the regime not being able to function effectively at the strategic level.

NOTES

1. United States Department of Defense, *Conduct of the Persian Gulf War*, pp. 73–4.
2. Ibid., p. 96.
3. Ibid., pp. 95–6; Schwarzkopf with Petre, *It Doesn't Take a Hero*, pp. 318–19; Atkinson, *Crusade*, pp. 272–4 and 473; Gordon and Trainor, *The Generals' War*, pp. 100, 137–8, 313–14 and 410–11; and Cohen *et al.*, *Gulf War Air Power Survey: Effects and Effectiveness*, pp. 276–7.
4. Deptula, 'Parallel Warfare'. On the definition of parallel attacks, see also Fadok, 'John Boyd and John Warden', p. 374.
5. Karsh and Rautsi, *Saddam Hussein*, p. 218; Brigadier General Tawfiq al-Yasiri, interview with author, tape-recording, London, 6 August 1998; and Colonel Muhammed Ali, interview with author, tape-recording, London, 23 August 1998.
6. Hamed al-Jabouri, interview with author, tape-recording, London, 15 August 1998; General Wafiq Samarrai, interview with author, tape-recording, London, 28 October 1999; and Brigadier General Tawfiq al-Yasiri, interview with author, tape-recording, London, 6 August 1998.
7. Hamid al-Jabouri, interview with author, tape-recording, London, 15 August 1998.
8. According to Latif Nusseif Jasim: 'If fire breaks out with an immense force now, the flames will reach the sky and sparks will fly in all directions ... Heaps of corpses will be seen in the desert. For us death is an honor. We would be martyrs. As for them [the United States], they have no cause ... I would like to seize the opportunity to warn foreign and US pilots that they might be eaten up by the people when their aircraft are downed.' See Latif Nusseif Jasim, interview with *Der Spiegel* (Hamburg), 8 October 1990, cited in Karsh and Rautsi, *Saddam Hussein*, p. 222.
9. Hazim Abd al-Razzaq al-Ayyubi, *Forty-Three Missiles on the Zionist Entity*, first published in Amman *al-Arab al-Yawm*, translated by *Foreign Broadcast Information Service (FBIS)* (25 October 1998 – 12 November 1998), p. 12. Confirmed by General Wafiq Samarrai, interview with author, tape-recording, London, 28 October 1999; and Brigadier General Tawfiq al-Yasiri, interview with author, tape-recording, London, 6 August 1998. According to the media: 'Iraq's brave men at the front of rightness have their fingers on the trigger while awaiting the zero hour for engaging in the most honourable epic in the history – the mother of all battles.' See 'Paper Says Army Ready for "Zero Hours", Baghdad Iraqi News Agency, 16 January 1991, cited in *FBIS-NES-91-011*, 16 January 1991, p. 17.
10. Denis Warner, 'Saddam's Strategy Rested on US Casualties', *Asia-Pacific Defence Reporter* (March 1991), p. 19; and the *Baghdad Observer*, 1 September 1990, p. 1.

11. *FBIS-NES-90-243*, 18 December 1990, p. 30, cited in Norman Cigar, 'Iraq's Strategic Mindset and the Gulf War: Blueprint for Defeat', *Journal of Strategic Studies* 15, No. 1 (March 1992), p. 4.

12. *Al-Jumhuriyya* (Baghdad), 2 August 1990, p. 3, cited in Norman Cigar, 'Iraq's Strategic Mindset and the Gulf War', p. 3; and Heikal, *Illusions of Triumph*, p. 264.

13. In late December 1990 the Iraqi Ambassador to Washington warned, 'it is an illusion if anyone thinks that an Egyptian or a Syrian or a Moroccan will fight the Iraqis'. See *Jordanian Times* (Amman), 31 December 1990, *FBIS-NES-90-251*, 31 December 1990, cited in Cigar, 'Iraq's Strategic Mindset and the Gulf War', p. 11. Note that when the ground war was about to start, the Syrians decided not to join the offensive.

14. *Baghdad Observer*, 18 September 1990, p. 1; and 21 September 1990, p. 1; George J. Church, 'Saddam's Strategies', *Time Magazine*, 1 October 1990, pp. 32–4; and 'Terror: Iraq's Second Front', *Newsweek*, 28 January 1991, pp. 32–3.

15. *Baghdad Observer*, 29 September 1990, p. 1.

16. Baghdad Iraqi News Agency, 8 and 28 August 1990: 'If war breaks out, the oil-fields in Iraq would not be the only ones to be set on fire, but also those in other areas ... Should this happen, a good deal of the amount allotted to the West would be cut off, because when oil is ablaze it cannot flow to France, England or Japan', as cited in Karsh and Rautsi, *Saddam Hussein*, p. 232. See also *Baghdad Observer*, 24 September 1990, p. 1.

17. *Al-Jumhuriyya* (Baghdad), 14 August 1990, p. 4, cited in Cigar, 'Iraq's Strategic Mindset and the Gulf War', p. 3.

18. *Baghdad Observer*, 24 September 1990, p. 1.

19. General Wafiq Samarrai, interview with author, tape-recording, London, 28 October 1999; and General Wafiq Samarrai, interview with BBC Frontline, transcript, p. 22.

20. *Baghdad Observer*, 8 November 1990, p. 1; 9 November 1990, p. 1; 16 November, p. 1.

21. George Galluo Jr and Frank Newport, 'Approval Ratings of Bush and Congress at New Lows', *Gallup Poll Monthly* (October 1990), pp. 34–45.

22. Fouad Ajami, 'Inside Saddam's bunker', *U.S. News and World Report*, 3 December 1990, p. 30. Note that as late as 15 January 1991 the *New York Times–CBS News* poll showed that the American people were almost divided in half over the issue of war: 47 per cent in favour of a war and 46 per cent for continued sanctions. See Andrew Rosenthal, 'Americans Don't Expect Short War', *New York Times*, 15 January 1991.

23. Tariq Aziz, interview with BBC Frontline, transcript, pp. 10–11; and *Baghdad Observer*, 1 September 1990, p. 1. On uncertainty of US action, see also Walter Laqueur, 'Is Appeasement Better Than War?', *Los Angeles Times*, 11 December 1990; Walter Laqueur, 'What Do Arabs Want', *Los Angeles Times*, 12 December; Tom Hundley, 'Arabs Think Diplomacy Will Resolve Gulf Crisis', *Chicago Tribune*, 13 December 1990; Joseph C. Harsch, 'Saddam Hussein's Nuclear Threat Is No Reason for War', *Christian Science Monitor* 30 November 1990, p. 7; Linda Feldmann, 'Capitol Hill Urges Patience in Gulf', *Christian Science Monitor* 30 November 1990, p. 3; 'Jan. 15 Deadline Need not Mean War', *USA Today*, 30 November 1990; 'Has Bush Blinked at Baghdad?', *Washington Times*, 5 December 1990; Anthony Lewis, 'Patience Is Strength', *New York Times*, 2 November 1990; Andrew Rosenthal, 'Weighing Balance Between War and Diplomacy', *New York Times*, 7 October 1990. See also Heath, *The Course of My Life*, p. 657.

24. *Baghdad Observer*, 29 October 1990, p. 1.

25. Ibid., 6 December 1990, p. 1.

26. Ibid., p. 1.

27. Ibid., p. 1.

28. 'I would clearly say that Kuwait is Iraqi [territory], and this is not an invention. Neither is Saddam Hussein the only Iraqi ruler who says and believes Kuwait is Iraq. All kings and leaders who ruled Iraq had adopted measures and stances affirming that Kuwait is Iraqi.' See *Baghdad Observer*, 24 December 1990, p. 1.

29. According to the *Baghdad Observer*, 1 million evacuated Baghdad for a few hours, and with 4,238 civil defence centres throughout the country the Iraqi people were well prepared for war. See *Baghdad Observer*, 27 December 1990, p. 1; and Cockburn and Cockburn, *Out of the Ashes*, p. 10.

30. *Baghdad Observer*, 28 December 1990, p. 1; 29 December 1990, p. 1.

31. Ibid., 31 December 1990, p. 1.

32. Richard Lacayo, 'Five Decisive Moments', *Time Magazine*, 11 March 1991, p. 32.

33. Theodore Draper and others have characterised this as a deliberate approach to permit presidential war-making without congressional consent. See Theodore Draper, 'The True Story of the Gulf War', *New York Review of Books* 39, No. 3 (30 January 1992); and Duffey *et al.*, *Triumph Without Victory*, pp. viii, 414–15.

34. Hamed al-Jabouri, interview with author, tape-recording, London, 15 August 1998; and Colonel Hamed Salem al-Zyadi, interview with author, tape-recording, London, 25 January 1999.

35. *FBIS-NES-90-232*, 3 December 1990, p. 20, noted in Cigar, 'Iraq's Strategic Mindset and the Gulf War', p. 3.

36. General Wafiq Samarrai, BBC Frontline, transcript, p. 14. This perception is supported by Colonel Muhammed Ali, interview with author, London, 23 August 1998.

37. In late December Saddam Hussein admitted that 'it is natural that we are surprised ... The positions of the USSR were neither fair nor decent in this regard, and we did not expect this [the Soviet Union supporting the United States].' See Patrick E. Tyler, 'US Says Early Attacks Caught Iraq Off Guard', *New York Times*, 18 January 1991.

38. Saddam Hussein, in *FBIS-NES*, 11 and 13 February 1992, cited in Baram, 'Calculation and Miscalculation in Baghdad', p. 34.

39. Associated Press, 'Hussein Recalls Gulf War Strategy', *Philadelphia Inquirer: International*, 27 July 1997.

40. Brigadier General Tawfiq al-Yasiri, interview with author, tape-recording, London, 6 August 1998.

41. Colonel Muhammed Ali, interview with author, tape-recording, London, 23 August 1998.

42. General Wafiq Samarrai, interview with author, tape-recording, London, 28 October 1999.

43. General Wafiq Samarrai, interview with BBC Frontline, cited in Witness Statement of General Charles A. Horner in the Case of Kuwait Airways Corporation and Iraqi Airways Company in the High Court of Justice Queen's Bench Division Commercial Court, London, October–December 1999, review of Air Vice Marshall R. A. Mason's report of 4 June 19991, Appendix D, pp. 13–15 (selected transcripts have been made available to the author).

44. *Al-Iraq* (Baghdad), 7 January 1991, p. 3, cited in Cigar, 'Iraq's Strategic Mindset and the Gulf War', p. 5. Note that there were reports of Libya mobilising to support Iraq militarily. See Gregory Copley, 'Qadhafi Moves Military Forces to Support Iraq', *Defense and Foreign Affairs Weekly*, 16 December 1990, p. 2.

45. 'Largest Demonstrations Ever Support Saddam', Baghdad Domestic Service, 15 January 1991, cited in *FBIS-NES-91-011*, 16 January 1991, p. 15.

46. 'Saddam Visits Battlefront, Speaks to Troops', Baghdad Domestic Service, 16 January 1991, cited in *FBIS-NES-91-011*, 16 January 1991, p. 15.

47. 'Saddam Message to President Bush', Baghdad Domestic Service, 17 January 1991, cited in *FBIS-NES-91-011*, 17 January 1991, pp. 17–19. For similar statements by Saddam Hussein: 'whenever someone wants to expel a combatant from some country he will rely on the "groundpounder" [lit. 'a soldier who walks on the ground'] and will come with a hand grenade and a rifle with a bayonet to fight against the soldier in the trench', in *Sawt al-Shaub* (Amman), 12 January 1991, p. 44, cited in Norman Cigar, 'Iraq's Strategic Mindset and the Gulf War', p. 15. See Saddam Hussein, in *al-Thawra* (Baghdad), 14 January 1991, p. 3, cited in Norman Cigar, 'Iraq's Strategic Mindset and the Gulf War', p. 15.

48. General Wafiq Samarrai, interview with author, tape-recording, London, 28 October 1999; and General Wafiq Samarrai, interview with author, notes, 20 July 1999; David Fulghum, 'U.S. Lays Groundwork for Possible Offensive', *Aviation Week and Space Technology* 133, No. 9 (27 August 1990), p. 17; Rowan Scarborough, 'Shields Won't Deter Attack', *Washington Post*, 2 November 1990; and Aras Habib, interview with author, tape-recording, London, 14 May 1998.

49. General Wafiq Samarrai, interview with author, tape-recording, London, 28 October 1999 and notes, 20 July 1999.

50. Witness Statement of General Fehed Abdul Baki Mohammed in the Case of Kuwait Airways Corporation and Iraqi Airways Company in the High Court of Justice Queen's Bench Division Commercial Court, London, October–December 1999, p. 2; and General Wafiq Samarrai quoted in Witness Statement of Christopher Christon, pp. 2–3 (selected transcripts have been made available to the author).

51. William Arkin, 'The Urban Sanctuary in Desert Storm', *Airpower Journal* 11, No. 1 (Spring 1997), pp. 13–15.

52. Patrick E. Tyler, 'Iraqi Government to Leave Baghdad', *New York Times*, 4 January 1991; Tariq Aziz, BBC Frontline, transcript, pp. 8–9; and United States Department of Defense, *Conduct of the Persian Gulf War*, p. 73.

53. Arkin, 'The Urban Sanctuary in Desert Storm', pp. 13–15.

54. Aras Habib, interview with author, tape-recording, London, 2 April 1998; General Wafiq Samarrai, interview with author, tape-recording, London, 28 October 1999; and Colonel Muhammed Ali, interview with author, tape-recording, London, 23 August 1998.

55. Staff Brigadier Muhammed al-Zumayri, in *al-Jumhuriyya* (Baghdad), 5 December 1990, p. 3, cited in Cigar, 'Iraq's Strategic Mindset and the Gulf War', p. 18.

56. Cigar, 'Iraq's Strategic Mindset and the Gulf War', p. 19.

57. Ibid., p. 18.

58. Faleh al-Jabber, 'Why the Intifada Failed', p. 104; and 'Why the Uprising Failed', *Middle East Report* (May–June 1992), p. 7.

59. *New York Times*, 20 November 1990, pp. A-1 and A-13; and the *Washington Post*, 20 November 1990, p. A-10.

60. *Baghdad Observer*, 16 October, p. 1; 17 October 1990, p. 1.

61. Keaney and Cohen, *Gulf War Air Power Survey: Summary Report*, p. 9; United States Department of Defense, *Conduct of the Persian Gulf War*, pp. 11–13 and 84–5; and the *Washington Post*, 17 March 1991, pp. A-1, A-24.

62. United States Department of Defense, *Conduct of the Persian Gulf War*, pp. 110–12;. Keaney and Cohen, *Gulf War Air Power Survey: Summary Report*, pp. 9–10; John M. Broder, 'Iraqi Defenses Take a Cue From History', *Los Angeles Times*, 13 October 1990.

63. al-Bazzaz, cited in Samaan and Muhareb, *An Aggression on the Mind*, pp. 129–30.
64. Associated Press, 'Hussein Recalls Gulf War Strategy', *Philadelphia Inquirer: International*, 27 July 1997.
65. 'Iraq: TV Carries Saddam Remarks on Gulf War', cited in *FBIS-NES-97-208*, 5 August 1997, p. 1; and Christopher Dickey, 'Rope-a-Dope in Baghdad', *Newsweek*, 4 February 1991, pp. 26–7.
66. Cordesman and Wagner, *The Lessons of Modern War, Vol. II*, p. 593.
67. *Baghdad Observer*, 6 September 1990, p. 1.
68. Tariq Aziz, cited in Cigar, 'Iraq's Strategic Mindset and the Gulf War', p. 21; General Wafiq Samarrai, telephone interview with author, notes, 11 October 1999; and Cohen *et al.*, *Gulf War Air Power Survey: Operations*, p. 127.
69. United States Department of Defense, *Conduct of the Persian Gulf War*, p. 74.
70. Ibid., p. 75.
71. Winnefeld, Johnson and Niblack, *A League of Airmen*, p. 118.
72. See for example, James P. Coyne, 'A Strike by Stealth: The F-117 Pilot who Dropped the First Bomb Recounts the Opening of Operation Desert Storm', *Air Force Magazine* 75, No. 3 (March 1992), pp. 38–45.
73. Cohen *et al.*, *Gulf War Air Power Survey: A Statistical Compendium*, pp. 517–39.
74. Bill Gertz, 'Missiles Strike against Iraq mulled on Hill', *Washington Post*, 10 September 1990.
75. Atkinson, *Crusade*, p. 15.
76. Vice Admiral Stanley Arthur, interview with BBC Frontline, part one, pp. 15–16; and Atkinson, *Crusade*, pp. 15–16.
77. Freedman and Karsh, *The Gulf Conflict 1990–91*, p. 313; John Schwartz *et al.*, 'The Mind of a Missile', *Newsweek*, 18 February 1991, pp. 22–5.
78. Norman Friedman contends that 297 missiles were actually fired, but nine failed to leave the tube and six fell into the water after leaving the tube. He further argues that at least two, but possibly six were shut down by the Iraqis. See, Friedman, *Desert Victory*, p. 339. Additionally, 35 conventional air-launched cruise missiles were employed by B-52s on the first night of operations: half against electricity and half against command, control and communication targets. See Keaney and Cohen, *Revolution in Warfare?*, p. 190; and Keaney and Cohen, *Gulf War Air Power Survey: Summary Report*, p. 224.
79. Deptula, interview with author, tape-recording, Incirlik (Turkey), 19 and 20 August 1999.
80. Coyne, *Airpower in the Gulf*, pp. 50, 71, 94.
81. Clancy with Horner, *Every Man a Tiger*, p. 352; Murray with Thompson, *Air War in the Persian Gulf*, p. 141; and United States Department of Defense, *Conduct of the Persian Gulf War*, p. 202.
82. Keaney and Cohen, *Gulf War Air Power Survey: Summary Report*, pp. 55 and 76; Cohen *et al.*, *Gulf War Air Power Survey: Operations*, p. 93; and United States Department of Defense, *Conduct of the Persian Gulf War*, pp. 74, 95.
83. Atkinson, *Crusade*, p. 30.
84. Davis, *Decisive Force*, p. 34.
85. Murray with Thompson, *Air War in the Persian Gulf*, p. 109; Davis, *Decisive Force*, p. 39; and Ramadan, *In the Shadow of Saddam*, p. 221.
86. 'Saddam Visits Air Force Command', Baghdad Domestic Service, 17 January 1991, cited in *FBIS-NES-90 [sic]-012*, 17 January 1990 [sic], p. 21; 'Communiqué No. 4', Baghdad Domestic Service, 18 January 1991, cited in *FBIS-NES-91-013*, 18 January 1991, p. 26; and 'Communiqués Claim Shootdowns, Outline Views: Communiqué No. 3', Baghdad Iraqi News Agency, 17 January 1991, cited in *FBIS-NES-91-013*, 18 January 1991, p. 25.

87. Michael Evans, 'Saddam "Foiled Coup Attempts by Air Force Chiefs"', *The Times* (London), 30 January 1991.

88. It should be noted that there is a distinction between strikes and sorties. Sorties reflect the number of flights, while strikes reflect the number of targets attacked. Note that if for example an F-111 drops four bombs on four different targets, one has one sortie and four strikes. However, if two of those bombs attack the same target, one has one sortie and three strikes. If the mission is aborted after take-off, one has one sortie and zero strikes. Despite this distinction, 95 per cent of aircraft sorties equated strikes. Note further that tankers and support aircraft will account for sorties flown, but they will not be counted for as strikes. As for F-117s, which carried two bombs each, a total of 1,299 bombs were dropped, but it amounted to 1,788 strikes. See Cohen *et al.*, *Gulf War Air Power Survey: A Statistical Compendium*, p. 403.

89. The aircraft that formed the 'heart and soul' of the strategic air campaign were those with precision guided weapons: 64 F-111Fs, 46 F-15s and 36 (later increased to 42) F-117s. In total the USAF deployed some 700 combat aircraft and 450 support aircraft. The USN and USMC supplied 724 more, the Arabs 490 and members of Nato added another 146. See Davis, *Decisive Force*, p. 28.

90. Cohen *et al.*, *Gulf War Air Power Survey: A Statistical Compendium*, p. 518: and Cohen *et al.*, *Gulf War Air Power Survey: Effects and Effectiveness*, p. 388.

91. Murray with Thompson, *Air War in the Persian Gulf*, pp. 141–2; and Davis, *Decisive Force*, p. 42. Altogether, in the first two days, Coalition air attackers struck 169 of 298 potential strategic targets.

92. Cohen *et al.*, *Gulf War Air Power Survey: Operations*, pp. 147, 191; and Deptula, interview with author, tape-recording, Incirlik (Turkey), 19 August 1999.

93. Warden, interview, *Desert Story Collection*, 10 December 1991, p. 86; Cohen *et al.*, *Gulf War Air Power Survey: Operations*, pp. 138, 156; and Horner, interview with author, notes, 20 August 1999.

94. 'Commander Cables Saddam', Baghdad Domestic Service, 18 January 1991, cited in *FBIS-NES-91-013*, 18 January 1991, p. 27.

95. Tom Post *et al.*, 'Keep Smiling, Israel', *Newsweek*, 28 January 1991, pp. 20–1.

96. Warden, interview, *Desert Story Collection*, 10 December 1991, p. 112.

97. Ibid.

98. al-Ayyubi, *Forty-Three Missiles on the Zionist Entity*, pp. 1–5.

99. Ibid., p. 27.

100. Ibid., p. 33.

101. Ibid., p. 13.

102. Baker with DeFrank, *The Politics of Diplomacy*, p. 359; Baghdad Iraqi News Agency broadcasts, 9–13 January 1992, in *FBIS-NES-92-009*; Amatzia Baram, 'Israeli Deterrence, Iraqi Responses', *Orbis* 31, No. 2 (Summer 1992), pp. 399–401; interview with Hussein Kamel, 'Inside Saddam's Brutal Regime', *Time Magazine*, 18 September 1995, p. 53; Colonel Hamed Salem al-Zyadi, interview with author, tape-recording, London, 25 January 1999; and Tariq Aziz, interview with BBC Frontline, transcript, p. 19.

103. On the misperception at the time, see for example, Marvin Leibstone, 'Operation Desert Storm: Phase One – The Early Days', *Military Technology* 15 (February 1991), pp. 80–2; and Russell Watson and Gregg Easterbrook, 'Desert Storm', *Newsweek*, 28 January 1991, p. 11. Note that some 17,000 precision guided munitions were expended, while by comparison some 210,000 unguided bombs were dropped in Desert Storm. See Keaney and Cohen, *Gulf War Air Power Survey: Summary Report*, p. 226.

104. The Scud killed 28 and wounded 98 more. It was the largest single incident of US losses of the war. In total 148 US service members were killed in action and

35 of these died by 'friendly fire'. Of 467 wounded, 72 were hit by 'friendly fire'. (Note alternative words for 'friendly fire': 'blue-on-blue' or 'fratricide'.) See Swain, *'Lucky War'*, pp. 177, 181.

105. Glenn Frankel, 'Iraqi Rebels Say Air Raids Hit Iraqi Industry Hard', *Washington Post*, 22 January 1991.
106. Russell Watson and Gregg Easterbrook, 'Desert Storm', *Newsweek*, 18 February 1991, p. 12; and Russell Watson and Gregg Easterbrook, 'War's New Science', *Newsweek*, 18 February 1991, pp. 20–1.
107. Henry Kissinger, 'A Postwar Agenda', *Newsweek*, 28 January 1991, pp. 26–9.
108. Arkin, 'The Urban Sanctuary in Desert Storm', pp. 13–15. Confirmed by General Wafiq Samarrai, interview with author, tape-recording, London, 28 October 1999.
109. Faleh al-Jabber, 'Why the Intifada Failed', p. 105.
110. Murray with Thompson, *Air War in the Persian Gulf*, p. 148.
111. Keaney and Cohen, *Gulf War Air Power Survey: Summary Report*, p. 144; Cohen *et al.*, *Gulf War Air Power Survey: Operations*, p. 163; and Peter Bacque, 'When Weather Is an Enemy', *Air Force Magazine* 75, No. 4 (April 1992), p. 68.
112. See Cohen *et al.*, *Gulf War Air Power Survey: Operations*, p. 193. These observations did also appear in print at the time. See for example 'Hard Days Ahead', *Newsweek*, 4 February 1991, p. 18.
113. Keaney and Cohen, *Gulf War Air Power Survey: Summary Report*, p. 14.
114. Peter Bacque, 'When Weather Is an Enemy', p. 71; and Keaney and Cohen, *Gulf War Air Power Survey: Summary Report*, p. 146.
115. General Wafiq Samarrai, interview with author, tape-recording, London, 28 October 1999.
116. Duffey *et al.*, *Triumph Without Victory*, p. 262; and Sharon Begley, 'Saddam's Ecoterror', *Newsweek*, 4 February 1991, pp. 22–5. Both argue Saddam Hussein's purpose was to enlist Western media in a campaign against the war because of the environmental damage.
117. General Colin Powell, interview with BBC Frontline, part 1, pp. 21–2; and Warden, interview, *Desert Story Collection*, 10 December 1991, p. 96.
118. Tony Capaccio, 'Despite Directives, Off-Limits Iraqi Power Plant Gear was Hit', *Jane's Defense Weekly* 16, No. 2 (13 January 1992).
119. Colin Powell, interview with BBC Frontline, part 1, pp. 21–2.
120. Baghdad Iraqi News Agency, 24 January 1991, cited in *FBIS-NES-91-016*, p. 22.
121. 'Saddam Ministers Set "Ground Offensive Plan"', Baghdad Domestic Service, 30 January 1991, cited in *FBIS-NES-91-020*, 30 January 1991, p. 20. According to USAF historian Richard P. Hallion, Saddam Hussein began his preparations as early as 22 January. See Hallion, *Storm over Iraq*, p. 220.
122. 'Visits Al-Basrah Governate 27 Jan', Baghdad Iraqi News Agency, 30 January 1991, cited in *FBIS-NES-91-020*, 30 January 1991, p. 20.
123. 'Paper Says Bush Will Lose Everything', Baghdad Iraqi News Agency, 27 January 1991, cited in *FBIS-NES-91-020*, 30 January 1991, p. 26.
124. 'Paper: Technology Cannot Defeat "Iraqi Resolve"', Baghdad Iraqi News Agency, 26 January 1991, cited in *FBIS-NES-91-020*, 30 January 1991, p. 26.
125. Glosson, interview with BBC Frontline, part one, pp. 15–16.
126. Brigadier General Tawfiq al-Yasiri, interview with author, tape-recording, London, 6 August 1998; and Gordon and Trainor, *The Generals' War*, pp. 272–8.
127. On 1 February an Iraqi Military Communiqué stated that the attack on al-Khafji was a great success and that the Iraqi units had withdrawn from Saudi territory. See 'Units Withdraw From Al-Khafji', Baghdad Domestic Service, 1 February 1991, cited in *FBIS-NES-91-022*, 1 February 1991, pp. 21–2; and 'Action "Not

Occupation"', Baghdad Mother of Battles Radio, 30 January 1991, cited in *FBIS-NES-91-020*, 30 January 1991, p. 22.

128. 'Assembly Speaker Comments on Plans for Long War', *Amman SAWT Al-Shab*, 2 February 1991, pp. 1, 15, cited in *FBIS-NES-91-023*, 4 February 1991, pp. 30–1; and 'Al-Khafji Battle Called Part of "War Strategy"', Baghdad Iraqi News Agency, 4 February 1991, cited in *FBIS-NES-91-023*, 4 February 1991, p. 45.

129. 'Commander comments on Al-Khafji "Operation Storm"', Baghdad Mother of Battles Radio, 2 February 1991, cited in *FBIS-NES-91-023*, 4 February 1991, pp. 31–2. According to General Wafiq Samarrai, Saddam Hussein said: 'capture for me 4,000 or 5,000 American, English and French troops and we'll use them as human shields. We will tie them to our tanks and overrun the Saudi oil wells. If we do this, the allied jets won't attack.' See General Wafiq Samarrai, BBC Frontline, transcript, p. 22.

130. Brigadier General Tawfiq al-Yasiri, interview with author, tape-recording, London, 6 August 1998; Colonel Muhammed Ali, interview with author, tape-recording, London, 23 August 1998; and Trainor, 'War by Miscalculation', in Joseph S. Nye Jr. and Roger K. Smith (eds), *After the Storm: Lessons From the Gulf War* (Lanham, MD: Madison Books, 1992), p. 210.

131. Clancy with Horner, *Every Man a Tiger*, p. 432; and Aras Habib, telephone interview with author, notes, 28 January 2000.

132. General Wafiq Samarrai, interview with author, tape-recording, London, 28 October 1999.

133. 'Talk Questions Whether Air Strikes Can Win War', Baghdad Domestic Service, 3 February 1991, cited in *FBIS-NES-91-023*, 4 February 1991, p. 45.

134. Meilinger, 'Towards a New Airpower Lexicon or Interdiction', pp. 40–1; Hallion, *Storm over Iraq*, pp. 219–23; and Gordon and Trainor, *The Generals' War*, pp. 288.

135. Friedman, *Desert Victory*, p. 197.

136. General Wafiq Samarrai, interview with author, tape-recording, London, 28 October 1999.

137. 'The Gulf War: Battered, Hunkered Down, but Iraq's Army is Undefeated', *The Economist*, 26 January 1991, p. 19; and 'Hunkering in the Bunkers', *Newsweek*, 4 February 1991, p. 28.

138. Colonel John A. Warden, transcript of interview with Suzanne B. Gehri, *Desert Story Collection*, 10 December 1991, p. 96; and Hallion, *Storm over Iraq*, p. 219.

139. James Bruce, 'Iraq Lists 148 Aircraft in Iran', *Jane's Defence Weekly* 15, No. 17 (27 April 1991), p. 684.

140. Tariq Aziz, interview with BBC Frontline, transcript, p. 18. According to Iraqi media: 'Last night, 25 January, several of our planes were forced to land in Iran. Contacts are being carried out, in accordance with accepted norms, to return the planes and the pilots to their homeland.' See 'Statement on Planes' Landing in Iran', Baghdad Domestic Service, 26 January 1991, cited in *FBIS-NES-91-018*, 28 January 1991, p. 31.

141. Witness Statement of Muhammed Hamza al-Zubaidi, in the Case of Kuwait Airways Corporation and Iraqi Airways Company in the High Court of Justice Queen's Bench Division Commercial Court, London, October–December 1999, p. 13.

142. Davis, *Decisive Force*, p. 46; and United States Department of Defense, *Conduct of the Persian Gulf War*, p. 154.

143. Davis, *Decisive Force*, p. 47.

144. Ibid.

145. Cohen *et al.*, *Gulf War Air Power Survey: Operations*, pp. 197–9.

146. Glosson, interview with BBC Frontline, part one, p. 2.
147. Murray with Thompson, *Air War in the Persian Gulf*, p. 206; and Deptula, interview with author, tape-recording, Incirlik (Turkey), 19 August 1999.
148. Glosson, interview, *Desert Story Collection*, 29 May 1991, p. 83.
149. Ibid., p. 94. Horner argued that Powell's decision was based on the cost: Horner, 'What We Should Have Learned in Desert Storm, But Didn't', *Air Force Magazine* 79, No. 12 (December 1996), p. 56; Murray with Thompson, *Air War in the Persian Gulf*, p. 205.
150. Glosson, interview, *Desert Story Collection*, 29 May 1991, p. 95.
151. According to Table 163, 'TLAM: USN Sorties by Mission Type', the distribution of the 282 sorties were as follows: 17 January (122), 18 January (58), 19 January (32), 20 January (8), 22 January (8), 24 January (6), 25 January (11), 26 January (7), 28 January (2), 29 January (3), 31 January (19) and 1 February (6), in Cohen *et al.*, *Gulf War Air Power Survey: A Statistical Compendium*, p. 386.
152. Powell with Persico, *My American Journey*, p. 500.
153. Davis, *Decisive Force*, p. 48.
154. Deptula, interview with author, tape-recording, Washington, DC, 11 March 1998.
155. Glosson, interview, *Desert Story Collection*, 29 May 1991, p. 84.
156. Note that Powell defined Baghdad as off limits, while the Black Hole planners intentionally interpreted it as central Baghdad being off limits. After a few debacles between Glosson and Schwarzkopf the former succeeded. See Deptula, interview, *Desert Story Collection*, 23 May 1991, p. 67; and Warden, interview, *Desert Story Collection*, 10 December 1991, p. 108.
157. Glosson, interview, *Desert Story Collection*, 29 May 1991, pp. 86, 118–19; Deptula, interview, *Desert Story Collection*, 23 May 1991, pp. 71–2. See also 'Bush and the Generals', *Newsweek*, 4 February 1991, p. 17. Note that Schwarzkopf ordered the Black Hole planners to prepare a 72-hour bombing effort against the remaining NBC targets 'in the event a cease-fire is declared and only seventy-two hours remain prior to implementation'. See Murray with Thompson, *Air War in the Persian Gulf*, p. 207.
158. Keaney and Cohen, *Gulf War Air Power Survey: Summary Report*, p. 219.
159. The targets were the Regional Headquarters of Iraqi Intelligence Services; the Headquarters for the Special Security Services; the Ministry of Strategic Industry and Planning building (responsible for NBC development); the Ministry of Defence building adjacent to Ministry of Petroleum; the Republican Guard Headquarters; and the Headquarters of the Ministry of Military Planning. The former two were approved by Schwarzkopf, but the Republican Guard HQ was rejected on the grounds that it had either been bombed or moved.
160. Deptula, interview, *Desert Story Collection*, 23 May 1991, p. 77.
161. Ibid., p. 78.
162. Murray with Thompson, *Air War in the Persian Gulf*, p. 226.
163. Deptula, interview, *Desert Story Collection*, 23 May 1991, p. 76.
164. Davis, *Decisive Force*, p. 82, n.52.
165. Swain, '*Lucky War*', p. 182.
166. Warden, interview, *Desert Story Collection*, 10 December 1991, p. 49.
167. Schwarzkopf, *It Doesn't Take a Hero*, pp. 511–14. (emphasis in original).
168. Henderson, *Instant Empire*, pp. 229–30.
169. Cohen *et al.*, *Gulf War Air Power Survey: A Statistical Compendium*, pp. 517–39.
170. Ibid.
171. Cohen, *et al.*, *Gulf War Air Power Survey: Effects and Effectiveness*, pp. 277–8; and Colonel Muhammed Ali, interview with author, tape-recording, London, 23 August 1998.

172. Note that F-117s conducted 173 strikes and the TLAM 61 out of 264. The other strikes were conducted by F-16 (16 on the third day of war and 12 on the fifth) and F-111F (two on the first day of war). See Cohen *et al.*, *Gulf War Air Power Survey: Statistical Compendium*, pp. 517–39.
173. Davis, *Decisive Force*, p. 43.
174. Atkinson, *Crusade*, pp. 288–9; and Powell with Persico, *My American Journey*, p. 513.
175. Powell with Persico, *My American Journey*, p. 499; and Deptula, interview, *Desert Story Collection*, 23 May 1991, pp. 66–7.
176. Cordesman and Wagner, *The Lessons of Modern War, Volume IV: The Gulf War*, p. 499; and Freedman and Karsh, *The Gulf Conflict 1990–1991*, p. 329.
177. Baram, 'Calculations and Miscalculations in Baghdad', p. 46.
178. Interview with Lawrence Eagleburger, BBC Television, *The Washington Version*, 18 January 1992, cited in Freedman and Karsh, *The Gulf Conflict 1990–1991*, p. 329. According to Aras Habib, a woman reportedly hit a Ba'ath official in the face when he arrived at the scene. This action was unprecedented and supports King Hassan's observation that the incident turned the people against the regime rather than uniting around it. Aras Habib, interviews with author, tape-recordings, London, 2 April and 14 May 1998.
179. Eliot Cohen, interview with author, tape-recording, Washington, DC, 23 February 1999.
180. 'Conscripts Said Serving "Against Their Will"', *al-Sharq al-Awsat* (London), 17 January 1991, p. 6, cited in *FBIS-NES-91-013*, 18 January 1991, p. 34; and Cordesman and Wagner, *The Lessons of Modern War*, Vol. 4, p. 499.
181. Freedman and Karsh, *The Gulf Conflict 1990–1991*, p. 325; and Aras Habib, interviews with author, tape-recordings, London, 2 April and 14 May 1998.
182. Colonel Muhammed Ali, interview with author, tape-recording, London, 23 August 1998; and General Wafiq Samarrai, interview with author, tape-recording, London, 28 October 1999.
183. al-Ayyubi, *Forty-Three Missiles on the Zionist Entity*.
184. General Wafiq Samarrai, interview with author, tape-recording, London, 28 October 1999.
185. Ibid., General Wafiq Samarrai, interview with author, tape-recording, London, 28 October 1999; Tariq Aziz, interview with BBC Frontline Show (BBC I), *No. 1407T* (part one), air date 28 January 1997, transcript, p. 17.
186. al-Bazzaz, *The Ashes of Wars*, p. 28.
187. Arkin, 'Baghdad: The Urban Sanctuary in Desert Storm', p. 17; and General Sir Peter de la Billiere, cited in Freedman and Karsh, *The Gulf Conflict 1990–1991*, p. 325.
188. Colonel Muhammed Ali, interview with author, tape-recording, London, 23 August 1998.
189. Pape, *Bombing to Win*, p. 230.
190. Lieutenant Colonel William Brurner, interview with author, tape-recording, Washington, DC, 18 February 1998.
191. Yahia and Wendel, *I Was Saddam's Son*, p. 225; Aras Habib, interview with author, tape-recording, London, 14 May 1998; Tashin Mualla, Iraqi National Accord, interview with author, tape-recording, London, 14 August 1998.
192. Nabeel Musawi, interview with author, notes, London, 13 July 2001; and Tahsin Mualla, interview with author, tape-recording, 14 August 1998.
193. Makiya, *Cruelty and Silence*, p. 77; and Aras Habib, interview with author, tape-recording, London, 14 May 1998.
194. Tashin Mualla, interview with author, tape-recording, London, 14 August 1998.

195. Arkin, 'Baghdad: The Urban Sanctuary in Desert Storm', p. 176.
196. Tashin Mualla, interview with author, tape-recording, London, 14 August 1998.
197. Yevgeni Primakov, interview with BBC Frontline Show (BBC I), *No. 1407T* (part 1), air date 28 January 1997, p. 3; and Ken Fireman, 'Hussein's Peace Feeler: Says He'll Cooperate with Soviets', *The New York Newsday*, 13 February 1991.
198. General Wafiq Samarrai, interview with author, tape-recording, London, 28 October 1999.
199. al-Ayyubi, *Forty-Three Missiles on the Zionist Entity*.
200. Cohen *et al.*, *The Gulf War Air Power Survey: Effects and Effectiveness*, p. 337.
201. al-Ayyubi, *Forty-Three Missiles on the Zionist Entity*.
202. al-Bazzaz, *The Ashes of Wars*, p. 23.
203. General Wafiq Samarrai, interview with author, tape-recording, London, 28 October 1999.
204. United States Department of Defense, *Conduct of the Persian Gulf War*, p. 199.
205. Rick Francona, *Ally to Adversary: An Eyewitness Account of Iraq's Fall from Grace* (Annapolis, MD: Naval Institute Press, 1999), pp. 82–3.
206. al-Bazzaz, 'Inside the Belly of the Beast', www.meforum.org/wires/bazzaz.html
207. Brigadier General Tawfiq al-Yasiri, interview with author, tape-recording, London, 6 August 1998.
208. al-Bazzaz, *The Ashes of Wars,* p. 8.
209. 'Iraq: TV Carries Saddam Remarks on Gulf War', cited in *FBIS-NES-97-208*, 5 August 1997, p. 1; and Christopher Dickey, 'Rope-a-Dope in Baghdad', *Newsweek*, 4 February 1991, pp. 26–7.
210. Meilinger, 'Air Targeting Strategies: An Overview', in Hallion, *Air Power Confronts an Unstable World*, p. 62.
211. Chris Hedges, 'After the War: Iraq in Growing Disarray, Iraqis Fight Iraqis', *New York Times*, 10 March 1991, pp. 1, 14.
212. Makiya, *Cruelty and Silence*, p. 62.
213. Makiya, *The Republic of Fear*, p. xix.
214. Amatzia Baram, *Policy Watch*, No. 218, pp. 3–5.
215. Baram, 'Calculations and Miscalculations in Baghdad', pp. 49–50.
216. 'Envoy in France: Iraq "Ready to Negotiate"', Tripoli Voice of Greater Arab Homeland, 18 January 1991; and 'Further Comments by Iraqi Envoy in Spain', Madrid Domestic Service, 17 January 1991, both cited in *FBIS-NES-91-013*, 18 January 1991, p. 30.
217. 'Gorbachev Letter Proposes Withdrawal From Kuwait', Baghdad Domestic Service, 21 January 1991, cited in *FBIS-NES-91-014*, 22 January 1991, p. 37.
218. '"Text" of Saddam's Reply' [to Gorbachev's letter], Baghdad Iraqi News Agency, 21 January 1991, cited in *FBIS-NES-91-014*, 22 January 1991, p. 37.
219. Yevgeni Primakov, interview with BBC Frontline, part one, p 3; and Ken Fireman, 'Hussein's Peace Feeler: Says he'll Cooperate with Soviets', *New York Newsday*, 13 February 1991.
220. Alison Mitchell, 'Soviets Press Bid for Peace in Gulf', *New York Newsday*, 15 February 1991, p. 14; Timothy M. Phelps, 'A Major Shift by Baghdad, Or Hussein's "Cruel Hoax"', *New York Newsday*, 16 February 1991.
221. 'Saddam Addresses Nation on Initiative 21 Feb', Baghdad Domestic Service, 21 February 1991, in *FBIS-NES-91-035*, 21 February 1991, pp. 21–3; 'INA Reports Aziz Moscow News Conference', Baghdad Iraqi News Agency, 23 February 1991, in *FBIS-NES-91-037*, 25 February 1991, p. 35; and Freedman and Karsh, *The Gulf Conflict 1990–1991*, pp. 377–81.
222. Byman, Pollack and Waxman, 'Coercing Saddam Hussein', pp. 133.
223. Warden, interview, *Desert Story Collection*, 10 December 1991, pp. 115–16.

224. 'Soviets Say Iraq Accepts Kuwaiti Pullout', *New York Times*, 22 February 1991, p. 1.
225. 'Bush Keeps a Date Set 2 Weeks Ago', *New York Newsday*, 25 February 1991, pp. 7, 17.
226. Rick Atkinson and Ann Devroy, 'Bush: No Immediate Plan to Start Ground War U.S. Will Rely "For a While" On Air Power Against Iraqis', *Washington Post*, 12 February 1991; Susan Page, 'Bush: We'll Bomb Them Some More', *New York Newsday*, 12 February 1991; and R. W. Apple Jr, 'Allies Step Up Gulf Air Offensive; Strikes Focus on Iraqis in Kuwait', *New York Times*, 12 February 1991.
227. Timothy Clifford and Kurt Royce, 'Risk of Ground War Delay', *New York Newsday*, 12 February 1991.
228. Molly Moore and Guy Gugliotta, 'Allies to Step Up Air Strikes Against Iraqi Ground Forces', *Washington Post* and 8 February 1991; Susan Sachs, 'Ground Assault "Inevitable"', *New York Newsday*, 8 February 1991.
229. Saul Friedman, 'Gulf War Escalating, Analysts Fear', *New York Newsday*, 4 February 1991; Josh Friedman, 'He'll [Rafsanjani] Play Mediator: Offers to Hold Talk with U.S.', *New York Newsday*, 5 February 1991; and Josh Friedman, 'Iraq Responds to Iran's Peace Plan', *New York Newsday*, 10 February 1991.
230. Peter Faber, 'The Evolution of Airpower Doctrine in the United States', pp. 30–3; Peter Faber, interview with author, tape-recording, Washington, DC, 19 February 1998; and Major Howard D. Belote, 'Warden and the Air Corps Tactical School: What Goes Around Comes Around', *Airpower Journal* 13, No. 3 (Fall 1999), pp. 39–47.
231. United States Air Force, 'Global Reach Global Power', p. 5. Note that there is a substantial distinction between war-making and war-fighting capability. See for example H. P. Willmott, who notes that the Germans proved that they were good at fighting, but not very good at waging war, in *The Great Crusade: A New Complete History of the Second World* War (New York: Free Press, 1989), p. xi,
232. David A. Deptula, 'Firing for Effect: Change in the Nature of Warfare', Defense and Airpower Series (Arlington, VA: Aerospace Education Foundation, 1995), pp. 8–9.
233. Belote, 'Warden and the Air Corps Tactical School', pp. 40–4.
234. Cohen, 'Strategic Paralysis: Social Scientists Make Bad Generals', *American Spectator* (November 1980), p. 27; and Cohen, interview with author, tape-recording, Washington, DC, 23 February 1999.
235. Deptula, interview with author, tape-recording, Washington, DC, 11 March 1988; and Warden, telephone-interview with author, notes, 12 April 1999.
236. Luttwak, correspondence with author, transcript, 15 November 2000.
237. Alan Stephens, 'Asymmetric Advantage and Homeland Defence', in John Andreas Olsen (ed.), *The Asymmetric Approach*, Militærteoretisk skriftserie No. 4 (FSTS: Oslo, 2002).
238. Richard Szafranski and Lieutenant Colonel Peter W. W. Wijninga, 'Beyond Infrastructure Targeting: Toward Axiological Aerospace Operations', *Aerospace Journal* 14, No. 4 (Winter 2000), pp. 45–59.
239. APN Lambert, 'Air Power and Coercion' in Olsen (ed.), *From Manoeuvre Warfare to Kosovo?* (Trondheim: The Royal Norwegian Air Force Academy, 2001), p. 240.
240. Schelling, *Arms and Influence*, p. 3.
241. Paul Watzlawick, John H. Weakland and Richard Fiusch, *Change: Principles of Problem Formation and Problem Resolution* (New York: W. W. Norton & Company, 1973), pp. 1–12.

Conclusions

Air Vice Marshal (ret.) Tony Mason observed in 1987 that 'It has frequently been the fate of airmen to be criticised for failing to meet their promises rather than be congratulated on the reality of their actual achievements.'[1] Although the Black Hole and Checkmate contribution to the success of air power in 1991 is celebrated in some circles, it none the less falls neatly in line with the fate of various predecessors. In many ways Mason's observation can be extended to suggest that it is the negative aspect of the strategic air campaign against Saddam Hussein that commands most attention. It is inevitably easier to deal with what air power did not accomplish. Air power has limitations for sure, but so does every other mechanism used by states to try to achieve their aims.[2] According to H. P. Willmott, it is 'one of those unfortunate aspects of air power that it always seems to have to defend its record, specifically its failings, in a way that armies and navies somehow seem to avoid'.[3] Part of the explanation might be that air power visionaries, since the days of Douhet, Mitchell and de Seversky, have always claimed more than they could justify, and consequently any promise in 1990 was to be viewed with suspicion.

Another aspect might be the 'nature of the beast'. While armies occupy territory air power does not, and therefore one lacks the traditional reference of advance and retreat, which often indicates success and failure. Moreover, the whole notion of air power is far less tangible and definable compared to actions by its sister services, and as David Gates has observed: 'Every bomb dropped has the potential to cause an explosion which is as political as it is physical.'[4] As one moves into the strategic realm it becomes increasingly difficult to measure effects, and the lethality of air power has political repercussions whether applied successfully or not. The reality is that the potential and limitations of air power remain little understood, even among airmen, in part because those educated in planning and executing air campaigns have little or no knowledge about the enemy system, which they ultimately seek to influence.

Robert A. Pape has attempted to examine the use of air power comparatively through several case studies.[5] He argues that strategic air power failed in the Iraqi case because Saddam Hussein survived and was not coerced prior to extensive air operations against the Iraqi forces occupying Kuwait. The fact that Saddam survived does not indicate, however, that the concept of 'strategic paralysis' was ineffectual. One might have to settle for less absolute criteria of assessment as wars historically tend to change and reduce rather than solve problems. Measuring the effectiveness of strategic air power remains an incredibly complex process, as one cannot easily weigh the relative importance of human factors, technology and strategy in what at the end of the day is a political endeavour. Furthermore, the uniqueness of the 1991 air campaign, fought as it was under specific military and political circumstances, makes it dangerous to generalise and suggest certainties for the future. In this respect it is difficult to determine how much the strategic air offensive contributed to the overall military victory, and even more so to suggest its concrete influence on the Iraqi leadership's decision-making process. This research has explored the impressions of high-ranking Iraqi officials and officers, and although interviewees agree that the regime was partly paralysed, observations and reflections are indeed subjective. As always, where you stand depends on where you sit. While findings have suggested that the Black Hole and Checkmate planners reached for something that was beyond their grasp, one question that has been dealt with throughout this study needs further elaboration: was the Iraqi regime's political power structure one that air attacks could not alter?

It has been argued that while the US manoeuvres in the Middle East throughout the Cold War ensured the primary aims of denying the Soviet Union a stronghold in the region and ensuring the flow of oil at reasonable prices, one clear side-effect was that several Arab regimes came into possession of considerable amounts of military equipment. As key Arab states underwent a period of increased nationalism, militarisation and radicalisation, in no small part because of the creation of Israel, violent means emerged as a very real option for dealing with domestic and regional problems that undermined democratic developments and diplomatic solutions. The growing friction throughout the Middle East resulted in states such as Iraq witnessing a hardening of attitudes and in the process it established a highly authoritarian regime with considerable durability. In the case of Iraq the strengthening of the political power structure took place from the early seventies and within a decade Saddam Hussein had absolute control, as he sustained power by the creation of a pervasive and seemingly omnipotent internal security and intelligence network which was based on kinship relations, strengthened by wider control of the republic through the Ba'ath Party, the government and the military institutions. The depth and strength of that system possessed a certain force of its own, created as it was from four decades of turmoil in the region and the high degree of patriotism engendered during the war with Iran. There was a common bond that held together an ethnically and religiously diverse society, and the demands of the war ensured a degree of both control over society, and redundancy within the political system, that Washington did not comprehend. While the air planners sought to isolate the Iraqi leadership from the outside world, its own people and its own military forces, they did not take into account the all-persuasive security agencies within the regime. Most notably, the Mukhabarat and the Amn al-Amm ensured state security, while the Amn al-Khass and the Special Republican Guard ensured personal protection for the Iraqi leadership. These agencies coincided with the wider Party apparatus, and with other separations of power they probably prevented the regime from collapsing. With no powerful organised opposition inside the country, eliminated as it was in the course of two decades of repression, the bombing of military and political headquarters weakened the regime, but it did not succeed in changing it. Then again, one must remember that changing the regime was not a Coalition objective, and therefore the intelligence effort and application of resources that would have to be applied to such an endeavour for it to succeed were absent.

Nevertheless, Instant Thunder represented the birth of a new air power concept. It was, as presented between 9 and 20 August 1990, bold, imaginative and innovative, but not in accord with the reality of what was politically acceptable and operationally attainable. It proposed victory through the strategic bombing of a small number of targets deep inside the Iraqi homeland in the hope of isolating the regime from its political and military control structures, thus leading to its overthrow or 'strategic paralysis', either of which would force Iraqi forces to abandon Kuwait. As it turned out, 43 days of bombing against several hundred targets did not bring about the collapse of the regime's command and control systems. The orderly withdrawal of the Republican Guard and the subsequent ability to put down two internal revolts illustrate the fact that the regime's domestic control was far from shattered. Despite this, Instant Thunder importantly provided the political and military establishment with a *philosophy* that remained at the heart of what became the strategic air campaign, the first phase of Operation Desert Storm. It was only one part of the final war plan, but it has had repercussions for the formulation of strategy throughout the decade that followed. In the aftermath of Operation Allied Force, the Chief of the Air Staff, General Michael Ryan, who strongly opposed the Instant Thunder concept in 1990, argued that current air power doctrine was to go after the enemy with massive force from the opening moment.[6] He referred to this as 'classic air power doctrine'.[7] The air commander, Lieutenant General Michael Short, also argued for a

Warden-like strategy, stating 'I would have gone for the head of the snake [Milosevic] on the first night.'[8]

When reflecting on the significance of Instant Thunder as an approach to warfare, one must recollect that it was developed not only in a short period of time with very limited information and resources, but also in a partly hostile environment. Those closely involved with the Checkmate effort suggested a possible course of action at a time when no other organisation or individual was capable of drafting a proposal. At the time, the USAF was too imbued with Cold War thinking that assumed that it would start on the defensive. The USAF as an institution was essentially hamstrung by the alliance between TAC and the Army's TADOC.[9] The Black Hole and Checkmate team in effect changed the whole direction of planning, and by reintroducing conventional air power as a distinct instrument of policy they offered the political and military command a means of action that would carry considerable weight without jeopardising huge numbers of Coalition forces. Schwarzkopf's immediate concern when he was tasked with executing Operation Desert Shield was the possibility of a bloodbath between the opposing ground forces. With Instant Thunder he realised that the national objectives could be achieved without unacceptable casualties. In a time of great chaos, Instant Thunder suggested not only a way around an immediate over-riding problem, but it was the only military option that could be executed in a short period of time. In a matter of days, the extended Checkmate group had not only reintroduced the notion of conventional strategic air power, but convinced the military and political command that air power should be given a dominant role if it came to war – something that strongly contradicted the AirLand Battle doctrine. Importantly, the airmen added an *offensive* aspect to the problem solving which was almost absent in then current military thinking. Operation Desert Storm did in the end validate the Air Force's vision articulated in Global Reach Global Power.[10]

Warden proved himself to be a unique conceptualiser with great foresight in the early part of the crisis. While imperative in developing and presenting Instant Thunder to Schwarzkopf and Powell in August 1990, the concept survived in theatre first and foremost because of Deptula's dedication, insight and position, and secondly because Glosson became an advocate. Deptula was the crucial link, as he had taken part in forming Instant Thunder and then became a key member of the Black Hole planning cell. From that position he was able to control the planning process by adapting the concept into a workable plan acceptable to Horner, Schwarzkopf and Powell. He managed to keep in touch with Warden's Checkmate group in Washington at the same time as obstacles in theatre were solved. He was the person who kept the

Instant Thunder idea alive in the crucial days of late August 1990. As the planning unfolded, Glosson assumed responsibility for the overall air campaign effort, and with support from Checkmate, Glosson and Deptula were able to select the targets they were convinced would best meet the military and political objectives.

While Instant Thunder was modified in the process, it should not be forgotten that initially Warden viewed it as sufficient to compel Saddam Hussein to withdraw from Kuwait. As Colonel Peter Faber has observed, 'Warden is like all theorists and like all visionaries: the architectural elegance of the argument takes precedence over the reality.'[11] He was, however, given only a limited chance to prove his concept, as it was not executed in sequence, and thus the strategic air campaign had to share responsibility with the KTO campaign from the beginning. Additionally, time told against Instant Thunder: the Iraqi regime was less prepared for strategic attacks in early September 1990 than four months later, and the onset of winter brought weather inimical to operational effectiveness. Moreover, in its original form Instant Thunder was presented as a twin approach where the physical bombing was supposed to be complemented by strategic psychological operations: as it turned out the strategic air campaign was executed without such an addition. Finally, Warden insisted that there should be a war-termination resolution that could guide their actions. Despite these factors, the final version of the strategic air campaign plan was a huge improvement on the initial concept, and it is unreasonable to argue that Instant Thunder as it stood in late August 1990 would have been more effective than the offensive that was launched in January 1991.

Warden knew, from the day he entered the planning scene, that he would be involved in political and both inter- and intra-service battles in order to get his ideas approved. His presence was resented by the Joint Staff (J-3) in Washington, which looked upon itself as the rightful venue for such planning. CENTCOM, CENTAF and TAC resented Warden's initiative on the same grounds: he was encroaching on their turf. The mere fact that the idea was interesting and embraced by Schwarzkopf does not seem to have lessened that opposition. In Warden's mind *demnant quod non intelligunt* (they condemn what they do not understand). One should therefore credit the Checkmate group for their ability to reintroduce the concept of offensive air power under such circumstances, and acknowledge that they had great insight as far as aircraft and precision guided weapons were concerned. The major problem with Instant Thunder lies elsewhere: the planners knew little about the regime they were fighting beyond locations of buildings and communications. Moreover, the planners did not have suggestions as to how the regime should be overthrown beyond assuming that if they managed to paralyse the regime such an outcome was inevitable. This was in fact Powell's major criticism of the concept, as he told the Senate in December 1990: 'Such strategies are designed to hope to win; they are not designed to win.'[12] In an ethnically diverse and volatile country, who would be the preferred successor: a Kurd, a Shia, a Sunni, a Ba'athist, a Tikriti or a strong nationalist? It was not the case that Saddam Hussein was the one 'bad guy' and all other options were preferred by Washington. Moreover, what was preferred by the United States might not be what the Iraqis themselves wanted. The whole presumption is that the replacement would accede to Coalition demands, and as one official objective was to maintain balance of power in the region it would require a strong man to accept withdrawing from Kuwait unconditionally and immediately. In a region where face-saving is a real factor in politics one meets a point of contradiction: no new leader could afford to make the concessions demanded of him, as he would have to appear strong before his own people. Thus, from a strategy-formulation point of view, one cannot simply stop the political considerations at the threshold of military success. These are fundamental challenges when one examines any strategy, and in this case the air planners assumed that the existing regime would collapse in light of US military success.

It is not surprising that the air planners did not have details about the Iraqi regime, but the principle of the Praetorian Guard is hardly new, and neither was the nature of the Iraqi regime. Moreover, Checkmate established an informal relationship with the intelligence community, and given that a sufficient picture of the Iraqi political power structure did not emerge indicates that the structure was beyond Washington's comprehension. Whether the intelligence agencies could not or would not provide the details that the air planners needed to succeed, the White House was not ready to commit itself to overthrowing Saddam Hussein, and thus the philosophy of Instant Thunder was not given the basis required for success. Although the air planners did the best they could with a limited understanding of Iraq, they assumed that the intelligence institution would adopt the proper means of measuring results. While the planners introduced a new air power concept where bombing for political effect – or effects-based operations – was the primary focus, where every bomb was to have a political purpose, they relied too much on the institutional intelligence process to provide appropriate damage assessment criteria. This might well have been part of the reason why there was so much tension between the Black Hole planners and the intelligence agency in Riyadh, but the planners essentially assumed that the latter would adhere to the new way of thinking. In the end, the only circumstances in which the air planners' ideas could be realised would therefore require that Baghdad, and both the political leadership and its intelligence agencies in Washington, conformed to the air planners' consideration and value judgement.

The concept of 'strategic paralysis' was, nonetheless, an attempt to deal directly with the problem, Saddam Hussein's regime, rather than with mere symptoms, the Iraqi ground forces occupying Kuwait. One is reminded of Basil Henry Liddell Hart's observation on the outcome of the Second World War:

> They did not look beyond the immediate strategic aim of 'winning the war', and were content to assume that military victory would assure peace – an assumption contrary to the general experience of history. The outcome has been the latest of many lessons that pure military strategy needs to be guided by the longer and wider view from the higher plane of 'grand strategy'.[13]

While victory on the battlefield has historically resulted in partial solutions,[14] the Black Hole and Checkmate planners suggested that strategic air power would enable a second-order change. One may suggest that war is such a complex endeavour that the solution for peace does not reside within the military terms of reference, that is, a military victory on the battlefield does not ensure political victory or a stable peace. It is, after all, the state that wages war, and troops only fight it. For all the shortcomings found within the strategic air power concept, the planners managed to look beyond the battlefield. The concept of *inside-out warfare* was truly a brilliant one as it changed the perspective of planning and execution, but it also had its flaws. While the strength of the Five Ring Model is that it is simple in concept, therein, also, resides its weakness. One might agree that the national leadership is the enemy's most important centre of gravity, but the planners were unable to identify targets beyond the physical realm of buildings and communication lines. Warden himself was vague on the point. He referred to the objective of attacking the inner ring as killing Saddam Hussein (assassination from the air), creating conditions for a coup or uprising and rendering the decision-making process more difficult by injecting fog and friction. While there is consistency on the conceptual level, Warden did not have in-depth knowledge of how to go beyond the abstract. Moreover, the model did not allow for such complexities, but at least it provided overriding guidance at a time of great uncertainty. It does, importantly, provide a common option for detailed planning with a clearly defined strategic orientation.

According to the Iraqi troops interviewed, 'more of the same' in terms of targeting the 'inner ring' would not have made much difference. While the Scud hunt, the bad weather, the 'tank-plinking', the 'shelter-busting', the nine-day halt in bombing central Baghdad and the lack of sustained effort against the Republican Guard surely weakened the effects of the strategic air campaign, these diversions do not suggest that a greater operational commitment would have altered the impact on the Iraqi leadership's decision-making. Necessary improvements to challenge such a regime reside predominately in political dedication and knowledge of the regime itself. While the complexities of the multilayered Iraqi system suggest the difficulties of changing such a regime through air power alone, this research has shown that the strategic air campaign induced fog, friction and uncertainty into the Iraqi decision-making apparatus, reducing its effectiveness. Furthermore, the experience of Kosovo in 1999 and Afghanistan two years later proves that regime change can indeed be accomplished by air power, demonstrating the importance of declaring regime change as an objective, and appropriately focusing intelligence and resources to achieve that outcome.

Increased leverage resides, in many ways, outside the operational aspects of the strategic air campaign. Two decades of strong repression by the Ba'ath Party served to prevent discontent from surfacing. By the 1980s all organised opposition to the regime had been driven from the country. Individuals were jailed or executed on mere suspicion of action against the regime. Severe suppression was effective, as discontent was muted and those with reservations about the system kept their views to themselves. Without any means of organised opposition inside Iraq, whatever opposition to the regime existed did so outside the country and was weak, faction-ridden and without coherence and unity. Moreover, Washington had yet to define its post-war agenda. According to Gordon Brown, General Schwarzkopf's chief foreign policy advisor, the Bush administration 'never did have a plan to terminate the war'.[15] It was Schwarzkopf, a military officer, who was sent to dictate the cease-fire agreement without instructions from the Department of State. While the Black Hole and Checkmate team developed a strategic air campaign in military terms, and they recognised in part the political aspect of how such military achievements should be translated into political action, their efforts were rebuffed by senior military leaders who held that 'war termination is not our job'. In the end, while the air campaign planners tried to define the post-war political agenda, the effort was stopped by the traditional military mind-set, and therefore no one addressed this important subject. The question of why the US State Department and National Security Council failed to address this critical issue remains unanswered to this day. Indeed, the lack of a grand strategy for the region was striking: there was no political policy or military plan to deal with such an occupation, and while Warden came up with an option he did so in both a political and a military vacuum.

An added psychological campaign at the strategic level would most likely have strengthened the case for 'strategic paralysis'. The idea was launched in Instant Thunder but never explored, again because it became entangled in politics. Such operations could possibly, however, have focused on convincing the Iraqi people to take matters into their own hands from the early days of the war. It may well have encouraged them to rise up, and informed them of how they could possibly end the war. Such an effort from within would surely have put more pressure on the regime, as the decision-makers were able to conduct meetings and hide throughout Baghdad without such concerns. Interviews conducted in this research with Iraqis suggest that although they were ready to defect, they did not know what to do but hide in the country-side. Furthermore, when the bombing started large parts of Baghdad were evacuated. One group that did not have the means to leave was the poor Shia population of Saddam City. Had this group been armed at the time with nothing more than light weapons, or merely encouraged to take specific action, it would have put immense pressure on the capital. The ultimate challenge, however, would be how to follow that up, as any such attempt would include the risk of going down a blind alley. As it happened, Bush encouraged the Iraqi people to take matters into their own hands in late February 1991 but did not act on it, leaving the Iraqi people collectively with a deep sense of betrayal that prevails to this day. There was in the end only so much air power could do against a regime as long as the Iraqis remained passive, and when parts of the populace chose to take action the bombing had stopped. While the regime witnessed pressure from the air the Iraqi leadership was allowed to deal with one political problem at a time.

In the final analysis, the Bush administration was afraid of ruining a great military victory by getting involved in Iraqi politics. Having committed 5,000 troops to the region, risking the loss of thousands of human lives, declaring that the regime and not the people was the enemy as 60,000 tonnage of bombs were released, it seemed surreal not to want to get involved in internal Iraqi affairs. While the Americans clearly distinguished between war and peace, the Iraqi leader viewed events in terms of the notion of struggle, which blurred such a distinction. The overwhelming military victory not leading to the desired political outcome in 1991 is partly the result echoed in Carl von Clausewitz's *On War*:

> First, therefore, it is clear that war should never be thought of as *some-*
> *thing autonomous* but always as an instrument of policy; otherwise the
> entire history of war would contradict us ... The first, the supreme, the
> most far-reaching act of judgement that the statesman and commander
> have to make is to establish by that test the kind of war on which they

are embarking; neither mistaking it for, nor trying to turn it into, something that is alien to its nature. This is the first of all strategic questions and the most comprehensive.[16]

Lastly, even the ultimate outcome of a war is not always to be regarded as final. The defeated state often considers the outcome merely as a transitory evil, for which a remedy may still be found in political considerations at some later date.[17]

For all the limitations of Saddam Hussein as a commander, he might well have instinctively understood these dictums better than his opponents. It is perhaps indicative that he referred to the endeavour as the 'Mother of all Battles' rather than the 'Mother of all Wars'. At the end of the day his overarching goal of personal survival was fulfilled, albeit short of regional dominance. He lived to fight another day, as witnessed over the last 12 years.

Although air power alone was not given sufficient support to alter the Iraqi regime, it did facilitate the required conditions for 'a better state of peace'. The power of the Iraqi regime was compromised and in that fact is a partial explanation of the uprisings that followed in its wake: how far this uprising can be explained in terms of perceived weakness of the regime or the perception of national defeat is problematic. For the first time during the Ba'ath era, Iraqi citizens succeeded in taking action against the regime. The strategic air campaign was therefore successful in incapacitating the regime only in relative terms: it prevented it from exploring decisive offensive action, but it did not prevent the regime from taking the necessary precautions to secure its survival. Such a distinction is worth emphasising when one discusses whether strategic bombing worked or not.

In conclusion, the attacks against the 'inner ring', which included only 2 per cent of the overall air effort, had the redeeming feature of addressing the real problem, and not merely the manifestation of it. The strategy suggested an unprecedented political leverage that Washington was not capable of appreciating. Without a clear idea of which group should replace the leader, the desired ends were never within reach. One way to improve strategic bombing beyond delivery systems is to study the nature of potential enemies, including their culture, and develop an understanding of how the value and power systems of these states work. Importantly, 'strategic paralysis' is not a surgical exercise with identifiable cause–effect links. The strategy may provide leverage in warfare, but it surely cannot succeed without political commitment to see the problem through and a comprehensive understanding of 'the enemy as a system'. One may suggest that the need for political and military establishments to cooperate in order to maximise the potential of air power is getting ever more essential to succeed in warfare.

NOTES

1. Mason, 'The Decade of Opportunity: Air Power in the 1990s', *Airpower Journal* 1, No. 2 (Fall 1987), p. 4.
2. Stephen P. Aubin, 'The Self-Imposed Limits of Air Power', *Strategic Review* 26, No. 4 (Fall 1998), pp. 42–51.
3. Willmott, 'When Men Lost Faith in Reason', p. 31.
4. David Gates, 'Air Power and Aspects of Civil–Military Relations', in Stuart Peach (ed.), *Perspectives On Air Power: Air Power in its Wider Context* (London: Her Majesty's Stationary Office, 1998), p. 30.
5. Pape, *Bombing to Win*. For alternative discussions on coercion in relation to air power, see Michael Clarke, 'Air Power, Force and Coercion', in Andrew Lambert and Arthur C. Williamson (eds), *The Dynamics of Air Power* (Bracknell, Berkshire: Her Majesty's Stationary Office, 1996), pp. 67–85; and David Gates, 'Air Power and the Theory and Practice of Coercion', *Defense Analysis* 13, No. 3 (1997), pp. 239–54.
6. Earl H. Tilford Jr, 'Operation Allied Force and the Role of Air Power', *Parameters* 29, No. 4 (Winter 1999–2000), pp. 24–38.
7. General Michael E. Ryan, 'Air Power is Working in Kosovo', *Washington Post*, 4 June 1999.
8. John A. Tirpak, 'Washington Watch: Short's View of the Air Campaign', *Air Force Magazine* 82, No. 9 (September 1999), pp. 43–9; and Dana Priest, 'Air Chief Faults Kosovo Strategy', *Washington Post*, 22 October 1999.
9. Edward C. Mann, correspondence with author, transcript, 19 September 1999.
10. United States Air Force, 'Airpower in Operation Desert Storm', *USAF Fact Sheet 91-03 Special Edition* (May 1991), pp. 1–2; John M. Loh, 'Advocating Mission Needs in Tomorrow's World', pp. 4–13; and Dennis M. Drew, 'Desert Storm as a Symbol: Implications of the Air War in the Desert', *Airpower Journal* 6, No. 3 (Fall 1992), pp. 4–13.
11. Peter Faber, interview with author, tape-recording, Washington, DC, 19 February 1998.
12. Congress, General Colin Powell speaking on the Crisis in the Persian Gulf Region, pt. 663.
13. B. H. Liddell Hart, *Strategy* (London: Meridian Books, 1957), p. xvii.
14. Raymond Aron, *Peace and War: A Theory of International Relations* (London: Doubleday, 1966), p. 577.
15. Gordon Brown, cited in Gordon and Trainor, *The Generals' War*, p. 461.
16. von Clausewitz, *On War*, p. 110.
17. Ibid., p. 89.

Appendix I: Transcripts of *The Desert Story Collection*

Lieutenant Colonels Suzanne B. Gehri, Edward C. Mann and Richard T. Reynolds conducted the interviews. All transcripts are available on microfilm at the Historical Research Agency (AFHRA) at the Air University, Maxwell AFB, Alabama.

Name/Rank[1]	Relevance to air campaign	Date[2]	Reference[3]
Adams, James, Lt. Gen.	Deputy Chief of Staff, Plans and Operations (XO)	03/02/92	28034/876228
Alexander, Robert, Maj. Gen.	Director of Plans (XOX)	30/05/91	28034/876230
		30/06/92	28034/876232
		30/06/92	28034/876234
Baptiste, Sam, Lt. Col.	Head of KTO cell in Riyadh. Weapons expert at the Tactical Air Command (TAC)	24/09/92	28034/876237
Blackburn, Jim, Col.	Air Staff Intelligence Director for targets	21/04/92	28034/876239
		21/04/92	28034/876241
Bristow, Richard, Col.	Deputy of Air/Land Forces Application Agency (ALFAA), at TAC	09/11/92	28034/876242
Caruana, Patrick, Br. Gen.	CENTAF strategic forces advisor	15/08/91	28034/876244
Chain, Jack, Gen.	Commander Strategic Air Command (SAC)	12/08/91	28034/876250
Crigger, James, Col.	CENTAF director of operations and TACC director	02/12/91	28035/876254
		04/12/91	28035/876254
Deptula, David, Lt. Col. & Rogers, Mark, Maj.	(see individual interview)	22/05/91	28035/876256
Deptula, David, Lt. Col.	Member of Secretary of the Air Force's Staff Group, major contributor of Instant Thunder and principal architect of the strategic air campaign from the Special Planning Cell (SPG)	23/05/91	28035/876258
		10/12/91	28035/876260
		11/12/91	28035/876262
		12/12/91	28035/876264

Dugan, Michael, Gen.	USAF Chief of Staff, fired on 17 September 1990	15/08/91	28035/876268
Glosson, Buster, Br. Gen.	Deputy Commander of the Middle East Force (MFE) in Persian Gulf and responsible for the SPG	29/05/91 29/05/91 04/06/92 04/06/92	28035/876272 28035/876274 28035/876275 28035/876277
Griffith, Thomas, Br. Gen.	Deputy Chief of Staff for Plans (TAC/XP)	26/09/91	28035/876276
Henry, Larry, Br. Gen.	CENTAF, Electronic warfare expert	02/06/92	28035/876280
Horner, Charles, Lt. Gen.	Central Command Air Force (CENTAF)	02/12/91 04/03/92	28036/876282 28036/876284
Karnes, Dave, Maj.	CENTAF member and member of the SPG	21/08/91	28036/876286
Loh, John, Gen.	Vice Chief of Staff of the Air Force	26/09/91 16/10/91	28036/876288 28036/876290
May, Charles, Lt. Gen.	Assistant Deputy Chief of Staff, Plans & Operations	21/08/92	28036/876292
Moore, Burton, Maj. Gen.	USCENTCOM director of operations (J-3)	23/10/91 21/09/92	28036/876294 28036/876296
Rice, Donald, civilian	Secretary of the Air Force	11/12/91 11/12/91	28036/876300 28036/876301
Rogers, Mark, Maj.	Member of XOXW and member of the SPG	04/06/91 04/06/91	28036/876303 28036/876305
Russ, Robert, Gen.	Commander, TAC	09/12/91 09/03/92	28036/876306 28036/876308
Ryan, Michael, Maj. Gen.	Director of Operations at TAC, CENTAF/Rear	04/09/92	28036/876310
Smith, Perry, Maj. Gen. (Ret.)	Military expert for CNN	18/06/92	28036/876314
Standfill, Ronnie, Lt. Col.	Key member of Checkmate	03/06/91	28037/876316
Warden, John, Col.	The initiator and principal architect of Instant Thunder; Director of XOXW	30/05/91 22/10/91 10/12/92	28037/876324 28037/876326 28037/876328
Wilson, Steve, Col.	Member of the Air Staff, and the first to brief Gen. Horner on Instant Thunder	11/12/91	28037/876330

[1]The listed military rank refers to the time of the Persian Gulf War (many had been promoted by the time of interview).
[2]Time of interview.
[3]The first number refers to the 'Roll Index', and the second to the actual 'IRIS' identification.

Appendix II: BBC Frontline: The Gulf War

Name	Nationality	Title
Atkinson, Richard	US	Author of *The Crusade*
Aziz, Tariq	Iraq	Foreign Minister
Baker, James	US	Secretary of State
Billiere, Peter de la (Gen.)	UK	Senior Commander
Cheney, Richard	US	Secretary of Defense
Gates, Robert	US	Deputy National Security Advisor
Glosson, Buster (Br. Gen.)	US	Chief of the Offensive Air Campaign
Gorbachev, Mikhail	USSR	President
Haass, Richard	US	National Security Council Director for Near East and South Asian Affairs
Horner, Charles (Lt. Gen.)	US	US Ninth Air Force Commander (JAFAC)
Powell, Colin (Gen.)	US	Chairman of the Joint Chiefs of Staff (CJCS)
Samarrai, Wafiq (Gen.)	Iraq	Head of Military Intelligence
Schwarzkopf, Norman (Gen.)		US Commander-in-Chiefs of Central Command (CINC)
Scowcroft, Brent	US	National Security Advisor
Thatcher, Margaret	UK	Prime Minister
Trainor, Bernard	US	Author of *The Generals' War*
Waller, Calvin (Lt. Gen.)	US	Deputy Commander of Central Command (DCINC)

BBC Frontline Show (BBC I), No. 1407T (part 1), air date 28 January 1997 and No. 1408T (part 2), air date 4 February 1997. Complete transcripts were provided by *Journal Graphics*. These transcripts contain three parts: (1) extracts of interviews that were on the show on 28 January 1997 (part 1); (2) extracts of interviews that were on the show on 4 February 1997 (part 2); and (3) transcripts of interview that contain information not on the show (transcript). This author has chosen to refer to the respective page number of the specific interview by identifying whether it was in part 1, part 2 or the separate transcript made available to the author.

Note on Sources

The history of war is seldom generous to the vanquished, and this is also the case with the current literature on Operation Desert Storm. While there is a vast amount published on the 1991 Gulf War, there is far less on military operations and comparatively little from 'the other side of the hill'. As far as air power is concerned, the most comprehensive and analytical accounts derive from authors closely associated with the USAF, and these accounts do not account for what the Iraqis thought, how they responded and how effective they believed their responses to be.

The USAF Historical Research Agency (AFHRA) at Maxwell AFB, Alabama, is the repository of most of the historically significant documentation with regard to US air operations, but virtually all of its content is classified. Moreover, many of the significant discussions during the campaign were conducted by secure telephone with little or no recording. Although no official account of the USAF role in the war has been published, the author benefited from draft versions and extensive tape-recorded discussions with historians at the USAF Historical Branch, Bolling AFB. These historians conducted independent research that included their own interviews with US airmen. The most authoritative and extensive analysis of the air war in print is the *Gulf War Air Power Survey (GWAPS)*. Although restricted to limited distribution, that study reviews most aspects of the air war, and with its 11 reports amounting to some 4,000 pages it was of great significance to this research.

While some operational and technological aspects of the bombing can be examined without considering Iraqi perceptions, analysing the political effects on the Iraqi regime cannot. Examining the validity of the concept behind the strategy therefore requires consultation with the air planners and those who experienced the bombing. The single most important source on the air campaign planning process is the *Desert Story Collection*. It includes some 200 interviews with USAF officers who participated in the planning and execution of Operation Desert Storm. The project, which was conducted by Lieutenant Colonels Suzanne B. Gehri, Edward C. Mann and Richard T. Reynolds, was undertaken separately from the *GWAPS* research, and since most of the interviews took place in the months immediately after the war, they complemented the author's personal interviews conducted some seven to nine years later. Although these interviews are not published, transcripts are available at the AFHRA (see Appendix 1). While those interviews focus on USAF officers, another source is the BBC Frontline's extensive interviews with military and political leaders who participated in the conflict. Extracts from these interviews can be found in the BBC's 4-hour long video, but more importantly, the full transcripts of all interviews were made available to the author (see Appendix II). In total, these sources, combined with the author's correspondence with participants and experts, formed the basis for the disclosure of the origins, evolution and execution of the strategic air campaign that formed the basis for assessing the theoretical concept's applicability. Personal accounts in professional military journals were useful additional sources, and finally, autobiographies from military and political leaders have been consulted together with the vast amount of secondary literature (see Bibliography).

Since the objective of the thesis is to establish not only the strategic air power concept, but the political utility of that concept, the Iraqi perceptions have been examined. There is little written documentation available to support Iraqi decision-making and its perception of the events, but some insight has been gained by exploring Iraqi news, and statements by senior officials, and engaging in numerous interviews with Iraqi opposition groups in London. Particular attention has been given to Iraqi officers who participated in the war, individuals who had a strong relationship with Baghdad at the time, and individuals who have good access to the inner workings of the regime. The main Iraqi opposition groups proved to be extremely helpful in developing an understanding of the Iraqi political power structure, as they have a good knowledge of the regime that they are intent on overthrowing. This 'political' insight was developed further by interviews with Iraqi military officers who are now in exile and Middle East experts such as Amatzia Baram and Michael Eisenstadt. Iraqi news reports translated by *Foreign Broadcast Information Service* (*FBIS*) and newspaper articles from the *Baghdad Observer* further supplemented the verbatim accounts. The *FBIS* translates news from all over the world, and a complete record is available at the Library of Congress in Washington, DC, while most of the newspaper editions prior to 17 January 1991 are available at the British Library in London. Finally, three Iraqi sources added particular insight into the Iraqi leadership's mind-set during the air campaign: General Wafiq Samarrai, former Chief of Military Intelligence; Saad al-Bazzaz, former editor-in-chief of *al-Jumhuriya* and author of the unofficial Iraqi account of the war; and Staff Lieutenant General Hazim Abd al-Razzaq al-Ayyubi, the missile commander who was in charge of the Scuds launches.

The chief problem in relying on personal interviews to reconstruct past events is that memories fade and after-the-fact rationalisations emerge, but given the lack of official records, recourse to interviews were necessary in order to add to existing knowledge on the subject. While 'oral history' is a profession in its own right, the purpose of interviewing a number of participants was to open avenues not explored in the current literature. While the interviewees were biased, their stories and observations are just as valid as the written word. One exercised caution in seeking to present only conclusions that can be based on reasoned and critical interpretation. The chosen method for presenting the argument is thus the analytical narrative account, based on empirical research with different layers of analysis. As details and events are considered, and given the fact that this thesis is not a history of the Gulf War, emphasis is given to the view that warns against drawing general principles from this one conflict. Collectively the mentioned sources contributed to an increased understanding of Operation Desert Storm.

Bibliography

Aburish, Said K., *A Brutal Friendship: The West and the Arab Elite* (London: Victor Gollancz, 1997)

—— *Saddam Hussein: The Politics of Revenge* (New York: Bloomsbury, 2000)

Acheson, Dean, *Present at the Creation: My Years in the State Department* (New York: W. W. Norton & Co., 1969)

al-Ayyubi, Hazim Abd al-Razzaq, *Forty-Three Missiles on the Zionist Entity*, first published in Amman al-Arab al-Yawm, transl. Foreign Broadcast Information Service (FBIS) (25 October 1998–12 November 1998)

Algosaibi, Ghazi A., *The Gulf Crisis: An Attempt to Understand*, 1st edn 1993 (London: Kegan Paul International, 1998)

Ambrose, Stephen E., *Eisenhower*, Vol. II (New York: Simon & Schuster, 1984)

Armitage, M. J. and R. A. Mason, *Air Power In the Nuclear Age, 1945–84: Theory and Practice* (London: Macmillan, 1985)

Aron, Raymond, *Peace and War: A Theory of International Relations* (London: Doubleday, 1966)

Aspin, Les, *The Aspin Papers: Sanctions, Diplomacy, and War in the Persian Gulf* (Washington, DC: Center for Strategic and International Studies, 1991)

Aspin, Les, and William Dickinson, *Defense for a New Era: Lessons of the Persian Gulf War*, House of Armed Services Committee (New York: Brassey's, 1992)

Atkinson, Rick, *Crusade: The Untold Story of the Gulf War* (London: HarperCollins Publishers, 1994)

Baker, James A. III with Thomas M. DeFrank, *The Politics of Diplomacy: Revolution, War, and Peace 1989–1992* (New York: G. P. Putnam's Sons, 1995)

Balfour-Paul, Glen, *The End of Empire in the Middle East: Britain's Relinquishment of Power in her Last Three Arab Dependencies* (Cambridge: Cambridge University Press, 1994)

Baram, Amatzia, *Building Toward Crisis: Saddam Husayn's Strategy for Survival* (Washington, DC: The Washington Institute for Near East Policy, 1988)

Baram, Amatzia, *Culture History and Ideology in the Formation of Ba'thist Iraq: 1968–1969* (London: Macmillan, 1991)

Baram, Amatzia and Barry Rubin (eds), *Iraq's Road to War* (London: Macmillan, 1993)

Batatu, Hanna, *The Old Social Classes and the Revolutionary Movements of Iraq: A Study of Iraq's Old Landed and Commercial Classes and of its Communities, Ba'thists and Free Officers* (Princeton, NJ: Princeton University Press, 1978)

Battle, Joyce (ed.), *Iraqgate: Saddam Hussein, US Policy and the Prelude to the Persian Gulf War (1980–1994)* (Alexandria, VA: Chadwyck-Healey, 1994)

Beck, Robert J., *The Grenada Invasion: Politics, Law, and Foreign Policy Decisionmaking* (Boulder, CO: Westview Press, 1993)

Bengio, Ofra, *Saddam's Word: Political Discourse in Iraq* (New York: Oxford University Press, 1998)

—— *Saddam Speaks on the Gulf Crisis: A Collection of Documents* (Syracuse, NY: Syracuse University Press, 1992)

Bennis, Phyllis and Michel Moushabeck (ed.), *Beyond the Storm: A Gulf Crisis Reader* (New York: Olive Branch Press, 1991)

Bergquist, Ronald, *The Role of Airpower in the Iran–Iraq War* (Maxwell Air Force Base, AL: Air University Press, 1988)

Blackwell, James, *Thunder in the Desert: The Strategy and Tactics of the Persian Gulf War* (New York: Bantam Books, 1991)

Boudreault, Jody, Emma Naughton and Yasser Salaam (eds), *U.S. Official Statements: U.N. Security Council Resolution 242* (Washington, DC: Institute for Palestinian Studies, 1992)

Braybrook, Roy, *Air Power: The Coalition and Iraqi Air Forces*, Desert Storm Special 2 (London: Osprey Publishing, 1991)

Brittan, Victoria (ed.), *The Gulf Between Us: The Gulf War and Beyond* (London: Virago Press, 1991)

Brodie, Bernard, *Strategy in the Missile Age* (Princeton, NJ: Princeton University Press, 1959)

—— *War and Politics* (New York: Macmillan, 1973)

Brown, Gordon, *Coalition, Coercion and Compromise: Diplomacy of the Gulf Crisis, 1990–1991*, The Institute for Study of Diplomacy, Edmund A. Walsh School of Foreign Service (Washington, DC: Georgetown University Press, 1997)

Brzezinski, Zbigniew, *Power and Principle: Memories of National Security Advisor, 1977–1981* (New York: Farrar Straus & Giroux, 1985)

—— 'The Premature Partnership', *Foreign Affairs* 73, No. 2 (March/April 1994)

Builder, Carl H., *The Icarus Syndrome: The Role of Air Power Theory in the Evolution and Fate of the U.S. Air Force*, 4th edn (New Brunswick, NJ: Transaction Publishers, 1998)

—— *The Masks of War: American Military Styles in Strategy and Analysis* (Baltimore, MD: Johns Hopkins University Press, 1989)

Bulloch, John and Harvey Morris, *Saddam's War: The Origins of the Kuwait Conflict and the International Response* (London: Faber and Faber, 1991)

Bush, George, *Public Papers of the Presidents of the United States: George Bush, 1990* (Washington, DC: Government Printing Office, 1991)

Bush, George and Brent Scowcroft, *A World Transformed* (New York: Alfred A. Knopf, 1998)

Cable, Larry, *Unholy Grail: The US and Wars in Vietnam, 1965–1968* (London: Routledge & Kegan Paul, 1991)

Cappelluti, Frank J., 'The Life and Thought of Giulio Douhet', Ph.D. Dissertation 1967. (University of Michigan)

CARDRI, *Saddam's Iraq: Revolution or Reaction?*, 2nd edn (London: Zed Books, 1990)

CARDRI, *Iraq Since the Gulf War: Prospects for Democracy* (London: Zed Books, 1994)

Christison, Kathleen, *Perceptions of Palestine: Their Influence on U.S. Middle East Policy* (Berkeley, CA: University of California Press, 1998)

Chubin, Sharam and Charles Tripp, *Iran and Iraq at War* (Boulder, CO: Westview Press, 1988)

Clancy, Tom, *Armoured Warfare: A Guided Tour of an Armoured Cavalry* (London: HarperCollins, 1996)

—— *Fighter Wing: A Guided Tour of an Air Force Combat Wing* (New York: Berkley Books, 1995)

Clancy, Tom with Chuck Horner, *Every Man a Tiger* (New York: G. P. Putnam's Sons, 1999)

Clausewitz, Carl von, *On War*, Michael Howard and Peter Paret (trans. and eds) (London: Everyman's Library, 1993)

Cleveland, William L., *A History of the Modern Middle East* (Boulder, CO: Westview Press, 1994)

Clodfelter, Mark *The Limits of Air Power: The American Bombing of North Vietnam* (New York: Free Press, 1989)

Cockburn, Andrew and Patrick Cockburn, *Out of the Ashes: The Resurrection of Saddam Hussein* (New York: HarperCollins, 1999)

Cody, James R., *AWPD-42 to Instant Thunder: Consistent, Evolutionary Thought or Revolutionary Change?* (Maxwell Air Force Base, AL: Air University Press, 1996)

Cohen, Aharon, *Israel and the Arab World* (London: W. H. Allen, 1970)

Cohen, Eliot A., *et al.*, *Gulf War Air Power Survey: Volume I: Part I: Planning* (Washington, DC: Government Printing Office, 1993)

—— *Gulf War Air Power Survey: Volume II: Part I: Operations* (Washington DC: Government Printing Office, 1993)

—— *Gulf War Air Power Survey: Volume II: Part II: Effects and Effectiveness* (Washington, DC: Government Printing Office, 1993)

—— *Gulf War Air Power Survey: Volume V: Part A: A Statistical Compendium* (Washington, DC: Government Printing Office, 1993)

Conniff, Michael L., *Panama and the United States: The Forced Alliance* (Athens, GA: University of Georgia Press, 1992)

Cordesman, Anthony H. and Abraham R. Wagner, *The Lessons of Modern War, Volume II: The Iran–Iraq War* (Boulder, CO: Westview Press, 1990)

—— *The Lessons of Modern War, Volume IV: The Gulf War* (Boulder, CO: Westview Press, 1996)

Coyne, James P., *Airpower in the Gulf* (Arlington, VA: Air Force Association Book, 1992)

Creveld, Martin van, *Command in War* (Cambridge, MA: Harvard University Press, 1985)

—— *The Transformation of War* (New York: The Free Press, 1991)

D'Olier, Franklin, *et al.*, *The United States Strategic Bombing Surveys: Summary Report (European War) (Pacific War)*, 1st ed 1945 (Maxwell Air Force Base, AL: Air University Press, 1987)

Danchev, Alex and Dan Keohane (eds), *International Perspectives on the Gulf Conflict 1990–1991* (London: Macmillan, 1994)

Darwish, Adel and Gregory Alexander, *Unholy Babylon: The Secret History of Saddam's War* (New York: St. Martin's Press, 1991)

Davis, Brian Lee, *Qaddafi, Terrorism, and the Origins of the U.S. Attack on Libya* (New York: Praeger, 1990)

Davis, Richard G., *Decisive Force: Strategic Bombing in the Gulf War* (Washington, DC: Air Force History and Museums Program, 1996)

—— *The 31 Initiatives: A Study of Air Force–Army Cooperation* (Washington, DC: Office of USAF History, 1987)

Department of the Army, Field Manual (FM) 100-5, *Operations* (Washington, DC: Government Printing Office, 1982)

Deptula, David A., 'Firing for Effect: Change in the Nature of Warfare', *Defense and Airpower Series* (Arlington, VA: Aerospace Education Foundation, 1995)

de Seversky, Alexander P., *Victory Through Air Power* (New York: Simon and Schuster, 1942)

Dickie, John, *'Special' No More: Anglo-American Relations: Rhetoric and Reality* (London: Weidenfeld & Nicolson, 1994)

Donnelly, Thomas, Margaret Roth and Caleb Baker, *Operation Just Cause: The Storming of Panama* (New York: Lexington Books, 1991)

Douhet, Giulio, *The Command of The Air*, transl. Dino Ferrari (New York: Coward-McCann, 1984)

Drew, Dennis M. and Donald M. Snow, *Rolling Thunder 1965: Anatomy or Failure* (Maxwell Air Force Base, AL: Air University Press, 1986)

Duffey, Brian, *et al.*, *Triumph Without Victory: The Unreported History of the Persian Gulf War* (New York: Times Books, 1992)

Dunnigan, James F. and Austin Bay, *From Shield to Storm: High-Tech Weapons, Military Strategy, and Coalition Warfare in the Persian Gulf* (New York: William Morrow and Company, 1992)

Eisenstadt, Michael, 'Like a Phoenix From the Ashes: The Future of Iraqi Military Power', *Washington Institute for Near East Policy* 36 (1993)

—— '"The Sword of the Arabs": Iraq's Strategic Weapons', *The Washington Institute for Near East Policy* 21 (1990)

el-Kikhia, Mansour, *Libya's Qaddafi: The Politics of Contradiction* (Gainesville, FL, University Press of Florida, 1997)

Fadok, David S., *John Boyd and John A. Warden: Air Power's Quest for Strategic Paralysis* (Maxwell Air Force Base, AL: Air University Press, 1995)

Farid, Abdel Magid, *Nasser: The Final Years* (Reading: Ithaca Press, 1994)

Farouk-Sluglett, Marion and Peter Sluglett, *Iraq Since 1958: From Revolution to Dictatorship* 2nd edn (London: I. B. Tauris & Co, 1990)

Francona, Rick. *Ally to Adversary: An Eyewitness Account of Iraq's Fall from Grace* (Annapolis, MD: Naval Institute Press, 1999)

Freedman, Lawrence, *The Cold War: A Military History* (London: Cassell, 2001)

Freedman, Lawrence (ed.), *War* (Oxford: Oxford University Press, 1994)

Freedman, Lawrence and Efraim Karsh, *The Gulf Conflict 1990–1991: Diplomacy and War in the New World Order*, updated with new preface (London: Faber and Faber, 1994)

Freedman, Robert O. (ed.), *The Middle East After the Israeli Invasion of Lebanon* (Syracuse, NY: Syracuse University Press, 1986)

Friedman, Alan: *Spider's Web: Bush, Saddam, Thatcher and the Decade of Deceit* (London: Faber and Faber, 1993)

Friedman, Norman, *Desert Victory: The War for Kuwait*, 1st edn 1992 (Annapolis, MD: The Naval Institute Press, 1993)

Futell, Robert F., *Concepts, Ideas, Doctrine: Basic Thinking in the USAF 1907–1960*, Vol. I (Maxwell Air Force Base, AL: Air University Press, 1989)

Gaddis, John Lewis, *Strategies of Containment: A Critical Appraisal of Postwar American National Security Policy* (New York: Oxford University Press, 1985)

Galbraith, John Kenneth, *The Affluent Society* (London: Hamish Hamilton, 1958)

Garrett, Stephen, *Ethics and Airpower in World War Two* (New York: St. Martin's, 1993)

Gaston, James C., *Planning the American Air War: Four Men and Nine Days in 1941* (Washington DC: National Defense University Press, 1982)

Gat, Azar, *Fascists and Liberal Visions of War: Fuller, Liddell Hart, Douhet, and other Modernists* (Oxford: Clarendon Press, 1998)

Gentile, Gian P., *How Effective is Strategic Bombing? Lessons Learned from World War II to Kosovo* (New York: New York University Press, 2001)

George, Alexander, L. *Bridging the Gap: Theory and Practice in Foreign Policy* (Washington, DC: United States Institute of Peace, 1993)

George, Alexander L., and William E. Simons (eds), *The Limits of Coercive Diplomacy* (Boulder, CO: Westview Press, 1994)

George, Alexander L. and Richard Smoke (eds), *Deterrence in American Foreign Policy: Theory and Practice* (New York: Columbia University Press, 1974)

Gilchrist, Peter, *Sea Power: The Coalition and Iraqi Navies*, Desert Storm Special 1 (London: Osprey Publishing, 1991)

Gooch, John (ed.), *Airpower: Theory and Practice* (London: Frank Cass, 1995)

Gordon, Michael R. and Bernard E. Trainor, *The Generals' War: The Inside Story of the Conflict in the Gulf* (Boston, MA: Little, Brown and Company, 1995)

The Government of the Hashemite Kingdom of Jordan, 'Jordan and the Gulf Crisis August 1990–March 1991', *White Paper*, Amman (1991).

Gray, Colin S., *Explorations in Strategy* (Westport, CT: Greenwood Press, 1996)

Gray, Peter W. (ed.), *Air Power 21: Challenges for the New Century* (Norwich: The Stationery Office, 2000)

Grossman, Mark, *Encyclopaedia of the Persian Gulf War* (Santa Barbara, CA: ABC-CLIO, 1995)

Halberstam, David, *War in a Time of Peace: Bush, Clinton and the Generals* (London: Bloomsbury, 2002)

Hallion, Richard P., *Storm over Iraq: Air Power and the Gulf War* (Washington DC: Smithsonian Institution Press, 1992)

Hallion, Richard P. (ed.), *Air Power Confronts an Unstable World* (London: Brassey's, 1997)

Hamza, Khidhir with Jeff Stein, *Saddam's Bombmaker* (London: Simon & Schuster, 2000)

Hansell Jr., Haywood S., *The Air Plan That Defeated Hitler*, 1st edn 1972 (New York: Higgins-McArthur/Longino & Porter, 1980)

Head, William and Earl H. Tilford Jr. (eds.), *The Eagle in the Desert: Looking Back on U.S. Involvement in the Persian Gulf War* (Westport, CT: Praeger, 1996)

Heath, Edward, *The Course of My Life: My Autobiography* (London: Hodder and Stoughton, 1998)

Heikal, Mohamed, *Illusions of Triumph: An Arab View of the Gulf War* (London: HarperCollins, 1993)

Helms, Robert F. and Robert H. Dorff (eds), *The Persian Gulf Crisis: Power in the Post-Cold War World* (London: Praeger, 1993)

Henderson, Simon, *Instant Empire: Saddam Hussein's Ambition for Iraq* (San Francisco, CA: Mercury House, 1991)

Higham, Robin, *Air Power: A Concise History* (London: Macdonald, 1972)

Hiro, Dilip, *Desert Shield to Desert Storm: The Second Gulf War* (London: Paladin, 1992)

Hogan, Michael J. (ed.), *America in the World: The Historiography of American Foreign Relations Since 1941* (Cambridge: Cambridge University Press, 1995)

Hutchinson, Kevin Don, *Operation Desert Shield/Desert Storm: Chronology and Fact Book* (London: Greenwood Press, 1995)

The Insight Team of the Sunday Times, *The Yom Kippur War* (London: André Deutch, 1975)

Iskander, Amir, *Saddam Hussein: The Fighter, the Thinker and the Man*, transl. Hassan Selim (Paris: Hachette Realities, 1980)

Israelyan, Victor, *Inside the Kremlin During the Yom Kippur War* (University Park, PA: Pennsylvania State University Press, 1995)

Jabber, Faleh A., Ahmad Shikara and Keiko Sakai, *From Storm to Thunder: Unfinished Showdown Between Iraq and the U.S.* (Tokyo: Institute of Developing Economics, 1998)

Jentleson, Bruce W., *With Friends Like These: Reagan, Bush, and Saddam, 1982–1990* (New York: W. W. Norton & Company, 1994)

Karsh, Efraim (ed.), *The Iran–Iraq War: Impact and Implications* (London: Macmillan, 1989)

Karsh, Efraim and Inari Rautsi, *Saddam Hussein: A Political Biography* (London: Brassey's, 1991)

Kaufman, Burton I., *The Arab Middle East and the United States: Inter-Arab Rivalry and Superpower Diplomacy* (New York: Twayne Publishers, 1996)

Keaney, Thomas A. and Eliot A. Cohen, *Gulf War Air Power Survey: Summary Report* (Washington, DC: Government Printing Office, 1993)

—— *Revolution in Warfare? Air Power in the Persian Gulf* (Annapolis, MA: Naval Institute Press, 1995)

Kennan, George F., *American Diplomacy*, 1st edn 1951; expanded edn (Chicago, IL: University of Chicago Press, 1984)

Khadduri, Majid and Edmund Ghareeb, *War in the Gulf, 1990–1991: The Iraq–Kuwait Conflict and its Implications* (New York: Oxford University Press, 1997)

Kissinger, Henry, *White House Years* (Boston, MA: Little, Brown and Company, 1979)

Klare, Michael, *Rogue States and Nuclear Outlaws: America's Search for a New Foreign Policy* (New York: Hill and Wang, 1995)

Kolko, Gabriel, *Century of War: Politics, Conflicts, and Society Since 1914* (New York: The New Press, 1994)

Kuniholm, Bruce R., *The Origins of the Cold War in the Near East: Great Power Conflict and Diplomacy in Iran, Turkey, and Greece* (Princeton, NJ: Princeton University Press, 1980)

Kuniholm, Bruce R. and Michael Rubner, *The Palestinian Problem and United States Policy: A Guide to Issues and References* (Claremont, CA: Regina Books, 1986)

Lambert, Andrew and Arthur C. Williamson (eds), *The Dynamics of Air Power* (Bracknell, Berkshire: Her Majesty's Stationary Office, 1996)

Lamy, Perry L., *Barrel Roll: An Air Campaign in Support of National Policy, 1968–73* (Maxwell Air Force Base, AL: Air University Press, 1996)

Lauterpacht, E., C. J. Greenwood, M. Weller and D. Bethlehem, *The Kuwait Crisis: Basic Documents*, Cambridge International Documents Series, Vol. I (Cambridge: Grotius Publications, 1991)

Leffler, Melvyn P., *A Preponderance of Power: National Security, the Truman Administration, and the Cold War* (Stanford, CA: Stanford University Press, 1992)

LeMay, Curtis E. with MacKinlay Kantor, *Mission with LeMay* (Garden City, NY: Doubleday Books, 1965)

Liddell Hart, B. H., *Strategy* (London: Meridian Books, 1957)

Lucas, W. Scott, *Divided We Stand: Britain, the US, and the Suez Crisis* (London: Hodder and Stoughton, 1991)

Luttwak, Edward N., *Strategy: The Logic of War and Peace*, 4th edn (Cambridge, MA: Belknap Press, Harvard University Press, 1995)

Magyar, Karl P. (ed.), *Challenge and Response: Anticipating US Military Security Concerns* (Maxwell Air Force Base, AL: Air University Press, 1994)

—— *Global Security Concerns: Anticipating the Twenty-First Century* (Maxwell Air Force Base, AL: Air University Press, 1996)

Makiya, Kanan, *Cruelty and Silence: War, Tyranny, Uprising, and the Arab World*, paperback edn (New York: W. W. Norton & Company, 1994)

—— *Republic of Fear: The Politics of Modern Iraq*, updated version with a new introduction (Berkeley, CA: University Press of California, 1998)

Mandeles, Mark D., Thomas C. Hone and Terry S. Sanford, *Managing 'Command and Control' in the Persian Gulf War* (Westport, CT: Greenwood Publishing Group, 1996)

Mann, Edward C., *Thunder and Lightning: Desert Storm and the Airpower Debates* (Maxwell Air Force Base, AL: Air University Press, 1995)

Marr, Phebe, *A Modern History of Iraq* (Boulder, CO: Westview Press, 1988)

Mason, R. A., *Air Power: A Centennial Appraisal* (London: Brassey's 1994)

Matar, Faud, *Saddam Hussein: The Man, the Cause and the Future* (London: Third World Centre, 1981)

Matthews, Ken, *The Gulf Conflict and International Relations* (London: Routledge, 1993)

McKinnon, Dan, *Bullseye One Reactor* (San Diego, CA: House of Hits, 1987)

McPeak, Merrill A., *Selected Works 1990–1994* (Maxwell Air Force Base, AL: Air University Press, 1995)

Meilinger, Phillip S. (ed.), *The Paths of Heaven: The Evolution of Airpower Theory* (Maxwell Air Force Base, AL, Air University Press, 1997)

Mets, David R., *The Air Campaign: John Warden and the Classical Airpower Theorists* (Maxwell Air Force Base, AL: Air University Press, 1998)

_____ *The Long Search for a Surgical Strike: Precision Munitions and the Revolution in Military Affairs*, CADRE Paper No. 12 (Maxwell Air Force Base, AL: Air University Press, 2001)

Metz, Helen Chapin *et al.*, *Iraq: A Country Study*, 4th edn (Washington, DC: Government Printing Office, 1993)

Miller, Aaron David, *Search for Security: Saudi Arabian Oil and American Foreign Policy* (Chapel Hill: University of South Carolina Press, 1980)

Mitchell, William, *Skyways: A Book on Modern Aeronautics* (Philadelphia, PA: J. B. Lippincott, 1930)

—— *Winged Defense: The Development and Possibilities of Modern Air Power Economic and Military*, 1st edn 1925 (New York: Dover Publications, 1988)

Mohamedou, Mohammad-Mahmoud, *Iraq and the Second Gulf War: State Building and Regime Security* (Bethesda, MD: Austin & Winfield, 1998)

Monroe, Elizabeth, *Britain's Moment in the Middle East, 1914–1971*, 2nd edn (London: Chatto & Windus, 1981)

Moore, John Norton (ed.), *The Arab–Israeli Conflict: Readings and Documents*, abridged and revised edn (Princeton, NJ: Princeton University Press, 1977)

Moran, Daniel, *Wars of National Liberation* (London: Cassell, 2001)

Munro, Alan, *An Arabian Affair: Politics and Diplomacy behind the Gulf War* (London: Brassey's, 1996)

Murray, Williamson with Wayne W. Thompson, *Air War in the Persian Gulf*, 2nd edn (Baltimore, MA: The Nautical & Aviation Publishing Company of America, 1995)

Musallam, Ali Mussalam, *The Iraqi Invasion of Kuwait: Saddam Hussein, his State and International Power Politics* (London: British Academic Press, 1996)

Mylroie, Laurie, 'The Future of Iraq', *The Washington Institute for Near East Policy* 24 (1991)

Neff, Donald, *Fallen Pillars: U.S. Policy towards Palestine and Israel since 1945* (Washington, DC: Institute for Palestinian Studies, 1995)

Nixon, Richard M., *Public Papers of the Presidents of the United States: Richard M. Nixon, 1969* (Washington, DC: Government Printing Office, 1971)

—— *Public Papers of the Presidents of the United States: Richard M. Nixon, 1970* (Washington, DC: Government Printing Office, 1972)

Noorani, A. G., *The Gulf Wars: Documents and Analysis* (New Delhi: Konark Publishers Pvt, 1991)

Nye, Joseph S. and Roger K. Smith (eds), *After the Storm: Lessons from the Gulf War* (Lanham, MA: Madison Books, 1992)

O'Ballance, Edgar, *The Second Gulf War: About the Liberation of Kuwait (August 1990–March 1991)* (Bromely, Kent: Galago, 1992)

O'Shaughnessy, Hugh, *Grenada: Revolution, Invasion and Aftermath* (London: Sphere Books with *The Observer*, 1983)

Olsen, John Andreas (ed.), *From Manoeuvre Warfare to Kosovo?* (Trondheim: The Royal Norwegian Air Force Academy, 2001)

Osgood, Charles, *An Alternative to War and Surrender* (Champaign-Urbana, IL: University of Illinois Press, 1962)

Overy, Richard, *Why the Allies Won* (London: W. W. Norton & Company, 1995)

Palmer, Michael P. A., *On Course to Desert Storm: The United States Navy and the Persian Gulf* (Washington, DC: Naval Historical Center, 1992)

Pape, Robert A., *Bombing to Win: Air Power and Coercion in War* (Ithaca, NY: Cornell University Press, 1996)

Paret, Peter (ed.), *Makers of Modern Strategy: from Machiavelli to the Nuclear Age*, reprint (Oxford: Oxford University Press, 1994)

Parker, Richard B. (ed.), *The Six-Day War: A Retrospective* (Gainesville, FL: University Press of Florida, 1996)

Peach, Stuart (ed.), *Perspectives On Air Power: Air Power in its Wider Context* (London: Her Majesty's Stationary Office, 1998)

Persson, Magnus, *Great Britain, the United States and the Security of the Middle East: The Formation of the Baghdad Pact*, Lund Studies in International History, No. 3 (Stockholm: Almquiest & Wiksell Intl., 1998)

Pimlott, J. L., *Vietnam: History and Tactics* (London: Orbis, 1982)

Pimlott, John and Stephen Badsey (eds), *The Gulf War Assessed* (London: Arms and Armour, 1992)

Powell, Colin with Joseph E. Persico, *My American Journey* (New York: Ballantine Books, 1995)

Quandt, William B., *Camp David: Peacemaking and Politics* (Washington, DC: The Brookings Institute, 1986)

Rabinovich, Itamar, *Waging Peace: Israel and the Arabs at the End of the Century* (New York: Farrar, Straus and Giroux, 1999)

Ramadan, Mikhael, *In the Shadow of Saddam: Saddam Hussein's Former Double* (Auckland: GreeNZone, 1999)

Rashid, Nasser Ibrahim and Esber Ibrahim Shaheen, *Saudi Arabia and the Gulf War* (Joplin, MO: International Institute of Technology, 1994)

Reagan, Ronald, *An American Life: The Autobiography* (London: Arrow Books, 1991)

Record, Jeffrey, *Hollow Victory: A Contrary View of the Gulf War* (McLean, VA: Brassey's, 1993)

Renshon, Stanley A., *The Political Psychology of the Gulf War: Leaders, Publics, and the Process of Conflict* (London: University of Pittsburg Press, 1993)

Reynolds, Richard T., *Heart of the Storm: The Genesis of the Air Campaign Against Iraq* (Maxwell Air Force Base, AL: Air University Press, 1995)

Ridgeway, James (ed.), *The March to War* (New York: Four Walls Eight Windows, 1991)

Ripley, Tim, *Land Power: the Coalition and Iraqi Armies*, Desert Storm Special 3 (London: Osprey Publishing, 1991)

Ritter, Scott, *Endgame: Solving the Iraq Problem – Once and for All* (New York: Simon & Schuster, 1999)

Romjue, John L., *From Active Defense to AirLand Battle: The Development of Army 1973–1982* (Fort Monroe, VA: U.S. Army Training and Doctrine Command, 1984)

Rosensaft, Menachem Z., *Not Backward to Belligerency: A Study of Events Surrounding the 'Six-Day War' of June, 1967* (New York: Thomas Yoseloff, 1969)

Rubner, Michael, *The Palestinian Problem and United States Policy: A Guide to Issue and References* (Claremont, CA: Regina Books, 1986)

Salinger, Pierre with Eric Laurent, *Secret Dossier: The Hidden Agenda Behind the Gulf War* (London: Penguin Books, 1991)

Samaan, Samaan B. and Abdullah H. Muhareb (eds), *An Aggression on the Mind: A Critical Study of Sa'd al-Bazzaz's Book 'A War Gives Birth to Another'*, trans. Mohammad Sami Anwar (Kuwait City: Center for Research and Studies on Kuwait, 1995)

Sayigh, Yezid and Avi Shlaim (eds), *The Cold War and the Middle East* (New York: Oxford University Press, 1994)

Scales, Robert H., *Certain Victory: The U.S. Army in the Gulf War*, paperback edn (London: Brassey's, 1997)

Schelling, Thomas C., *Arms and Influence* (New Haven, CT: Yale University Press, 1966)
—— *The Strategy of Conflict*, (Cambridge, MA: Harvard University Press, 1997)
Schofield, Richard, *Kuwait and Iraq: Historical Claims and Territorial Disputes*, 2nd edn (London: Royal Institute of International Affairs, 1993)
Schwarzkopf, H. Norman with Peter Petre, *It Doesn't Take a Hero* (London: Bantam Books, 1993)
Sciolino, Elaine, *The Outlaw State: Saddam Hussein's Quest for Power and the Gulf Crisis* (New York: John Wiley & Sons, 1991)
Scranton, Margaret E., *The Noriega Years: U.S.–Panamanian Relations, 1981–1990* (Boulder, CO: Lynne Rienner Publishers, 1991)
Seldon, Anthony with Lewis Baston, *Major: A Political Life* (London: Phoenix, 1998)
Shafik, Fouad Fahmy (trans.), *The Iraqi Interim Constitution* (Dobbs Ferry, NY: Oceana Publication, 1990)
Sherry, Michael S., *The Rise of American Air Power: The Creation of Armageddon* (New Haven, CT: Yale University Press, 1987)
Shlaim, Avi, *War and Peace in the Middle East: A Concise History*, revised and updated (New York: Penguin Books, 1995)
Shultz, George P. *Turmoil and Triumph: My Years as Secretary of State* (New York: Charles Scribner's Sons, 1993)
Shultz Jr., Richard H. and Robert L. Pfaltzgraff Jr. (eds), *The Future of Air Power in the Aftermath of the Gulf War* (Maxwell Air Force Base, AL: Air University Press, 1992)
Simons, Geoff, *Iraq: From Sumer to Saddam* (Basingstoke: Macmillan, 1994)
—— *Libya: The Struggle for Survival* (London: Macmillan, 1993)
Simpson, John, *From the House of War* (London: Arrow Books, 1991)
Spector, Ronald H., *After Tet: The Bloodiest Year in Vietnam* (New York: Free Press, 1993)
Spiegel, Steven P., *The Other Arab–Israeli Conflict: Making America's Middle East Policy from Truman to Reagan* (Chicago, IL: Chicago University Press, 1985)
Steinberg, S. H. (ed.), *Statesman's Year-Book: Statistical and Historical Annual of the States for the Year 1957* (London: Macmillan, 1957)
Stephens, Alan (ed.), *The War in the Air 1914–1994* (Fairbairn, Canberra: RAAF Air Power Studies Centre, 1994)
—— *The Implications of Modern Air Power for Defence Strategy*, No. 5 (Fairbairn, Canberra: RAAF Air Power Studies Centre, 1992)
Stock, Ernest, *Israel on the Road to Sinai, 1949–1956* (Ithaca, NY: Cornell University Press, 1967)
Sultan, Khaled Bin with Patrick Seale, *Desert Warrior: A Personal View of the Gulf War by the Joint Forces Commander* (London: HarperCollins, 1995)
Sumaida, Hussein with Carole Jerome, *Circle of Fear: A Renegade's Journey from the Mossad to the Iraqi Secret Service* (Toronto: Stoddart, 1991)
Summers Jr., Harry G., *On Strategy II: A Critical Analysis of the Gulf War* (New York: Dell Publishing, 1992)
—— *The New World Strategy: A Military Policy for America's Future* (New York: Simon & Schuster, 1995)
Swain, Richard M., *'Lucky War': Third Army in Desert Storm* (Fort Leavenworth, KS: United States Army Command and General Staff College Press, 1997)
Tarock, Adam, *The Superpowers' Involvement in the Iran–Iraq War* (Commack, NY: Nova Science Publishers, 1998)
Taylor, Philip M., *War and the Media: Propaganda and Persuasion in the Gulf War* (Manchester: Manchester University Press, 1992)
Timmermann, Kenneth R., *The Death Lobby: How the West Armed Iraq* (London: Bantam Books, 1992)

Toffler, Alvin and Heidi Toffler, *War and Anti-War: Making Sense of Today's Global Chaos*, reprint (London: Warner Books, 1995)

Trost, Carlise A. H., 'Maritime Strategy of the 1990s', *US Naval Institute Proceedings* (May 1990)

Tzu, Sun, *The Art of War* (London: Hodder and Stoughton, 1995)

Udovitch, A. L. (ed.) *The Middle East: Oil, Conflict and Hope* (Lexington, MA: Lexington Books, 1976)

United States Air Force, *Air Force Manual 1-1: Basic Aerospace Doctrine of the United States Air Force* (Washington, DC: Government Printing Office, 1984)

—— *Air Force Manual 1-1: Basic Aerospace Doctrine of the United States Air Force*, (Washington, DC: Government Printing Office, 1992)

—— 'Global Reach Global Power: Reshaping for the Future', *USAF White Paper* (Washington, DC: United States Air Force, 1991)

United States Army, *The Iraqi Army: Organization and Tactics* (Boulder, CO: Paladin Press, 1991)

United States Department of Defense, *Conduct of the Persian Gulf War: An Interim Report to Congress* (Washington, DC: Government Printing Office, 1991)

—— *Conduct of the Persian Gulf War: Final Report to Congress* (Washington, DC: Government Printing Office, 1992)

United States Government Accounting Office, *Operation Desert Storm: Evaluation of the Air Campaign* (Washington, DC: Diane Publishing Co., 1997)

Vaux, Kenneth L., *Ethics and the Gulf War: Religion, Rhetoric, and Righteousness* (Boulder, CO: Westview Press, 1992)

Warden, John A. III, *The Air Campaign: Planning for Combat*, revised edn (New York: toExcel, 1998)

—— 'The Grand Alliance: Strategy and Decision' (MA thesis, Texas Tech University, 1975)

Warden, John A. and Leland A. Russell, *Winning in FastTime: Harness the Competitive Advantage of Prometheus in Business and Life* (Montgomery, AL: Venturist Publishing, 2001)

Waters, Gary, *Gulf Lesson One – The Value of Air Power: Doctrinal Lessons for Australia* (Fairbairn, Canberra: RAAF Air Power Studies Centre, 1992)

Watzlawick, Paul, John H. Weakland and Richard Fiusch, *Change: Principles of Problem Formation and Problem Resolution* (New York: W. W. Norton & Company, 1973)

Weinberger, Casper, *Fighting for Peace: Seven Critical Years in the Pentagon* (New York: Warner Books, 1990)

Willmott, H. P., *The Great Crusade: A New Complete History of the Second World War* (New York: The Free Press, 1989)

Winnefeld, James A., Dana J. Johnson and Preston Niblack, *A League of Airmen: U.S. Air Power in the Gulf War* (Santa Monica, CA: RAND, 1994)

Woodward, Bob, *The Commanders* (New York: Simon & Schuster, 1991)

Yahia, Latif and Karl Wendel, I *Was Saddam's Son*, 1st edn. 1994 (New York: Arcade Publishing, 1997)

Yergin, Daniel, *The Prize: The Epic Quest for Oil, Money and Power* (New York: Simon & Schuster, 1991)

Young, John W., *The Foreign Policy of Churchill's Peacetime Administration 1951–1955* (Worcester: Leicester University Press, 1988)

Index